Novelists in a Changing World

Novelists in a Changing World

Meredith, James, and the Transformation
of English Fiction in the 1880's

Donald David Stone

Harvard University Press   Cambridge, Massachusetts   1972

Publication of this book has been aided by a grant from the Hyder Edward
Rollins Fund
Library of Congress Catalog Card Number 75–169861
SBN 674–62830–6
Printed in the United States of America

Permission to quote has been granted by Charles Scribner's Sons, New
York, for *The Letters of Henry James*, edited by Percy Lubbock, copyright
1920, renewed 1948 by William James and Margaret James Porter; by the
trustees of the Hardy estate, Macmillan Company, Canada, and Macmillan
Company, London and Basingstoke, for Florence Emily Hardy's *The Life of
Thomas Hardy*; by the Clarendon Press, London, for *The Collected Letters of
George Meredith*, edited by C. L. Cline, copyright 1970; by Oxford University
Press, New York, for Henry James's *Notebooks*, copyright 1948; by Alexander
James (c/o Paul Reynolds, Inc.).

*To My Mother and Father
for their respect for and devotion to those most
precious and increasingly rare of intangibles,
civilized human values*

Contents

Preface

The problematic nature of the novelist's relationship to his society and his art in a time of change is the subject of this book. During the decade of the 1880's there occurred in England a profound transformation of social, political, and philosophical values which prematurely opened the way to the twentieth century. The relatively stable beliefs of the Victorians—stable as a result of willful individual efforts as much as of popular inertia—were replaced by a new set of values, indeterminate in scope and subjective in orientation. Although the full implications of such major changes of attitude as the revolt against authority and the loss of former certainties (Nietzsche's announcement of the death of God, for example, was made in 1882) were not widely realized for at least another decade, one can find in the philosophers and, perhaps above all, in the novelists of the 1880's ample evidence of the awareness that the Victorian age was ending and a new period, the modern age, was beginning.

In the first section of this book, I consider the nature of the transformation in the 1880's, as demonstrated by the major historical events and the philosophical revolution, and as reflected in the works of the major English novelists of the period. I have selected, in the second and third parts of the book, the figures of George Meredith and Henry James for close examination, not only because they seem to me to be the two greatest novelists at work in the 1880's but also because they exemplify differing reactions to the changes of the period and they offer opposing views of the role of the novelist in an age of change. Both novelists reached their literary peaks as Victorian novelists when the decade started: Meredith in *The Egoist* (1879), James in *The Portrait of a Lady* (1881). Thereafter, Meredith suffered in an attempt to perpetuate Victorian values in a post-Victorian world; James, after struggling for a time to write in the Victorian mode, gave way to a combination of romantic instincts and modern self-assertiveness. In the same decade that Meredith, despite declining health and powers, finally attained popular recognition, James, despite anxious bids for popular acceptance, became increasingly divorced in attitude from the age. The result of Meredith's decline and James's withdrawal was of crucial significance for the future of fiction. Although by managing to adjust the nature of the novel and by changing the role of the novelist to suit himself James at least enabled the novel to survive in a post-Victorian setting, the novel was, nevertheless, henceforth deprived of many of the qualities which had given it its distinction and made it so remarkable and powerful a social and cultural force in the past.

Far more authors, teachers, students, and friends have provided me with advice and assistance as I worked on this study than can be listed here. Pre-eminent among them has been Professor Jerome Hamilton Buckley, a generous and illuminating guide; I wish to thank him and Mrs. Buckley for their help and encouragement. I would also like to thank Professors Monroe Engel, Robert Bloom, and Adrienne Koch, who helped direct the various transmutations of this work while I was an undergraduate at the University of California at Berkeley and a graduate student at Harvard University. Everyone who has read and studied James knows and appreciates the work done by Leon Edel, and I am grateful that two invaluable works devoted to Meredith—C. L. Cline's excellent edition of the *Collected Letters* and V. S. Pritchett's brilliant lectures on *George Meredith and English Comedy*—reached me during the final phase of my work on this book. (James is hardly at a loss for enthusiasts nowadays, and I have tried to examine him with more critical perspective than is usually achieved by his admirers; critical enthusiasm for Meredith in recent years has, on the other hand, been both uncommon and long overdue.) To Howard Mumford Jones I am conscious of many debts of gratitude, among them for his gracious comments on the earlier draft of this book and for the honor of its being awarded the literary prize which he established at Harvard. I am extremely grateful to my sisters, Nadine and Diana, and to my friends—among whom I must mention the late Daniel Zerfoss—who listened patiently and advised beneficially, and I wish to thank Nadine for the typing of the manuscript. One last word of thanks is in order here—to the staff of the Harvard Press, and especially to my editor, M. Rita Howe, for their expert and amiable assistance in the final preparations of this book.

[1] Introduction: Two Novelists

Settled in England in 1880, Henry James might have applied to himself the description which he later made of Dumas the Younger: "he came into the world at the moment in all our time that was for a man of letters the most amusing and beguiling—the moment exactly when he could see the end of one era and the beginning of another and join hands luxuriously with each."[1] The 1880's is the period of English history in which the dissolution of the Victorian world and the reorientation toward the modern sensibility can best be traced, side by side. As the great Victorian spokesmen passed away, one after another, a new variety of influential and increasingly subjective philosophers took their place; similarly, with the deaths of the established Victorian novelists, not only a younger group of novelists, but an entirely new set of attitudes toward fiction appeared. In this decade of "transition England" (as Mrs. Humphry Ward called it),[2] a number of new novelists—George Gissing, William Hale White, Richard Jefferies, and Olive Schreiner, among them—chose to describe the major conflicts of the time in realistic books. Others—Robert Louis Stevenson, Rudyard Kipling, and Oscar Wilde, for example—determined either to ignore or escape the problems of the period by cultivating a new form of romanticism: not the larger romanticism which Sir Walter Scott or Goethe, early in the nineteenth century, had offered as a means of reconciling the opposing claims and half-truths of their time, but a romanticism which urged aesthetic solipsism or escapism to exotic and remote places. In George Moore, the transitional nature of the decade found its readiest experimenter, and in Mrs. Ward's account of the deconversion of Robert Elsmere the decade produced its most popular novel. Meanwhile, Thomas Hardy simultaneously depicted in his fiction a vanished rural England, which corresponded more, perhaps, to his imaginative desires than to an actual place or people, and a new breed of self-conscious and self-destructive individuals born out of their due time and perhaps unhappy in any place or period. Among all the novelists whose life and work embody the opposing trends of the decade, George Meredith and Henry James are the best representatives for the literary historian, in addition to being the two finest novelists.

In January 1880, James, replying to William Dean Howells' "protest against the idea that it takes an old civilization to set a novelist in motion," which he had argued in his biography of Hawthorne, lamented the absence in America of the "paraphernalia" required by a novelist who might aspire to belong "to the company of Balzac and Thackeray." "It is on manners, customs, usages, habits, forms, upon all these things matured and established, that a novelist lives," James maintained, "—they are the very stuff his work is made of";[3] and what America lacked, England appeared to have in profusion. From his point of view "as an artist and as a bachelor," James claimed that, for himself, "as one who has the passion of observation and whose business is the study of human life," London offered the greatest opportunities to the novelist.[4] James realized from the moment he decided to settle there that the material advantages of England were being threatened, that a period of social crisis had begun, but he found in "the 'decline' of England" a "tremendous and even, almost, an inspiring spectacle," and he awaited the aesthetic satisfaction of witnessing firsthand what seemed "the greatest drama in history!" In 1885 the English troubles with Ireland and the Sudan led James to reflect:

> The possible *malheurs*—reverses, dangers, embarrassments, the "decline," in a word, of old England, go to my heart, and I can imagine no spectacle more touching, more thrilling and even dramatic, than to see this great precarious, artificial empire, on behalf of which, nevertheless, so much of the strongest and finest stuff of the greatest race (for such they are) has been expended, struggling with forces which perhaps, in the long run, will prove too many for it. If she will only struggle, and not collapse and surrender and give up a part which, looking at Europe as it is to-day, still may be great, the drama will be well worth watching from [such] a good, near standpoint as I have here.[5]

James would have agreed with Gissing's view, arrived at from a vantage point considerably closer to the social miseries of the mid-1880's than James's: "Human life has little interest to me, on the whole—save as material for artistic presentation."[6] James looked to England to provide materials for the novelist, and he sought to convert the "drama" of the crisis of the eighties into subject matter for his fiction in that period. Like Gissing, he came increasingly to assert the superiority of the artistic-minded individual to his historical background.

In the 1880's Meredith at long last began to receive the praise due him as a novelist. Upon the death of George Eliot in 1880, and especially after the publication of *Diana of the Crossways* in 1885, Meredith rightly emerged as the greatest living English novelist. And while the charge of "obscurity" continued to be raised against him, he spent his last twenty years admired as (in James's words) "a quite splendid and rather strange, Exhibition."[7] When, in 1892, he was elected president of the Society of Authors to succeed Tennyson, the honor "carried with it implicit acknowledgement that he was England's most distinguished author."[8] Recognition arrived, however, at a time when Meredith could not fully appreciate its value. The death of his second wife and the collapse of his health occurred at a time when the act of writing was often physical agony, and the novels and poems of the last period very often appear tortured in style and diction. For all that, Meredith struggled to promote worthy ideals—ideals with Victorian roots—in an age of change. In the cottage built on the slope above his house at Box Hill, Meredith could look up from his writing and enjoy the sight of the Surrey countryside, and the major themes of his works, expressed often with brilliant wit or with lyric beauty, deal with the need for selfless perspective, achieved with the help of the Comic Spirit, and for harmony with nature. Where James looked to a picturesque Victorian society to provide him with the materials for fiction, Meredith devoted much of his writing to warning of the social and personal dangers of egoism, thereby countering the forces of disintegration. In *Beauchamp's Career* he criticized the general indifference toward the need for helpful changes; while he felt that England still carried influence as a

civilized nation, Meredith was distressed "to observe [his] countrymen bemuddled by their alarms and selfish temporary interests."[9]

Although the two novelists were devoted friends in their later
years, James berated Meredith, after his death, for having allowed
social and moral themes to overshadow his aesthetic responsibilities. "The fantastic and the mannered in him were as nothing,"
James conceded to Edmund Gosse, compared ". . . to the intimately
sane and straight; just as the artist was nothing to the good citizen and the liberalised bourgeois."[10] To their contemporaries' eyes,
Meredith and James seemed more alike than now appears the case.
They were both notorious for their stylistic mannerisms and their
heterodox methods—their mutual interest, for example, in describing characters in terms of complex psychological analysis rather
than in creating the kinds of character portraits Victorian readers
loved to identify with. Both were intellectual novelists, and each
became the object of a philosophical or aesthetic cult. Moreover,
both were Romantic artists with aspirations to realism, who asserted their own personality and their own ideals in their work.
But their intellectual ideals were opposed, as was their particular
form of romanticism. Meredith's aim, like his idol Goethe's before
him, was to reconcile the claims of realism and romanticism: the
truthfulness of "Earth" with the "atmosphere" of idealism. To
the end of his life he asserted that his philosophy amounted to the
realization "that a frank acceptance of Reality is the firm basis of
the Ideal."[11] If Meredith introduced himself into his novels, he did
so to reveal his own weaknesses, to expose his delusions of grandeur to the purifying laughter of the Comic Spirit. Although James
made a point, in his early works, of caricaturing the weaknesses
of the detached, Jamesian individual, he chose, in his later works,
to celebrate the very limitations he had revealed in such figures
as Louis Leverett in "A Bundle of Letters" and Ralph Touchett in
The Portrait of a Lady. Beginning as an "analytical" novelist—as
he was tagged by critics who considered him the head of the school
of American realism—in revolt against the romance tradition in
America, he later reverted to a romantic position, Emersonian in
origin and Pateresque in its aesthetic quality. If he criticized the
American lack of "paraphernalia" which had denied Hawthorne
the resources and stature of an English novelist, James also even-

tually rejected the English trappings and society he had earlier envied and insisted, instead, upon the primacy of his own inner life as the only standard of artistic excellence and gauge of reality.

Comparing their work in 1904, Stanislaus Joyce recognized Meredith's superior powers of style and imagination, but he viewed James's work as "a much more important contribution to the modern conscience than Meredith's." Finely pinpointing the nature of Meredith's limitations for the modern reader as well as the source of James's modernity, he noted: "The emotion Meredith harps loudly on is love, in Henry James it is freedom."[12] In all his writings, and especially in the sequence of novels extending from *Beauchamp's Career* (1877) to *One of Our Conquerors* (1891), Meredith addressed himself to the theme that Victorian society needs the talents of its individualists even as those individuals need the self-transcending opportunities offered by the Victorian community. But as the age dismayingly went to pieces, Meredith found it increasingly difficult to express himself in the medium traditionally concerned with the reconciliation between self and society, and with the symbolic celebration of marital love. He admitted to his older son in 1881 that he found himself, "as a describer of nature and natural emotions, a constant sufferer in dealing with a language part of which is dead matter."[13] Not only the language but the age itself thwarted his best efforts. James, in the 1880's, attempted initially to mirror the Victorian society of which he had chosen to be the spectator. As that society made demands on the individuals in his novels, however, he turned increasingly to the theme that the individual—specifically, the Jamesian artist—must be free from the claims of society or history or even personal ties. If Meredith went to pieces along with the Victorian era, James at least managed to escape the Victorian shipwreck—although at a substantial cost, as it proved, for the history of the novel.

Part I.   The English Novel
in the 1880's

[2] The Old Order Changes

> *There is not a creed which is not shaken,*
> *not an accredited dogma which is not shown*
> *to be questionable, not a received tradition*
> *which does not threaten to dissolve.*
> *(Matthew Arnold, 1879)*

> *The civilized world is trembling on the verge of*
> *a great movement. Either it must be a leap*
> *upward, which will open the way to advances yet*
> *undreamed of, or it must be a plunge downward*
> *which will carry us back toward barbarism.*
> *(Henry George,* Progress and Poverty, *1879)*

In the late 1870's a sense that England had passed its peak and was rapidly declining had begun to take hold. A major economic depression was felt at the same time that the political and religious certainties which had served in the past to stabilize and unify the country began to crumble. Suddenly, as if in confirmation of the passing of an era, the great Victorian leaders and moralists, the architects of the Victorian Compromise and the inspirers of the Victorian conscience and confidence, began to disappear in the 1880's: Disraeli and John Bright, Darwin and Newman, Arnold and Browning, George Eliot and Trollope. At the death of perhaps the most revered of the great Victorians, Thomas Carlyle, in 1881, Gissing wondered: "Does it not seem now as if all our really great men were leaving us, and, what is worse, without much prospect as yet of any to take their place. Where are the novelists to succeed Thackeray, Dickens, George Eliot? What poets will follow upon Tennyson and Browning when they, as must shortly be the case, leave their places empty? Nay, what *really great* men of any kind can honestly be said to have given tokens of their coming?" Four years later Gissing made an exception in the case of Meredith, who, he insisted, despite widespread neglect, had "For the last thirty years . . . been producing work unspeakably above the best of any living writer . . ."[1] Although Meredith had finally gained an audience, he found himself unable to convince his age of the need for restraint as well as responsible individualism. Horrified by "the ravings of the Tory Press for War" in 1885, Meredith wrote to a close friend that at such times he felt "the curse of an impotent voice."[2]

The few surviving eminent Victorians who witnessed the changes of the eighties did so with mounting frustration. Herbert Spencer, who continued his ambitious and preposterous attempt at a synthesis of all knowledge in an age of dissolution, was alarmed by the rise of imperialism and the increasing power of the state in direct proportion to the decline of individual responsibility. In *The Man Versus the State* (1885) he warned that what was being celebrated in some quarters as an increase in personal freedom was being attained at the price of the individual's contribution to the welfare of the community—at the price, ultimately, of the individual's control over his own destiny. Gladstone served two terms as Prime Minister during the 1880's, but, despite his energetic efforts to achieve peace at home and justice in Ireland, his ministry from 1880 to 1885 "never gave the impression," as his biographer notes, "of controlling events; it seemed to be at their mercy." Gladstone's faith in the masses, for whom he had successfully worked to extend the franchise, was linked to his sentimental belief that, in contrast to the frivolousness and selfishness of the upper classes, they would exhibit powers of "self-command, self-control, respect for order, patience under suffering, confidence in the law, regard for superiors."[3] Instead, the widened electorate exhibited a lack of interest in, and often opposition to, the reform measures needed at home and in Ireland; the new voters proved most responsive to the appeals of the imperialist crusaders.

In February 1884, Gissing heard John Ruskin deliver the most apocalyptic warning of the age: "In his lecture the other night on a new kind of storm-cloud he believes only to have appeared of late years, Ruskin more than hints that the degradation of the heavens is due to men's iniquity." Admonishing his audience "like a Hebrew prophet,"[4] Ruskin sensed signs of cosmic disorder, and, reflecting on the seasonal harmony of the past, he proclaimed:

"That harmony is now broken, and broken the world round: fragments, indeed, of what existed still exist, and hours of what is past still return; but month by month the darkness gains upon the day, and the ashes of the Antipodes glare through the night." Ruskin blamed, among others, the "tutors" of the new, Darwinian science, who were inferring that men "are nothing more than brute beasts driven by brute forces."[5]

The Poet Laureate, meanwhile, in better mental condition than Ruskin but equally gloomy, saw the end of his hopes for England; and in "Locksley Hall Sixty Years After" (1886), Tennyson sarcastically attacked the purveyors of materialism and determinism in the new philosophy, science, and literature:

> Tumble Nature heel o'er head, and, yelling with the yelling street,
> Set the feet above the brain and swear the brain is in the feet.
>
> Bring the old dark ages back without the faith, without the hope,
> Break the State, the Church, the Throne, and roll their ruins down the slope.

The lure of material progress obscured the growing poverty of all sustaining, transcendent ideals, and, as economic depression gripped the country, the cities filled to overflowing with new generations of citizenry bereft of any reason for hope. Written on the eve of the Jubilee year, Tennyson's poem recognized, as had Henry George's great tract before him, that progress and poverty were inseparable modern companions:

> Is it well that while we range with Science, glorying in the Time,
> City children soak and blacken soul and sense in city slime?

The social history of the 1880's constituted in many ways a climax to the Victorian belief in progress, but it also reflected a sudden poverty of all things needful—spiritual, intellectual, idealistic.

Recent historians have tended to idealize as the "High Noon of Victorianism" the years from 1840 to 1875 when a balance between opposing forces produced a degree of social calm in England

unknown elsewhere in Europe.[6] While the great historian Jacob
Burckhardt was assuring his students at Basel, in 1871, that "everything up to our day is fundamentally nothing but an age of revolution,"[7] England seemed secure from the distemper of the times.
The Victorian "age of equipoise," with its triumphant sense of
"unity transcending diversity" (the phrases of two historians),[8]
was as much a result, perhaps, of an ingrained stolidity of the
imagination, a provincial feeling of self-sufficiency and self-righteousness, as it was of continuing agricultural prosperity and indus-
trial progress. Mid-Victorian England looked to itself as the source
of all material things necessary, and to its past for a feeling of
spiritual reassurance. Before 1880, as H. V. Routh claims, the Victorians "for the most part looked back to the older culture as their
source of spiritual strength and clung to its well-tried wisdom as
a guiding-light in their perplexities and as an inspiration to compensate for their disillusionments." The Victorian literature of
this period, whether the work of Tennyson, Ruskin, or George
Eliot, "though full of conflicting creeds, and incompatible ideals,
has preserved . . . this one common quality—the affectation of
adjustment."[9]

In later decades of the nineteenth century, history seemed less
assuring. The agricultural depression which began in the 1870's
intensified in the 1880's, and, with the gradual enfranchisement of
the male working-class population between 1867 and 1884, the
presence of large numbers of unemployed workers seemed to pose
the threat of a socialist revolution. Matthew Arnold feared the
accession to power of uneducated "Numbers," and he opposed the
stabilizing power of culture to the threat of anarchy; for Carlyle,
the future after the Second Reform Bill appeared a vision of "Practical Chaos (with dirt, disorder, nomadism, disobedience, folly and
confusion)."[10] The end result of the rule of numbers, however,
proved not to be disorder or anarchy so much as a trivialization of
the quality of life—less the fault of the working classes than of
those to whom they looked and who ignored their real needs. In
the quest for material necessities, as Gissing realized, "the things
of the heart and mind" were overlooked. "The struggle for existence
is so hard," he wrote in *Thyrza*, "that we grow more and more
material: the tendency is to regard it as the end of life to make

money . . . Our social state, in short, has converted the means of life into its end."[11] In *Demos*, Gissing warned that power was being given "to the class which not only postpones everything to material wellbeing, but more and more regards intellectual refinement as an obstacle in the way of progress." Gissing hoped to increase the awareness of the masses to civilized values and to a sense of their responsibilities through "spiritual education."[12] but the Victorians' faith in the effects of education was severely tried by the unforeseen consequences of the National Education Act of 1870. To meet the necessities of mass education, children were taught the mechanics of reading but not the reason for education; with the rise of literacy came an "increase in gullibility, as well as of enlightenment among the masses."[13] The schools prepared new millions of readers for popular journalism—and popular journalism helped spread the gospel of imperialism.

In *Progress and Poverty*, Henry George prophesied that the education of "men who must be condemned to poverty, is but to make them restive; to base on a state of most glaring social inequality political institutions under which men are theoretically equal, is to stand a pyramid on its apex."[14] The threat of social revolution hovered over the 1880's and was utilized as a literary theme by Gissing in *Demos* and by James in *The Princess Casamassima*. Despite such developments as a large gathering of the unemployed at Trafalgar Square in 1886, however, the revolution never materialized. In one historian's thesis (written in the 1930's), the emergence to political power of the laboring classes was a triumphant landmark "in the recurrent struggle for individual freedom."[15] Notwithstanding the efforts of the various reformist groups founded in the 1880's—H. M. Hyndman's Social Democratic Federation in 1881, the Fabian Society in 1883, the Independent Labor Party in 1887—it came as a shock to many reformers of the period to discover that the working classes were not immune to the stolid conservatism, egoism, and materialism of the other classes. Much of the energy of the reformers was spent in attacking one another, and, in spite of dreams of an English Revolution in 1889 (to coincide with the centennial of the fall of the Bastille), the populace proved unresponsive.[16] In this time of domestic crisis, much intellectual energy and popular sentiment were diverted to a cause which, although it may have seemed an economic solution at the time, now appears to have been a form of romantic escapism. Publication of J. R. Seeley's *The Expansion of England* in 1883, the formation in the following year of the Imperial Federation League, plus the literary endeavors of a group of young writers—all served to intensify imperialist fervor. The death of General Gordon at Khartoum in 1885 diverted public interest and support from Gladstone's attempts toward a Home Rule Bill and helped to sentimentalize the imperialist mission. In 1887, according to the *Annual Register*, "The domestic history . . . , so far as politics were concerned, might be summed up in two words, 'impotence' and 'unrest.' "[17] The hero of Edward Bellamy's *Looking Backward* pointed to 1887, with its sense of social drift and chronic unemployment, as the period just before the great universal social revolution, but many Victorians chose instead to look to India for distraction from the critical problems at home. The year 1887 proved a landmark for romantic manifestos, in terms of both fiction and politics; during that Jubilee year of Victoria's reign, over five and a half million people attended the Colonial and Indian Exhibition.

If the social reformers of the 1880's were unsuccessful in their mission, so were the efforts of two other groups: the feminists and the Irish. "The case with women resembles that of the Irish," Meredith observed to Mrs. Leslie Stephen in 1889. "We have played fast and loose with them, until now they are encouraged to demand what they know not how to use, but have a just right to claim."[18] Largely ignored by politicians, the cause of women's rights was taken up in several novels of the decade. In *Diana of the Crossways* (1885) Meredith defended the rights of women and the Irish simultaneously in the figure of his Irish heroine. In *A Drama in Muslin* (1886) George Moore suggestively and sympathetically dealt with the plight of the surplus of unmarried women in modern society. Gissing and Hardy, too, considered the frustrated ambitions of the "New Women," and in *The Story of an African Farm* (1883) Olive Schreiner powerfully described the self-destructive rebellion of her heroine against social barriers. Although James treated the ambitions of the feminists satirically in *The Bostonians*, elsewhere he respected the strivings of his heroines (like Isabel Archer) for freedom. Far more disturbing in the eighties, and the major topic of news in the papers, were the activities of Irish supporters of Home Rule. The threat of Parnell's Land League to deprive English landowners of their Irish rents and a number of highly publicized terrorist threats, climaxed in 1882 by the assassination of the Chief Secretary for Ireland and his Undersecretary in Phoenix Park, constituted evidence of Celtic barbarism in the public mind. Fear of terrorist activities at home provoked a reporter to write in 1883 that "attempts of a gang of Irish Americans to blow up the Local Government Board and the *Times* office . . . , although unattended with loss of life, produced a feeling of insecurity bordering on panic, not only in London but throughout the United Kingdom. Alarming stories of the discovery of arms and explosives were greedily swallowed, and the fears of the public were daily fostered by sensational reports of the most trivial circumstances."[19]

England had undergone periods of crisis before, to be sure, but the national confidence of preceding years was fatally weakened by a general sense that no benign deity would henceforth come to her aid. Perhaps the most essential element in preserving the Victorian balance, while it lasted, was the unifying force of a national religious sentiment.[20] Even the influential mid-Victorian nonbelievers translated the religious commandments of their ancestors into one or another "religion of humanity"; if they could not believe in God or immortality, as George Eliot averred, they believed the more strongly in their duties to society. Whether Darwin shattered or merely confirmed, in some cases, belief in a kindly Providence, it soon became evident that with the decline of religion came a weakening of belief in the individual's obligations to society. Despite a resurgence of evangelical religiosity in the 1860's and 1870's, there was far too little room in the existing churches for the expanding population; by 1880 John Bright informed Parliament (which was refusing to seat Charles Bradlaugh on account of his avowed atheism) that "to a large extent the working people of the country do not care any more for the dogmas of Christianity than the upper classes care for the practice of that religion."[21] "The working man's Bible," as one of Gissing's characters says, "is his Sunday Newspaper,"[22] and Gissing was obsessed by the destructive ability of politicians and journalists to fill listeners' and readers' minds with dogmas, which formerly only religion had had the power to do. The volume of religious books, which accounted for the highest percentage of new books to appear in 1880, slipped steadily during the decade, and novels began to take their place in importance, rising from about ten to over twenty percent of the total of new books released from 1880 to 1890. In 1888 Hardy observed "that young people nowadays go to novels for their sentiments, their religion, and their morals."[23]

A modern observer of the 1880's has the advantage, like the man of 2000 portrayed in Edward Bellamy's *Looking Backward*, of being able to foresee where society was drifting. "The singular blindness" of the people of the eighties "to the signs of the times is a phenomenon commented on by many of our historians," says Doctor Leete, who finds it impossible to believe that the economic distress of the period did not seem like "obvious and unmistakable . . . indications . . . of the transformation about to come to pass."[24] Despite the decline of national religious sentiment and the increase in suffrage, and despite all the agitation of socialists, Irish Home Rulers, and feminists in that decade, it may well be the most striking fact of the 1880's that a revolution did not visibly take place. Many historians, as a result, have pointed to the more colorful and dramatic events of the 1890's or to the First World War as proof that the Victorian period continued for a few more years after the 1880's. In truth, the decade of the eighties was a watershed in which the impotent idealism of the previous era and the emergent subjective forces of the modern world can be viewed together, whether in politics or philosophy or, what is most relevant here, the novel. "The fact of a new idea having come to one man," John Morley argued, "is a sign that it is in the air. The innovator is as much the son of his generation as the conservative." The handful of major figures, philosophers and novelists, discussed in the next two sections represent those who, in a decade of change and re-orientation of attitudes, participated in what James characterized as "the battle of the old and the new, the past and the future, of the ideas that arrive with the ideas that linger."[25]

New Philosophies: Liberty, Subjectivity, and Aestheticism

While a social revolution did not materialize in the 1880's, there was a quiet but decisive philosophical revolution. Alfred North Whitehead has dismissed the last two decades of the nineteenth century as "one of the dullest stages of thought since the time of the First Crusade,"[26] but the ideas of Nietzsche and Walter Pater testify to the presence of powerful and subversive elements in European thought. Before the end of the decade, such crucial modern ideas as the death of God, the need for a reassessment of all values, the recognition of the relativist spirit, and the pre-eminence of the individual appeared in their writings. What G. K. Chesterton praised as the "Victorian Compromise" he saw ending "roughly somewhere about 1880, when the two great positive enthusiasms of Western Europe had for the time exhausted each other—Christianity and the French Revolution."[27] The ebbing of religious belief coincided with the decline of the liberal tradition, with its faith in reason and reasoning individualism. The spirit of John Henry Newman and John Stuart Mill, the two finest exemplars of the religious and liberal counterspirits in Victorian England, continued to exert a strong influence at the end of the century, but they had been reinterpreted to such a degree that Newman's sense of "tradition" and Mill's belief in "liberty" had become, for Pater, merely aesthetic and subjective attitudes.

When in 1882 Nietzsche first announced the death of God, he did so to reveal a *fait accompli*. In the second part of his *Life of Carlyle,* published in 1884, J. A. Froude contrasted the traumatic loss of faith among the early Victorian notables, especially Carlyle and Tennyson, with the modern sense of religious alienation: "The present generation which has grown up in an open spiritual ocean, which has got used to it and has learned to swim for itself, will never know what it was to find the lights all drifting, the compasses all awry, and nothing left to steer by except the stars. In this condition," Froude continues, "the best and bravest of my own contemporaries determined to have done with insincerity, to find ground under their feet, to let the uncertain remain uncertain, but to learn how much and what we could honestly regard as true, and believe that and live by it."[28] By the 1880's it was no longer certain, to many writers, that there remained anything "true" to hold onto save the certainty of uncertainty, or what Gissing called the "Hope of Pessimism." A number of writers emulated Arnold's attempt "to recast religion,"[29] and several novelists of the 1880's, such as J. H. Shorthouse, William Hale White, Mrs. Humphry Ward, and Pater, attempted to show, in lesser or greater degrees, how much of the spirit of religion was practicable in an age of disbelief.

"The craving for a strong faith is no proof of a strong faith, but quite the contrary." Nietzsche's dismissal of Carlyle, along with all other influential Victorians, in *Twilight of the Idols* (1888) was part of his attempt to revaluate the intellectual heritage up to his time. At the same time that Herbert Spencer was trying to synthesize all of knowledge, Nietzsche saw only the spuriousness of most intellectual values and all systems, intellectual or political. Nothing remained secure, not even language: "Whatever we have words for, that we have already got beyond."[30] Insisting that he was not himself a nihilist, Nietzsche viewed his era as the prologue to an age of nihilism, and in an effort to combat it, he argued the necessity for absolute intellectual honesty and for the overcoming of self. In his desire to take upon himself so formidable an intellectual burden, which included the salvaging of the most enduring elements of European culture, and by reason of his extraordinary integrity of mind, Nietzsche seems in many ways the last of the great idealistic Western philosophers. Both the vastness of his goal and the self-destructiveness of his intellectual energies link him with Meredith, who shared something of Nietzsche's robust sense of humor, along with his physical disabilities, but who managed to escape the philosopher's mental fate. While Meredith championed the taming of the ego for the sake of society, Nietzsche constantly turned, according to Walter Kaufmann, to "the theme of the antipolitical individual who seeks self-perfection far from the modern world."[31] The emphasis on perfecting one's self rather than one's world connects Nietzsche with Pater, both of whom, unaware of the other but reacting to similar historical pressures upon similarly sensitive natures, saw in art the one redeeming quality of history. "Art and nothing but art!" Nietzsche proclaimed in the late 1880's. "It is the great means of making life possible, the great seduction to life, the great stimulant of life." Works of art, Pater declared in 1888, serve as "a sort of cloistral refuge, from a certain vulgarity in the actual world."[32] But what was treated as a tonic by Nietzsche was considered an opiate by Pater.

"Modern thought is distinguished from ancient," wrote Pater in his essay on Coleridge (1865, revised 1880), "by its cultivation of the 'relative' spirit in place of the 'absolute.' "[33] Envious, like Nietzsche, of the Hellenic ideal of harmony, Pater, too, distrusted the modern spirit of systematization, though he could never quite accept historical flux as the only philosophical absolute, as did Nietzsche in his theory of "eternal recurrence" or Meredith in his celebration of process. Agreeing with Burckhardt that "The chief phenomenon of our days is the sense of the provisional,"[34] Pater nevertheless sought a sense of permanence; the major English relativist of his time, he was willing even to consider the possibility that relativity itself was relative. In his shift of emphasis from the primacy of objective reality to the primacy of the individual's singular awareness of reality, Pater had an enormous impact upon the formation of modern sensibility. As the values of the past appeared increasingly relative and dubious, only one thing seemed indisputably real: one's own subjectivity. H. Stuart Hughes has pointed to the 1890's as the decade in which subjectivity became a major philosophical and sociological concern, but the process was already evident in the philosophers and novelists (Pater was both) of the 1880's who attempted, as George Moore noted of his own achievement, "the rescue and the individualization of the ego."[35]

"All eras in a state of decline and dissolution are subjective," Goethe remarked in the early part of the nineteenth century, and he claimed that German writers in particular were driven by a thirst for originality and personal freedom, by the desire to go their own way and satisfy only themselves without bothering with others, "from which comes much excellence, but also much absurdity."[36] In the later part of the century, the tenets of German romanticism, filtered through the views of French aestheticians, arrived full force in England by way of Pater, and the "culte de moi" (in Maurice Barrès' phrase) became as pervasive among English writers as among their continental and American colleagues. The aesthetic views of Hegel, Erich Heller maintains, were instrumental in pointing the way to the modern "artist's journey into the interior." Henceforth, the artist had his choice of realistically or satirically coming to grips with an elusive or menacing external world, or of withdrawing instead into the safety and superior reality of his inner world.[37] In the philosophies of Nietzsche and Pater, William James and Henri Bergson, in particular, the individual became both the standard and the source of reality. If systems were false, one's subjective reality was always verifiable.

The modernity of James's and Bergson's philosophies has become evident in recent years. In his *Essai sur les données immédiates de la conscience* (1889), Bergson attempted to prove the freedom of the will from all external agencies by distinguishing between the individual's outer or public self and his inner or private self. But instead of indicating, as Kant had done, the validity of both selves, Bergson claimed authenticity only for the private self: the public self exists in an artificial world of measured spatiality and is "fixed" by public conventions of language and decorum, but the private self is formless and free, reducing time and externality to whatever it chooses to make of them. In many of his novels and poems Meredith suggested the difference between the masks we wear and the sentimental ego concealed underneath, but he did so in an effort to subdue egoism and unite the public and private selves. James's amusing parable of "The Private Life," on the other hand, is devoted to the theme that one chooses to be one of two selves: either a public face, without personal freedom or identity, or a private self, which is the equivalent of being a Jamesian artist. The conflict between individual freedom and those social pressures which serve to fix one in place as a lifeless "portrait" is memorably depicted in James's great novel, *The Portrait of a Lady.* Just as the novelist insisted upon the need for artistic freedom, his brother, William James, recognized the universal existence of solipsism in *The Principles of Psychology* (1890) and *The Varieties of Religious Experience* (1902). "The axis of reality," as he noted in the latter book, "runs solely through the egotistic places,—they are strung upon it like so many beads."[38] But the popularizer of pragmatism saw as clearly as Meredith the need for

useful activity as a means of minimizing the dangers of subjectivity. For, as a recent authority on European romanticism has shown, the freeing of the ego from external limitations left many romantics the choice ultimately between nihilism or religious orthodoxy,[39] the option—as proved to be the case with Nietzsche, on the one hand, and Pater, on the other—between willfully destroying themselves or passively denying themselves.

If Darwin and Mill are viewed as the key intellectual forces in England in the two decades following 1859, Pater in many ways seems to have become the key figure by the last two decades of the century insofar as English literature is concerned. To study the various strands that make up his philosophy would necessitate undertaking an intellectual history of the nineteenth century, yet Pater remains both unique and modern in the use that he made of his sources. Between the years 1858 and 1862 while he was an undergraduate at Oxford, English intellectuals were embattled in religious and scientific controversies. And, in the miraculous year of 1859, with the publication of such works as Darwin's *Origin of Species* and Mill's *On Liberty*, England entered—or it was recognized that she had entered—"an age of crisis."[40] As a young man, Pater was already marked by a compelling need for beauty, which he found, for example, in Catholic ritual; he was also swayed by a sense of fatalism, which was heightened by his study of Hegelian historicism. But Pater never surrendered himself to the views of one philosopher or one system; the works of Darwin and Mill appeared on the scene in time to confirm his sense of historical determinism, against which the individual was incapable of exerting an influence, and of the need, nevertheless, for personal freedom. Darwin's claim for the infinite variations in nature was translated by Pater into an aesthetic injunction for helpless man at least to enjoy, through observation and analysis, the marvelous "subtleties of effect" of an unstable universe.[41]

Pater's indebtedness to Darwin, Newman, and Arnold have been discussed elsewhere,[42] but it should be noted that he transmuted Mill's plea for liberty into the "Conclusion" to the *Renaissance*, where it reappeared as an aesthetic appeal to the reader not to become the victim of any single, dogmatic way of looking at the world, including one's own. Read in the context of 1859, *On*

Liberty is a rational, balanced, Victorian book, a defense of intellectual freedom and an attempt (as has been noted) "to release the human mind from every other influence except logic."[43] Mill believed, above all, in the primacy of reason, and he cautioned, "No one pretends that actions should be as free as opinions." Read with the background of the 1880's in mind, however, *On Liberty* seems considerably more radical than its author intended. Mill agreed with John Sterling to the effect that " 'Pagan self-assertion' is one of the elements of human worth, as well as 'Christian self-denial,' " but where Mill was interested in balancing and combining the opposing half-truths, a later generation noted only the approval of "self-assertion." Mill's pronouncement that "the individual is not accountable to society for his actions, insofar as these concern the interests of no person but himself,"[44] is obvious enough, but it could seem revolutionary indeed when taken out of context. For Meredith as for Mill, the need for individual expression in society was ultimately for the sake of that society. But it was precisely the effect of the freeing of the ego from his societal bonds which, combined with the new materialistic philosophies,[45] insured the emergence of modern man.

In *The New Republic* (1877), W. H. Mallock imagined a situation in which such influential Victorians as Ruskin, Arnold, and Huxley (under assumed names) converse on the subject of how culture, faith, and philosophy can be made to serve in the present, critical situation. One man alone among the guests takes the line that the collapse of society would not be such a bad thing:

> "I," said Mr. Rose, "look upon social dissolution as the true condition of the most perfect life. For the centre of life is in the individual, and it is only through dissolution that the individual can re-emerge. All the warrings of endless doubts, all the questionings of matter and of spirit, which I have myself known, I value only because, remembering the weariness of them, I take a profounder and more exquisite pleasure in the colour of a crocus, the pulsations of a chord of music, or a picture of Sandro Botticelli's."

Mr. Rose, whose two subjects are "self-indulgence and art,"[46] was modeled upon Pater; and if Mallock was unfair to one of the most complex figures in English literature, he did present the image of Pater that was becoming accepted and idolized by a new genera-

tion. Pater had written his first version of the Coleridge essay in 1865 and what was to become the "Conclusion" to the *Renaissance* in 1868, but his modernity was not sufficiently realized until the late 1870's.[47] In the same year that Mallock recognized the social danger of his philosophy, Pater himself suppressed the "Conclusion," fearing that its call for aesthetic hedonism might be misinterpreted as an active ideal.

Despite his criticism of Coleridge's unwillingness to abandon a life of single-minded aspiration and to commit himself to the "relative spirit," Pater could not restrain his sympathy for a desire so close to his own. "Coleridge," he wrote, "by what he did, what he was, and what he failed to do, represents that inexhaustible discontent, languor, and home-sickness, that endless regret, the chords of which ring all through our modern literature."[48] In the essay on "Winckelmann" (1867), which reappeared in the *Renaissance*, Pater contrasted the Greek achievement of harmony and repose reflected in Hellenic art with the "modern world, with its conflicting claims, its entangled interests," and its inability to arrive at a sense of "unity." "Yet, not less than ever," he declared, "the intellect demands completeness, centrality." Tormented by his awareness of a deterministic, fragmented modern world, Pater sought consolation in the appreciation of works of art. Only in art, he hinted in the "Winckelmann" essay, can one receive "an equivalent for the sense of freedom";[49] for Pater, however, art provided this saving illusion only for the onlooker, not for the modern artist.

In the essay on "Wordsworth" (1874), he defined the great Romantic poet's great achievement in terms of his outlook—"impassioned contemplation"—rather than his creativity. "That the end of life is not action but contemplation—*being* as distinct from *doing*—a certain disposition of the mind," Pater stressed, "is, in some shape or other, the principle of all the higher morality." But "being" for Pater meant observing, absorbing, taking in impressions—treating life, in short, as a work of art, and contemplation as the only activity worth pursuing. "To treat life in the spirit of art," he proposed, "is to make life a thing in which means and ends are identified."[50] The famous "Conclusion" to the *Renaissance*, with its appeal "to be for ever curiously testing new opinions and courting new impressions," is underlined by a belief in human limitations rather than addressed to the question of human possi-

bilities in an age of change. All forms of activity—even artistic creation—are doomed to frustration, and only through contemplation can one achieve some measure of success. In the late essay on "Mérimée" (1890), Pater argued that for the artist born into the modern world—everywhere detecting "the hollow ring of fundamental nothingness under the apparent surface of things"[51]—there is a choice only of succumbing to nihilism or else creating works of narrowly subjective interest.

Nietzsche and Pater, the two major philosophers of the 1880's, both proclaimed the freedom of the will—freedom from all past theories and all systems—and the pre-eminent value of art. For Nietzsche, however, the will was seen as an instrument of power, and the will to power meant the will to *create*; for Pater, the will existed, at best, as *vision*. The Pateresque individual, hence, is a receptacle of impressions, not a transmitter. The danger of Pater, as Yeats realized, was that he placed too high a value upon passivity: "The soul becomes a mirror not a brazier." Yeats called his artistic associates of the late 1880's and 1890's members of the "tragic generation," and he wistfully recalled that "we looked consciously to Pater for our philosophy." "It taught us," Yeats said of Pater's novel *Marius the Epicurean*, "to walk upon a rope, tightly stretched through serene air, and we were left to keep our feet upon a swaying rope in a storm."[52] Pater exerted a crucial influence upon the modern novel through his insistence upon the primacy of subjective over objective reality: the world exists only to be observed, he implied, and the single measure of reality is subjective consciousness. George Moore and Oscar Wilde enthusiastically claimed Pater as their teacher, but it was an American, Henry James, who, in his theory of the novel and through the creation in his novels of hero-observers like Hyacinth Robinson or Lambert Strether, immortalized the Pateresque lesson.

Responses to Change in the Novel: Romanticism versus Realism

Despite the sense of historical transformation and drift evident in the 1880's, the rise of imperialism, aestheticism, and philosophical solipsism in that decade attests in varying ways to the un-

willingness of many Englishmen to face or endure the changing scene about them. The need for realistic solutions was met instead by a number of romantic evasions, and this split between realism and romance in politics was reflected in the split between realism and romance in the novel. Where English novelists had traditionally employed a dialectical process whereby they chose to mirror reality but to select and heighten their materials in a subjective fashion, they now found themselves, with the exception of Meredith, choosing between one or the other: "The last two decades of the century," as Kenneth Graham has shown, saw "the rise of a new school of realism and a rival school of romance," and the result was that "dialectic" was replaced by "warfare."[53] The documented romanticism of Sir Walter Scott gave way to the exotic romanticizing of H. Rider Haggard, just as the sympathetic realism of George Eliot was replaced by the detached, analytical realism (as critics complained) of her disciple Henry James. Meredith alone, among novelists of the 1880's, sought to combine realism with idealism in the manner of Goethe.

In *A History of Our Own Time,* which appeared in 1880, Justin McCarthy argued that the practice of realism had gone as far as it could or should go: "Its close details, its trivial round of common cares and ambitions, its petty trials and easy loves, seem now at last to have spent their attractive power, and to urge with their fading breath the need of some new departure for the novelist." In an age of realism, McCarthy proposed that fiction "be dipped once again in the old holy well of romance."[54] The "Romantic Revival" which materialized in the 1880's did so despite—and in opposition to—the fact that it was not a romantic age. The major literary force of the period, in fact, was a superrealist, Émile Zola, and, at the same time that Haggard and Kipling and Robert Louis Stevenson were diverting the imaginations of their readers toward far-off places, an impressive group of realistic American, French, and Russian novels and novelists were appearing in England. Meanwhile, in the last years of his life, Anthony Trollope, the "High Priest of Victorian realism,"[55] surveyed his changing world with a mixture of stoicism and regret.

From one point of view, the English novel may be seen to have exhausted itself in the 1880's with the death of George Eliot in

1880 and Trollope in 1882; from another point of view, the novel was "reborn" with the birth, in that decade, of Joyce, Virginia Woolf, and D. H. Lawrence. The Victorian novel reached its climax in *Middlemarch* (1872), the most notable English novel to balance the aspirations of the individual will against the demands of society. But, it should be remembered that George Eliot set her greatest book in the England of the 1830's, at the time when signs were appearing—along with the Reform Bill—of forces that would prove destructive to Victorian stability. In *Daniel Deronda* (1876), her last and "only novel of contemporary life,"[56] she depicted an England already disintegrating as a result of the interrelated forces of materialism and egoism. Victorian individualism, which customarily channeled its energy in social directions, could no longer find a place for itself in England. Deronda's voyage to the East may remind us of the Victorian hunger for assured religious roots, but there was obviously no outlet for him in England. And for Gwendolen Harleth, there were neither roots nor missions to satisfy her half-articulated needs. Could George Eliot have continued to write fiction in the 1880's? James asserted that in form *Middlemarch* "sets a limit . . . to the development of the old-fashioned English novel."[57] In its subject matter, too, and in its author's appeal to individual self-denial and sympathy, the novel reflects an attitude no longer tenable in a decade when self-realization or escapism were becoming the only standards. Only Meredith in the eighties attempted bravely to graft the theme of "the old-fashioned English novel" onto a new language. Ultimately, however, both theme and language proved incapable of survival.

After her death, critics of the time favorably compared George Eliot's "realism," with its compassion for as well as fidelity to real life, to the new, scientific realism of James and Zola. While George Eliot seemed the exemplary realistic novelist, Scott was unquestionably the novelist critics were fondest of holding up as a model to aspiring writers. In 1878 he was the first novelist to be included in the English Men of Letters series, and his capable if uninspiring biographer, R. H. Hutton, who found little but pessimism and the depiction of aimlessness in those works of James which he reviewed for the *Spectator*, drew attention to "the tonic influence, the large instructiveness, the stimulating intellectual air, of Scott's historic tales."[58] In *Fiction, Fair and Foul* (1880), Ruskin compared the Waverley novelist to the new writers, whose work seemed to him ugly and without principles. Ruskin was appalled by what he considered the modern novelists' celebration of self-indulgence. The great literature of the past, prose or poetry, he argued, revealed "absolute command over all passion, however intense," a language completely clear and straightforward, with the "utmost spiritual contents in the words." "Scott," he affirmed, "lived in a country and time, when, from highest to lowest, but chiefly in that dignified and nobly severe middle class to which he himself belonged, a habit of serene and stainless thought was as natural to the people as their mountain air."[59] In his autobiography, H. G. Wells alluded to Scott as an "exponent" of the earlier "prevalent sense of social stability," "a man of intensely conservative quality" who never doubted "what was right or wrong, handsome or ungracious, just or mean," who saw "events therefore as a play of individualities in a rigid frame of values never more to be questioned or permanently changed":

> Throughout the broad smooth flow of nineteenth century life in Great Britain, the art of fiction floated on this same assumption of social fixity. The Novel in English was produced in an atmosphere of security for the entertainment of secure people who liked to feel established and safe for good. Its standards were established within that apparently permanent frame and the criticism of it began to be irritated and perplexed when, through a new instability, the splintering frame began to get into the picture.[60]

Wells exaggerated the degree of "security" found among the English of the early nineteenth century. The sense of balance in mid-Victorian fiction was the result very often of painful efforts on the part of the major novelists to resist the increasing feeling of individual solitude and despair, and to create—to invent, if necessary —a community to which the individual could relate. Still, history is not only what happens but what people at the time and just afterward think happened, and for many elder Victorians like Ruskin who found themselves in the 1880's, the illusion of security in Scott was preferable to the fact of changing times.

"The famous English novelists have passed away, and have left no successors of like fame," Arnold declared in 1887,[61] and, while he looked to Tolstoy to carry on in fiction the tradition of high seriousness, other Victorians were uneasy about the simultaneous convergence from abroad of introspective Russian novelists, French naturalists, and analytical Americans. By far the most discussed and feared novelist of the eighties was Zola, and Zolaism came to stand for the various threats of materialism, barbarism, and socialism. Tennyson, in the *Idylls of the King,* had warned that modern man was giving signs of returning "to the beast"; Zola seemed to glorify *la bête humaine.* Because of his noisy artistic and pseudo-scientific theorizing, and because of the lengths to which his fanatical belief in realism led him, Zola seemed *the* literary theorist and realist of the age. "It is owing to him," Edmund Gosse declared in 1890, "that the threads of Flaubert and Daudet, Dostoiefsky and Tolstoi, Howells and Henry James can be drawn into anything like a single system."[62] Fiercely opposed to romantic idealism, Zola in 1880 preached "the lofty lesson of the real," and he argued that "nothing is so dangerous as the romantic vein; such works, depicting the world in false colors, throw imaginations out of gear and lead people astray." Promoting naturalism as a fictional method, he insisted that only by seeing what really exists can readers "try to come to terms with it. We are only scientists, analysts, anatomists . . . and our works have the certainty, the solidity, and the practical application of works of science. I know of no school which is more moral or more austere."[63]

The self-confident tone of the theoretician, however, was often belied by the novelist's doubts. In *L'Oeuvre* (1886), the painter Bongrand, modelled upon Zola's idol Manet, admits to a loss of faith in everything but art itself and suggestively broods upon whether creation is possible in an age of doubt, a worry shared by Pater in his essay on Mérimée and by Hardy:

> We're living in a bad season, in a vitiated atmosphere, with
> the century coming to an end and everything in process of
> demolition; buildings torn down wholesale; every field being
> ploughed and reploughed and every mortal thing stinking of
> death. How can anybody expect to be healthy? The nerves
> go to pieces, general neurosis sets in, and art begins to totter,
> faced with a free-for-all, with anarchy to follow, and
> personality fighting tooth and nail for self-assertion.

At this point, Zola's mouthpiece, Sandoz, while agreeing that "the century has been a failure," urges that through faith in science, but above all in artistic work, artists can resist the dual temptations of abandonment to nihilism or "supernaturalism." "We are not an end," Sandoz affirms, "we are a transition, the beginning only of something new . . . And it's that sets my mind at rest, and somehow encourages me: to know we are moving towards the reason and solidity that only science can give . . ."[64]

In England, Zola was denounced for his political and social danger. (The downfall of Parnell, for example, was traced to motives, according to the London *Times*, which Zola had popularized in France.) Tennyson imagined the consequences of "maiden fancies wallowing in the troughs of Zolaism," and in the late 1880's, Henry Vizetelly, the publisher of Zola, Flaubert, the Russian novelists, and George Moore, was persecuted and imprisoned for publishing such books as *La Terre*, the substance of which, as was argued in Parliament, "was of such a leprous character that it would be impossible for any young man who had not learned the Divine secret of self-control to have read it without committing some form of outward sin within twenty-four hours after."[65] The "troughs of Zolaism" were one more sign of the democratization, the "Americanization" of English principles. In a hysterical attack upon "The New Naturalism," a critic writing in the *Fortnightly Review* in 1885 identified it with Darwinism and blamed Zolaism for the decline of the West: "It is beyond question—look at France if you want overwhelming demonstration of it—that the issue of what M. Zola calls the Naturalistic Evolution is the banishing from human life of all that gives it glory and honour: the victory of fact over principle, of mechanism over imagination, of appetites, dignified as rights, over duties, of sensation over intellect, of the belly over the heart, of fatalism over moral freedom, of brute force over justice, in a word, of matter over mind."[66]

Meredith, while no admirer of realism divorced from idealism, nevertheless called the French writers' "Realism" a "corrective of the more corruptingly vapourous with its tickling hints at sensuality."[67] The practitioners of naturalism may have resorted to excesses, but, as Meredith realized, the English determination to ignore reality and to conceal brutal egoism under sentimental rhetoric was far more serious. Criticizing George Sand's reliance on sentimentalism, James concluded "that something even better in a novelist is that tender appreciation of actuality which makes even the application of a single coat of rose-colour seem an act of violence." In a letter to Howells in 1884, he declared that Zola and his colleagues were doing "the only kind of work, to-day, that I respect; and in spite of their ferocious pessimism and their handling of unclean things, they are at least serious and honest."[68] With the publication of *French Poets and Novelists* (the first of his books to be published in England) in 1878, James was confused in critics' minds with the disciples of the French realists. A British reviewer of *Roderick Hudson,* which appeared in England the following year, enunciated a theme which was to echo through criticisms of James made in the eighties: he was tagged as a master of "subtle but somewhat morbid analysis"; his work was considered "cynical" and pessimistic in tone; his novels were regarded as "painful" reading.[69] In a by no means unsympathetic account of "Modern Fiction," which appeared in the *Atlantic* in 1883, Charles Dudley Warner warned against the danger to American optimism of James's and Howells' (among others) use of a realistic technique which discounted the existence of ideals:

> The characteristics which are prominent, when we think of our recent fiction, are a wholly unidealized view of human society, which has got the name of realism; a delight in representing the worst phases of social life; an extreme analysis of persons and motives; the sacrifice of action to psychological study; the substitution of studies of character for anything like a story; a notion that it is not artistic, and that it is untrue to nature to bring any novel to a definite consummation, and especially to end it happily; and a despondent tone about society, politics, and the whole drift of modern life.[70]

The effect of James' stories, another critic declared in 1885, is a uniform "impression, not of the tragic pathos of life, but of its general futility."[71] James was abused not only for not being George Eliot, but—and this was even more serious—for not being Sir Walter Scott.

In his much-abused essay in praise of James, which appeared in 1882, Howells declared, "The art of fiction has, in fact, become a finer art in our day than it was with Dickens and Thackeray."

While citing James as the triumphant heir to George Eliot and Hawthorne, Howells emphasized the need for the abandonment of such Victorianisms as the use of plot or happy endings. "In one manner or another," he argued, "the stories were all told long ago; and now we want merely to know what the novelist thinks about persons and situations."[72] The defense of novelistic artistry was interpreted as an endorsement of literary egoism and a repudiation of tradition. Howells' unfortunately worded eulogy had the effect of turning a large segment of the critical press against the pretensions of the Jamesian novel; and James's reputation was severely damaged at a time when the sales of his work were beginning to decline. In 1887, H. Rider Haggard protested the "laboured nothingness of this new American school of fiction," and praised instead "the swiftness, and strength, and directness of the great English writers of the past."[73]

James himself paid tribute to the passing of George Eliot, just as he praised the achievement of Zola, in a superlative essay on each. His study of Trollope, in particular, is an eloquent estimate of one of the last major Victorian novelists by one of the greatest modern novelists. "He accepted all the common restrictions," James asserted, "and found that even within the barriers there was plenty of material."[74] Trollope did not compose his novels with the logic of a historian, with a sense of artistic necessity, but his works do contain the most detailed record of Victorian society, James declared. When he decided to write a novel in the Victorian manner—*The Tragic Muse*—James took Trollope as his model, although his theme was one that Trollope would have found inimical. James's tributary essay was written before the posthumous appearance of the *Autobiography*, which revealed more than James had suspected of how little Trollope took himself seriously as an artist. Trollope's matter-of-fact account of how he wrote literature as a trade—producing so many pages a day, beginning a new novel if he had a working hour left over—seemed reprehensible at a time when writers were considering the "art" of fiction. Gissing, who knew better, depicted the successful literary man, in Jasper Milvain of *New Grub Street*, as an advocate of the "trade" of fiction, capable of turning away from a conversation with the declaration, "I can get two hours' work before going to bed."[75]

While Scott seemed the exemplar of idealistic normalcy to the Victorian age, Trollope best embodied the age he lived in, just as he best described it in his novels. Incapable of understanding the desires of a Dorothea Brooke or a Daniel Deronda to surmount the limitations of or to escape from their society, Trollope was content to remain in that society and to keep his characters within Victorian limits. Although he could, on occasion, create studies of psychological aberration beyond the reach of any of his English contemporaries, he preferred to be considered, as a modern admirer describes him, "the articulate perfection of [the] normal quality" of mid-Victorian England.[76] "A more convincing impression of what everyday life was like in England in the middle Victorian years," Asa Briggs declares, pairing Trollope with Bagehot, "can be gathered from their pages than from any other source."[77]

It may well be true, however, that "the well-organized and substantial world that he presented so matter-of-factly," as Harry Levin observes, "was a dream of order, a mirage of solidity, an oasis of comfort in a desert of anxieties not dissimilar to our own."[78] The stability of the Victorian world was all the more coveted by Trollope as a result of his Bohemian upbringing. The improvidence of his family, their life of exile in Belgium are candidly portrayed in the *Autobiography:* "A sadder household never was held together. They were all dying; except my mother, who would sit up night after night nursing the dying ones and writing novels the while,—so that there might be a decent roof for them to die under." The Trollope family was emotional to a fault, and the energetic Mrs. Trollope judged all things from the heart. Endowed with "a genuine feeling for romance," the son admitted, "she was neither clear-sighted nor accurate; and in her attempts to describe morals, manners, and even facts, was unable to avoid the pitfalls of exaggeration."[79] Throughout his life and work, Trollope successfully avoided those pitfalls, but the remembrance of personal insecurity found inverted expression in his celebration of Victorian communal ties. As an outsider, originally, he cherished the Victorian balance, and his novels repeatedly stress the dangers of self-indulgence.

In his later novels Trollope became preoccupied with the theme of loosening Victorian ties. A recent writer has commented on the discovery in late Trollope that "the forces that pull people apart" had become "stronger than the cohesive forces" in the Victorian world. As a novelist whose subject was contemporary England, Trollope, in a period of change, "made change his predominant subject matter."[80] The same year he began his memoirs, in 1875, he published *The Way We Live Now,* and the figure of Melmotte, the Continental Jewish speculator who wins a seat in Parliament, constitutes Trollope's most stringent symbolical portrait of what he considered the foreign and materialistic threats to English society. It is a common bond among the great Victorian novelists that the creation of images of a stable society, which they venerated and feared losing, was the result of lives that were not stable in origin. Dickens, George Eliot, Thackeray, Meredith, Trollope, and Hardy were all outsiders in terms of their background or social status; yet, paradoxically we look to them for a depiction of Victorian equilibrium and to their late novels for an account of the dangers of modern materialism and egoism.

If Melmotte represented the forces of change to Trollope, his favorite character among his creations was Plantagenet Palliser, the dutiful future Prime Minister of the political novels. Palliser is the Victorian novelist's equivalent to Tennyson's Arthur in the *Idylls of the King*—the unglamorous but selfless ruler of society. But if the poet's Camelot is doomed because of emergent selfish assertiveness, the novelist's Victorian world is most clearly endangered by excesses depicted in *The Way We Live Now.* In his biography of Lord Palmerston, which appeared in 1882, Trollope paid homage to the antireform leader who had maintained only established views and whose followers always knew where they stood with him. Appalled by the current political scene, he drew a nostalgic image of an older, stable order.

In his final works, Trollope attempted to deal with rather more liberal themes than he had used before. In the last of the political novels, *The Duke's Children* (1880), youth chooses its own destiny, however erratic, and Palliser gives in to it. In *Dr. Wortle's School* (1881), a bigamous union is condoned—the bigamy is accidental rather than deliberate, and ultimately not bigamous at all—and the libelled Mrs. Peacocke calls the "hardness" of her accusers "at any rate as bad as my impurity."[81] The recognition of the relativity of morality in special cases is one of the major ideas in Trollope's last works, such as *Dr. Scarborough's Family* (published in 1883). In his last completed novel, *An Old Man's Love* (published in 1884), an older man gives up his fiancée—whom he loves, we are told, as Arthur loved Guinevere—to a young man whose major advantage is that he is young. In his last years, Trollope recognized the claims of youth, even if he noticed a decline in responsibility among the supplanting generation. His unfinished novel *The Land Leaguers*, however, attacked Parnell's endeavors in Ireland and challenged the plea for Home Rule on the ground that "Never were a people less fitted to exercise such dominion without control."[82] Home Rule seemed to him a romantic idea rather than a realistic proposal, and no doubt Trollope intended—in his strangest novel and his one attempt at science fiction, *The Fixed Period* (1882)—to suggest that the efforts of a future liberated British colony to enforce a policy of euthanasia for its elderly citizens symbolized what might happen if the Irish went their own way without England's civilizing influence. Trollope associated the dangers of the new democracy with the vestiges of romantic egoism. In the biography of Palmerston, he wistfully looked back to the days when "democratic enmity to order was not at work in England."[83]

Trollope's political writings, as Briggs observes, were confessed "substitutes for political action,"[84] but the novelist's very conception of the trade of fiction was an attempt to transform a Bohemian diversion into a respectable profession. In his biography of Thackeray for the English Men of Letters series (1879), he noted that his great predecessor had been "a man of fits and starts, who, not having been in his early years drilled to method, never achieved it in his career." Once Trollope made up his mind to undertake the writing of novels as a full-time job, he tried to escape from such instability. "I found it to be expedient," he recalled, "to bind myself by certain self-imposed laws," such as the production of so many pages a week. "I have been told," he added, "that such appliances are beneath the notice of a man of genius. I have never fancied myself to be a man of genius, but had I been so I think I might well have subjected myself to these trammels."[85] Despite his radically different conception of fiction as a sacred craft, James praised Trollope for having preserved the record of his time in a more convincing manner than the French naturalists. But Trollope's realistic theme and objective style were anachronisms in the eighties, and in his *Confessions of a Young Man,* published six years after Trollope's death, George Moore declared, "The healthy school is played out in England; all that could be said has been said." In *Avowals* he wittily characterized Trollope as "a great revolutionary" to the extent that he "carried commonplace further than anyone dreamed it could be carried," thereby necessitating a "reaction."[86] Henceforth, Moore deemed, a new language, a new method, and a freeing of the ego were necessary if the novel were to continue.

[3] The Freeing of the Ego

*The individual is something quite new which
creates new things, something absolute; all his
acts are entirely his own.
Ultimately, the individual derives the values of
his acts from himself; because he has to
interpret in a quite individual way even the
words he has inherited.*
(*Nietzsche,* The Will to Power)

*[H]e was ready now to concede, somewhat more
easily than others, the first point of his new
lesson, that the individual is to himself the
measure of all things, and to rely on the exclusive
certainty to himself of his own impressions.*
(*Pater,* Marius the Epicurean)

When Rousseau announced at the
opening of his *Confessions* that he was "commencing an undertaking, hitherto without precedent, and which will never find an
imitator," he could scarcely have anticipated how commonplace
such a project would appear in the course of two centuries. Before
Rousseau, the writing of confessions had been reserved, for the
most part, for religious purposes—to show, in Bunyan's words,
"the merciful working of God upon my soul." St. Augustine and
Pascal memorably exposed how their anguished souls found comfort in God, but the exhibition of one's self mattered only insofar
as the self was surrendered to God. Pater, who hovered near the
possibility of such a renunciation in his last years, remarked of
Pascal that "he interests us as precisely an inversion of what is
called the aesthetic life," but George Moore, willing to divorce
style from purpose in preparing his own secular *Confessions*,
claimed that "The whole theory and practice of modern literature"
evolved from St. Augustine's use of "psychological analysis."[1]

With the disappearance of fixed standards of the past—religious, political, social—writers increasingly found themselves either constructing subjective standards to take their place or else attempting, in one way or another, to escape the new burden on the self. The 1880's witnessed a rise simultaneously in the creation of fictional autobiographies, which described the loss of and the need for new spiritual values, and in romantic invitations to various forms of withdrawal or escapism. Whether they chose to celebrate their rejection of Victorianism, like Samuel Butler and Moore, to determine if some "sort of religious phase [was] possible for the modern mind" (in Pater's phrase),[2] like William Hale White and Pater, or to cultivate interest in exotic places or aesthetic masks, like Stevenson and Wilde, the new novelists all responded to the great fact of the liberation of the modern ego. The implications of this freeing of individuality had been realized by Kierkegaard and Dostoevsky as a terrible burden if disconnected from religion. In *The Brothers Karamazov*, which appeared in 1880, Dostoevsky deplored the effects of "this terrible individualism": "For everyone strives to keep his individuality, everyone wants to secure the greatest possible fullness of life for himself. But meantime all his efforts result not in attaining fullness of life but self-destruction, for instead of self-realization he ends by arriving at complete solitude."[3] Stendhal, the greatest and most self-knowing of literary egoists, had predicted that his time would come in 1880, but the decade revealed a triumph of the ego which might have surprised and appalled one who had repeatedly shown in his novels "that egoism is self-destroying."[4] In *The Egoist* (1879), Meredith explored the dangers to society and self of a devotion to self, but, for Henry James, the need for and the theme of individual freedom proved irresistible.

Many of the great Victorians have left behind records of their lives:[5] in 1868 Gladstone published *A Chapter of Autobiography;* Mill's *Autobiography*, which dates back to the 1850's, appeared posthumously in 1873; Darwin's autobiographical sketch was largely finished in 1876, the same year Trollope put aside his own memoirs. Although the tone of these autobiographies was generally nostalgic, mention need only be made of Samuel Butler's

The Way of All Flesh, begun in 1873, to indicate that a new, iconoclastic spirit was also appearing. If Trollope had endeavored to fit himself into the Victorian picture, it was to be Butler's goal to extricate himself from his age. Where Mill had stressed his typicality—insisting that, under similar training, anyone could learn as he had—later autobiographers emphasized their singularity. The autobiographies of the eighties were very often portraits of the individual as outsider, as spectator, as observant artist, or even as, in Whistler's case, enemy of the Victorian world.

As the author of the *Confessions of a Young Man* (1888), George Moore may be said to have inaugurated the "be all my sins remembered" school of English literature. Yet the cultivated egoism of Moore makes an interesting contrast to the unabashed candor of Trollope. At the beginning of his *Autobiography*, Trollope declares that he will not, and cannot, confess everything: "That I, or any man, should tell everything of himself, I hold to be impossible. Who could endure to own the doing of a mean thing? Who is there that has done none?" Yet he fulfills the promise "that nothing that I say shall be untrue."[6] There is more unvarnished, if often cynical, truth in the Victorian's memoirs, written at twice Moore's age, than in the aesthete's. Trollope knew himself as if he had been one of his own characters, and he exposed his weaknesses mercilessly and humorously, thereby providing all the ammunition needed for the anti-Trollope crusade that followed. G. K. Chesterton shrewdly observes of Moore that, in his attempt always to be and to unmask himself, he was forced to resort to posing. His constant effort at being self-conscious destroyed the possibility that there could ever be a stable self capable of self-revelation. For all his devotion to putting himself down on paper, Moore, as well as Butler, affords proof of Nietzsche's epigram: "Talking much about oneself can also be a means to conceal oneself."[7]

"Every man's work," Butler wrote, "whether it be literature or music or pictures or architecture or anything else, is always a portrait of himself, and the more he tries to conceal himself the more clearly will his character appear in spite of him."[8] Butler finished *The Way of All Flesh* in 1885, although nearly twenty years were to pass before it was published posthumously. His reticence, in this respect, was Victorian, and, although the work itself was intended as an assault upon Victorianism, the point of the satire is meaningless without an awareness of the world that it attacks. U. C. Knoepflmacher has suggestively commented on the modernity of Butler, arguing that, with his interest in the unconscious, he is a bridge between the Victorians and later vitalists like Shaw and Lawrence.[9] Yet Butler, who was born before James or Pater, can be seen from another point of view as one of the last Victorians to offer definite answers to the perplexing questions raised in the late nineteenth century with regard to the validity of Darwin's findings. Nevertheless, compared with Ruskin's autobiography, *Praeterita*, which began to appear in the year that Butler's fictional memoir was finished, *The Way of All Flesh* is undeniably an important document in the emergence of modern sensibility.

In some respects, Ruskin and Butler were strikingly similar. Bachelors all their lives (excepting Ruskin's brief, unfortunate marriage), they were both solitary men who found an emotional outlet in scientific and artistic studies. Temperamentally aloof, they each formulated a philosophy in response to the scientific and mechanistic findings of the age which stressed man's ability to will some form of creative evolution. Ruskin's ideal society was found in the communality of the medieval past, to be sure, while Butler's dream was of the freedom of the remote future; yet, despite their efforts to reform the world, Butler's admission, as expressed by Ernest Pontifex, holds true for them both: "I am an Ishmael by instinct as much as by accident of circumstances, but if I keep out of society I shall be less vulnerable than Ishmaels generally are."[10] Whereas Butler recounted his past life in an effort at self-justification, Ruskin very often pinpointed those moments in his past when everything went astray. Brought up in solitary conditions, Ruskin found himself very early becoming a sympathetic "spectator," but also a man unable to love. "My entire delight," he noted, "was in observing without being myself noticed,—if I could have been invisible, all the better." Ruskin regretted how much he had lost "of time, chance, and—duty, (a duty missed is the worst of loss)," but he also defended the detached nature of his upbringing for having provoked feelings of general, if not particular, sympathy:

> We [he says of his parents and himself] did not travel for
> adventures, nor for company, but to see with our eyes, and to
> measure with our hearts. If you have sympathy, the aspect of
> humanity is more true to the depths of it than its words; and
> even in my own land, the things in which I have been least
> deceived are those which I have learned as their Spectator.

In his depiction of himself as incapacitated observer, Ruskin shows
affinities with Pater, just as he pointed the way to his greatest
modern admirer, Proust. Looking backward, during a lucid interval
in the frenzied last decades of his life, Ruskin observed: "in the
total of me, I am but the same youth, disappointed and rheumatic."[11]

For the purposes of his fictional autobiography, Butler presented
himself as both the developing Ernest Pontifex and his older, cynical patron, Overton. Whereas Ruskin seemed disturbed to discover
what he had become and why, Butler was pleased to see himself
having turned out for the best: "those who know him intimately,"
as Overton smugly remarks at the end of the book, "do not know
that they wish him greatly different from what he actually is."
From a master of irony, the understatement seems curiously uni-
ronic, perhaps unfortunately so. For if *The Way of All Flesh* is an
attack upon the various hypocritical masks worn by the Victorians,
it turns into an apologia for the cynical, all-knowing mask of
Overton-Butler. "If people would dare to speak to one another un-
reservedly," reflects Ernest, "there would be a good deal less sor-
row in the world a hundred years hence." Butler intended his hero
to defy the laws of environmental and hereditary determinism and
settle down to "a quiet, unobtrusive life of self-indulgence."[12] But
the social and physical laws operating against his hero—economic
necessity, the workings of the unconscious, sexual impulses—work
against the belief in vitalism. Ernest not only seems predestined
to become Overton, but Overton appears unable to cast off his
mask of cynical contemplation. Where Ruskin and Butler disagree
most strongly is with regard to the one's belief in self-denial and
the other's defense of self-assertion.

In another major work written in 1885—perhaps the decisive
year for English fiction as far as the transition from Victorianism
to modernism is concerned—Pater attempted to reconcile his own
conflicting drives toward assertion and renunciation. *Marius the*

Epicurean is the most important of Pater's several spiritual auto-biographies, which, beginning with "The Child in the House" (1878), he cast into a new form that combines elements of fiction and the essay. Pater's "Imaginary Portraits," as he labeled four such sketches, are all intellectual self-portraits, revelations of the author's simultaneous desire for the security of inertia and for a "stirring of the senses," which seems, while it lasts, like a real exertion of will. In an early essay on "Aesthetic Poetry" (1868), he described the lure of aestheticism as "that inversion of homesickness known to some, that incurable thirst for the sense of escape, which no actual form of life satisfies";[13] in "The Child in the House," on the other hand, he apotheosized the memory of his "old house" as "a citadel of peace in the heart of the trouble." When the "larger world without" appears to Florian Deleal, the former child is confronted by the joint spectacle of tangible beauty, heightened by a sense of pain and of ubiquitous human suffering. In the desire to escape the suffering of existence, Pater looked back to home as a womb-like "place 'inclosed' and 'sealed,' "[14] or else he looked to a means which provided a momentary illusion of freedom. The famous appeal in the "Conclusion" to the *Renaissance* to be always "getting as many pulsations as possible into the given time" was based on the premise that only through such aesthetic experience can one seem to "set the spirit free for a moment."[15] In *Marius*, the first in a projected trilogy of novels, Pater attempted to find a means to set his spirit free and at rest at the same time.

T. S. Eliot described *Marius* as the culminating "chimerical" effort of the Victorians to arrive at a substitute for religion in an age characterized by the "dissolution of thought,"[16] but Pater's career is impressive for its continuous questioning spirit and for the refusal to settle for any arbitrary form of orthodoxy. The realization of the need for religious assurance and the recognition that his efforts in that direction were hampered by the contradictory impulses of his mind did not put a stop to his wish for some form of synthesis. If he ultimately made of religion a vehicle for aesthetic enjoyment (in *Marius*), he at least did not offer his subjective faith as the only solution open to others, but stressed the singular circumstances which had led him to it. Pater's version of Christianity might be termed pragmatic expediency. While he intimated to Vernon Lee that he sought in *Marius* to express an alternative to the choices of aesthetic pessimism, positivism, and Voltairean optimism which she had cited as the only possible faiths in an age of unbelief, he suggested to Mrs. Humphry Ward that Christianity was at least "a workable hypothesis."[17] Whereas Ruskin claimed that by becoming a spectator he had developed feelings of human sympathy, Pater realized that the limited faculties of observation and the workings of solitary reflection were only too likely to narrow the scope of human understanding and to focus the mind, self-destructively, upon itself. Man is perpetually at the mercy, Pater warns, of committing himself to wrong and limiting doctrines, and he must be absolutely certain that he chooses his way of life wisely. The point of the "Conclusion" to the *Renaissance* is to prod the reader not to dwarf himself "into the narrow chamber of the individual mind," but to cultivate enough impressions so that he will not be at the mercy of his "own dream of a world": the aim of "for ever curiously testing new opinions and courting new impressions" is to prevent oneself from ever "acquiescing in a facile orthodoxy of Comte, or of Hegel, or of our own."[18] Unfortunately, the "Conclusion" was interpreted by many as the presentation of a new, hedonistic dogma, a new way of life. In the second edition of the *Renaissance* (1877), Pater removed it from the book, only to restore it in the 1888 edition with a footnote directing the reader to *Marius* for a fuller discussion.

The message of the "Conclusion," one discovers in *Marius*, is an echo of the Cyrenaic doctrine: "an 'aesthetic' education, as it might now be termed."[19] The aim is not personal "pleasure, but a general completeness of life"—what Coleridge had found only in religion and Winckelmann in Greek art. The quality of aesthetic experience and religious assurance are thereby combined, and Pater holds up "Insight" as "the most direct and effective auxiliary" "towards such a full or complete life, a life of various yet select sensation." The freeing of the individual "from all partial and misrepresentative doctrine" prepares him for "the real business of education—insight, insight through culture, into all that the present moment holds in trust for us, as we stand so briefly in its presence." Hence, Pater concludes (for the moment, at least), that "From that maxim of *Life as the end of life,* followed, as a practical consequence, the desirableness of refining all the instruments of inward and outward intuition, of developing all their capacities, of testing and exercising one's self in them, till one's whole nature became one complex medium of reception, towards the vision—the 'beatific vision,' if we really cared to make it such—of our actual experience in the world."[20] Although Marius absorbs many varieties of intellectual belief, it is this account of the individual as a "complex medium of reception" in search of a "beatific vision" which characterizes him and his creator throughout. The vision of Christian serenity received by Marius carries finality only because it comes at the end of his life and at the end of the novel. The "pilgrimage ends," as has been observed, "with an exaltation of the same feelings with which [Marius] began his journey."[21]

Pater's advocacy of the cultivation of sensations was interpreted by Wilde and Moore, among others, as being an end rather than a means. Moore proudly described himself, in the opening sentence of the *Confessions of a Young Man,* as a human sponge, whose soul "has very kindly taken colour and form from the many various modes of life that self-will and an impetuous temperament have forced me to indulge in."[22] Like Huysmans' *A Rebours,* published in the preceding year, *Marius* was worshipped not for its intellectual warning but for its ornate style. Overlooked was the notice, in the subtitle of the novel, that Marius had "ideas" as well as "sensations." In "A Bundle of Letters" (1879), James satirized the Pateresque young man trying to make of life a fine art, or at least saying so. Of Florimond Daintry, a parody in name as well as manner of one of Pater's self-portraitures in "A New England Winter" (1884), James acidly declares that "he really saw with great intensity; and the reader will probably feel that he was welcome to this ambiguous privilege."[23] By the time of *The Princess Casamassima* (1886), however, James's semiautobiographical protagonist is an expansion of Florian Deleal into a Jamesian tragic hero. Florian's dual sensibility—its awareness of the "spectacle of suffering" as well as its "fascination" with aesthetic beauty—is intensified in Hyacinth Robinson until he is driven to the self-destructiveness reminiscent of many of Pater's imaginary portraits.

Despite his search for a "beatific vision," Pater realized the unlikeliness of such an event occurring, especially in light of the limitations of human nature as he saw it and of the chaotic nature of the age. The heroes of his fictional sketches are all victims of transitional periods—aside from Hellenic Greece, Pater seemed to find only transitional periods in history—and of their restless minds. Every quest is frustrated, and the desire for "home" becomes a death wish. In the portrait of Sebastian Van Storck, for example, Pater studied the self-destructiveness of the mind. In the scholar's search for truth in Spinoza's Holland, he succumbs inevitably to a metaphorical "disease then coming into the world; disease begotten by the fogs of that country—waters, he [Sebastian's doctor] observed, not in their place, 'above the firmament'— on people grown somewhat over-delicate in their nature by the effects of modern luxury."[24] Sebastian is exposed to what Ruskin had described as the storm cloud of the nineteenth century and what Arnold (in "The Scholar Gypsy") claimed as the "strange disease of modern life." In the unfinished chapters of *Gaston de Latour* (1889), which had been intended as a sequel to *Marius*, Pater's hero witnesses, in late sixteenth-century France, the futility alike of aestheticism, represented in Ronsard's decision to become a monk, of enlightened self-consciousness, expressed in Montaigne's failure to look for meaning in life, and of the blind surrender to experience, reflected in Bruno's incapacity to make ethical as well as aesthetic distinctions. Addicted to a life of thought whose ultimate conclusion was the futility of thought, Pater best described himself in the portrait of Watteau, printed in the same year as *Marius*: "He was always a seeker after something in the world that is there in no satisfying measure, or not at all."[25]

Pater had an unintentional but crucial influence upon the aesthetic movement and is generally grouped with it, but in his search for a practicable religion to ward off the temptation of nihilism he is close to the remarkable author of the Mark Rutherford novels. According to Ramon Fernandez, Pater had a lethal influence because of his inability to lose himself in objective reality; he did not place any trust in action, for example, and thus *"did not allow the mind to escape from itself."*[26] But Pater was only the most gifted of a group of writers in the eighties who, at the mercy of their subjective intellects, sought distraction from what Gissing's biographer has aptly termed "the anguish of the unknowable."[27] "One-fourth of life is intelligible," according to the fictive editor of *The Autobiography of Mark Rutherford*; "the other three-fourths is unintelligible darkness; and our earliest duty is to cultivate the habit of not looking round the corner."[28]

The Autobiography of Mark Rutherford (1881) is the first half of William Hale White's fictional autobiography, which deals with the loss of faith of a Dissenting minister. White's tone is dispassionate throughout; unable to find emotional fulfillment in his religious vocation, he reaches the serenity desired by Pater only by accepting with finality the conclusion that the universe is a closed book and man's mission a generally futile one. It is not clear whether the "deliverance" referred to in the sequel to the *Auto-biography—Mark Rutherford's Deliverance* (1885)—is that provided by the protagonist's relatively happy marriage, by his acceptance of a religion devoted to personal relationships, or simply by the fact of his death. Less impressive as a thinker than Pater, less striking in his use of similar materials than Gissing, White commands respect for what André Gide called his "wonderful integrity."[29] He refused to minimize the implications of the decline of religion, just as he refused to magnify himself into a tragic victim of the times (as Gissing often chose to do). As White's sensitive biographer, Irvin Stock, notes, the *Autobiography* is more "intimate" a confessional work than, for example, Rousseau's. He discards "what Rousseau would never go without: his spiritual pride. He confesses what it is most difficult to confess: weakness, need, pain, and humiliation."[30]

"One thing is certain," White wrote in his notebook, "that there is not a single code now in existence which is not false," but he added that there was no need, thus, to "hand ourselves over to a despotism with no Divine right, even if there be a risk of anarchy." In his essay on Marcus Aurelius (1880), however, White observed that, with the decline of religion, "our difficulties are increased and the solitude is deepened."[31] Where Pater studied the problems of a select few—all projections of himself—White realized the effects of such a loss of faith on the common man. In *Mark Rutherford's Deliverance*, he urged the necessity of providing men with the means not only to endure but to find "joy." The poverty of life in Drury Lane, he shows, is the poverty of the will to live if deprived of imagination. As Rutherford says,

> The desire to decorate existence in some way or other with more or less care is nearly universal. The most sensual and the meanest almost always manifest an indisposition to be content with mere material satisfaction. I have known selfish, gluttonous, drunken men spend their leisure moments in trimming a bed of scarlet geraniums, and the vulgarest and most commonplace of mortals considers it a necessity to put a picture in the room or an ornament on the mantelpiece. The instinct, even in its lowest forms, is divine. It is the commentary on the text that man shall not live by bread alone. It is evidence of an acknowledged compulsion—of which art is the highest manifestation —to *escape*. In the alleys behind Drury Lane this instinct, the very salt of life, was dead, crushed out utterly, a symptom which seemed to me ominous, and even awful to the last degree.

Like Henry George in *Progress and Poverty*, White was disturbed by the precarious nature of modern civilization: "Our civilization seemed nothing but a thin film or crust lying over a volcanic pit, and I often wondered whether some day the pit would not break up through it and destroy us all." In such circumstances, the religious faith which Rutherford and his friend McKay bring to the inhabitants of Drury Lane is emptied of doctrine but aimed at man's need to be reconciled to some source of sympathy outside of himself. Since one can no more be certain of the absolute truth of atheism than of the old dogmas, there is a hope remaining in the admission of one's frailty: "The proper attitude, the attitude enjoined by the severest exercise of the reason is, *I do not know;* and in this there is an element of hope, now rising and now falling, but always sufficient to prevent that blank despair which we must feel if we consider it as settled that when we lie down under the grass there is an absolute end."[32]

In *The Revolution in Tanner's Lane* (1887) White turned from fictionalized autobiography to the form of historical semiautobiographical novel which George Eliot had used in *Romola* and Pater in *Marius*. In such a work the author evokes a historical past either to find a creed which might prove of service to the present or to depict an age whose problems resemble those of the present. White looked back to the early decades of the nineteenth century to trace the decline of the evangelical movement, just as Pater had looked back to Rome on the eve of decline in *Marius*. By contrast, Joseph Henry Shorthouse's *John Inglesant* (1880) is set in an age of crisis and opportunity, when the individual could still hope to learn from history. Shorthouse's hero wanders through seventeenth-century England, France, and Italy only to discover the efficacy of compromise, whether in his personal relations or in his celebration of the Church of England. Inglesant has the good fortune to meet such supporting characters in the novel as Charles I, Archbishop Laud, Hobbes, George Herbert, and Milton. Witnessing the state of "waste" to which religious and political controversies have brought England, Inglesant—with an eye prophetically toward Mill—offers to renounce freedom for himself after having seen "the evil which the possession of it works among others and in the state."[33] Born a Quaker, Shorthouse's sympathy for quietist religions is evident in his interesting depiction of Nicholas Ferrar's community of Little Gidding. Shorthouse subtitled his work a "philosophical Romance," hoping to make his religious theme more palatable by serving it in the form of an adventure story. To his surprise, the novel proved to be one of the most popular novels of the 1880's, and it has been called "the one great religious novel of the English language."[34]

The "most widely circulated" novel of the decade (James's phrase)[35] deals with a theme similar to that of the Mark Rutherford books, but its conclusions are as hopeful as Shorthouse's. Mrs. Humphry Ward, Arnold's niece, wrote *Robert Elsmere* (1888) to show how, in an age of transition—marked by "a changing social order and a vanishing past"—a new way of life and a new faith could be achieved. "I wanted," she noted in her memoirs, "to show how a man of sensitive and noble character, born for religion, comes to throw off the orthodoxies of his day and moment, and to go out into the wilderness where all is experiment, and spiritual life begins again."[36] In their reviews of the novel, Gladstone and Pater were alike disturbed by the ease with which the minister-hero abandons his former faith. A sign of the times, however, was the extraordinary commercial success of the book.

Mrs. Ward subjects her hero to as many of the major influences of the nineteenth century as she could get away with. Elsmere is initially shaken by the findings of Darwin and by the higher criticism; he takes refuge in a Wordsworthian celebration of nature, cultivates a hero worship of Christ in a Carlylean manner, and finally assumes the role of a Ruskin or a William Morris in his establishment of religious and cultural clubs for workingmen. While in terms of its scope the novel has the fascination of a veritable "Encyclopaedia Victoriana," it is hard for the reader to maintain much interest in characters who have been selected to serve as mouthpieces for the various clashing ideologies of the age. Wilde described the book as "simply Arnold's *Literature and Dogma* with the literature left out." As symbolic heir to an age of turmoil, Elsmere is made to stand for too much to seem credible. Only in the figures of Elsmere's sister-in-law, Rose, one of the more charming "New Women" in late Victorian fiction, and of Langham, the bookish Oxford tutor who is the victim of his mercilessly analytical intelligence (he may have been modelled on Pater), did Mrs. Ward create distinctive characters. The book is also flawed by its sentimental solution and by the romantic treatment of the "people." Elsmere founds a new faith, based on the need for emotional worship of *"something,"* and dies a saint, uttering platitudes on his deathbed. In contrast to the Mark Rutherford books, *Robert Elsmere* simultaneously exploits and sentimentalizes the religious and political anguish of the period. But of such simplifications, best sellers are made, as Walter Besant learned from happy experience and Gissing at bitter cost.

A similarly ambitious but flawed book of the period is Richard Jefferies' *The Story of My Heart* (1883), a spiritual autobiography which has, perhaps unfortunately, worn better than his novels. A collection of philosophical ruminations, *The Story of My Heart* describes the process by which the author passed through a period of depression over the loss of past values and finally attained a passionate communion with nature. Jefferies' book, a pastoral counterpart to *The City of Dreadful Night*, expresses the theme that, in a universe without God or discernible design, man is a free agent. "We must do for ourselves," he asserts, "what superstition has hitherto supposed an intelligence to do for us." Through the process of intellect Jefferies arrived, like Pater and Nietzsche, at an anti-intellectual position. "Nothing is of any use," he declares, "unless it gives me a stronger body and mind, a more beautiful body, a happy existence, and a soul-life now. The last phase of philosophy is equally useless with the rest."[37]

An autodidact, Jefferies wrote his last works under the shadow of premature death. A whining personal tone often damages the effectiveness of these works, but the author's love of nature and his compassion for simple, country people frequently results in passages of singular force. The following section from the novel *Amaryllis at the Fair* (1887), his last book, foreshadows Lawrence in style and theme. The Idens have traveled from Coombe Oaks to London, after thirty years spent entirely in the country, in order to attend a family funeral. In the evening, taking advantage of the trip, they visited the theater, for "the coldness of death alone could open the door to pleasure." Jefferies notes:

> They sat at the theatre with grey hearts. With the music and the song, the dancing, the colours and gay dresses, it was sadder there than in the silent rooms at the house where the dead had been. Old Flamma alone had been dead *there;* they were dead here. Dead in life—at the theatre.
> They had used to go joyously to the theatre thirty years before, when Iden came courting to town; from the edge of the grave they came back to look on their own buried lives.[38]

Despite a tendency to overcolor his feelings of natural mysticism —and a predilection for describing his heroines as Grecian goddesses or Italian madonnas—Jefferies can be eloquently unsentimental otherwise. In his finest novel, *The Dewy Morn* (1884), he depicted what no other contemporary novelist of stature had cared to discuss: the agricultural depression of the eighties. The image of country life in *The Dewy Morn* guarantees Jefferies a place alongside George Crabbe as one of the few authentic describers of pastoral reality.

Perhaps the most impressive of the autobiographical novels of the eighties dealing with the estrangement of man from God and with man's inability to find a compensatory ideal was written by an African expatriate. A discovery of Meredith, Olive Schreiner presented in *The Story of an African Farm* (1883) a study of blighted young lives on a Karroo farm. Despite the grimness of the theme and the occasional crudeness of the writing, the book is a memorable parable of human frustration and of the hope for release through communion with nature, through love, through artistic creativity, or through dreams. "When we lie and think, and think," Waldo remarks, "we see that there is nothing worth doing. The universe is so large, and man is so small . . ." "But we must not think so far," Lyndall replies, "it is madness; it is a disease."[39] Waldo and Lyndall, thwarted young people trying to assert themselves in a hostile world, are the kind of characters about whom romantic novels like *Wuthering Heights* are made, but Olive Schreiner was too devoted to the principle of literary realism to attempt to present her characters with any romantic trappings. Her hero and heroine are too much at the mercy of their environment and of their own self-destructive wills to indulge in fictional histrionics.

"Our dream saves us from going mad," the author suggests at one point;[40] but all efforts toward release only make the unbearable reality even more unbearable. In the chapter "Times and Seasons," the reflective turmoil of the ego at war with itself is momentarily subdued, and nature (as in Meredith) speaks the need for man's harmony with the earth and the taming of the will. But the will to be free proves too strong; with Lyndall's rebellion against the role demanded of her sex, the "New Woman" becomes a fixture in the English novel. Intellectually and sexually frustrated, Lyndall becomes an emancipated woman when society offers no outlet for her energies, and, in this respect, she belongs among an impressive number of fictional women of the period, including Meredith's Diana Warwick, James's Isabel Archer, and Hardy's Sue Bridehead, as well as Strindberg's Miss Julie and Ibsen's Hedda Gabler. But *The Story of an African Farm* is compelling less as a contribution to feminist liberation than for its depiction of a modern society in which man is condemned to self-alienation and self-destruction. Modern man is represented alone and at the mercy of his mind which has been liberated from all past beliefs but, as a result, is trapped within a limited range of possibilities: "each mind keeping," in Pater's memorable phrase, "as a solitary prisoner its own dream of a world."

In direct and almost violent contrast to the novels of social and individual analysis written in the eighties there were also in that period the products of what has justly been called a "Romantic

Revival." The decade began with Gladstone's political victory over Disraeli, which seemed to mark a setback for those who believed in imperialism. The new Prime Minister exulted that "the downfall of Beaconsfieldism is like the vanishing of some vast magnificent castle of Italian romance."[41] Despite H. Rider Haggard's contention in 1887 that his age was not actually a romantic one, the combined activities of Haggard, Kipling, and Robert Louis Stevenson went far toward satisfying a sudden public taste for romantic fiction as diversion from domestic and Irish problems. All three writers were the discoveries of William Ernest Henley, who, along with Andrew Lang, was the most influential literary critic of the period. For his role in popularizing the new literature of adventure, Henley has been accused of helping to prepare for the imperialism of the 1890's. "Crippled, chronically ill, restless, and subject to severe depressions," a historian notes, "he looked to the British Empire for the strength and good health that he personally lacked."[42] The mood of the 1880's, John Gross has recently said in respect to the "bookmen" of the period, was marked by "a widespread faltering of Victorian self-confidence, a new edginess and uncertainty about the future." And, while many literary critics addressed themselves to the problems of the age in a "mood of determined realism," the more common reaction, exemplified by Henley and Lang, "was withdrawal, a retreat into nostalgia, exoticism, fine writing, *belles-lettres*."[43] The gap between social and literary criticism, which Arnold had tried to bridge, widened, and the distinction between fiction as a mirror of life and as a distraction from life became more pronounced.

Scott had looked to the Scottish Highlands or to medieval England for the sources of native romance. The new writers began to tap the possibilities of India, Polynesia, Arabia, and Africa (as well as the underground and little-known sections of London). The eighties was an age of great travel books, like Doughty's *Travels in Arabia Deserta* (1888), and of variations on the *Arabian Nights*, which, along with Scott, was often held up as a literary model in opposition to the realistic books of the period. It took a famous traveler, Richard Burton, to produce the first unexpurgated translation of the *Arabian Nights* into English in 1885, and it is ironic that a type of story deemed appropriate for young people should have proved, in its "full, complete, unvarnished, uncastrated copy,"[44] considerably more erotic than anything dared by the French naturalists. Stevenson's first published works of fiction, which had gone unnoticed when they appeared earlier, were gathered together in 1882 as the *New Arabian Nights*. In Stevenson's case—an invalid with romantic dreams of freedom—it is especially appropriate that he should have used such a title, since the original tales of Scheherazade are related by the narrator as a means of postponing the continuing threat of death.

Haggard was as much a product of this period as Olive Schreiner, although he preferred to provide a distraction from the very conditions she chose to stress. The former civil servant in Africa found much to praise in *The Story of an African Farm*, singling it out in his essay "About Fiction" (1887) as one of the few recent books to excite his interest. Her novel, he noted, is "written from within" and conveys the impression of "inward personal suffering on the part of the writer"; its "key-note is a note of pain." Despite his praise, Haggard felt that another, more promising route lay open to the novelist: "the paths and calm retreats of pure imagination." Citing the example of the *Arabian Nights*, he affirmed that the impulses of fancy still provided subjects for the writer "bold enough to handle them."[45] There is an irony in Haggard's claim for the boldness of adventure fiction, especially in the light of his own achievement and of the very different boldness of Zola or Olive Schreiner or the unexpurgated *Arabian Nights*. As far as Andrew Lang was concerned, however, novels should be "about fighting rather than about free love." Lang dismissed *The Story of an African Farm* as a "woebegone work" in which "people were always tackling religious problems, or falling in love on new and heterodox lines, instead of shooting deer, and finding diamonds, or hunting up the archaeological remains of the Transvaal."[46]

Two more temperamentally different writers than Olive Shreiner and Haggard can scarcely be imagined, despite their common use of Africa as background for their novels. But where she used her African farm as a realistic symbol of modern society in transition, Haggard's Africa is a figment of the romantic imagination, an exotic landscape where moral values are assured and Englishmen in full control of any emergency. In the preface to her novel, Olive

Schreiner declares that to be true to life one must necessarily be woebegone: "Sadly he [the novelist] must squeeze the color from his brush, and dip it into the gray pigments around him." In his essay on fiction, Haggard says that it is only through "books and dreams" that men may attain a vision of "Beauty" and "Perfection."[47] *King Solomon's Mines* (1885), his first literary success, provides an escapist vision in which, as James protested, even the carnage seems beautiful.

For swiftness of narrative, variety of incident, and an appealing ingenuousness on the part of narrator and author as to what will happen next, *King Solomon's Mines* is still immensely readable; it also has historic value as a record, accidentally and deliberately amusing, of English attitudes in the nineteenth century. English pluck and "some merciful Power" enable the hunting party to survive and conquer where other nationalities have perished. The view of the English as "Chosen People" is an idea central to Haggard's novel and to imperialist theorists like J. R. Seeley. Stanley's popular account of his adventures—*In Darkest Africa*—published in the same year (1890) as General Booth's plea for the "submerged tenth"—*In Darkest England*—makes the most of "a gracious Providence who for some purpose of His own preserved us."[48] Although the African people in Haggard display courage, an overwhelming desire to sacrifice themselves for their masters, and even intelligence throughout, Allan Quatermain can only say of the Zulus lined up in his party's honor that "It really was very affecting, and not the sort of thing one is accustomed to meet with from natives." In contrast to the adventure novels of Kipling and Stevenson, Haggard's best work is infinitely less polished or calculated, but the ingenuous tone prevents moral ambiguities from arising. In Conrad's hands, the figures of the benign and successful Quatermain, Captain Good, and Sir Henry Curtis could easily be used to demonstrate the latent viciousness and dangerous smugness of the well-meaning imperialists. At one point Quatermain succumbs to the spirit of battle, acknowledging "a savage desire to kill and spare not,"[49] yet afterward he is exactly the same good-natured man as before. The Englishmen in Haggard's works march into the heart of darkness only to find a radiant "Wonderland" in which everything is theirs for the asking.

Haggard's immense popularity was soon overshadowed by another of Henley's discoveries. "We'll tell you all about Rudyard
Kipling—your nascent rival," James wrote to Stevenson in 1890,
"he has killed one immortal—Rider Haggard."[50] At one time James
thought that Kipling would become an English Balzac, but it soon
became evident that Kipling's gifts lay in other directions. Kipling
has been much maligned and much absolved for his share in the
imperialist fervor of the 1890's, and it is undeniable that, whatever the ambivalence in his work and thought, the English public's
worship of him was largely for jingoist as well as escapist reasons.
In any case, despite the appearance of *Plain Tales from the Hills*
in 1887, Kipling as a phenomenon of literary history belongs to
the 1890's rather than to the 1880's. James considered Robert Louis
Stevenson one of the most interesting literary "figures" of the
eighties. His major rival for public attention was Oscar Wilde.

Stevenson married Fanny Osbourne in 1880, after pursuing her
to California and losing his health in the process. In that year he
also wrote to a friend that the world needed another Scott or
Arabian Nights rather than a George Eliot or Balzac: "We want
incident, interest, action; to the devil with your philosophy. When
we are well again, and have an easy mind, we shall peruse your
important work; but what we want now is a drug."[51] Again and
again in his literary essays of the eighties, Stevenson pursued the
theme that the "true mark" of literature "is to satisfy the nameless
longings of the reader, and to obey the ideal laws of the day-
dream."[52] Although the subtitle of *Treasure Island* is *A Story for
Boys*, Stevenson intended that it be read also by the boy in man.
His "passion" for youth, as James noted, counts, "in the age in
which we live . . . as a sufficient philosophy."[53] In some ways a
younger version of Meredith, who used him as the model for
Gower Woodseer in *The Amazing Marriage*, Stevenson also stressed
the need for physical exertion in essays like "Aes Triplex" despite
his own physical disabilities. Meredith symbolically treated manly
sports as a means of integrating the individual with nature and
society; Stevenson, on the other hand, was impelled more by the
need to escape the proddings of his nihilistic intellect. The fear of
death and the threat of reality are constant themes in Stevenson's
work, and his revolt against the drab realism of his age and the

Calvinist determinism of his personal background took shape in a cultivation of romanticism that he knew to be illusive.

Stevenson is always in danger of being too closely tied to such critical pronouncements as the reply to James's claim for "The Art of Fiction": "The whole secret is that no art does 'compete with life' [as James originally wrote]. Man's one method, whether he reasons or creates, is to half-shut his eyes against the dazzle and confusion of reality."[54] Try though he might, Stevenson could not help keeping his eyes half open to that reality too. Like William Hale White, he felt that the unintelligible darkness of the world should be averted for man's own good, but in *The Strange Case of Dr. Jekyll and Mr. Hyde* (1886) and *The Master of Ballantrae* (1888), as well as in the brilliant tales included with *The Merry Men* (1887), Stevenson explored that area of darkness. In both novels he attempted, it is true, to suppress the inherent moral ambiguities of his theme, but, while he tried to avoid the extremes of realistic analysis or romantic persiflage, he managed to find dangers wherever he turned.

A key to the buried theme of *Jekyll and Hyde* is found in the other characters' inability to deal with the "monster" Hyde in a normal manner. Having taken a loathing to Hyde at first sight, Enfield and the others turn "white and sick with the desire to kill him," yet the narrator indicates that Hyde "gave an impression of deformity without any nameable malformation." Hyde is meant to represent the beast in man; because they are unwilling to recognize his integral source in them, Dr. Jekyll and the others become more culpable than he. Like Frankenstein and his monster, Jekyll and Hyde are counterparts. Each needs the other, and it is only when one is separated from the other that tragedy occurs. Dr. Jekyll is a portrait of the analytical intellect creating destruction for himself and others. As he plans suicide, Jekyll marvels that Hyde's "love of life is wonderful . . . I, who sicken and freeze at the mere thought of him, when I recall the abjection and passion of this attachment, and when I know how he fears my power to cut him off by suicide, I find it in my heart to pity him."[55] Hyde, the natural and unreflective man, is the instrument of destruction, but Jekyll has the controlling will. The expense of romantic passion tends to be destructive; realistic intellect is self-destructive.

So daring a theme is sabotaged by Jekyll's afterthought that his scientific experiment—to isolate the evil from the good in man for the sake of making him entirely benign—was thwarted only by an "unknown impurity which lent efficacy to the draught."[56] A psychological horror story is allowed, thus, to become merely a horror story. It has been argued that the moral element in *Jekyll and Hyde* is not intrinsic to it, that it was added at Mrs. Stevenson's urging.[57] Yet the paradox that good and evil are not only inseparable but the end products of one another is nearly explicit in the best of Stevenson's completed novels, although once again the author tried to evade the implications of his theme. The villainous Master of Ballantrae and his selfless brother, Henry Durie, tend to blur into one another in the manner of Jekyll and Hyde; at times the reader has the uncomfortable feeling that the definition of good or evil is at the mercy of the narrator. It was an interesting idea to have the romantic Master seen from the point of view of the pragmatic and old-maidish MacKellar. "I had never much natural sympathy for the passion of love," MacKellar admits at one point, and one wonders why Stevenson takes such pains to limit the character of his narrator. When the brothers' father declares that the Master always had "the more affectionate nature,"[58] the reader is left to consider this either a grim irony on the father's part or else a partial truth. In one respect Stevenson was attacking, in the figure of the Master, the archetype of the Romantic hero; in the process he may have realized that he was also attacking the basis of romance.

The Master's attractiveness is all the more perplexing in view of the length to which Stevenson goes to demonstrate how evil and selfish he is; the sordid account of his adventures, as told by Colonel Burke, is too obviously meant to direct the reader's sympathies away from him. Yet Stevenson is fascinated by the villainous brother to the point of having even MacKellar temporarily impressed: "He had all the gravity and something of the splendour of Satan in the *Paradise Lost*," he notes at one point,[59] yielding to the Romantic view of Satan. Meanwhile, Henry Durie decays into morbidity and impotence, and in the last chapters the theme is completely confused as Stevenson becomes undecided as to whether evil is stalking good or good is hunting down evil. The brothers are fittingly buried together, but the idea of the *Doppelgänger* has been abandoned along the way.

The abandoned and unfinished themes in Stevenson remain considerably more interesting than many of his more polished works. "Markheim" and "The Merry Men," to be sure, are among the greatest short stories ever written, and the moral theme is succinctly and compellingly articulated. But it is in the boys' books that Stevenson was probably the more secure and better artist. In *Treasure Island* and *Kidnapped*, for example, he knew exactly where the novels were heading, and he saw to it that they reached their destination. Any ambiguities that smuggle themselves aboard are made to walk the plank. In *Jekyll and Hyde* and *The Master of Ballantrae*, however, Stevenson gave way to the very things that he deplored in modern fiction: morbid psychological analysis and a sense of the complexity of reality. It has been argued that the novelist's real genius was smothered by his respectable wife,[60] yet Stevenson pursued Fanny as avidly as he sought to destroy his impulse toward outrageous behavior and intellectual nihilism. Had he not attempted to subdue his intellect, he might have suffered the agonies of a Gissing or Pater. Like a character in one of Pater's *Imaginary Portraits*, Stevenson, in a time of change, sought, as Robert Kiely has noted, "for a haven in the world."[61] By sailing to Samoa Stevenson seemed to his contemporaries to have escaped the moral problems at home, and, even if the artist's willed retreat was necessary to his health and to the further writing of books, his action was misinterpreted as symbolizing the adventuring spirit of English colonialists abroad. It was perhaps the boyishness of the adult readers of *Treasure Island* which led them to half shut their eyes against the confusions of reality at home and to transfer their attention to the treasure islands of empire.

In 1879, the year before Stevenson called for an artistic "drug" to stave off the problems of the age, Oscar Wilde settled in England, creating problems of his own. According to Max Beerbohm's witty essay, "1880," Wilde was responsible, amid the political "turbulence" of the day, for another "revolution": "Beauty had existed long before 1880. It was Mr. Oscar Wilde who managed her *début*."[62] Although Wilde's comedies belong to the 1890's, he should be remembered in the 1880's as a target of satire in Gilbert and Sullivan's *Patience* (1881), the defender of romance in "The Decay of Lying" (1889), and the author of *The Picture of Dorian Gray* (serialized in 1890). *Dorian Gray* uses the *Doppelgänger* motif of *Jekyll and Hyde*, but Wilde's novel exploits the problem of human dualism almost entirely for artistic effect, and for the sake of Lord Henry's aphorisms. In his favorable review Pater unconsciously put his finger on the amoral effect of Wilde's seemingly moralistic fable: "his story is . . . a vivid, though carefully considered, exposure of the corruption of a soul, with a very plain moral, pushed home, to the effect that vice and crime make people coarse and ugly."[63] In the sense that Wilde uses a moral dilemma merely as a resource for literature, he might be viewed as an exemplar of the triumph of artistic subjectivity. Holbrook Jackson has defined decadence as "a form of imperialism of the spirit, ambitious, arrogant, aggressive, waving the flag of human power over an ever wider and wider territory."[64] To the degree that Wilde, Whistler, and Moore, for example, attempted to replace the standards of the Victorian world with the standards of their own ambitious egos, they may be labeled "decadent" in Jackson's definition of the term. They took to heart Flaubert's injunction that in detachment lies the only basis for artistic creation, and from Pater they concocted a methodology whereby impressions were to be collected for their own sake. Henry James should be included in this category of writers who lived apart from their age as aesthetic spectators; whereas they willfully detached themselves, James and Whistler, as Emersonian, self-reliant Americans, were born independent.

In his witty defense of the practice of literary criticism, Wilde argued that criticism should be cultivated as an art in itself, whereby spectatorship could find a creative outlet. Wilde and Moore alluded to Pater with the sort of praise that had worried him into suppressing the "Conclusion" to the *Renaissance*. Ethics, for Wilde, was the logical outcome of aesthetics. "To be good," as Lord Henry says, "is to be in harmony with one's own self . . . One's own life —that is the important thing." Wilde converted Pater's definition of style as a reflection of the artist into a formula for artistic self-indulgence. "It is the spectator, and not life, that art really mirrors," he declared in the "Preface" to *Dorian Gray*.[65] Pater's ideas have a habit of changing their meaning as their context changes. The following passages, for example, both proceed from the "Conclusion" to the *Renaissance* (and from Mill's *On Liberty* before it), but, if the content is similar, the intent is different:

> Live! Live the wonderful life that is in you! Let nothing be lost upon you. Be always searching for new sensations. Be afraid of nothing . . . A new Hedonism—that is what our century wants.

> Live all you can; it's a mistake not to. It doesn't so much matter what you do in particular, so long as you have your life. If you haven't had that what *have* you had?[66]

The first passage is Lord Henry's advice to Dorian; the second is Lambert Strether's injunction to Little Bilham in *The Ambassadors*. Wilde may have remembered James's advice, in "The Art of Fiction": "to be one of the people on whom nothing is lost!" Yet for James the argument against theorizing was similar to Pater's: neither the artist nor the philosopher should be hemmed in by absolutes. For Wilde, as for Moore, relativity became a new absolute. As James indicated in the figure of Strether, however, the price of one's freedom to perceive is paid at an enormous cost to one's active individuality.

"The only quality of theirs which extorts my respect," one of Shaw's characters says of artists, "is a certain sublime selfishness which makes them willing to starve and to let their families starve sooner than do any work they dont like."[67] Shaw pressed his own "sublime selfishness" into the service of socialism in the eighties, but, like Wilde in "The Soul of Man under Socialism" (1890), Shaw saw in socialism a political means of freeing the individual for the sake of more self-expression. In his attack on Max Nordau's account of the degeneration of the 1880's and 1890's, Shaw asserted, "The whole progress of the world is from submission and obedience as safeguards against panic and incontinence, to wilfulness and self-assertion made safe by reason and self-control . . ."[68] In the most endurable of his novels, *An Unsocial Socialist* (1884), Shaw followed in the footsteps of Shorthouse's *John Inglesant* in the determination to present philosophy in the guise of fiction. But Shaw's economic theories make very dreary reading, and despite the existence of two interesting characters—Agathe Wylie, a "New Woman," and Sidney Trefusis, the author's mouthpiece—the "determination . . . to make something like a romance out of such very thin material" was deplored by Shaw himself afterward. The future playwright's predilection for antisentimentalism and for dogmatizing at the drop of a hat are already apparent in the novels. Shaw realized, in the words of Trefusis, "With my egotism, my charlatanry, my tongue, and my habit of having my own way, I am fit for no calling but that of saviour of mankind—just of the sort they like."[69] Despite their status as political subjects of Britain, a number of Irishmen discovered, in the 1880's, that as artists they were free and could take artistic revenge on their masters.

In the early part of the 1880's Trollope blamed Irish unrest on the Americans. With much greater cause the aesthetic disturbances later in the decade might be attributed to a number of Americans and Irishmen under the influence of Pater and Emerson: Wilde, Moore, Shaw, Whistler, and James. If Trollope had praised the virtue of self-restraint, they in turn promoted aesthetic versions of the Declaration of Independence. A major fact of the "aesthetic Eighties," as Jerome Hamilton Buckley has labeled the period, was the general acceptance of cultural disintegration, and in the retreat of the artist from society, "both art and society paid the price of independence."[70] In his famous lecture, the "Ten O'Clock" (1885), Whistler denied the idea of Ruskin and Taine that the artist is a product of, or in any way belongs to and has obligations to, his time and place: "The master stands in no relation to the moment at which he occurs—a monument of isolation—hinting at sadness —having no part in the progress of his fellow men."[71] If Victorian society was no longer perceptibly stable, the arts presented the opportunity to depict a substitute rather than reproduced unity, and to celebrate an internal rather than an objective version of reality.

[4] Artists of Change

*Human life has little interest to me, on the whole
—save as material for artistic presentation.*
(George Gissing)

It is no accident that novelists spoke more and more of the "art of fiction" in the decade when society seemed anything but coherent and the Victorian world seemed in pieces. "For some years," Gissing noted in 1903, "there has been a great deal of talk about Art in our country. It began, I suspect, when the veritable artistic impulse of the Victorian time had flagged, when the energy of a great time was all but exhausted. Principles always become a matter of vehement discussion when practice is at ebb."[1] What unites four of the five best novelists of this transitional period—the exception is Meredith, who remained defiantly Victorian—is their ability to find in the craft they practiced a workable substitute for the values that had been lost. Of the four, Thomas Hardy is most difficult to assess. In his choice of themes and in his treatment of them, he seems the most modern and the most Victorian of figures in turn. Hardy's ability to raise many issues important to men in an age of change is matched by his refusal, all too often, to come to terms with those issues. Responsible for several of the greatest characters and passages in fiction, he is also guilty of some of the most embarrassing literary effects. If Gissing was incapable of Hardy's poetic brilliance, he is often more convincing than Hardy in the depiction of modern man trapped under the pressures of modern life. Gissing's major subject was the fate of the "unclassed," such inhabitants of the nether world as overly sensitive workers or dedicated writers who fit nowhere into the scheme of society. For George Moore, on the other hand, the problem was not where to turn but what mask to assume next. The one novelist of the four with independent means, he was able, quipped Wilde, to conduct his education in public.

The most gifted of the quartet is Henry James, who was able to immerse himself in an extraordinarily diverse mixture of novelistic subjects and styles and come up with a synthesis completely his own, untouched by colleagues or predecessors. James, Moore, Gissing, and Hardy were champions of the artistic ego, for whom the world existed at best to provide materials for fiction. Despite their marriages—in many ways because of them—Hardy and Gissing joined the others in respecting the value of individual freedom, although both expressed this theme negatively by showing the devastating effects of marriage upon their characters. James, more than the others and even more than Samuel Butler, upon whom the title originally was bestowed, can be called the "incarnate bachelor"[2] both in terms of his life and the values espoused in his fiction. His opposite in this respect, as in so many others, is Meredith, for whom marriage represented, symbolically and personally, the reconciliation of self and society, the self and others. I have selected James for lengthy analysis because, among all the novelists at work in the eighties whose novels and whose life typify the emergence of modern themes and attitudes, his works are finer and more ambitious than the others'. His ability to exploit and escape the problems of his changing world is one of the most interesting literary adventures of the time. Meredith, too, merits an entire section in order to show why the Victorian masters were perhaps unable to survive the approach of the modern world, but also to indicate the corresponding loss to the modern novel and the modern world.

In 1880 George Moore settled in London after studying painting in Paris. He had left Ireland, as William Gaunt observes, "like a new sponge about to be dipped in water for the first time,"[3] and the process of saturation and resaturation was to become the story of Moore's life. The lack of any sustaining philosophy led Moore from one set of artistic standards to another, and his experiences partially resemble those of Pater's Marius, minus the "ideas." He passed through at least seven ways of life before he died; in this sense, his "adventures" may be said to "summarize this entire epoch of transition."[4] In the eighties Moore exhibited himself as a French naturalist and an English aesthete, the disciple of Zola as well as of Pater. To Moore belongs much of the credit for the transformation of Zola's literary-scientific theory, as expounded in *Le Roman expérimental*, into a topic of public scandal in England. In the process, he went beyond Zola, for whom literary objectivity was connected with social reform, and not aesthetic technique. Moore's *A Modern Lover* (1883) and *A Mummer's Wife* (1885) were the first "French" novels to be written in England, the first dealing with the adventures of an egotistical painter and the second with the inevitable deterioration of an English Emma Bovary when she is moved from a fixed to an unstable environment. One of Moore's chief beneficiaries, Arnold Bennett, praised *A Mummer's Wife* for the richness of detail achieved by the novelist, who had taken notes in the pottery town of Hanley, which would later reappear as one of Bennett's "five towns."[5]

A Modern Lover is subtitled *A Realistic Novel,* and modernity was intended to be equated with realism. Lewis Seymour, Moore's self-indulgent painter-hero, is more interesting for his artistic views than for his various love affairs (and in this fact may be surmised the flawed nature of the novel). Moore's artistic ideas, translated from French sources, have more life than most of the characters in the book. As Harding, the "modern" novelist, says:

> We do not always choose what you call unpleasant subjects, but we try to go to the roots of things; and, the basis of life being material and not spiritual, the analyst inevitably finds himself, sooner or later, handling what this sentimental age calls coarse . . . The novel, if it be anything, is contemporary history, an exact and complete reproduction of social surroundings of the age we live in.

While Moore's artists search for the formula that will result in what Lewis calls an "idealization of materialism,"[6] Moore himself lifted the materials of his plot from Balzac and others. In his next book, however, he showed a substantial improvement in originality of treatment and subject matter. The importance of *A Mummer's Wife,* the best of Moore's novels before *Esther Waters,* is dimmed when the two books are compared, but its documentary interest has insured it a place in literary history. So proudly passive a man himself, Moore tended to write about characters like Kate Ede, who are deprived of the power of volition. Like James, Moore seized upon Zola's theory of environmental determinism as a way of defending his passive nature. Kate's views are completely determined by her provincial background, by her absorption of cheap romance fiction, and by the life on the road as first an actor's wife and then an actress herself. Like Zola's Gervaise, she becomes an incurable alcoholic, although she is rarely allowed a chance to gain either author's or reader's sympathy in the manner of a Gervaise or an Esther Waters. Instead, Moore tries for a deadening objectivity, which results in the dehumanization of his characters. This can be seen in the following passage, which describes Kate's abiding hunger for romance: "By well-known ways the dog comes back to his kennel, the sheep to the fold, the horse to the stable, and even so did Kate return to her sentimental self."[7]

Anticipating that the subject matter of the novel would result in its being banned from the lending libraries, Moore and his publisher, Henry Vizetelly, took the daring step of issuing *A Mummer's Wife* in a single six-shilling volume. In his *Autobiography*, Trollope, remembering the comparative failure of *The Warden* when it was first issued as one volume, had observed that "Short novels are not popular with readers generally. Critics often complain of the ordinary length of novels,—of the three volumes to which they are subjected; but few novels which have attained great success in England have been told in fewer pages. The novel-writer who sticks to novel-writing as his profession will certainly find that this burden of length is incumbent on him."[8] "Anybody can write a three-volumed novel," Wilde uncharitably remarked. "It merely requires a complete ignorance of both life and literature."[9] For the great Victorian novelists, the "burden of length" was necessary to give them sufficient room to maintain a detailed and intimate representation of life—and also to run through a sufficient number of serial issues for the sake of economic satisfaction. Eventually, however, the three-volume novel became a novelist's major source of income: a large enough order from Mudie's or another of the lending libraries could result in a fairly comfortable income, based upon a percentage of the thirty-one-and-a-half-shilling cost of each triple-decker. Novelists were thereby forced, very often, to write the sorts of novels that would appeal to the subscribers of the lending libraries, and it was considered especially important not to offend "young people." Despite some appreciative critical response, Meredith's novels provide a case in point of the economic deprivations caused a major novelist as the result of discouragement on the part of lending libraries.

In his pamphlet of 1885, "Literature at Nurse, or Circulating Morals," Moore attacked Mudie's for having, among other offenses, impeded "the free development of our literature." In a flamboyantly gloomy overstatement, Moore predicted that "no novel written within the last ten years" would survive, as a result of Mudie's repressive strictures.[10] For the novelist to attempt to survive on the percentage of receipts from six-shilling editions meant a considerable risk, obviously. With the exceptionally good volume of copies of *A Mummer's Wife* sold, however, Moore's profits from the undertaking were highly satisfactory despite the substantial decrease in the margin of profit from each book sold. James, who was about to learn to count less and less upon the demand for his fiction, was unhappy at this loss of revenue, but Gissing was relieved by the prospect of the end of "the old three volume tradition."[11] It should be observed, however, that the novelist escaped the tyranny of the libraries' strictures only to be trapped into writing novels that the public would buy in large numbers.

Gissing's *New Grub Street* (1891) details the anguish of novelists who, unlike Moore, counted upon the revenue from their novels as their major source of income. Moore and Gissing both treated life as a source of materials for fiction, and, if they are the two major English novelists who described the lower classes in the 1880's and 1890's, they also ultimately sought refuge in ascetic aestheticism. Both were detached individualists in a manner unsuspected by Arnold or Mill. "I have never learnt to regard myself as a 'member of society,'" Gissing's autobiographical persona remarks in *The Private Papers of Henry Ryecroft*. "For me, there have always been two entities—myself and the world, and the normal relation between these two has been hostile."[12] If Wilde and Stevenson were the two imposing literary "figures" of the eighties —and it was Wilde who observed that the only way to succeed in a democracy is to cultivate one's individuality—Moore and

Gissing passively reflect, in their lives and choice of literary materials, the changing nature of the age itself.

The most common objection to Moore is that he was basically insincere, that he drifted from interest to interest with the same amount of conviction in each, and hence no real conviction. But Moore managed to survive comfortably, a feat denied Stevenson, Wilde, and Gissing. Despite the courting of notoriety, the exposure in the *Confessions* of all his youthful sins, it is the youthfulness and not the sins that memorably stands out. If a cultivated innocence is often the last resort of the depraved, in Moore's case a cultivated depravity could never conceal his essential innocence. Moreover, in *Esther Waters* Moore wrote one assured masterpiece. In Gissing's case, it is not so easy to make a comfortable judgment as to the merit of his work. One feels, at times, that he is Hardy's little Father Time grown old and become a novelist. Gissing's message is that the man of sensitivity must suffer in the modern world and that man is best-off unborn or, as an expedient, lobotomized. "What is the use of thought which can no longer serve to direct life?" Ryecroft ruminates. "Better, perhaps, to read and read incessantly, losing one's futile self in the activity of other minds."[13] Despite all the critical verbiage devoted to Hardy's pessimism, Hardy is an ardent optimist when set next to Gissing.

In her suggestive account of his modernity, Mrs. Leavis notes, "Gissing is an example of how disastrous it may be for a writer whose talent is not of the first order to be born into a bad tradition."[14] In Gissing's case, one might add, the "bad tradition" was really the residue of a Victorian world unable to survive under altered conditions. In his initial inability to break away from the three-volume format, Gissing adhered to Victorian convention, but, while the bulky size of the older novel permitted room for a variety of incidents and characters, Gissing could only spin out sagas of extended gloom and misfortune. Reardon's labors (in *New Grub Street*) at "laborious padding" on his three-volume novels obviously reflect Gissing's own anguish. Nevertheless, much remains to be said in favor of his flawed novels of the eighties.

Gissing described his plan for *Workers in the Dawn* (1880), his first novel, as follows: "It is a novel, you must know, of social questions, and the principal characters are earnest young people striving for improvement in, as it were, the dawn of a new phase of our civilization."[15] Rarely was an intention less fulfilled or a book title more ill chosen. "Workers in the Twilight" would have served much better for Gissing's account of a frustrated artist and his doomed love for a sickly idealist. Gissing's brief phase as Comtian positivist ended when he realized that he was interested neither in the working classes nor in possibilities for reform. Man's only resource, he noted in an unprinted essay on the "Hope of Pessimism," is that he is at least able to be aware of the unchangeable human tragedy. Such a view points toward Conrad, although Gissing suggested in his next work that hedonistic self-consciousness, the artist's prerogative, might serve as an alternative to Schopenhauer's stern injunction: the repudiation of the will.

Perhaps Gissing would have been well advised to flee, like Stevenson, to Samoa; instead, he became the victim of his nihilistic intellect. After bitter experience he dismissed the possibility of love as "mere turmoil" in *New Grub Street*. Only in art did he search for relief. In his second novel, *The Unclassed* (1884), Gissing allows his artist-hero to express for him how he abandoned positivism for a faith in his "artistic self-consciousness." "My philosophy," says Waymark, "I have come to see, was worth nothing; what philosophy is worth anything? It had its uses for myself, however; it made me by degrees self-conscious, and brought me to see that in art alone I could find full satisfaction."[16] Disliking the class of people he chose to write about, Gissing extended sympathy only to the sensitive and self-destructive intellectuals in his novels who spend their time talking about literature or, as in *Thyrza*, working for the construction of free libraries. "The values by which he judges the working class are literary in the narrowest sense," Walter Allen suggests; "at times one would think that the sole end of life was that men and women should read."[17] Gissing's contention that the depiction of sensitive young men—"well-educated, fairly bred, *but without money*"—constituted his distinctive contribution to the novel[18] has some truth. James's Hyacinth Robinson in *The Princess Casamassima* and, to some degree, E. M. Forster's Leonard Bast in *Howards End* are variations on the Gissing young man—like Gilbert Grail in *Thyrza*—for whom there is no way out from his misfortunes but the acceptance of suffering as a value in itself. James's modest praise for the seriousness of Gissing's work dates from 1897,[19] and it is impossible to know whether he was aware of *Workers in the Dawn* or *The Unclassed* at the time he wrote *The Princess Casamassima* (for one thing, James's notebooks from that period have disappeared). The working class milieu used by James and Gissing is strikingly similar, and both novelists look at human suffering—not involving artists, that is—in terms of literary picture taking. Linking the two novelists for a moment, Forrest Reid noted how little enjoyment Gissing the artist took in what he was doing, while James, using "material quite as sordid," expressed "joy in the making of the book, and his genius infused its darkest pages with the spirit of life and beauty."[20]

Whatever they lack in "joy," Gissing's early novels often make up for in earnestness. *The Unclassed*, the first of his books to show genuine talent, deals with those poor and sensitive people of London who cannot fit into their shabby surroundings but who have little opportunity of escaping. Waymark, the protagonist, plans to make use of his surroundings by mirroring them in fiction. At one point, he becomes a rent collector in a particularly dreary part of London so that he can collect "rich material" for his planned novel. "Art, nowadays, must be the mouthpiece of misery," he tells his consumptive friend Julian, "for misery is the key-note of modern life." "Let me get a little more experience," he declares, "and I will write a novel such as no one has yet ventured to write, at all events in England." Such a novel would "dig deeper" into the "social strata" untouched by Dickens; there should be no question of the book being for young people, but rather

> for men and women who like to look beneath the surface, and who understand that only as artistic material has human life any significance. Yes, that is the conclusion I am working round to. The artist is the only sane man. Life for its own sake?— no; I would drink a pint of laudanum to-night. But life as the source of splendid pictures, inexhaustible material for effects— *that* can reconcile me to existence, and that only.

Waymark is hardly as callous as such a remark suggests—his aestheticism is a desperate remedy—but Gissing himself came to see the value of this view, which Nietzsche and James were expressing in their works at about the same time. Waymark's book,

Julian suggests, "will do more good than half a dozen religious societies," but nobody reads it when it is published, and the critics dismiss the novel as one of the "unsavoury productions of the so-called naturalist school."[21] It would be true of Gissing's work in the eighties, too, that it would be largely ignored, but Gissing was learning, like James after him, to turn the fact of his unsalability into a literary theme.

Demos (1886), which appeared on the eve of the Trafalgar Square riots, reflects the growing fear in the eighties that the rise to power of the working classes would mean an end to English culture. The new classes, Gissing warned, will be freed from all social obligations, but they will allow themselves to be led by the yellow press and by socialist demagogues. Here, too, Gissing presented in his novels what Nietzsche and Burckhardt were protesting in their philosophical writings. But, for Gissing, there were no overmen to look forward to; man is rooted in personal weakness, and his intellect can only reveal to him the lowliness of his condition. Hence, "we are interesting in proportion to our capacity for suffering, and dignity comes of misery nobly borne." The plot of *Demos* centers about the inheritance of a country estate, but Gissing suggests that the real issue is the inheritance of England, either by Richard Mutimer, a half-educated socialist who would turn the estate into a communally run coal mine, or by Hubert Eldon, an impoverished aristocrat with aesthetic leanings who would restore the land to its pastoral beauty. "Then you think grass and trees of more importance than human lives?" the heroine rebukes Eldon. "I had rather say," he replies, "that I see no value in human lives in a world from which grass and trees have vanished."[22]

The new men, Gissing warns, are possessed of only material desires. In a cynical aside, he foresees "the age when free thought—in the popular sense—will have become universal, when art shall have lost its meaning, worship its holiness, when the Bible will only exist in 'comic' editions, and Shakespeare be downcried by 'most sweet voices' as a mountebank of reactionary tendencies."[23] In *Thyrza* (1887), his next and best novel before *New Grub Street*, Gissing indicated the need for a spiritual education of the working classes, but he realized that the frailties within the more sensitive reformers could also work against genuine reform. Gissing's hero, Egremont, hopes to bring spiritual nourishment to the lower classes in the form of a free lending library. Yet Egremont's weaknesses, which derive from his sensitivity, destroy the effectiveness of his scheme; it is left, ironically, to Dalmaine, a selfish and thoroughly Philistine member of Parliament, to do real good for people he despises for the sake of self-profit and votes. In a flash of bitter insight, Gissing realized that the very purity of motive of an idealistic liberal like Egremont would keep him from resolving a complex situation, would in fact force him into a position of uncompromising self-righteousness, and would doom his efforts in working with and for others. By far the most sympathetically and best drawn of the characters in *Thyrza* is Gilbert Grail, a working man who by "mere grace" has developed a redeeming passion for literature. "To Gilbert, a printed page was as the fountain of life; he loved literature passionately, and hungered to know the history of man's mind through all the ages." Grail's hopeless poverty, however, is such that at times he aches for the ability to "lose consciousness of the burden of life."[24] A few years later Hardy would deal with such a character in a more masterly but hardly more convincing fashion in *Jude the Obscure*.

Despite the fact that Gissing gained his position in literary history by introducing the working classes into fiction, he was ultimately interested in only one sort of work and one sort of individual: a writer like himself. "No man ever lived," Henry Ryecroft protests, "who was, in every fibre, more vehemently an individualist."[25] Gissing's egoism may have prompted his best novels. Once he stopped writing as a spectator and wrote instead from experience, Frank Swinnerton argues, he created memorable works.[26] In the novels of the eighties, the objective materials became distorted into outlets for subjective self-pitying, as in his portrait of Julian in *The Unclassed*. In *New Grub Street* and *Henry Ryecroft* he explored his own problems as a writer and thinker with a merciless and strangely objective force. Reardon, his autobiographical representative in *New Grub Street*, is presented as knowingly courting his own downfall. In contrast, the callow Amy Reardon and the enterprising Jasper Milvain have a vitality that allows them to survive amid the Darwinian world of struggle in modern England. The capacity to survive is not, to be sure, one of Gissing's ideals; in this respect he is at one with Hardy and James. Filled with compassion and, in Gissing's words, "savage truths,"[27] *New Grub Street* remains the best novel in English on the subject of the day-to-day life of writers.

Gissing was a "modern" in his ability to mirror his own suffering as an image of general misery. "For it is the mind which creates the world about us," as Ryecroft muses, "and even though we stand side by side in the same meadow, my eyes will never see what is beheld by yours, my heart will never stir to the emotions with which yours is touched."[28] In Hardy no less than Gissing or James we also observe a case of the artist as solipsist. As a young man, Hardy noted, "The poetry of a scene varies with the minds of the perceivers. Indeed, it does not lie in the scene at all." Two decades later, in 1886, he called attention to the "suggestive" implications of Impressionist painting for literature: the importance of a particular scene depends on what appeals to the artist's *"individual eye and heart in particular."*[29] For Hardy, as for the older Victorian novelists, the tragic limitations that derive from each man's singular point of view would be a major theme, but he agreed with his younger colleagues in the impossibility of changing the situation—of attempting to broaden his readers' outlook, for example. Like the new novelists, he turned to literary creation as a means of consoling himself—and to the making of plots as a way of attaining a substitute power—for the realization of human helplessness. Gissing, who had sent him a copy of *The Unclassed*, admitted to what was a common goal: "In literature my interests begin and end; I hope to make my life and all my acquirements subservient to my ideal of artistic creation."[30] While Gissing complained that the necessity of writing for a public forced the novelist, at times, to substitute "reticences and superficialities" in place of "honest work," Hardy was drawn by opposing desires to be frank and reticent at the same time. Hardy was willing to bowdlerize his texts for the sake of serial publication so long as he had control over the final copy of the book, but, in the selection and handling of his topics, he was occasionally led into equivocations and ambiguities that seem to reflect an unwillingness to recognize the moral issues raised.

Six of Hardy's novels were published in the years between 1880 (*The Trumpet-Major*) and 1891 (*Tess of the d'Urbervilles*), and various essays on fiction testify to Hardy's interest in the development of the novel, even if he was given to ambivalent positions. In "The Profitable Reading of Fiction" (1889), he argued that novels should be true to life—even the unpleasant facts of life—but that, "despite the claims of realism, . . . the best fiction . . . is more true, so to put it, than history or nature can be."[31] In the more interesting piece on "Candour in English Fiction" (1890), Hardy attacked the insincerity of most contemporary fiction. Speaking as the author of *Tess*, which had just been rejected for serialization for the second time, he defended the use of unhappy endings and observed: "The crash of broken commandments is as necessary an accompaniment to the catastrophe of a tragedy as the noise of drum and cymbals to a triumphant march." Advocating the need for the "explicit novel," Hardy observed that, while the novel should never "exhibit lax views of that purity of life upon which the well-being of society depends," it could reveal something like "the position of man and woman in nature, and the position of belief in the minds of man and woman—things which everybody is thinking but nobody is saying."[32]

The most useful source of Hardy's comments on fiction, however, is the biography which his second wife assembled from his personal writings. It is here that Hardy's conflicting desires as a novelist—his wish to explore the tragedies of modern life and yet to provide a means of fictional pleasure—are most fully articulated. "The writer's problem," he wrote in 1881, "is, how to strike the balance between the uncommon and the ordinary so as on the one hand to give interest, on the other to give reality."[33] The answer, he decided, lay in separating the fabrication of plot from the creation of character: as long as one's characters were true to life, there was no need to worry about improbabilities or coincidences or melodramatic conventions in one's choice of story. But the predilection for lively plots often led Hardy to distort or falsify his characters in the process, and the contradiction between what a character is and what a character does, as in the case of his "pure woman," Tess, has led critics to doubt both his moral and his artistic integrity.[34]

No biographer of Hardy has yet managed to explain how this dispassionate, harmless, amiable, mildly morbid man, who disliked being touched and who found in writing a refuge from human involvement, nevertheless managed to write several of the world's great novels. Hardy has been praised as both realist and traditionalist devoted to the enduring simplicities of nature; he has also been hailed as an "anti-realist" determined to show cosmic absurdity at work in his intentionally irrational plots. One critic has even defended Hardy's generally crude use of coincidence as a way of saying "through the workings of chance what later writers" chose "to say through the vocabulary of the unconscious."[35] Hardy lends himself to a variety of interpretations because of the split in his purposes and the contradictions in his views. In an age of transition, he saw the traumatic effects on men's consciousness of their estrangement from their environment and of their lack of compensating ideals. Yet nature, he realized, was capable of being cruel as well as comforting, and it was man's right to assert himself, even if assertion necessarily led to acts of self-destruction. Hardy resolved this dualism by writing novels in which he could create an artistic *image* of nature—Hardy's Dorset is as much an illusion of the continuity of simple rural life as Trollope's Barset was an illusion of the Victorian balance—and a *drama* of man's futile attempts toward heroism. As an artist, he created situations which demand the useless expenditure of will, but Hardy reserved his deepest sympathies for characters who are powerless to act.

Asked late in life to recommend one of his books to be set up in braille, Hardy recommended *The Trumpet-Major* on the assumption that "scenes of action rather than those of reflection or analysis" were desired.[36] Hardy regarded the writing of fiction as a trade, and in his early novels he often seemed disposed to grant his readers and editors whatever they wished. His male heroes are generally noble, passive, and almost embarrassingly self-sacrificing —born victims rather than the sports of malign fortune. John Loveday, the trumpet-major, is one of these: he sacrifices the woman he loves and ultimately his life so that his mindless and fickle brother will live happily ever after with her. Loveday's unselfishness may have pleased contemporary readers, but one wonders to what degree, if any, Hardy conceived of Brother Bob as a case of the blissfulness of a life without imagination or thought or comprehension of any sort. *A Laodicean* (1881) is a considerably better novel than its predecessor in terms of the issues it raises and the brilliance of the opening chapters. Hardy drew upon autobiography for his portrait of the sensitive young architect, George Somerset, who courts one of the most potentially interesting women in Victorian fiction. Paula Power, a railway contractor's daughter and "New Woman" with a "prédilection d'artiste" for the past and the aristocracy, is one of the author's most ambitiously conceived women; yet Paula's complexity and human indecisiveness are wasted as the novel turns into a trivial, comic melodrama. Although Hardy's illness during the composition of parts of this book has been offered as an excuse for the bathos of the later sections, it is possible that, when dealing with real people and real dilemmas in his work, Hardy often did not know (or chose not to know) what to do with them.

Perhaps the saddest of all the failures of the period was *Two on a Tower* (1882), which seems a far better work upon reflection than upon examination. In the contrast between Swithin St. Cleeve, the self-absorbed young scientist, and Lady Constantine, the romantic older woman who sacrifices herself for him, Hardy set up an antithesis of temperaments that might have provided far more than the occasion for so trivial a plot. Swithin's dedication to astronomy parallels, at times, Hardy's dedication to writing. Swithin observes, for example, that the sky is filled with stars invisible to man—proof of how "nothing is made for man," of how essentially unintelligible is the universe and how irrelevant is man.[37] Once stated, however, this thought never again disturbs the young man's self-confidence in his ability to decipher the universe through his telescope. The philosophy, with its hints of Pascal and Schopenhauer, is detachable, and the scientist and novelist seem more proud of their discovery and rhetoric than they seem fully conscious of the implications. Hardy looked back on the novel, in his preface of 1895, as "the emotional history of two infinitesimal lives against the stupendous background of the stellar universe,"[38] but what he presented was the same situation he had used elsewhere: the waste of human sensitivity and the destructiveness of human will.

In *The Mayor of Casterbridge* (1886), Hardy combined this dualism in the figure of a single character, producing his most unified novel. For once the battle between assertiveness and self-denial takes place in a single individual, and the source of Michael Henchard's strength is also the occasion for tragedy. Henchard represents, Irving Howe says, "the heroism and futility of the human will,"[39] but the only role open to such a being is self-destruction. Yet while Hardy seems to be confirming Schopenhauer's view of the negative and even evil effects of the assertion of will, he deliberately allows so little possibility of choice or resistance to his characters that hostile critics have customarily blamed him for playing the part of the "Immanent Will" to an assortment of puppets. Like James, Hardy found in the practice of his art a means of power and an illusion of freedom barred to the characters he chose to create out of passive materials.

The Woodlanders (1887) is perhaps the most satisfying of all the Hardy novels of the eighties in the comparative ease of style and plainness of theme. For a change, Hardy manages to remain unambivalent in his attitude toward the superiority of the simple and uncultivated life. The sophisticated education which Grace Melbury receives only makes her unhappy with herself and detached in her relations with others. The theme is anti-intellectual, but in terms of the people involved a loss of intellect, or the postures of intellect, is scarcely to be missed. In the figures of Giles Winterborne and Marty South Hardy created perhaps the only convincing examples in his fiction of characters who are interesting as well as simple and who maintain harmonious relations with nature. But characters with more complicated natures, who have been corrupted by knowledge and worldly experience, intrude into Hardy's Edenic world, and woodlanders and aliens alike are ultimately frustrated. Hardy later spoke of the novel as a contribution to the marriage question, but, while the depiction of the unhappy marriage between Grace and Dr. Fitzpiers affords proof of the need for more lenient divorce laws, Hardy was constitutionally incapable of depicting a happy marriage in his novels. If the Victorian writers tended to treat marriage as a symbolic gesture of unity and reconciliation, Hardy depicted marriage as a fatal combination of dissimilar individuals already divided against themselves and now split against each other as well.

Tess of the d'Urbervilles (1891) and *Jude the Obscure* (1896) are Hardy's most impressive novels; while artistic flaws and dogmatic lapses of intelligence abound as usual, the novels contain scenes and characters impossible to forget. It was part of Hardy's Victorianism that he should have desired his readers to forget that his characters are only literary creations, and it is both an irony and a testament to Hardy's genius that criticisms are so often made by readers who resent the novelist's treatment of Tess or Jude— as if they were flesh and blood persons whom Hardy was inexcusably tampering with. Meredith, for example, complained that Tess, "at one time so real to me," becomes "a smudge in vapour" at the end because of the novelist's "sudden hurry to round the story."[40] Hardy's ability to put "real" people into impossible situations causes much discomfort, but the novelist's greatest characters transcend their plots and become something like symbolic forces.

In the case of Jude, alienation is transformed into poetry by the power of Hardy's artistry. Jude, who bears any number of similarities to Gissing's frustrated heroes, not only cannot will his life, but he is unable existentially to will his own death as well. In the great scene where he tries to crack through the frozen pond and drown himself, the ice refuses to break. While Jude is Hardy's greatest depiction of human frustration, Tess is his major example of the strength of fortitude. Tess suffers as a result of the willfulness and stupidity of others, but the most remarkable aspect of her fate is not her death (one of the clumsy touches in the book), but her resistance under the pressures to which Hardy subjects her, her determination to persevere in spite of her misfortunes. "The business of the poet and novelist," Hardy declared in 1885, "is to show the sorriness underlying the grandest things, and the grandeur underlying the sorriest things."[41] While he succumbed to the temptation to prove the first part of this statement in *The Dynasts*, he achieved the latter ambition in *Tess*.

In the last years of their lives, Hardy and Meredith were sometimes bracketed together as expounders of antithetical viewpoints:
pessimism versus optimism, or, in G. K. Chesterton's comparison
of the two, Pandiabolism and Pantheism. "The subtle and sad
change that was passing like twilight across the English brain"
at the end of the Victorian period, noted Chesterton in 1913, "is
very well expressed in the fact that men have come to mention
the great name of Meredith in the same breath as Thomas Hardy."[42]
Both novelists responded to the Darwinian discoveries, but where
the one found cosmic muddle, the other celebrated cosmic plenitude. Nevertheless, Hardy's irrational President of the Immortals
has worn better as a credible deity than Meredith's benign Comic
Spirit, and Hardy's "twilight view of life" (in Meredith's words),[43]
his depiction of human helplessness before the forces of internal
and external determinism, has eclipsed Meredith's confidence in the
human ability to transform one's environment and oneself sanely
and honestly. Where Meredith turned to fiction, as his predecessors
among the great Victorian novelists had done before him, in order
to express a social philosophy, Hardy and James devoted themselves to fiction for its own sake and for their own sake.

James's dislike of *Tess* and his patronizing attitude toward Hardy
are familiar enough,[44] but the similarities between the two novelists
are not always noted. Both began writing at about the same time,
and one of James's early essays was a caustic review of *Far from
the Madding Crowd*, which appalled him for its verbal padding, its
clumsy construction, and its unpleasantly aggressive heroine. James
and Hardy were both repelled by the same type of vigorous woman
—compare Arabella in *Jude* with Mona Brigstock in *The Spoils of
Poynton*, for example—and attracted to passive, selfless, and suffering young men (and women, in James's case). In the review of
Hardy just mentioned, James put his finger on one of his own
weaknesses: "he rarely gets beyond ambitious artifice—the mechanical simulation of heat and depth and wisdom that are absent."[45] Both novelists made craftsmanship try to serve, at times,
in place of a significant subject, and Hardy complained of James's
The Reverberator that, while written with care, it remained trivial
in theme.[46]

Hardy's contribution to the modern novel matches that of James in his disregard for happy endings, especially happy marriages— a Victorian convention with social as well as literary implications. D. H. Lawrence draws attention to the fact that Hardy's major characters are cut off from society, that they are forced to live in the modern desert away from the old codes of conduct. Of course, one of Hardy's major themes is the psychological catastrophe which results from this alienation of man from the human community and from nature, but he saw that alienation was an inescapable fact of history and that no effort at reintegration could purposefully succeed. In the fine short story, "A Few Crusted Characters" (1891), Hardy looks at the simple, rooted countryfolk through the eyes of one who has travelled too far from them ever to come home again, but Hardy's enduring countryside was an artistic creation and not an actual place. In his suggestive essay on Hardy, Lawrence defines modern individualism in a way obviously closer to Lawrence's views than to Hardy's but not so different from James's conception:

> By individualist is meant, not a selfish or greedy person, anxious to satisfy appetites, but a man of distinct being, who must act in his own particular way to fulfill his own individual nature. He is a man who, being beyond the average, chooses to rule his own life to his own completion, and as such is an aristocrat.[47]

The definition scarcely has anything to do with Jude or Henchard or Tess, but, if the word "artist" is substituted for "aristocrat," Lawrence can be seen as a colleague, to some degree, of Hardy and, to a greater extent, of Henry James.

If it has rarely seemed necessary to place James in his time in order to trace his nineteenth-century roots, the reason may well be that the American novelist in England is readily detachable. He does not "date," H. G. Wells once complained. Being an inhabitant of no easily mapped region, however, James has proved even more impossible to examine objectively than Hardy. James' description of Delacroix can be applied to himself: "Like all really great masters, . . . he can be described only by seeming paradoxes and contradictions."[48] He cherished his contradictoriness, especially as a young man with unlimited ambitions, a realist with romantic views, a cosmopolite with an American subject. Simplicity was impossible for the new American or new Englishman as a result of the shifts in intellectual and political history. In his memoirs, James compared the mood of sincerity in mid-Victorian England with the skepticism of the present; while he admired the transitional figure of Arnold, he also characterized Victorian novelists, in "The Art of Fiction," as being unself-conscious, incomplete, "*naïf*." In his study of Hawthorne (1879) James spoke of the modernity of the modern world—specifically of America, but with application to England, too—in terms of the growth of complexity in point of view. With the Civil War, the old, simple world to which Hawthorne belonged passed away, and into the "national consciousness" was introduced "a certain sense of proportion and relation, of the world being a more complicated place than it had hitherto seemed, the future more treacherous, success more difficult." The "good American," James declared, "will be a more critical person than his complacent and confident grandfather. He has eaten of the tree of knowledge," but instead of becoming a "sceptic" or "cynic," he will compensate for the new state of affairs by becoming, "without discredit to his well-known capacity for action, an observer."[49]

What James foresaw happening to his fellow Americans had already come true in his own case. James's family, his travels, his readings—all determined that his would be no simple life. "We wholesomely breathed inconsistency and ate and drank contradictions," he later said of his extraordinary upbringing.[50] If the rootlessness and the child's unhampered development of a view of the world drawn from romances never allowed him to enter fully into the life of his time, or into what one generally considers everyday life, it did provide him very early with an Arnoldian disinterestedness, a detachment which encouraged an untroubled free play of the mind. It helped make him perhaps the most complacent and least socially committed major writer of his time, confident of his powers, his artistic future, his integrity and singularity and uninvolved in any of the political, religious, or social disputes of his troubled times. The historical disruptions of the period, as F. W. Dupee has noted, "seem to have left James's mind as inviolable to doctrine as ever; and even his continued adherence to a native self-reliance and empiricism may well have been instinctive."[51] If life was complex, was a battle between fixed opposing forces, as he declared in the fine 1874 essay on Turgenev, there was a source of consolation which outweighed everything. There is no disguising the fact that "Evil is insolent and strong; beauty enchanting but rare; goodness very apt to be weak; folly very apt to be defiant; wickedness to carry the day," and so on.

> But the world as it stands is no illusion, no phantasm, no evil
> dream of a night; we wake up to it again for ever and ever;
> we can neither forget it nor deny it nor dispense with it. We
> can welcome experience as it comes, and give it what it demands,
> in exchange for something which it is idle to call much or
> little so long as it contributes to swell the volume of
> consciousness.

In both phrasing and idea, James exhibits a kinship here with Pater, although he continues by pointing to "a visible rule, that bids us learn to will" as well as "seek to understand."[52]

The complexity of the new American has made him an "observer," and the battle of life is a feast for one's "consciousness." If the philosophy is slightly superficial and the attitude somewhat rhetorical, still the focus is not on the complications of life but on the delight in one's observations. Without sharing, or aspiring to share, in the tangled issues of the day, James regarded the political disruptions as a source of "entertainment" and opportunity for the artist. As noted at the beginning of this book, England's loss of prestige in the late 1870's moved James to write that "the 'decline' of England seems to me a tremendous and even, almost, an inspiring spectacle." In 1888 he examined Guy de Maupassant's theory that everyone sees life in a different way and forms a "particular illusion," but the worries of Pater, Gissing, and Hardy caused no anxiety for James:

> It is of secondary importance that our impression should be
> called, or not called, an illusion; what is excellent is that
> our author has stated more neatly than we have lately seen
> it done that the value of the artist resides in the clearness with
> which he gives forth that impression.[53]

Wylie Sypher, discussing the "imperialism" of Romantic art, notes that it "asserts its authority not by method but rather by subduing things to the painter's eye," and Ortega y Gasset has stressed the importance of Impressionist painting in directing the artist's point of view away from the world and "into himself."[54] In this sense, James may be described as the Impressionist novelist *par excellence*. "He was only an eye," Cézanne declared of Monet, and what Cézanne added might also be said of James: "but what an eye!" Perhaps the key terms in James's aesthetic theory are "consciousness" and "point of view." The ease with which personal consciousness was translated into artistic means and artistic power is important to an understanding of James's faith in art.

In one of the great passages of religious stoicism, Pascal speaks of the superiority of thinking man to the circumstances which destroy him. Man is a thinking reed and "knows that he dies and the advantage which the universe has over him; the universe knows nothing of this. All our dignity consists, then, in thought." Two centuries later, Pater (whose last essay was on Pascal) transferred Pascal's maxim into the language of moral aestheticism. Where Pascal sought consolation in a stern religion, Pater turned to aesthetic consciousness. Thought became for Pater, as Ramon Fernandez noted, a matter of artistic feeling, a matter of sensuous consciousness. Intelligence became a form of subjective response, the object being perceived subordinate to the observer instead of the reverse.[55] Pater's importance in nineteenth-century thought and his legacy to the detached young men of the 1880's and 1890's was immense, as has been indicated earlier, but Pater's legacy to James has rarely been studied. James's few direct references to Pater were generally satirical or subdued. Like Moore, James admired Pater's ability to leave for others no trace of himself save the mask he wore. "Faint, pale, embarrassed, exquisite Pater!" he ticked off to his friend Edmund Gosse.[56] That there are sufficient affinities between the two men should be apparent by now, despite James's occasional parodies in his fiction of Pateresque young men.

James maintained as an artist a "religion of consciousness" (the phrase is F. O. Matthiessen's)[57] which kept him secure from worries all his life. Even his mother's death contributed "hours of exquisite pain" and "certain supreme impressions," he confided to his notebook.[58] To a despondent friend, James sounded "the voice of stoicism," as he knew it, arguing that "life is the most valuable thing we know anything about" and it would be "a great mistake to surrender it while there is any yet left in the cup."

> In other words consciousness is an illimitable power, and though at times it may seem to be all consciousness of misery, yet in the way it propagates itself from wave to wave, so that we never cease to feel, and though at moments we appear to, try to, pray to, there is something that holds one in one's place, makes it a standpoint in the universe which it is probably good not to forsake.[59]

A more confident age had declared that knowledge is power; James, no less confident, insisted that art alone can defy the malign power of history. Repeatedly he affirmed that art makes life, embalms experience; art is the product of consciousness and the fruit of the artist's point of view.

It may be argued, however, that for James consciousness was only eye-deep. Although in 1880 he praised the "wiser" artists and "finer" geniuses who are able "to conceive of other points of view, other ways of looking at things, than [their] own,"[60] he later created characters whose superior virtue consists precisely in a similarity to their creator: detached, observant, somewhat self-righteous in their aesthetic perceptiveness. James's fiction in the 1880's forms a special unit in his long career because of his willingess to deal with the value of separate points of views other than the single one that dominates his later work. The decade that begins with *The Portrait of a Lady* (1881), and ends with *The Tragic Muse* (1890), reveals James's fullest concession to the traditional and recent forms of the novel as he found it. The period up to 1880 may be seen as his years of apprenticeship in the Anglo-European novel; in the decade following, he participated in the fictional worlds of Dickens as well as Zola, George Eliot and Turgenev, Trollope and Pater. In creating novels whose topics dealt, very often, with the major philosophical and historical changes of the period, James placed increasing emphasis on the need for the individual to free himself from all nets placed in the way of his freedom. The concept of freedom changed from a Pateresque wish not to be limited in point of view to the desire, expressed later in the decade, to be free in a particular, pre-eminently Jamesian manner. Increasingly, James projected his own needs and his own values into his novels in such a way as to subvert the customary balance between self and society that was present in the Victorian novel. In James we find personified the shift from the Victorian novel, which reconciled the individual to the world, to the modern novel, which has tended to emphasize the individual over his world and the individual author over anything referential. With justice, Ernest A. Baker has spoken of James's "subversive effect upon the methods of other novelists, and even upon the general conception and status of the art."[61]

Although there is some disagreement as to whether James was essentially an American romancer or an English novelist, it might well be claimed for him that he helped to Americanize in theme, as well as to Europeanize in technique, the English novel.* "America is the land of romanticism par excellence," Jacques Barzun has aptly remarked;[62] and, as far as fiction is concerned, the American novelist traditionally sees all things in relation to himself, while the English Victorian novelist sees everything, including himself, in some context. If James was personally solipsistic, he did not produce a "solipsist fiction," according to Raymond Williams.[63] In his late essay on the "New Novel" (1914), in fact, James was not entirely pleased to observe that the new writer "is ideally immersed in his own body of reference."[64] But if James was, as he repeatedly claimed, saturated in "life," he treated life only as potential material for fiction; James's revolutionary effect on the novel, as Wells noted and as Williams has recently reminded us, was that he related everything, including himself, only to the novel—although that meant, in effect, to the Jamesian novel. It is not so much that James had no "historic sense," as W. C. Brownell protested in 1905 (in an essay which holds up as a valid critique of the Jamesian methodology),[65] as that he saw no place for the human element in history.

---

* If, as in some historians' views, the signs of the nineties are reflected in the establishment of *The Yellow Book* and the Yellow Press, it might be noted that both were American imports, the former the creation of the American expatriate Henry Harland (featuring James's "The Death of the Lion" at the head of the first issue).

History is a mirage, for James's main characters, which they escape by disavowing. The theme of *The Tragic Muse*, the novel which marks the turning point in James's career, is that history is unreal and only art has validity.

Despite their criticisms of each other's literary methods, Meredith and James were devoted friends from the 1880's until Meredith's death in 1908. In the minds of hostile critics, they were guilty of many of the same literary sins: psychological overanalysis, stylistic mannerisms, and unintelligibility. In terms of their very personal styles, both are "moderns"; in what they conceived to be the role of the novelist and in what they chose to write about, however, they belong to opposing literary worlds. Beginning with *Beauchamp's Career* and reaching its highest glory in *The Egoist*, Meredith's literary aim was to write novels that would speak out against the dangerous prevalencies of the age. After *The Egoist* Meredith's health and writing power declined and his struggle in the eighties to assert himself as a Victorian novelist best illustrates for the literary historian of the period both the value of Victorian idealism and its inability to survive in an age of dissolution. James, too, it seems to me, reached his peak as a novelist of stature at the beginning of the decade with *The Portrait of a Lady*. While his novels cannot be said to have declined afterward, they nevertheless changed direction. In the course of the period, James's themes shifted into a modern mode, and simultaneous with the end of the decade, while Meredith was struggling for the last time in *One of Our Conquerors* to write a novel in the tradition of *Middlemarch*, James argued in *The Tragic Muse* for the absolute freedom of the artist from any responsibilities whatsoever, save to his craft. Meredith's and James's novels of the eighties reflect opposing attitudes toward the artist's responsibilities in an age of change. If Meredith appears, as a result, typical of the Victorian novelists' inability to survive "transition England," James is the decisive example of an author passing out of a dying era into a new age.

Part II. George Meredith at the Victorian Crossways

Introduction

"I had with him no sense of reciprocity," Henry James wrote Edmund Gosse in 1912, explaining the dearth of correspondence between himself and Meredith; "he remained for me always a charming, a quite splendid and rather strange, Exhibition, so content itself to *be* one, all genially and glitteringly, but all exclusively, that I simply sat before him till the curtain fell, and then came again when I felt I should find it up." With the publication of a selection of Meredith's letters in that year, James noted regretfully that Meredith's "whole aesthetic range, understanding that in a big sense, strikes me as meagre and short; he clearly lived even less than one had the sense of his doing in the world of art . . ." The presence of "many beautiful felicities of wit and vision" scarcely sufficed as compensations; in his letters, as in his novels and his life, James declared, Meredith revealed the limitations of one who had presumed to deny the superiority of art to all other values. The artist in Meredith "was nothing to the good citizen and the liberalised bourgeois."[1] For all his verbal and philosophical daring, Meredith, it was discovered after his death, had been a consummately Victorian novelist.

In a memorable passage of Edith Wharton's memoirs, James is remembered for having exploded in the midst of a discussion of Meredith, protesting the "unconscious insincerity" of his art:

> Words—words—poetic imagery, metaphors, epigrams, descriptive passages! How much did any of them weigh in the baggage of the authentic novelist? (By this time he was on his feet, swaying agitatedly to and fro before the fire.) Meredith, he continued, was a sentimental rhetorician, whose natural indolence or congenital insufficiency, or both, made him, in life as in his art, shirk every climax, dodge around it, and veil its absence in a fog of eloquence.

Elsewhere James could comment on the force of that "eloquence," but, as Edith Wharton concluded, "when the sacred question of the craft was touched upon, all personal sympathies seemed irrelevant, and our friend pronounced his judgments without regard to them."[2] It is curious to find the elderly James criticizing another author on the grounds of stylistic camouflage; yet neither novelist, despite their personal friendship, could really appreciate or understand the other's conception of the purpose of the novel. In the most often quoted of James's remarks on Meredith—apropos, it should be added, of one of his worst novels, *Lord Ormont and His Aminta*— the American was moved to "a critical rage, an artistic fury" when confronted by the difficulties of the style and by what he felt to be the banality of Meredith's theme:

> . . . not a difficulty met, not a figure presented, not a scene constituted—not a dim shadow condensing once either into audible or into visible reality—making you hear for an instant the tap of its feet on the earth. Of course there are pretty things, but for what they are they come so much too dear, and so many of the profundities and tortuosities prove when threshed out to be only pretentious statements of the very simplest propositions.[3]

It will not do to cite Virginia Woolf's defense of the muscular style of *Lord Ormont* here, for James is generally right in his feelings toward this novel. But as the author of *The Ordeal of Richard Feverel, Harry Richmond, Beauchamp's Career*, and, above all, *The Egoist*, Meredith cannot be dismissed so easily from consideration as a major novelist as historians and critics of the novel, under James's influence, have intimated.

Meredith is the most intelligent of Victorian novelists after George Eliot, and he has the richest imagination of any Victorian novelist aside from Dickens; yet he raises more hostile feelings among readers than perhaps any other major English novelist on account of both his artistic weaknesses and the extent of his Victorianism. Aside from a degree of popularity that began in the 1880's and lasted until just after his death, Meredith's relationship with the reading public has hardly ever been happy or secure. In his early novels and poems he addressed himself in an outlandish style to themes of psychological complexity, which baffled or outraged readers who wanted an uncomplicated reflection of life more in keeping with the Victorian "balance." However, as the Victorian age went to pieces, Meredith ignored the example of those literary colleagues—Moore, Gissing, Hardy, and James—who turned to the craft of fiction as a substitute for the dying values of the period, or of those admirers—Stevenson, Conan Doyle, Wilde—who sought by a cultivation of romantic escapism to half shut their eyes to the dismal realities. Instead, in the sequence of novels beginning with *Beauchamp's Career* (1877) and culminating in *One of Our Conquerors* (1891), Meredith apotheosized a sense of social balance which allowed room for human complexity as well as individual longings for freedom.

The differences between Meredith and James are considerably more complex than a convenient comparison, along James's lines, of the one as "Exhibition" and the other as critical "Consciousness." The two novelists were very close in many ways, sharing an interest in detailed psychological analysis and even sharing much the same select reading audience during their lifetimes. But while he would have echoed Meredith's proud claim, made late in life, that he had "never written a word to please the public"[4] (at least, in James's novels after 1890), James could never have agreed with Meredith's assumption that it is the novelist's duty to "civilize" the public. The Victorian writer counted upon a developing society, which it was the novelist's obligation to inform and help in its development, while the American expatriate looked to a stable England to provide the necessary materials for his fiction which America lacked. As it happened, both men were disappointed. English society did change very drastically in the last two decades of the nineteenth century—shattering the image which James had first discovered in Thackeray and hoped to utilize for himself—but not in the positive direction Meredith had envisaged. While James gradually withdrew into the increasingly subjective confines of his art, Meredith intensified, during the eighties, his battle against the forces of egoism. It was Meredith's awareness of his own egomania and his own predilection toward rhetorical evasiveness (which he labelled "sentimentalism") that enabled him to lash out at these dangers, as he saw them, to responsible individualism and social cohesion.

Although exasperated by Meredith's artistic lapses, James also declared, in praise, that his great colleague had harnessed "winged horses to the chariot of his prose."[5] If he was not born to be a novelist, Meredith nevertheless managed to make the novel perform tricks it had never performed before. The thesis of Virginia Woolf's essay on Meredith is that, if he had not come along when he did, the novel might have expired. In her view, which was shared by many critics around the turn of the century, the novel had reached formal perfection with Jane Austen and Trollope; afterward the form could survive only by becoming something else. If, as Virginia Woolf declares, "George Eliot, Meredith, and Hardy were all imperfect novelists largely because they insisted upon introducing qualities, of thought and of poetry, that are perhaps incompatible with fiction at its most perfect,"[6] nevertheless, these qualities when added to fiction demonstrated the contrary truth of James's claim for the novel as "the most independent, most elastic, most prodigious of literary forms." It is only fitting that Meredith, above all—the most highly endowed novelist of his time—should have shown that the novel could be the most richly endowed of literary forms, even if he could not always successfully show how in his own works.

[5] A Strange and Splendid Exhibition

Ah! Meredith! Who can define him?
(Oscar Wilde)

I have never felt the unity of personality running
through my life. I have been six different
men, six at least.
(Meredith)

To be at one's best is to be Meredithian.
(Siegfried Sassoon)

Despite the existence in his works of enough literary sins to sink the reputations of a half-dozen novelists, the extraordinary virtues in those works have guaranteed the name of George Meredith a prospect of survival in the time yet remaining for the sufferance of civilized values. V. S. Pritchett, in the best study of this "most perplexing of our novelists in the nineteenth century" to have appeared in recent years, finds difficulties and weaknesses in profusion; yet he concludes that Meredith

> is a storehouse of ways and means, a fine diagnostician in his field as a poet will be; and rather hard and intelligently merciless—which is refreshing in the nineteenth century. And if he looks askance at many pretended virtues, the virtues he preaches (and happily by implication) are truthfulness and fortitude in the romantic disaster. He is a hot-house stoic and perhaps we should look upon him, first and last, as one of the startling temperaments of a very temperamental age.[1]

A master at comedy, a fine lyric poet, and an acute psychologist, Meredith attempted to combine, though he often wasted, these gifts under the cover of philosophy. "No English writer of his century cast a wider net," J. B. Priestley maintained, and Priestley was not alone among Meredith's admirers, so often "overpowered by his breadth and force," who found in his singular combination of imaginative gifts "the only writer of the last two centuries who can be placed by the side of Shakespeare."[2]

Meredith awed and dismayed many of his contemporaries by the prodigality of his talents and the strangeness of his mannerisms. "He is not an easy man to be yourself with," his admirer and "too apt pupil" (in James's phrase), Robert Louis Stevenson, complained to James in 1888; "there is so much of him, and the veracity and the high athletic intellectual humbug are so intermixed."[3] In the late 1870's and the 1880's, Stevenson joined forces with such diverse company as Gissing, Wilde, and James Thomson in acknowledging Meredith as "the greatest force in English letters."[4] However, the same decade which witnessed his emergence as the acknowledged master among living novelists after three decades of comparative neglect also witnessed a weakening of his health and creative powers. It is at this time, as if to compensate for the loss by demonstrating in his person what he had previously conveyed in his fiction and poetry, that Meredith began to take refuge behind the mask of a "dramatic personality" (in the words of his biographer): "a flawless structure which had become his second nature." To such friends as James and Stevenson, "he created the effect of a perpetual and consummate theatrical performance";[5] meanwhile, a growing number of reporters and admirers from France and America as well as England began to make pilgrimages to Box Hill in order to hear what the last remaining great Victorian sage and individualist had to say in the way of reassurance for the future.

One reason for Meredith's continuing fascination is the liveliness of his attempt to understand and embrace the universe at so many points. In a critical mood, one might direct Meredith's own Comic Spirit against those of his admirers who celebrated, as a philosophical panacea for the doubts and crises of their times, his attempt to reconcile in a single system an acceptance and love of nature and society with the need for human mastery of environment and one's own nature. What seemed to his devotees a masterful philosophical fusion has come to seem more like aesthetic confusion or wishful thinking, and they often ended by embracing

an idol rather than a practicable idealism, leaving a later generation unsympathetically aware of clay feet. A Platonist and a realist,
a believer in Utopia who nevertheless accepted the validity of
Darwin's findings, Meredith based his belief (like Mill before him)
in man's potential or innate strength of rational behavior and
thought. He sought, in the manner of a Victorian universal man
like Herbert Spencer, to synthesize all knowledge. As in Spencer's
case, what seemed like synthesis to his contemporaries more often
resembles something merely synthetic and subjective now. Unlike
Spencer, Meredith was able to make up for the occasional "hollowness" of the philosophy, in E. M. Forster's view,[6] by means of the
artistry in his fiction. Although not the Complete Artist that James
called for, Meredith is a match for James in analyzing the psychological complexity of his characters, and he surpasses James as a
writer of comedy and poetry.

In the first chapter of *Diana of the Crossways* (1885), Meredith
made a once much-quoted outcry on the need for philosophical
"brainstuff" in fiction: "The forecast may be hazarded," he said,
"that if we do not speedily embrace Philosophy in fiction, the Art
is doomed to extinction, under the shining multitude of its professors."[7] Meredith did not fear the extinction of the novel form so
much as he feared, at a time of intense change, that the ideal of
civilization which England had pursued but never yet fully attained might be abandoned. The need for social change coincided
with, and depended upon, the need for self-enlightenment. "Close
knowledge of our fellows," he wrote in 1887 to an admirer at Harvard, "discernment of the laws of existence, these lead to great
civilization. I have supposed that the novel, exposing and illus-
trating the natural history of man, may help us to such sustaining
roadside gifts."[8] Meredith's confidence in the possibilities open
alike to mankind and to fiction impressed even so pessimistic a
writer as Gissing, who marvelled at his "high culture, and most
liberal mind" (a combination which brings only frustration to the
people in Gissing's novels): "His philosophy is wonderfully bright
and hopeful," he noted in 1895, contrasting him advantageously to
Hardy. "A scholar, he yet thinks the best of Democracy, and
believes that emancipated human-kind will do greater things than
the old civilizations permitted. There is a fine dignity about him,

and I feel proud to sit in his room."[9] A radical in politics, Meredith nevertheless believed that literature should be aristocratic—that it should help to ennoble the minds of readers rather than address itself to the lowest common denominator.

The rejection of Meredith, which began during the First World War, accompanied the increasing disbelief among intellectuals in the durability of civilized values, in the transforming capabilities of the individual will, or in the intrinsically rational construction of society—three of Meredith's key ideas. Hardy supplanted him in popularity, for Hardy's pessimistic views of an irrational universe filled with passive individuals seemed closer to historical fact than Meredith's beliefs. Young writers turned to James's lesson, first enunciated in England by Pater, that the artist's power of consciousness is a more than sufficient replacement for the use of the will. In 1911 Joseph Warren Beach praised Meredith for having produced "the noblest philosophy of our day," but in 1918 Beach turned to James, about whom he admitted: "His greatest appeal is perhaps to those whose lives have yielded the minimum of realization, to those who have the least control over the gross materials of life." In the choice of titles for his studies of the two novelists, Beach typifies a shift in critical values: from *The Comic Spirit in George Meredith*, he moved to a celebration of *The Method of Henry James*.[10]

It is ironical that the novelist whose first major work was excluded from the lending libraries for its immorality should seem so thoroughly "bourgeois" (James's description) after all; yet Meredith essentially wrote with the aim, in his own words, of making "John Bull understand himself."[11] Despite his occasional inability to make himself understood at all, Meredith relied upon comedy as a means of providing a sense of perspective for his readers—enabling them to perceive and thereby abandon their human flaws. The aim of comedy, Meredith declared in his lecture on comedy, is to show "the signification of living in society," and he noted that Aristophanes, for examples, demonstrates in his works "the idea of Good Citizenship."[12] Jacques Barzun has observed that Meredith and James are "antithetical" novelists, despite superficial similarities, because "Meredith takes the comic view" and regards man as a social animal bound by the rational laws of society, whereas in James's "melodramatic" world man's passions are irrational and forever threaten to subject him to unnamed, personal horrors.[13] The distinction Barzun alludes to might be applied to the essential difference between novel and romance: in the novel the norms and sanctions are social, and offenders are reminded of these limitations by means of comedy; in the romance man is the arbiter of his own fate, of his own damnation if need be. (A comparison of *The Egoist* with *The Portrait of a Lady* would easily establish this basic distinction.) The object of the Meredithian novel, accordingly, is to direct the reader's attention away from the novel and toward social consciousness, but for James the process is reversed—which is why it is more important for James's characters to act in accordance with the logic of the novel rather than in a manner "true to life."

Meredith's allegiance to the laws of society over the rules of art creates obvious problems in his novels; at times, however, he allowed his artistic impulses to conquer his social philosophy. As a comic theorist, he praised comedy for exposing those human weaknesses which it is perhaps a function of art to camouflage, but Meredith unwillingly sympathized with the desire for rhetorical defenses. If the function of the Comic Spirit is to force one to laugh himself out of his humor, the one novel of Meredith's where the Spirit plays a direct role contains as its protagonist an unregenerate Egoist from beginning to end. The comedy at the end of *The Egoist* depends upon Sir Willoughby Patterne's inability to see himself for what he really is. Willoughby's mask is the source of the novel's humor, and Meredith's portraits of sentimental maskers account for the artistic success of many of his books. The philosopher in Meredith who urges the removal of these masks (in *Sandra Belloni*, for example) turns out to be the enemy of novelistic artistry. One of the paradoxes in one's admiration of Meredith is that it is the sanity of the novelist which compels us to admire him, but it is often the irrationality of many of his best characters that makes his novels memorable.

"Meredith has always suffered from the curse of too much ability," Arthur Symons once observed. "He thinks in flashes, and writes in shorthand. He has an intellectual passion for words, but he has never been able to accustom his mind to the slowness of their service."[14] In trying to express John Bull to himself, as he claimed, Meredith tried to do more with words than had yet been accomplished in the novel in order to describe both the general human condition and the most intricate of human emotions, to show what we think we mean when we express ourselves in language and what in fact we really feel. In the ambitious attempt to unravel psychological cobwebs, as he once put it, as well as to create historical epics, he of necessity failed to write coherent novels. In evaluating Meredith's contributions to literature, one should not confuse the nature of his aim with the fact of his actual achievement. Confusion of the two led to the wild exaggeration of his accomplishments sixty years ago, which helped in turn to provoke the correspondingly too-hostile rejection that followed. The nature of Meredith's hold and lack of hold upon his readers is a matter of real interest to the cultural historian. It was possible sixty years ago for a distinguished literary critic to say, "Tolstoy does not deserve comparison with Meredith." In 1910 a respected German scholar called Meredith the most "brilliant and universal intellect" since Goethe, and the fine French critic Ramon Fernandez in 1926 urged the disciples of Proust to heed "the message of Meredith." Commentary on Meredith has always tended to run to extremes, and it is not uncommon to find both extremes in the same commentator. "I hate and admire him," grumbled Henley, after having written four appreciative reviews of *The Egoist*.[15] The question of Meredith's literary position, while hardly the philosophical issue of a half century ago, has never been satisfactorily settled. For over a century, in fact, his admirers have found it as hard to accept satisfactory explanations for the overwhelming neglect of Meredith as his detractors have found it difficult to accept the fact of his extraordinary survival.

Meredith has been assailed from every conceivable angle. In 1886 W. L. Courtney wrote in the *Fortnightly Review*, which had just serialized *Diana of the Crossways*, bemoaning Meredith's inability to tell a story as indicative both of the decline of the novel and of the decade's uneasy preoccupation with critical self-analysis and social doubt: "Only in such an age as ours could a novelist like

Mr. George Meredith be acceptable, for only in such an age could his peculiar gifts win for themselves recognition or even tolerance." In a generally appreciative essay, written a decade before he published his famous study *The Craft of Fiction*, Percy Lubbock admitted that Meredith was certainly no artist by modern (and admittedly Jamesian) standards: "the restraining hand, the deliberate design, the critical sense of perfection, these are not to be found [in his work]. More comprehensive still, the single-minded attitude of the artist before his work, his unqualified homage to it and it alone—this too was wanting." In a postscript added ten years later to his study of Meredith (which, in 1889, was the first book devoted to him), Richard Le Gallienne confessed that, while he held "Mr. Meredith's greatness to be even greater than" he had earlier, he had come "to see that it is perhaps more a philosopher's and less an artist's greatness than I could have been brought to admit at twenty-three." Perhaps the most devoted of all Meredith's admirers, the historian G. M. Trevelyan, admitted in 1954, fifty years after his pioneering work on Meredith's poetry and philosophy, that while Meredith possessed "more intellectual power and finesse, and stronger imagination than any other of the Victorians," only in a few poems "did he know how to employ them perfectly."[16]

It would be too tedious a task to call attention to all the various critical advances and retreats in the army of unutterable lore devoted to Meredith. Perhaps the best introduction to the problem of Meredith is that of the exasperated speaker in Oscar Wilde's "The Decay of Lying": "Ah! Meredith! Who can define him? His style is chaos illumined by flashes of lightning. As a writer he has mastered everything except language: as a novelist he can do everything, except tell a story: as an artist he is everything except articulate." Beyond the immediate desire to shine in epigrams, Wilde was more sensitive than most of Meredith's critics in dealing with the novelist's strengths and weaknesses. In "The Soul of Man under Socialism," Wilde made one of the earliest references to Meredith's distinction as a philosophical novelist: "to him belongs philosophy in fiction. His people not merely live, but they live in thought."[17] Wilde called attention to Meredith's greatest strength, the plenitude of his gifts, and to his greatest weakness, the inability all too often to channel superabundant energies into conventional forms.

Meredith's biography and bibliography alike can be understood only in terms of paradox and profusion. He was born in 1828 and died in 1909, overlapping the Victorian age by nearly a decade on both sides. Simultaneously the most and the least of Victorians, Meredith joined the ranks of the great Victorian critics and individualists—Carlyle, Arnold, and Ruskin—by maintaining a continual rebellion against the blindness and false values of the age. Like so many of his fellow novelists—Thackeray, George Eliot, and Trollope immediately come to mind—he was brought up outside the Victorian establishment and remained temperamentally divorced from the very social values he idealized in his fiction. Meredith's biographers have sought to explain his career by stressing various early influences: his lonely and initially spoiled childhood, his schooling in Germany under altruistic Moravians, his shame at his father's tailor shop, his disastrous first marriage to Thomas Love Peacock's daughter. Undoubtedly these do account for certain aspects of his development; yet part of his aim as a writer was to remake his biography. In a novel like *Evan Harrington* he transformed the most intimate of personal details into pure fiction, but in life he attempted to re-create into fact the fictional persona of George Meredith, Celtic Dauphin. The Egoist, as Meredith remarks apropos of Sir Willoughby Patterne, is his own father, but (and here Meredith suggests Joyce) so is the artist.

"Confound the *Press* for its impudence in calling me a pupil of anybody!" the proud young author wrote to a friend.[18] But Meredith was not altogether his own invention. Strong literary influences include Carlyle, Goethe, Molière, Gibbon, Keats, Tennyson, Browning, and the *Arabian Nights*. He agreed with Carlyle in holding up Goethe as "the pattern for all who would have a directing hold of themselves," and he deferred to Molière, in his lecture on comedy, as the exemplar of comic writing. It was Carlyle, however, "the greatest of the Britons of his time," with whom he maintained the closest identification. In 1882 he might have been describing himself when he said of Carlyle that "The efforts after verification of matters of fact, and to present things distinctly in language, were incessant; they cost him his health, swallowed up his leisure." Although "he did no perfect work, he had lightning's power to strike out marvellous pictures and reach to the inmost of men with a phrase."[19] Meredith apparently did not, like the young Dickens or James, devour novels as a child. The only English novelist he remembered having read was Scott, and it was Scott's ability to reproduce the psychology of an entire society that Meredith emulated in novels like *Vittoria*, although he also attempted to analyze the conflicting motivations of each individual character as well. A love of romance combined in Meredith with a mistrust of romantic evasions of reality. In his first novel, accordingly, he encased, in an *Arabian Nights* form of plot, an attack on the forces of illusion.

The Shaving of Shagpat (1856) contains many of Meredith's lifelong themes. The hero of the novel, deliberately conceived in a nonheroic manner, is a vain barber who is called upon to expose a popular Illusion. Carlyle's "clothes philosophy" of *Sartor Resartus* is transformed into a cult of hairiness, apotheosized in the figure of the public favorite, Shagpat. Only when the hero can conquer his own egoism, aided by repeated thwackings and by a wise heroine, can he perform service to society by shaving Shagpat, which symbolizes the exposure of humbug. Only belatedly, and with the aid of laughter, does the populace recognize the service, but, as Meredith warns at the end of the book, it will not be long before "a fresh Illusion springeth to befool mankind." In his lecture on comedy, delivered two decades later, Meredith invoked "the Comic idea" as a means of dealing with the phenomenon of "Folly perpetually sliding into new shapes in a society possessed of wealth and leisure, with many whims, many strange ailments and strange doctors."[20] The message of the need for self-discipline found expression in an extraordinarily imaginative, if undisciplined, style, and, while George Eliot recognized the "genius" of the novel, other readers were merely baffled by it, and the book was generally ignored. In his brief second novel, *Farina* (1857), Meredith turned from the *Arabian Nights* to medieval Cologne, but the theme is once again the development of a middle-class hero. His villain is a comic version of Satan; and the devil henceforth shows up on occasion in Meredith's novels and poetry as the personification of egoism.

If his first two works of fiction were charming *jeux d'esprit*, his next novel indicated the extent and daring of his genius. *The Ordeal of Richard Feverel* (1859) mainly shocked its few initial readers, and certainly its first reviewers, by subverting their expectations of what a novel traditionally entailed. In a new form, resembling at times an extended essay, Meredith ignored the conventions of plot and characters and concentrated on the intimate and contradictory details of his characters' developing or regressing minds and feelings. Like *Shagpat*, it is a novel without a conventional "hero." Its two male protagonists, Sir Austin Feverel and his son Richard, are both egoists, the one of a scientific and the other of a romantic nature, and, in their contrasting determination to play Providence or to submit to it in a Byronic-chivalric-fatalistic manner, they bring tragedy in their wake. The denizens of Raynham Abbey are conceived in comic terms. Once they are allowed to prowl beyond the confines of Abbey and comedy alike, however, they face the mingled possibilities of romance and tragedy. Both women whose adoration Richard accepts as a matter of course—his bride Lucy and his cousin Clare—perish as a result of his inability to throw off the "heroic" pose. Similarly, Sir Austin thwarts nature by first imposing a System upon his son and then imposing a mask upon his own paternal feelings.

The dialectic between the truth of nature and rhetorical posture in the novel is evidenced when one compares the chapter "Nursing the Devil," in which Sir Austin hardens his heart and nurses his pride, with the lyrical chapter "Nature Speaks," where Richard momentarily realizes the communal bonds of nature. While Nature speaks with eloquence, the Devil ultimately conquers. Optimistic as Meredith was about the possibility of communication between man and nature, and hence man and man, he was realistic enough to follow the logic of his fable to its obvious conclusion. "Beware the little knowledge of one's self!" reads one of Sir Austin's epigrams for *The Pilgrim's Scrip*. It is a characteristic Meredithian irony that Sir Austin can articulate into epigrams what he cannot face in real life. " 'The reason why men and women are mysterious to us, and prove disappointing,' we learn from THE PILGRIM'S SCRIP, 'is, that we will read them from our own book; just as we are perplexed by reading ourselves from theirs.' "[21]

The Ordeal of Richard Feverel contains a powerful message, which could be comprehended neither by the main characters in the novel nor by its earliest readers. Meredith found himself trying to articulate a simple theme never fully explored in the novel before: the existence of social masks, which separate man from man and man from woman, and of psychological masks, which keep man from understanding himself. Later in the century Henri Bergson would use the idea of public versus private selves as the basis for his explanation of the freedom of the will, but Bergson failed to comment on the division within the private self. Meredith attempted to make his readers see beyond the limited perspectives of the characters in the novel, but the difficulty of this undertaking obliged him to introduce into the novel the language and methods of poetry and philosophy, as well as to rummage among all the resources of fiction then available. He combined poetic symbolism with devices borrowed from the epistolary novel of Richardson. He even experimented with narrative point of view, shifting from one character's perspective to another's in the attempt to show their mutual incomprehension. At one point he quotes from Clare's diary, discovered after her tragic death, in order to demonstrate, ironically, the individual's inability to understand himself even in the privacy of a personal journal: "Even to herself Clare was not over-communicative." Halfway through the novel, as if suddenly realizing the revolutionary nature of his undertaking, Meredith intrudes and attempts to articulate what as a novelist he is presenting:

> At present, I am aware, an audience impatient for blood and glory scorns the stress I am putting on incidents so minute, a picture so little imposing. An audience will come to whom it will be given to see the elementary machinery at work: who, as it were, from some slight hint of the straws, will feel the winds of March when they do not blow. To them will nothing be trivial, seeing that they will have in their eyes the invisible conflict going on around us, whose features a nod, a smile, a laugh of ours perpetually changes. And they will perceive, moreover, that in real life all hangs together: the train is laid in the lifting of an eyebrow, that bursts upon the field of

thousands. They will see the links of things as they pass, and wonder not, as foolish people now do, that this great matter came out of that small one.[22]

Published in the year of the *Origin of Species* and *On Liberty*, Meredith's novel created a revolution of its own, even if the full effects were not felt for many years afterward. In many respects the modern English novel, with its psychological intricacies and subjective language, begins with *The Ordeal of Richard Feverel*.

None of Meredith's novels written in the 1860's approximates the stature of *Richard Feverel*, partly because he attempted, in works like *Evan Harrington* and *Rhoda Fleming*, to produce a popular success by working with subjects not altogether congenial to his abilities. Perhaps when *Richard Feverel* was banned from Mudie's lending libraries, cutting off the possibility of sales, Meredith decided to restrain his natural bent. In his next book, *Evan Harrington* (1860), he played with the label of the "gentleman" (a subject of controversy at the time) just as he had contended with the idea of the "hero" in *Richard Feverel*. Evan is a tailor's son raised to be a gentleman, who learns that he cannot escape his tradesman's background. The novel is flawed in conception as a result of Meredith's desire for his hero to face the truth of his birth but also to be rewarded in the eyes of society for having done so. What begins as a satire directed against the accepted view of the gentleman goes to pieces as Evan turns out to be a gentleman in fact. The attentive reader is treated to the rather uninteresting heroine's discovery that her beloved is a gentleman by nature, but it is impossible to feel concern for either of them.

One obvious reason for the clumsy handling of the protagonist stems from Meredith's autobiographical identification with him. In his biography of the novelist, Meredith's cousin, S. M. Ellis, revealed that in *Evan Harrington* Meredith not only used his grandparents and aunts as his models but he also in many cases borrowed their actual names.[23] The great Mel, Evan's tailor-father, was drawn from Meredith's grandfather Melchizedek, a Portsmouth naval outfitter. Many of the tradesmen referred to in the novel were actual acquaintances. Evan resembles George Meredith, who as a Portsmouth youth had been raised as an aristocrat and dubbed by classmates "Gentleman Georgy." Those characters in the novel not drawn from life were, as often as not, drawn from other novels. The Cogglesby Brothers, for example, are an embarrassing copy of Dickens' Cheeryble Brothers. It may be a sign of temporary inventive exhaustion on Meredith's part that he should have felt the need to resort to his early life and to other novels in search of literary materials. Nevertheless, he presented three of his most suggestive originals in the novel. Evan's father, the Great Mel, even though he dies before the book begins, memorably hovers over the ensuing chapters like a humorist's version of Hamlet's ghostly father. In the sickly Juliana Bonner, Meredith sketched a convincing, if slightly cruel, study of a diseased sensibility—in direct contrast to the sickly young maidens of Victorian literature, from Little Nell to Milly Theale, who are somehow purified by their physical suffering. The one really unforgettable character in the novel, however, is Evan's sister Louisa (actually Meredith's Aunt Louisa), the Countess of Saldar.

Whatever led so secretive a man as Meredith to write so autobiographical a novel is open to speculation. J. B. Priestley suggests that the central contradiction in Meredith's life was to camouflage as a man what he exposed as an artist; thus, he was at once the agent and the object of his satire.[24] But in a figure like the Countess, Meredith unconsciously defended his own secretiveness and his attempt to mask the facts of his personal life. Her determination to sustain an illusion about her and her brother's upbringing is akin to Meredith's elaborate descriptions of himself as being of Celtic ancestry. One should laugh at the Countess' vain attempts— and one does—but one also sympathizes with her in the process. The ambivalence on Meredith's part destroys the philosophical theme of the novel, but it ensures an artistic fascination otherwise lacking. Like the Baroness in James's *The Europeans*, the Countess seems more of an artist with words than a simple *poseuse*. Whatever Meredith's philosophical sympathies with his hero's desire to uncover the truth, his artistic sympathies are with the one character who prefers her disguise. Meredith's lifelong mistrust of "art" was in keeping with his philosophical love of truth. Even the writing of novels meant a capitulation to the forces of illusion, though he stridently attacked these forces in his novels. Nevertheless, his major literary creations are, with a few notable exceptions, defenders of illusion, embodiments of irrational behavior, and unchangeable egoists. The Countess joins Richmond Roy and Sir Willoughby Patterne among the novelist's greatest creations, exuberantly romantic characters who are conceived along novelistic lines which Meredith generally eschewed. But if Meredith was aware of the lure of romantic persiflage, he was also aware of the danger to society and self which resulted from a life of illusion. In *Modern Love* he returned to the antiromantic mood of *Richard Feverel*.

In 1862 Meredith brought out, at his own expense, his second volume of poems, containing a number of skillful Browningesque monologues and one of the great Victorian achievements in verse. "The Tragedy of Modern Love," in its original title, was conceived as an attempt to deal with the causes of the breakup of his first marriage. *Modern Love* is the first and finest of modern "confessional" poems. Its theme, which Meredith used repeatedly in his fiction, though rarely to such concentrated effect, is the tragic incomprehension between man and woman, the inability of husband and wife to put off the masks they have donned to ward off or to disguise natural feelings. As Mrs. Berry in *Richard Feverel* admits, "it's all a puzzle, man and woman! and we perplex each other to the end." *Modern Love* ends with the suggestion that there are no ready answers for the tragedies of modern love and life, that at best one can discern hints of reality after one's ordeal is passed, but real perspective is hardly possible:

> Ah, what a dusty answer gets the soul
> When hot for certainties in this our life!—
> In tragic hints here see what evermore
> Moves dark as yonder midnight ocean's force,
> Thundering like ramping hosts of warrior horse,
> To throw that faint thin line upon the shore!

The spokesman for the Comic Spirit, who repeatedly argued the necessity for more brainstuff in order to attain true perspective, here in *Modern Love* and again in several of his best novels, admitted the insurmountable fact of human limitations.

The new volume of poems did not sell, and the title poem elicited unappreciative response. " 'Modern Love' as a dissection of the sentimental passion of these days," Meredith wrote to a friend, "could only be apprehended by the few who would read it many times. I have not looked for it to succeed." In the same letter, he went on to discuss his program as a novelist, his hope to graft idealism onto realism:

> Between realism and idealism, there is no natural conflict. This completes that. Realism is the basis of good composition: it implies study, observation, artistic power, and (in those who can do more) humility. Little writers should be realistic. They would then at least do solid work. They afflict the world because they will attempt what is given to none but noble workmen to achieve. A great genius must necessarily employ ideal means, for, a vast conception cannot be placed bodily before the eye, and remains to be suggested. Idealism is as an atmosphere whose effects of grandeur are wrought out through a series of illusions, that are illusions to the sense within us only when divorced from the groundwork of the Real. Need there be exclusion, the one of the other?

He continued by praising those authors—Shakespeare, Goethe, Molière, Cervantes—who are "Realists *au fond*," but who "have the broad arms of Idealism at command. They give us Earth; but it is Earth with an atmosphere."[25] Meredith's impatience with the kind of realistic analysis which often tends in his work to undermine any idealistic message may help explain his increasing turn to symbolic characters to embody the sort of ideal triumphs impossible for a figure treated realistically. The novels of the 1860's, at any rate, often show the inability of realism and idealism to coexist; one of the two tends to destroy the other.

Meredith's annoyance with "little writers" probably stemmed from his new duties as reader for Chapman and Hall, an occupation which strengthened his resistance to the tastes of a reading public which devoured the kinds of novels he despised and usually rejected. (Among the writers whose work he encouraged were Hardy, Gissing, and Olive Schreiner.) The preaching tone that crept into his letters and novels of the decade may be the unfortunate by-product of his position from 1860 to 1868 as editorial writer for the arch-Conservative *Ipswich Journal*. During that busy decade, he was forced to write political journalism in a manner opposed to his radical instincts and obliging him to assume a posture of political charlatanry, and to read intolerable manuscripts in order to make a living denied him by the meager sales of his fiction. Meanwhile, from 1860 to 1866 he published four novels and *Modern Love*, none of which met with the sort of critical appreciation that prods public interest. These biographical considerations need hardly excuse the fact that his works, aside from *Modern Love*, now began to reveal annoying mannerisms, but they help explain the mixed tone of defensiveness and belligerency in the novels.

Sandra Belloni (1864), originally published under the title *Emilia in England*, required more time and energy to write than any of its predecessors, and it demands more time and energy of the reader than may rationally be expected. Like *Richard Feverel*, the novel was planned along comic lines—as a comparison between a ridiculous family of English sentimentalists, the Poles, and a vocally gifted daughter of nature, half-Italian and half-Welsh. Once the logic of the plot is established, however, the only possible outcome is tragedy for the Pole family and escape to Italy for the heroine, Sandra. Speaking of the most unfortunate pair among the sentimentalists, Cornelia Pole and her proud, impoverished suitor, Purcell Barrett, Meredith asserts early in the book that one should not pity such beings: "they are right good comedy; for which I may say that I almost love them. Man is the laughing animal: and at the end of an infinite search, the philosopher finds himself clinging to laughter as the best of human fruit, purely human, and sane, and comforting. So let us be cordially thankful to those who furnish matter for sound embracing laughter."[26] But in the later chapter entitled "The Tragedy of Sentiment," Meredith finds it impossible to appeal to the reader's sense of humor; the paths of sentiment lead not to comic catharsis but to suicide. Cornelia's and Purcell's inability to understand either their own motives or those of one another leads them into "labyrinths of delusion," and the reader's final response to their tragedy is not "sound embracing laughter" but a mixed emotion of which pity and distaste are elements. Not happy with the ill-chosen assortment of characters in the novel, Meredith salvaged Sandra and a few others for a sequel novel of considerably more concentrated force.

Meredith had warned in a note to *Modern Love* that the work was not for "little people" or for "fools," but in *Sandra Belloni* and *Rhoda Fleming* he stressed the devastating importance of such individuals in life. Wilfrid Pole, especially, is subjected to merciless scrutiny, which Meredith defends on the ground that if his creation seems like a mere puppet it is because he has chosen to become one. Meredith compares his ready admission of the puppet-like qualities of Wilfrid with the confession of a professional puppeteer, who first pretends that his puppets are real and then, after the performance, destroys the illusion by showing the audience the dolls he has been using. Meredith insists that as a result of his frank admission, *in advance*, that he has a puppet in his hands, the reader will rationally accept the fact of the real puppet and then knowingly accept the idea of the character being represented by the doll. Despite such Brechtian admissions, however, the novel is weakened by the attempt to make philosophical-aesthetic generalizations of this sort. At war with the methods of the old-fashioned narrator is the "Philosopher," who intrudes into the novel at awkward moments to point out the reality of the situation. "He points proudly to the fact that our people in this comedy move themselves," Meredith asserts, "—are moved from their own impulsion,—and that no arbitrary hand has posted them to bring about any event and heap the catastrophe. In vain I tell him that he is meantime making tatters of the puppets' gold robe—illusion: that he is sucking the blood of their warm humanity out of them." The semicomic battle between Philosopher and narrator is fought to little purpose in the novel, which expires under the blows of the one's self-righteousness and the other's artistic confusion. "We are indeed in a sort of partnership," the narrator admits of himself and the Philosopher, "and it is useless for me to tell him that he is not popular and destroys my chance."[27]

Sandra Belloni has the same morbid fascination for the student of the novel that an architectural ruin exhibiting a variety of styles and many fascinating details might have for an architectural historian: among the rubble are intermingled traces of devastation and genius. The self-consciousness and artistic confusion of the novel may be partially explained by the author's personal difficulties during the time he worked on it and by his frantic attempt to unite elements of philosophy, psychology, comedy, and tragedy in such a way as to solve his difficulties with the form of fiction. Purcell Barrett speaks for Meredith in arguing the need for changes in the novel that would enable it to express better the complexity of reality: "Our language is not rich in subtleties for prose," he declares. "A writer who is not servile and has insight, must coin from his own mint. In poetry we are rich enough; but in prose also we owe everything to the license our poets have taken in the teeth of critics."[28]

Despite the confusion of purpose and effect in *Sandra Belloni*, its sequel, *Vittoria* (1867), is a sometimes magnificent romantic escape from Meredith's personal difficulties and from his accompanying awareness of the problems of English society. *Sandra Belloni* and *Rhoda Fleming* embody a distressed man's attempt to locate and to call for a rectification of social disorder. However, in the first novel the heroine must escape from society to find personal fulfillment; in the second, the sister heroines are both crushed by the forces of custom. Not until *Beauchamp's Career* did Meredith feel secure enough to return to the theme, and then only after the experience of a happy second marriage and two brilliant semiromantic novels. Planning *Vittoria*, Meredith blamed the defects of his past work on his predilection for "morbid emotion and exceptional positions . . . My love is for epical subjects—not for cobwebs in a putrid corner; though I know the fascination of unravelling them."[29]

Vittoria, happily, succeeds in both analytical details and epical scope. The subject, as Lionel Stevenson aptly observes, is "the psychology of revolution,"[30] and the heroine, out of place in her English setting, emerges as the personification here of heroic Italy straining to be free of her Austrian rulers and her own weaknesses. Sandra-Vittoria is also Meredith's first portrait of the "New Woman"; she has been called by a Marxist critic the first example in fiction of the "positive hero"[31] (in Meredith's case, it is usually the women who are heroic). She is a touchstone for the other characters in the novel, and misfortunes occur on almost every occasion that her advice is ignored. *Vittoria* stands halfway between the historical novels of Scott and Tolstoy, and, if it exhibits a brilliant mixture of historical drama and psychological intimacy, the novel also demonstrates Meredith's confidence in the individual's potential control over his own destiny. "The fates are within us," as Merthyr Powys (Meredith's Welsh spokesman) observes. "Those which are the forces of the outer world are as shadows to the power we have created within us." The major test for Meredith's characters is their ability to conquer egoism—and thereby to love. "By our manner of loving we are known," reflects the author of *Vittoria*.[32]

In *Rhoda Fleming* (1865), written between the two Sandra novels and apparently with the hope of repeating the recent success of George Eliot's country novels, Meredith relies heavily upon the role of chance and on the action of "little people" in producing tragedy. The heroine of the novel, Dahlia Fleming, is made to suffer from the improprieties and selfishness of her aristocratic lover, and then to suffer again from the proprieties and self-righteousness of her sister Rhoda. Neither country nor city provides a standard for the problems of life. "Ah, Lord!" as Rhoda's admirer Robert Eccles moans, "what miseries happen from our not looking straight at facts."[33] Nevertheless, the major and minor characters do not look at the facts, preferring to judge the problems of others in light of their own limited points of view.

Meredith effectively plays on these human limitations in the scene where Rhoda and Robert conduct a conversation that obscures their real feelings. "To each of them the second meaning stood shadowy behind the utterances," the novelist observes:

> "Now it's time to part." (Do you not see that there's a danger for me in remaining?)
> "Good night," (Behold, I am submissive.)
> "Good night, Rhoda." (You were the first to give the signal of parting.)
> "Good night." (I am simply submissive.)
> "Why not my name? Are you hurt with me?"
> Rhoda choked. The indirectness of speech had been a shelter to her, permitting her to hint at more than she dared clothe in words.
> Again the delicious dusky rose glowed beneath his eyes. But he had put his hand out to her, and she had not taken it.
> "What have I done to offend you? I really don't know, Rhoda."
> "Nothing." The flower had closed.[34]

Sixty years ago, Paul Elmer More cited this passage to prove Meredith's obscurity, noting that in his other novels no such explanatory comments are "added to guide the bewildered reader."[35] But Meredith's very point was that unless men and women changed drastically enough, by such means as more rational education, they would be unable to comprehend one another—or his novels, for that matter.

After the various labors of the 1860's in which he searched for a form of the novel congenial to his talents, Meredith hit his stride in the 1870's with three great novels: *Harry Richmond* (1871), *Beauchamp's Career* (1875), and *The Egoist* (1879). Meredith was in a more independent position as the decade began. He had recently switched from the *Ipswich Journal* to the *Fortnightly Review*, where he could at last express his authentic political beliefs, and he was enjoying the first years of a stable marriage. Of *The Adventures of Harry Richmond* Percy Lubbock observed, "it has been said that if Shakespeare revisited the globe and asked for a book of our times to read, this would be the volume to offer him, the book more likely than another to convince him at once that literature is still in our midst."[36]

Meredith's hero passes through various ordeals, expressed in forms of differing rhetoric, before he learns to accept the truth of man's divided nature. Because of the frequent use of romantic devices and episodes—Harry's experiences among gypsies, his adventures in Germany, his romance with the Princess Ottilia—some critics have concluded that Meredith's aim was to write a romance. While it is certain that the Romantic Revival of the 1880's and 1890's owed much to the author of *Harry Richmond*, it was Meredith's intention in the novel to educate his hero in the alternating disciplines of romantic adventure and pragmatic realism. The hero's assimilation of romance, under the guidance of his extravagant father, Richmond Roy, is tempered by his dawning realization of the need for practical action, as evidenced in the charitable behavior of his grandfather, Squire Beltham. In the words of a Meredithian heroine, "*The young who avoid that region* [of romance] *escape the title of Fool at the cost of a celestial crown.*"[37] Harry Richmond's career alternates between the theatrical world of his father, who believes himself to be the son of the Prince Regent, and the commonsensical world of his grandfather, who, under a veneer of verbal bluntness, is emotionally high strung. In the greatest scene of the novel, Beltham exposes Roy as a petty charlatan, but it is the unmasker who dies from the strain and the by now naturally theatrical father who wins the sympathy of those around him. Once again Meredith is dealing with the theme of masks, and, as in *Evan Harrington*, it is the romantic impostor who is most interesting. Richmond Roy, the master of verbal pyrotechnics, is appropriately destroyed in an explosion of real fireworks, and only with the opposing mentors of his life removed can the hero hope to develop.

At philosophical issue in the book is the dialectic between free will—the ability to change—and destiny. Roy and Beltham represent, in their different ways, fixed attitudes. The squire permits Harry freedom of political persuasion so long as he swears "never to change it." As Harry reflects, "He was a curious study to me, of the Tory mind, in its attachment to solidity, fixity, certainty." He recognizes his father, on the other hand, as "a tragic spectacle," whose utterances "were examples of downright unreason such as contemplation through the comic glass would have excused; the tragic could not. I knew, nevertheless, that to the rest of the world he was a progressive comedy: and the knowledge made him seem more tragic still. He clearly could not learn from misfortune; he was not to be contained . . . I chafed at his unteachable spirit, surely one of the most tragical things in life."[38]

Harry's two mentors are incapable of change, unlike the hero, and as such join the great "unteachable" creations of literature, like Falstaff or Don Quixote. The kind of hero Meredith was trying to present is obviously incapable of being pinned down in this fashion; he is not only capable of development, but, of necessity, he is unable to be captured in the pages of a novel. Thus, Meredith found himself once again proclaiming the impossibility of achieving full intelligibility, leaving the reader to conclude that reality is that which is unutterable: "my wits have been sharpened enough," as the hero concludes, "to know that there is more in men and women than the stuff they utter."[39] *Harry Richmond* is a memorable novel, however, largely because of the presence of

Richmond Roy and what his son calls his "rarely-abandoned seven-league boots of jargon." One of the truly mythic beings of literature, he is more real to us than his teachable son.

If Meredith's ironical triumph in *Harry Richmond* is the creation of the superbly irrational Richmond Roy, his achievement in *Beauchamp's Career* is the depiction of an entire irrational society. In a letter of 1874 he described the new novel as "philosophical-political":

> an attempt to show the forces round a young man of the present
> day, in England, who would move them, and finds them
> unalterably solid, though it is seen in the end that he does not
> altogether fail, has not lived quite in vain.—Of course, this is
> done in the concrete. A certain drama of self-conquest is
> gone through, for the hero is not perfect.

Nevil Beauchamp struggles for "the advancement of Humanity," but is ignored by a complacent society. "In this he is a type," Meredith adds. "And I think his History a picture of the time—taking its mental action, and material ease, and indifference, to be a necessary element of the picture."[40] On the eve of historical changes, England pretended not to notice, or really did not see, the need for constructive change. Meredith complained to G. W. Foote in 1880 that in England "the activity of the mind is regarded with distrust and men live happier when mated with compromises than with realities:—and the very sense of unsoundness resulting from their consequent position makes them all the more dread a breath of change."[41] It is possible that Meredith diverted his abandoned plan to write an autobiography into the conception of *Beauchamp's Career*. Although the radical politics of his hero, plus his tendency to run to extremes, was modeled upon that of Meredith's friend Captain Frederick Maxse, who had recently been defeated in a bid for election to Parliament, the more basic situation in the novel of an idealistic hero whose various "forlorn efforts to make himself understood" are continually thwarted suggests the author's own feelings at the lack of critical understanding of his work. As in *Sandra Belloni*, Meredith attempted to portray a society in which human incomprehension is insurmountable, using as his plot a comic situation that leads inevitably to the death of the protagonist.

Beauchamp is thwarted not only by the inertia of society and the resistance of his autocratic uncle but by his own inexperience.

Unfortunately, as Meredith notes, he "had not the faculty of reading inside men."[42] Meredith could easily have written a bitter novel (in the manner of Gissing) showing the self-destructive results of a life of futile idealism. Instead, he unified the book by means of comic irony, with the result that the book does not succumb to either of the possible extremes of bitter satire or downright tragedy. (To portray the English classes realistically, Meredith declared in 1881, a writer must resort to satire—the alternative is "romance of the wildest.")[43] Beauchamp's "career" is an entirely ironic one, and its single conspicuous success is the conquest of self, which enables him to resist the romantic temptation to run off with the married French Countess Renée. Early in the novel Meredith speaks of his radically new kind of protagonist, who does not seek to develop his sensibility in the Byronic fashion: "To be a public favourite is his last thought. Beauchampism, as one confronting him calls it, may be said to stand for nearly everything which is the obverse of Byronism, and rarely woos your sympathy, shuns the statuesque pathetic, or any kind of posturing." Beauchamp's failures are not even disguised as romantic bids for sympathy. "His faith is in working and fighting"; whereas he thinks he can succeed, Meredith knows otherwise.[44]

Having called forth an antihero to engage the reader's attention, Meredith insists that, to be true to life, he must let Beauchamp destroy himself if Beauchamp so wishes, taunted by the world's indifference. Only in a conventional *novel* can such a being survive:

> For me, I have so little command over him, that in spite of my nursery tastes, he drags me whither he lists. It is artless art and monstrous innovation to present so wilful a figure, but were I to create a striking fable for him, and set him off with scenic effects and contrasts, it would be only a momentary tonic to you, to him instant death. He could not live in such an atmosphere. The simple truth has to be told: how he loved his country, and for another and a broader love, growing out of his first passion, fought it; and being small by comparison, and finding no giant of the Philistines disposed to receive a stone in his fore-skull, pummelled the obmutescent mass, to the confusion of a conceivable epic. His indifferent England refused it to him.[45]

Assaulting the vestiges of Byronism, Meredith also contended with the new spirit of Darwinism by showing in his new novel that the survival of the fittest did not also mean the survival of the noblest. A realistic Victorian David would obviously not vanquish his Philistine antagonists—nor could a new St. Theresa find epical opportunities for her aspirations—except in a novel that was, in Meredith's or George Eliot's view, untrue to life. But whereas Dorothea Brooke achieves a symbolic triumph of sorts, however modest, Beauchamp's fate is to achieve his fixed goal by the aid of chance—it is through the illness of his uncle's pregnant wife and not Beauchamp's efforts that Romfrey finally makes his apology to Dr. Shrapnel—and then perish by accident.

Beauchamp's failure to understand others and make his aims understood can be partly blamed on his defective education. By birth and instinct a nobleman, he is in practice inarticulate. Like Meredith, he falls very early under the influence of Carlyle with devastating stylistic results plus a warped conception of the active possibilities open to real heroes. Beauchamp provides an interesting contrast to another disciple of Carlyle, Basil Ransom, in James's *The Bostonians*. While Ransom resembles the reactionary side of late Carlyle, however, both are united by a single-minded attempt to transform society even though neither has an understanding of human nature. If this disadvantage is used to fictionally comic advantage by James in a novel about the clash of opposing fixed viewpoints, the theme of incomprehension is treated as a historical lesson by Meredith. When asked by Carlyle why he did not become a historian, Meredith replied that he wrote history by creating novels. The keynote to his view of history is best expressed in a line of Dr. Shrapnel's concerning "The stench of the trail of Ego in our History."[46] *Beauchamp's Career* is a fine study of self-conquest in a self-oriented society. Having isolated the greatest social danger, as he felt, of the period, Meredith chose in his next novel to devote himself entirely to the theme of egoism, its cause, its cure, its comic possibilities, and its social dangers.

The publication of *Beauchamp's Career* marked the turning point in Meredith's fortunes. Like Henry James at about the same time, he found himself an object of growing critical interest in the late 1870's. Both novelists were difficult; each was an outsider of sorts. James's success, however, came at a substantially earlier point in his career: in 1871, when *Harry Richmond* was published, the twenty-eight-year-old American's first novel, *Watch and Ward*, was serialized. In 1875 *Roderick Hudson* and *Beauchamp's Career* were both serialized, and the striking differences in temperament and motivation between the two novelists are easily discernible in comparing the two works. It is as unlikely that Meredith would have chosen an artist as his hero as that James would have ever considered celebrating social altruism. Curiously, it was James, in a novel written to clarify his views of his possibilities as an artist, who wrote the more coherent and entertaining work; Meredith, directing his novel toward society, would not and could not condescend to write within accepted limits of fiction. Meredith refused to consider any "momentary tonic" for his reader. If Beauchamp were to be true to life, he could not possibly be described in conventional novelistic terms. A radical in politics, Meredith was a radical in his treatment of the novel as well. Victorian radicalism, however, has dated. With no commitments to society, James became for a while its darling. Yet it is precisely the lack of commitment to anything but the novel and his own impressions which set off the Jamesian revolution in fiction.

Even while working with conventional Victorian subjects, James was never really a Victorian novelist, temperamentally or philosophically. More of the decor of Victorian society can be found in James's fiction of the 1880's than in any of Meredith's novels, and more of the details of radical politics can be seen in *The Princess Casamassima* than in *Beauchamp's Career*. Yet what were artistic materials for James were values of major importance to Meredith, who struggled in the 1880's to defend those values from extinction. In his desire to change society, Meredith hoped thereby to conserve it in a manner similar to that of his friend John Morley. Both men hoped that England was stable and civilized enough to "resist all effort in a destructive direction." "If dissolvent ideas do make their way," Morley conceded, a year before the publication of *Beauchamp's Career*, "it is because the society was already ripe for dissolution."[47] In the frustrated effort to resist the forces of dissolution, Meredith labored, in his novels and poetry of the 1880's, to demonstrate the efficacy of the Victorian ideal of responcible and altruistic individualism; meanwhile, James's successful efforts to withdraw into a modern sensibility at least served to guarantee the continuing history of the novel.

The Limits of Comedy: The Egoist

> *Learn to laugh at yourselves as one must laugh!*
> (*Nietzsche,* Thus Spoke Zarathustra)

> *The chief consideration for us is, what particular*
> *practice of Art is the best for the perusal of*
> *the Book of our common wisdom; so that*
> *with clearer minds and livelier manners*
> *we may escape, as it were, into daylight and*
> *song from a land of foghorns.*
> (*Prelude to* The Egoist)

Meredith admitted of *The Egoist* in 1879 that "the whole cast of it is against the modern style,"[1] and indeed, at the beginning of an era in which the freeing of the ego from all external claims or responsibilities was accepted by the new philosophy, politics, and literature, Meredith's Victorian bias and stature were increasingly evident. The rise in egoism, curiously, corresponded to a reduction in size of the self. As the opportunity for notable individual efforts decreased (noted by Meredith in *Beauchamp's Career*), the Victorian individualist gave way to a modern invention: the personality. "Egolatry," the position of idolatry of the ego espoused by "the ill-starred philosophies," in Gabriel Marcel's words, of the Romantic and modern period, had the resultant effect of producing a harvest of *poseurs*. Enclosed in and burdened by one's self, the egoist finds himself constantly in need of performing, living for the effect he makes on others as proof that, in their eyes, he exists. The individualist, on the other hand, identifies and develops himself in terms of his relationship with others—wife, society, reality. Posturing appears most naturally in an environment which has become "artificial, unreal, and, in a certain sense, effeminate." This apparently Victorian explanation of egoism appears in Marcel's essay "The Ego and its Relation to Others" (1942), an admirable philosophical introduction to Meredith, which pays tribute to the novelist's "incomparable analyses" of the subject in *The Egoist*.[2] In no other novel does Meredith show himself so opposed in philosophy to James, who celebrated in his autobiography the necessary detachment of "a small boy" from "others" which had enabled him to become an artist. *The Egoist* is a novel about the need for attachment—to other people, to society, to such ideals as love and nature—and Meredith invokes the spirit of comedy in order to prod his heroine and his readers to the discovery of the splendid objective world of "daylight and song."

Comedy was Meredith's lifelong concern, not only as a favorite literary mode but as a leading theme. His first novel, *The Shaving of Shagpat*, had shown, in an extravagant comic allegory, the necessity for man to attain a truthful sense of perspective by means of laughter directed first of all against himself. The protagonist of *Shagpat* can subdue Illusion only after he has sufficiently disciplined himself to master the sword of Aklis, Meredith's first representation of what he would later call the "Sword of Common Sense": the Comic Spirit. When asked to lecture before the London Institute for the Advancement of Literature and the Diffusion of Useful Knowledge in 1877, Meredith chose to speak on "The Idea of Comedy and the Uses of the Comic Spirit." "An Essay on Comedy," as it was later retitled, might be better named "An Essay on Society." As Meredith's own title implies, the author is more concerned with the "idea" than the comedy, and most concerned of all with the potential uses of comedy as a civilizing force. In later years Meredith spoke of the essay as "a vindication of our intellect."[3]

"Sensitiveness to the comic laugh is a step in civilization," he argues in the lecture. "To shrink from being an object of it is a step in cultivation." An index to the stage of civilization a society has reached, he continues, is the kind of material that society laughs at and the "ring of the laugh." The higher the civilization, the more thoughtful is the laughter—until, one assumes, a future state is reached where laughter becomes altogether unnecessary. The ideal comic writer is Molière, whose plays provoke "no audible laughter," but rather "laughter of the mind." Meredith's ideal audience, it becomes clear at the outset, is "a society of cultivated men and women," and this group of properly educated men and women have the option of becoming citizens of "the selecter world," an undefined critical Utopia. In becoming one of the disinterested elite, the Meredithian critic-citizen tends to lose all differentiating personal identity, even sexual identity. "The comic poet dares to show us men and women coming to this mutual likeness," he solemnly declares.[4] Meredith belongs to the order of philosophers for whom ideas and ideal states are generally more real than their human approximations (in which respect he was similar to Mill and Morley). Unlike Plato, however, he seems to have thought man capable of reaching those ideal heights.

What limited Meredith's appreciation of the great comic writers of the past was the recognition of the frailty of human nature mirrored in their works and the reminder of the frail human response of their audiences. True comedy has traditionally shown us, he reflects, that life "is not a Comedy, but something strangely mixed; nor is Comedy a vile mask." But Meredith hoped for the sort of ideal world which he saw reflected in the purity and rationalism of Molière's dramatic world. "If life is likened to the comedy of Molière," he declares, "there is no scandal in the comparison." The French playwright's achievement, he argues again and again, was to have created characters drawn from "the idea," which is so generalized "as to make it permanently human."[5] The more a character becomes a universal type, the greater is his reality.

Whatever the abstractness of the section of the lecture devoted to "The Idea of Comedy," the section on "The Uses of the Comic Spirit" presents some positive guidelines that can be applied toward the discussion of Meredithian comedy. If history is a record of "the stench of the trail of Ego," then comedy is society's weapon of defense against egoism. "If the Comic idea prevailed with us,"

Meredith remarks in allusion to Aristophanes' success in inculcating "the idea of Good Citizenship," England would be changed from a nation of selfish merchants and self-pitying Byrons into a Germanic version of Greece: "There would be a bright and positive, clear Hellenic perception of facts. The vapours of Unreason and Sentimentalism would be blown away before they were productive. Where would Pessimist and Optimist be? They would in any case have a diminished audience."[6]

It is a typically unconscious Meredithian irony that in this ideal society there would be no real need for literature of any sort, just as Plato's Republic was wisely rid of any sort of emotional reminder, supplied by poetry, that man is guided by more than brainstuff. The lesson of the Comic Spirit is the need for the abandonment of individual proclivities in order to fit into a society governed by common sense. "If you believe that our civilization is founded in common-sense (and it is the first condition of sanity to believe it)," Meredith proclaims, "you will, when contemplating men, discern a Spirit overhead."[7] This is the Comic Spirit, who laughs at the excesses of men, and laughs them into their rightful roles as loyal citizens of their society. To be laughed out of one's humor is also to risk becoming less as well as more than human. As Macilente, the comic scourge in Ben Jonson's *Every Man Out of His Humor*, declares, once humor characters are deprived of their distinguishing characteristics, they become mere "vapors." At this point the comedy stops, but so does human life.

Fortunately for Meredith's theory, with regard to his fiction, he is dealing there not with an ideal future but with the irrational present. As a consequence, the most memorable of Meredith's creations are his irrationals, hopelessly unteachable—the Countess de Saldar, Sir Willoughby Patterne, and Richmond Roy. And it is the depiction of an irrational society, as in *Beauchamp's Career* or *One of Our Conquerors*, which is still accessible to generations that have long ago stopped believing in intellectual progress. Between the date of the lecture on comedy and the appearance of the novel which transformed some of the nebulous ideas into memorable concrete form, Meredith published three short novels. In their varying ways, they, too, serve as illustrations of his ideas, and they point toward the achievement of *The Egoist*.

The House on the Beach was begun over a decade earlier, but not published until 1877. The basic plot is similar to that of The Egoist: an inexperienced girl is engaged to a pompous egoist, partly through the efforts of her well-meaning but weak father, but she is eventually united with a satirical young journalist. Neither of the young lovers comes off for the reader, but, in Martin Tinman, Meredith drew an amusing portrait of the stolidly Saxon middle class. Tinman dreams of climbing the social ladder and, in the meantime, poses before the mirror in a court uniform. Although he appears as solidly rooted in place as Sir Willoughby, Tinman is actually in a position as unstable as his house on the beach; just as the house is destroyed by waves, he is demolished by laughter.

Also published in 1877, Meredith's The Case of General Ople and Lady Camper is a little-known gem of English fiction. General Ople is a more salvageable comic egoist than Tinman. He lives on a level of comfort not in keeping with his social station, is addicted to meaningless jargon, and is unaware of the suffering he causes his daughter by ignoring her infatuation with the nephew of their new neighbor. When Lady Camper, the neighbor, attempts to bring him round to view the situation of the young lovers, he is comically blind enough to assume that she is accepting his marriage proposal to her. For once, Meredith carries the theme of comic incomprehension to a comic conclusion. Lady Camper becomes a comic scourge, exposing his sentimental nature by drawing witty and cruel caricatures of him; she sees that the General is able finally to see himself and others for what they really are. If the means are cruel, the result is a more humane man. "You would not have cared one bit for a caricature," she tells him at the conclusion, "if you had not nursed the absurd idea of being one of our conquerors."[8] Meredith borrowed the latter phrase for the title of a novel in which a sentimental egoist is unable to see himself or others in perspective—with catastrophic results. Lady Camper is another of Meredith's "touch-stone" women, in his own phrase, who illustrates the efficacy of his statement in the lecture, "You may estimate your capacity for Comic perception by being able to detect the ridicule of them you love, without loving them less." His heroine marries the comically flawed General with the assurance that he will provide "a fund of amusement for her humour."[9]

A serious prelude to *The Egoist,* published in the same year (1879), *The Tale of Chloe* is a moving fable about an overly delicate heroine in an overly brutalized society. The setting is Bath in the eighteenth century: "the *milieu* of artificial manners and customs," as Siegfried Sassoon observes, "where a veneer of good breeding, elaborate courtesies, and persiflage thinly covered the coarse passions of human nature."[10] In this world, where a Duchess is a former milkmaid and her aristocratic lover is a scoundrel, the heroine immolates herself in order to break up the union with the woman, whom she is chaperoning, and the villain, by whom she was herself previously abandoned. "Hers was the unhappy lot," Meredith says, "of one gifted with poetic imagination to throb with the woman supplanting her, and share the fascination of the man who deceived." Chloe's is the tragedy of empathy in an otherwise uncomprehending world. Her poignant self-sacrifice guarantees that the society will continue to maintain its precarious sense of decorum. "Society," as the leader of Bath society warns Chloe, ". . . is a recommencement upon an upper level of the savage system; we must have our sacrifices."[11]

The themes of all three novellas, plus the lecture on comedy, coalesce in *The Egoist:* a sentimental egoist is exposed to the laughter of the Comic Spirit and revealed to be primitive man under his civilized costume. Having shown in Beauchamp's thwarted career an emblematic "picture of the time," Meredith turned in his next full-length novel to a symbolic depiction of the forces opposed to social amelioration: "a gentleman of our time and country, of wealth and station; a not flexile figure, do what we may with him." Sir Willoughby Patterne is a modern representation of "The Egoist, who is our original male in giant form."[12] He is in every way the obverse of Beauchamp:[13] incapable of change, he chooses to regress rather than learn. A fixed comic portrait, Willoughby is the only major character in the novel who at the end is exactly as he was at the beginning. Unlike Beauchamp, however, he survives, and, though he does not succeed in becoming a social conqueror, he does remain one of the unconquerables of artistic myth.

After hoping in novel after novel for a critical and popular success, Meredith apparently felt that he had not put enough ingredients into his new book. Writing to Robert Louis Stevenson, he doubted "if those who care for my work will take to it at all. . . It is a Comedy, with only half of me in it, unlikely, therefore, to take either the public or my friends."[14] Modesty aside, Meredith indeed limited the scope of his design and disciplined his energies in the new novel, making *The Egoist* the most manageable of Meredith's works. Characters and plot and themes do not swarm out of control, as they do in his usual novels. If *The Egoist* was not the popular success that *East Lynne* had been or *Robert Elsmere* would be, it was eagerly read at Oxford and Cambridge, and it confirmed Stevenson, among others, in the belief that Meredith was "built for immortality." Stevenson included the novel among the "Books Which Have Influenced Me," contending that, in the portrait of Willoughby, Meredith had achieved "an unmanly but a very serviceable exposure of myself." Meredith's portrait of Everyman as an irrationalist is one of the triumphs of the English novel; in attacking egoism in an embodied form, he made his most lasting contribution to modern mythology. Henley, who wrote four separate reviews of the novel, saw in Willoughby "a compendium of the Personal in man."[15]

In Victorian England egoism was seen as more than a comic butt; it was a philosophical, a political, a social threat. Matthew Arnold had presented culture as the necessary bulwark against anarchy, the unenlightened egoism of all classes; for him, the guardian of culture was criticism. With considerably more optimism, Meredith envisaged the possibility of an enlightened civilization, "a society of cultivated men and women," whose watchword would be harmony—a reconciliation of all the warring claims of the nineteenth century—and whose guardian would be the Comic Spirit. In a famous passage from the lecture on comedy, Meredith personified the Spirit as at once a lofty and a faun-like deity, imbued with the best of heaven and earth and concerned with men's "honesty and shapeliness in the present":

> whenever they wax out of proportion, overblown, affected, pretentious, bombastical, hypocritical, pedantic, fantastically delicate; whenever it sees them self-deceived or hoodwinked, given to run riot in idolatries, drifting into vanities, congregating in absurdities, planning short-sightedly, plotting dementedly; whenever they are at variance with their professions, and violate

the unwritten but perceptible laws binding them in consideration
one to another; whenever they offend sound reason, fair justice,
are false in humility or mined with conceit, individually, or
in the bulk—the Spirit overhead will look humanely malign,
and cast an oblique light on them, followed by volleys of silvery
laughter.[16]

Sir Willoughby Patterne is the most conspicuous example in the
novel of the comic overreacher, the emblematic menace to society
and all that society stands for, but the other major characters are
all egoists too, in one respect or another. Once Clara and Vernon
and Laetitia can see themselves for what they are, however, they
can choose to change if they wish. Laetitia, it might be argued,
becomes an intensified egoist by the end of the novel so that she
may be a perfect match for her husband, Willoughby. Clara and
Vernon, on the other hand, achieve full perspective and are last
seen high in the Alps. "Sitting beside them," Meredith observes,
"the Comic Muse is grave and sisterly" (XIV, 626).

The novel moves on at least two separate planes of development:
from the closed drawing rooms and laboratory of Patterne Hall to
the enlightened freedom of the mountains, as far as Clara is concerned, and from the autocratic freedom to roam the world at will
toward the status of mastered master of a provincial backwater,
in Willoughby's case. Accordingly, half of the novel takes place
on the level of a drawing room comedy; the tone for such scenes
is as theatrical as the Prelude to the novel intimates:

> Comedy is a game played to throw reflections upon social life,
> and it deals with human nature in the drawing-room of civilized
> men and women, where we have no dust of the struggling outer
> world, no mire, no violent crashes, to make the correctness of
> the representation convincing . . . The Comic Spirit conceives
> a definite situation for a number of characters, and rejects all
> accessories in the exclusive pursuit of them and their speech
> [XIII, 1].

The heavy use of dialogue—and its functional use in representing
members of a society who are active only verbally—does point
toward James's novel in dialogue, *The Awkward Age*. But *The
Egoist* is still another of Meredith's hybrid books, keeping to the
drawing room at times but often extending outside of Patterne

Hall into magnificent scenes in nature. What would have served as theatrical set pieces, like the dinner at Lady Mountstuart Jenkinson's, are occasionally only obliquely described by the characters afterward. Although the novel contains the most unified of Meredith's plots, the study of character and characters remains his principal interest. It might be argued that the novel is built on a series of stylistic levels, each appropriate to the particular character's point of view. Thus Willoughby is seen very early as a Restoration prince and wit; it is only appropriate that his place in the novel be confined to that of a character in a comedy. His comical poetic justice results from his inability to put off theatricalizing. Like Richmond Roy, he becomes the slave of his own rhetoric, and histrionics becomes second nature to him. In a strict sense, Willoughby and Clara belong to different literary genres. Hers is a discovery of the poetic truth of life, which enables her to see through the masquerade at Patterne Hall, just as Laetitia's discovery is of life's cold prose, which enables her to live with Patterne Hall.

Like James, Meredith is a master of the use of point of view in the novel. Whereas James preferred more often to confine the angle of vision to a single character for the sake of artistic coherence, however, Meredith capitalized on the differing points of view of his characters to make a thematic point. In this respect James's atypical *The Bostonians* is similar to *The Egoist*, where the theme and method are united to give a comic picture of human incomprehension. More generally in James, however, a single character, like Isabel Archer or Lambert Strether, grows in comprehension to the point where his or her angle of vision is not only the single one that the reader is given, it is also the *right* way of comprehending the experience undergone. At the end of *The Bostonians*, however, it is evident that none of the characters have seen the light. Such comic incomprehension allows James to make a negative philosophical point: in all likelihood neither the characters in *The Bostonians* nor the readers of the novel will attain the author's own point of view. In light of the subsequent critical haggling over the novel, James's point was well taken. In *The Egoist* all the major characters but Willoughby have gained a sense of perspective, and although he towers above the others as a symbolic menace, in terms of the immediate plot he is socially contained.

Unable to see himself as others see him, Willoughby is unable to see beyond his own conception of himself. Early in the novel we are told that, while looking into the then adoring eyes of Laetitia Dale, "He found the man he sought there, squeezed him passionately, and let her go" (XIII, 29–30). The reader's impression of Willoughby, for the first third of the novel, is both terrifying and misleading. He is presented as the absolute lord of his domain, admired by the surrounding world. From Clara Middleton's point of view, it at first seems perverse that she should want to break her engagement to such a man, even though she is terrified that she will be sacrificed to him against her wishes. The security of Willoughby's position is delusive, however. Having been jilted once before, he fears that the same thing will happen again, that the world will point an accusing and mocking finger at him. The "world," as it turns out in a succession of brilliant anticlimactic chapters, is no more than the prying Ladies Busshe and Culmer, and it is to impress them that he manages to bargain for a loveless marriage with Laetitia. Willoughby *Tyrannus* accordingly metamorphoses into the figure of a slave to his illusions, "enchained by the homage" of what he has defined for himself as the world; he becomes an actor forced to do what his audience expects from him.

A recent admirer of *The Egoist*, Louis Auchincloss, has explained Willoughby, in Dostoevskian terms, as a man with tragic problems: "He cannot love—one is almost tempted to see his drama as a tragedy of impotence."[17] But if hell, for the Russian novelist, is the inability to love, such a condition, for Meredith, is the occasion for comedy. In the context of the novel Willoughby is a comic creation, a comic threat to himself as well as others. One is relieved that Meredith did not yield to the temptation of tracing a comic pattern to its logical tragic conclusion, as he did in the case of Beauchamp, or of Purcell Barrett in *Sandra Belloni*. Instead of diffusing his interests, Meredith channeled them into an exclusively comic direction. A compressed comic character, with suggestions of a humors figure like Sir Epicure Mammon, Willoughby is amazingly suggestive. A "flat" character, unlike Clara or Vernon or

Laetitia, he is a vivid example that such fixed beings may be more vital and memorable than most three-dimensional beings. The danger of egoism, as Meredith realized, is that it reduces the individual to a personality. To develop, one needs a supple mind; Willoughby's limitation of mind necessarily leads to a limitation of his own freedom. The novel, as J. Hillis Miller has noted, "is a sophisticated investigation of the theme of self-fulfillment in a world where the individual needs other people, but also needs to be free to develop according to his own nature . . ."[18] Clara has the dilemma of choice in the novel because she is confronted by the examples of Willoughby's egoism and Vernon Whitford's individualism. The egoist is of necessity a performer, not an individual who can choose for himself and thereby change.

Willoughby's most conspicuous addiction is to sentimental rhetoric—that "sentiment," in Thomas Love Peacock's phrase, "which is canting egotism in the mask of refined feeling."[19] The donning of human masks, a major Meredithian concern, is demonstrated in the unconscious theatricalizing of Willoughby's thoughts and feelings. In one of the chapters devoted to his attempts at soul-unsearching, Willoughby grimly envisages what the loss of Clara will mean to his pride:

> Ten thousand furies thickened about him at a thought of her lying by the roadside without his having crushed all bloom and odour out of her which might tempt even the curiosity of the fiend, man.

He moves from this monstrous image to a sentimental staging of a future dialogue between the magnanimous hero and the repentant Clara. He imagines her, eternally cast off, in the act of reading from the script he has prepared for her:

> "My friend—I call you friend: you have ever been my friend, my best friend! Oh, that eyes had been mine to know the friend I had!—Willoughby, in the darkness of night, and during days that were as night to my soul, I have seen the inexorable finger pointing my solitary way through the wilderness from a Paradise forfeited by my most wilful, my wanton, sin. We have met. It is more than I have merited. We part. In mercy let it be for ever. Oh, terrible word! Coined by the passions of our youth, it

comes to us for our sole riches when we are bankrupt of earthly treasures, and is the passport given by Abnegation unto Woe that prays to quit this probationary sphere. Willoughby, we part. It is better so."

"Clara! one—one only—one last—one holy kiss!"

"If these poor lips, that once were sweet to you . . ."

The kiss, to continue the language of the imaginative composition of his time, favourite readings in which had inspired Sir Willoughby with a colloquy so pathetic, was imprinted [XIII, 270–271].

Never far from the rhetoric of Willoughby* is the inner sensualist; the thought of the "last" kiss immediately brings out the inner beast in him, and he refuses again to relinquish possession of Clara.

"The love-season is the carnival of egoism," Meredith observes, "and it brings the touchstone to our natures" (XIII, 130). In Willoughby's case, the ordeal is devastating. The idea of courtship to him is demonstrated to be an extension of fox hunting: his pursuit of Constantia Durham and Clara is described in metaphors drawn from the chase. Willoughby coats the essentially primitive nature of his action in an absurd rhetoric of lovemaking. When he tries to persuade Clara to withstand the "world" with him and to be his "beyond death" (XIII, 57), Willoughby attracts our disgust as well as hers. But when he repeats the same kind of rhetoric to Laetitia, many pages later, the effect is comic. Clara has changed in viewpoint, Laetitia is changing, and we have changed; Willoughby, however, is indefatigable: "We two against the world!" he recites from his lovers' litany, and so on (XIV, 485). "If Willoughby would open his heart to nature," as Clara muses in another context, "he would be relieved of his wretched opinion of the world" (XIII, 217). Instead, he is the victim of his rhetoric, a provincial pseudo-Byron, who achieves unknowingly, and by reason of his unknowingness, the stature of comic touchstone to the other characters. Willoughby has been criticized by mechanistic students of the novel for being "given" to the reader rather than adequately

---

* The inspired use of a character's own projected inner rhetoric to make a thematic point is one of Meredith's innovations in the novel. Critics who have dismissed his rhetorical style as overinflated seldom notice that it is inflated, very often, only at certain moments for certain precise, antirhetorical reasons. The passage excerpted above clearly points toward the Gerty MacDowell section of *Ulysses*.

explained,[20] but, in the first place, what is given is an anthropologi-
cal prototype, and, in the second place, he exists to "explain" the
other characters' development. "Miss Middleton owed it to Sir
Willoughby Patterne that she ceased to think like a girl," as Meredith points out (XIII, 111). To know him is a liberal education.

Set in opposition to him is Clara, who learns from his example
and, ironically, from his own words, "Beware of marrying an
Egoist" (XIII, 115), while she avoids becoming one herself. If
Willoughby ranks with Richmond Roy as Meredith's greatest
mythic achievement, Clara Middleton is surely his best human
figure. For Stevenson, she was "the best girl ever I saw anywhere,"
and it is still not impossible to echo the sentiment of Meredith's
early admirers that her only equals in literature are Shakespeare's
heroines. In explaining a sudden infatuation, the unfortunate hero
of Forster's *The Longest Journey* appeals to his friend to "read
poetry—not only Shelley. Understand Beatrice, and Clara Middleton, and Brunhilde." Clara's progress in the novel, like that of the
heroine of *A Room with a View*, is linked to the development of
her heart and brain. For both young ladies, the outcome calls to
mind Forster's final chapter title, "The End of the Middle Ages."
Personal development is equated with social progress. When, early
in Meredith's novel, Willoughby presents his rhetorical dream to
her that, "by love's transmutation," she might "literally be the man
she was to marry," she replies that she prefers "to be herself, with
the egoism of women!" (XIII, 54). Clara's discovery of her fiancé's
selfishness initially enforces a desire to act on her own authority.
She wants to sever the bonds of the engagement simply to be
free, but it is at the moments when Clara feels herself trapped
that she is most conventional. "Dreadful to think of!" she is
shocked to discover, "she was one of the creatures who are written
about" (XIII, 180).

Arguing with herself that she must be herself, Clara expresses
to Laetitia her fear of the confines of Patterne Hall: "I chafe at
restraint; hedges and palings everywhere! I should have to travel
ten years to sit down contented among these fortifications. Of
course I can read of this rich kind of English country with pleasure
in poetry. But it seems to me to require poetry. What would you
say of human beings requiring it?" (XIII, 183). If Laetitia, the

amateur poetess, changes during the course of the novel into a practical, prosaic woman, Clara moves in the opposite direction toward poetry, toward a life imbued with the poetry of earth. In one of the best scenes of the novel, a scene with obvious affinities to, and more crucial differences from, the chapter devoted to Isabel Archer's all-night meditation in James's *The Portrait of a Lady*, Clara contemplates all night the problem of her difficult situation and that of women in general. "Can a woman have an inner life apart from him she is yoked to?" she wonders (XIII, 329). But whereas Isabel finds refuge ultimately in the fact of her individuality, Clara detects the first hint of an answer in nature. She watches, in the early morning, the activities of the birds:

> The lovely morning breathed of sweet earth into her open window and made it painful, in the dense twitter, chirp, cheep, and song of the air, to resist the innocent intoxication. O to love! was not said by her, but if she had sung, as her nature prompted, it would have been. Her war with Willoughby sprang of a desire to love repelled by distaste. Her cry for freedom was a cry to be free to love [XIII, 244].

Clara is unsure as yet of the meaning of her discovery; she thinks more in terms of loving "unselfishness and helpfulness" at this time, but she soon discovers that these qualities are embodied in the figure of Vernon Whitford.

Clara's first instinct is to run away from her predicament, but she learns in time that to do so would be to succumb to the same unreasoning rashness by which she became engaged to Willoughby in the first place. "I have seen my own heart," she can tell Laetitia at the end of the novel. "It is a frightful spectre. I have seen a weakness in me that would have carried me anywhere" (XIV, 606). Clara learns, unlike Willoughby, "to be straightforwardly sincere in . . . speech" as well as in action. When she first articulates this wish to Laetitia, while explaining her repugnance toward her fiancé, Clara complains of her lack of "power to express ideas" in the manner of that accomplished poetess. "Miss Middleton, you have a dreadful power," replies Laetitia, whose own eyes have begun to open (XIII, 190–191).

Meredith chooses to describe his developing heroine in terms of the poetry of nature, just as he invests Willoughby with theatri-

cal trappings. The two rhetorics can be seen side by side in the
episode where Clara attempts, metaphorically and really, to escape
one of Willoughby's threatening bursts of sentiment:

> "You are cold, my love? you shivered."
> "I am not cold," said Clara. "Someone, I suppose, was walk-
> ing over my grave."
> The gulf of a caress hove in view like an enormous billow
> hovering under the curled ridge.
> She stooped to a buttercup; the monster swept by [XIII,
> 153].

Like Diana Warwick, Clara can be defined as "deeply a woman,
dumbly a poet."[22] One must distinguish between the poetic rhetoric
and the theatrical rhetoric in Meredith; the one tries to embody the
natural, the other succeeds in concealing the natural. If the Alps
come to stand for intellectual freedom, the symbol for harmony
with nature in the novel is the double-blossomed wild cherry tree.
Immediately after Clara discovers her fiancé to be an "immovable
stone-man" (XIII, 116), she finds a source of refuge in Vernon,
who represents "the world taken into her confidence" (XIII, 125).
In need of his rational guidance, she comes upon him sleeping
under the cherry tree:

> She turned her face to where the load of virginal blossom, whiter
> than summer-cloud on the sky, showered and drooped and
> clustered so thick as to claim colour and seem, like higher Alpine
> snows in noon-sunlight, a flush of white. From deep to deeper
> heavens of white, her eyes perched and soared. Wonder lived
> in her. Happiness in the beauty of the tree pressed to supplant
> it, and was more mortal and narrower. Reflection came, contract-
> ing her vision and weighing her to earth. Her reflection was:
> "He must be good who loves to lie and sleep beneath the
> branches of this tree!" [XIII, 134–135].

Clara's history in the novel is summarized in the movement from
wonder to reflection, from her first awareness of the poetry of earth
to her ability to articulate it and her identification of it with Vernon.
Once she is united with him, she has begun to learn how to reconcile the earth and the transcendental wonder. However, it is
beyond the reach of the novel to articulate the final achievement
satisfactorily. The problem arises that although Vernon can be

accepted as a symbol, he never seems a sufficiently human mate for Clara.

The heroes of the late Meredith novels—Vernon, Redworth in *Diana of the Crossways,* Dartrey Fenellan in *One of Our Conquerors,* Matey Weyburn in *Lord Ormont and His Aminta,* Gower Woodseer in *The Amazing Marriage*—are alike in their supposed ability to reconcile instinctive with intellectual reason, in their manliness, and in their common sense. Each of the heroes undergoes, or has undergone, an unfortunate experience with an ill-matched woman—a motif frequent in Meredith's works, no doubt suggested by his own unhappy first marriage. The author wishes them to embody such an impossible form of perfection that they fail to be credible literary characters. Having shown in *Beauchamp's Career* how a brilliantly endowed protagonist would of necessity not succeed in a human sphere, Meredith turned to a succession of symbolic victors, embodiments of his own views. While Vernon does fit the role called for in the scheme of the novel, at times he fails to convince the reader that such an embodied Meredithian symbol could survive beyond the limits of the book. And, as a representative of vitality, he is notably less vital than his cousin Willoughby.

Meredith contrasts the cousins very early in the novel, as they travel around the world together. We are informed of the liveliness of Willoughby's letters, and of the straightforwardness and absence of irony in Vernon's. Willoughby projects his personality wherever he goes; Vernon absorbs what he sees and hears. "One was the English gentleman wherever he went; the other was a new kind of thing, nondescript, produced in England of late, and not likely to come to much good himself, or do much good to the country" (XIII, 28). Despite this ironic modesty on Meredith's part, Vernon does embody for Clara the principle of useful, selfless work. A hiker and mountain climber, as well as a scholar, Vernon was partly intended as a tribute to Meredith's friend Leslie Stephen; his best scene in the novel, his pursuit of Clara through the woods during a rainstorm, suggests the best side of Stephen: "Let him be drenched, his heart will sing" (XIV, 314).

While Clara's "power" to express herself first reveals to Laetitia that her idol has feet of clay, it is Willoughby who turns Laetitia into a female egoist. In the chapter ironically entitled "Sir Willoughby Attempts and Achieves Pathos," the male Egoist tries to see if he still exerts power over his longtime worshiper by indulging in inflated, self-pitying histrionics. The result, which he is unable to detect, is that "He had, in fact, perhaps by sympathetic action, succeeded in striking the same springs of pathos in her which animated his lively endeavour to produce it in himself" (XIV, 385). Laetitia collapses in a fit of self-pity, realizing the painful waste of her years and energy. When Willoughby seeks her hand in the attempt to escape from the probable scorn of the "world" after Clara abandons him, he finds to his horror that she has changed, that her illusion has been destroyed and, with it, her career as a sentimental poetess.

When he finally coerces her into accepting him, it is at the very cost that had prompted Clara to break away from him: the prospect of a loveless marriage to an egoist. Not even General Ople has the discomfiting future that Willoughby faces with one who warns: "I am hard, materialistic; I have lost faith in romance, the skeleton is present with me all over life. And my health is not good. I crave for money. I should marry to be rich. I should not worship you. I should be a burden, barely a living one, irresponsive and cold. Conceive such a wife, Sir Willoughby!" But the addiction to rhetoric has become second nature to him, and he retorts, "It will be you!" Laetitia promises to be his "critic" and confesses that she has become, as a result of privation, a willful "Egoist." If Clara and Vernon are perfectly mated in theory, Willoughby and Laetitia are the perfect pair in fact: the unconscious and the conscious egoist. "But he had the lady with brains!" Meredith notes. "He had: and he was to learn the nature of that possession in the woman who is our wife" (XIV, 617–621).

For the purposes of the novel, at least, Willoughby is socially contained, and the set of marriages brings the comedy to its inevitable conclusion. Despite those satisfactions of the demands of society and fiction, Meredith hints at a number of disturbing issues that are beyond the scope of a comic novel and are taken up in his subsequent works. "If one must go through this," Clara wonders, "to be disentangled from an engagement, what must it be to the poor women seeking to be free of a marriage?" (XIII, 178). Later the author openly philosophizes on the "Condition of Woman" question, a matter most memorably argued by John Stuart Mill in the late 1860's and exemplified in the treatment of Meredith's own heroines. "They are to us what we hold of best or worst within," he says, from an enlightened male viewpoint. "By their state is our civilization judged" (XIII, 276–277). He had similarly argued in the lecture on comedy that the advancement of women is both a prerequisite for and a theme of comedy. In *One of Our Conquerors* he illustrates what happens when a sensitive woman is overpowered by an egoistic mate. That *The Egoist* occupies Meredith's consistently comic attention does not obscure the potentially grave underlying problems. Willoughby is another of Meredith's versions of the devil, a comic counterpart to Shakespeare's Richard III or Milton's Satan. It is a sign of Meredith's affirmative, societal philosophy that he felt such a being could be contained by social barriers, an "army of unalterable law." Modern readers, however, may very well decide that Willoughby is horrendously and delightfully unchangeable and may choose to disbelieve in either the corrective powers of comedy or the rational sanctions of society. Willoughby is at once an Arnoldian Barbarian and a Darwinian prehistoric man, who reminds us that the irrational not only survives in life, but poses a danger if unexposed.

Another disturbing theme implicit in the novel is Meredith's semiconscious fear that truth is not only incomprehensible to the many, but incapable of articulation by the few. In a comedy, the inability to comprehend or articulate can be used to advantage; in life, as Meredith showed in his next novel, the outcome is often tragic. It is especially gravely ironic that Meredith's own attempts to articulate his beliefs should so often have been unsuccessful. The "Prelude" to *The Egoist*, for example, is often criticized for its unintelligibility; yet its purpose is to warn the reader that the novel must be surveyed through a comic perspective. That comedy is difficult, however, unless one is prepared to read carefully and philosophically. In the "Prelude," Meredith makes one of the most eloquent defenses of the usefulness not only of comedy but of art. Those who look for answers from Darwinian science, he claims, will be informed but not enlightened; we remain "the same, and animals into the bargain":

Art is the specific. We have little to learn of apes, and they may
be left. The chief consideration for us is, what particular practice
of Art in letters is the best for the perusal of the Book of our
common wisdom; so that with clearer minds and livelier manners we may escape, as it were, into daylight and song from a
land of fog-horns.

Comedy, Meredith declares, is the best remedy: "She is the ultimate civilizer, the polisher, a sweet cook. If . . . she watches over
sentimentalism with a birch-rod, she is not opposed to romance.
You may love, and warmly love, so long as you are honest" (XIII,
3–4). The enemies of comedy, accordingly, are imposture and false
rhetoric.

Meredith chose to fight inflated rhetoric with poetic rhetoric,
and he often managed to confound the two in his reader's minds.
In attacking the narrow-minded cleverness of the Mrs. Mountstuart Jenkinsons, he did so with a cleverness that has made unsympathetic readers turn Meredith's admonition upon himself:
"You see how easy it is to deceive one who is an artist in phrases.
Avoid them . . . they dazzle the penetration of the composer. That
is why people of ability like Mrs. Mountstuart see so little; they
are bent on describing brilliantly" (XIV, 371–372). In effect, Meredith saw so much that he often found himself unable to articulate
adequately. If *The Egoist* is an attack upon the would-be "artist
in phrases," Meredith raises the possibility that, for the philoso-
pher-poet working in the novel form, language may not really be
able to make the intended gesture.

Such a problem would not have bothered James, for whom the
ability to articulate was never a matter for alarm. One's beliefs
hardly matter as long as one can express himself distinctly, as
James implies in his critical essays. Almost always readable in
expression and often ambiguous in theme, James compares curiously with Meredith, whose occasional inabilities to make himself
intelligible and his failure to be morally ambiguous have alike
worked against him. James, however, was supremely the artist
in fiction; he was always more interested in putting his impressions
to fictional use than in putting fiction to any outside use. Whereas
Meredith's ideal is a good citizen, James's ideal is the artist. If
James's intention was to transform his readers into spectators like

himself, Meredith's goal seems to have been to cure his readers of his own follies.

The Portrait of a Lady, which appeared between the publication dates of *The Egoist* and *Diana of the Crossways,* has obvious affinities with both novels in choice of subject matter and characterization, but, beyond the fact that a good many contemporary readers found all three books obscure, they were composed with radically different intentions in mind. There are many links between Isabel Archer and Clara. Both ladies are engaged to egoists, but, whereas Isabel's discovery of her mistake comes long after the marriage, Clara very quickly learns of her error and is enabled to escape. For James the moment of triumph is precisely the full awareness of the consciousness; for Meredith victory comes only when the reasoning consciousness has also *acted* affirmatively. Meredith's philosophical affirmation, as Ramon Fernandez admiringly points out, was to show that self-analysis is not the conclusion but the prerequisite for sane action; thus, for Meredith, analysis is part of a "dramatic" process.[23]

Clara sees the "frightful spectre" of her heart, but the self-recognition is not enough. For James's heroes, the heightening of sensibility is the goal in itself, although critics have been traditionally undecided as to whether a heroine like Isabel has really attained self-awareness or has only accepted an illusion of self-sufficiency. The Jamesian hero, at any rate, is, like his creator, his own law and standard, even if that standard is entirely passive. Such beings threaten to become what in Meredith's terminology would be egoists—or, by James's standard, artists. The desired goal of Meredith's heroes and their creator is to be engaged. Clara's "cry for freedom," she soon realizes, is really "a cry to be free to love"—to love unselfishness and useful work. The Meredithian heroine, in symbolic consequence, moves as inevitably toward as the Jamesian heroine moves away from marriage—or, one might add, the ability to love.

The illusion that she has freely chosen Osmond is as much a reason for Isabel's return to him at the end of the novel as her flawed apperception was responsible for her having chosen him in the first place. In any case, the marriage vow is arguably an aesthetic *donnée* rather than a real philosophical allegiance.

Dorothy Van Ghent has insisted that Osmond is a more successful figure than Willoughby because he has "internal relations"; he is not merely given to us. "Osmond," she asserts, "is incomparably a subtler evil, for he does represent values."[24] But these "values" are not real ones; they are, first, the products of Isabel's flawed perception, and, second, a necessity in the mechanics of the novel for causing her to return to him. Osmond is certainly more "evil," but in a deliberately melodramatic fashion. Take the passage in *The Portrait* where Osmond complains of Isabel's "one fault" to Madame Merle:

> "She has too many ideas."
> "I warned you she was clever."
> "Fortunately they are very bad ones," said Osmond.
> "Why is that fortunate?"
> "*Dame*, if they must be sacrificed!"[25]

This is a completely different sort of evil from that of Sir Willoughby Patterne, who also desires his bride to sacrifice her ideas. If he were only able to comprehend Clara, Meredith declares,

> He could have seen that she had a spirit with a natural love of liberty, and required the next thing to liberty, spaciousness, if she was to own allegiance. Those features, unhappily, instead of serving for an introduction to the within, were treated as the mirror of himself. They were indeed of an amiable sweetness to tempt an accepted lover to angle for the first person in the second. But he had made the discovery that their minds differed on one or two points, and a difference of view in his bride was obnoxious to his repose. He struck at it recurringly to show her error under various aspects. He desired to shape her character to the feminine of his own, and betrayed the surprise of a slight disappointment at her advocacy of her ideas. She said immediately: "It is not too late, Willoughby," and wounded him, for he wanted her simply to be material in his hands for him to mould her; he had no other thought. He lectured her on the theme of the infinity of love. How was it not too late? They were plighted; they were one eternally; they could not be parted. She listened gravely, conceiving the infinity as a narrow dwelling where a voice droned and ceased not. However, she listened. She became an attentive listener [XIII, 51–52].

The difference in tone and effect between the two passages is that between first-rate melodrama, engaged to occupy the reader's mind for a circumscribed period, and brilliant comedy, intended to convey the reader's mind beyond the book in his hand. To be sure, each author utilizes the method of the other to arouse false expectations. James eschewed the idea of the "happy ending" as much as Meredith disliked the prospect of a melodramatic or negative conclusion.

On occasion, however, each writer acted out of keeping with his personal preference in such matters: James capitulated to popular demand in *The Europeans* and *The Bostonians;* Meredith yielded to the idea of the irrationalism of society in *Sandra Belloni* and *Beauchamp's Career.* But, in general, James opted for the artistic and Meredith for the philosophical solution. The one aimed at absorbing his reader's attention into the logic of the novel, and the other aimed at directing the reader's viewpoint far beyond the novel and toward an active role in life. At times, when comparing their respective achievements, one is tempted to say that it is art rather than nature that never betrays the heart that loves her. Nevertheless, in his study of Sir Willoughby Patterne and Clara Middleton, Meredith created not only one of the great philosophical novels but one of the few perfect works of literary art as well.

The Limits of Tragedy: The Tragic Comedians *and* Diana of the Crossways

> *"In few things that we do, where self is concerned, will cowardice not be found. And the hallucination colours it to seem a lovely heroism . . . I am always at crossways."*
> (Diana Warwick, *in* Diana of the Crossways)

With the publication of *Diana of the Crossways* in 1885, Meredith was justly recognized as the greatest living Victorian novelist, although for the wrong book. Gissing described *Diana* as "Shakespeare in modern English"[26]—a title far better suited to *The Egoist.* Meredith's health and writing powers gave way in a decade of profound changes; in the two novels—*The Tragic Comedians* and *Diana*—which followed *The Egoist* Meredith attempted to study the effects of extreme psychological pressures upon characters drawn from history, but he succeeded mainly in showing the waste of intelligence and heroism. The frustrated career of Ferdinand Lassalle, whose death dealt a decisive blow to the fate of German Socialism, demonstrated with great force the need for self-awareness and self-discipline in modern leaders. The historical Lassalle, transformed into Meredith's Alvan in *The Tragic Comedians*, was in many ways a mixture of Nevil Beauchamp and Sir Willoughby Patterne, and his tragic downfall derived from comic motives: incomprehension of himself and others. Meredith "did not forget," Hardy remarked of him after his death, "(though he often conveniently veiled his perception of it), that, as I think Ruskin remarks, 'Comedy is Tragedy if you only look deep enough.' "[27] And history, especially modern history, as Meredith realized, is a depressing combination of the two.

If in *The Egoist* Meredith had hinted at tragic possibilities within his comic theme, in his next novel he chose to explore the interrelationship between comedy and tragedy. *The Tragic Comedians* was derived from a historical episode that had appeal for Meredith at this point in his career. The novel is not one of his major achievements, although there are admirers of its passionate subject and psychological intensity.[28] Meredith confided to a friend, "I fear you will not care for it. But it is history, and a curious chapter of human nature."[29] It is conceivable that he began work on the book because the prospect of a ready-made subject afforded relief to his inventive powers: Helene von Dönniges, the woman responsible for Lassalle's death, had just published a defense of her conduct in the affair. It is noteworthy that he set aside the manuscript of the optimistic *The Amazing Marriage*, not to be completed for another fifteen years, in order to turn to a study in historical ambiguity.

In *Vittoria*, Meredith had already attempted a historical novel, embodying in its heroine the spirit of Italy during the Risorgimento. During the dark days of the German invasion in 1870, he had written an ode to France in which he had expressed a philosophy of history. Like his own Dr. Shrapnel, he saw history as a reflection of the retarding work of egoism, but he set in opposition to this the successful efforts of selfless heroes. If Napoleon embodied the regressive egoism, the return to man's primitive state, Joan of Arc symbolized the conquering forces of altruism. In the figure of Vittoria Meredith embodied the latter spirit; in Sir Willoughby Patterne he drew a comic representation of the pretensions of the former. In the case of Lassalle, however, Meredith detected a perplexing combination of both types, a subject for both the Comic and the Tragic Muse. "He was neither fool nor madman, nor man to be adored," Meredith says of his fictional Alvan (Lassalle):

> his last temptation caught him in the season before he had subdued his blood, and amid the multitudinously simple of this world, stamped him a tragic comedian: that is, a grand pretender, a self-deceiver, one of the lively ludicrous, whom we cannot laugh at, but must contemplate, to distinguish where their character strikes the note of discord with life; for otherwise, in the reflection of their history, life will seem a thing demoniacally inclined by fits to antic and dive into gulfs. The characters of the hosts of men are of the simple order of the comic; not many are of a stature and a complexity calling for the junction of the two Muses to name them.[30]

The Tragic Comedians reflects Meredith's awareness that in history elements may be fatally intermixed to the point where positive development may not be an evolutionary inevitability. Part of Meredith's early affirmative belief had centered in the famous line from *Modern Love:* "We are betrayed by what is false within." If that were entirely so, human history would naturally progress upward so long as men and women were properly educated. But in Lassalle's tragicomic life, Meredith could not avoid noting the prominent role of chance in history. In contesting Carlyle's view of the importance of heroes in history, Tolstoy had shown in *War and Peace* that "heroes" are largely at the mercy of chance. Despite his continuing optimism toward man's possibilities and despite his enthusiasm for Carlyle, Meredith was not inclined to disagree. In many ways, Alvan's failure is Carlyle's—and that of the self-divided Romantic tradition behind him—but Alvan's problems resemble Meredith's in 1880.

The critical discovery of Meredith in the 1870's seems not to have pleased him as much as it discouraged him to find his message so often misinterpreted. "It is vexatious to see how judges from whom one looks for discernment miss the point," Meredith would say late in life,[31] but this habit of mind arose during the years of his popularity. It must be admitted that Meredith did not help matters very much during these years. The charge of obscurity began with his earliest works, and with *Beauchamp's Career* readers complained that he was writing in a deliberately obscure manner. By the time of *The Tragic Comedians*, the style can no longer be defended on the grounds of functional diffuseness. The obscurities in *One of Our Conquerors* can be partly forgiven on account of their relationship to the theme of that novel; in the other late novels, however, one often feels at one with James in his exasperation with *"the unspeakable Lord Ormont"*: "there are pretty things, but for what they are they come so much too dear, and so many of the profundities and tortuosities prove when threshed out to be only pretentious statements of the very simplest propositions."[32] It was on *The Tragic Comedians* that George Moore based his opinion of Meredith's style: there are "only sterile nuts, phrases that people would call epigrams, and it is impossible for me to call to mind a book more like a cockatoo than 'The Tragic Comedians'; it struts and screams just like one."[33] Meredith wrote the book in a period of personal depression and physical distress. His health had begun to give way at about the age of fifty, largely as a result of overwork and overexertion. At the same time that he began to hymn the spirit of "blood" and of youth in his poetry, he was becoming increasingly aware of his own disability and age. The songs to nature are heartfelt, but *The Tragic Comedians* reveals, as Sassoon notes, "an artificial vitality." "The brilliant brain was losing its sap. The mannerisms were becoming rigid. The sterility of expertly contrived writing was already apparent."[34] The celebrator of the song of "The Lark Ascending," free of the "taint of personality," was becoming the slave of his literary mannerisms and philosophical crotchets. And there is a reason to guess that he suspected as much himself.

In the figure of Alvan, Meredith found a case like his own, a victim of circumstance as well as of a tragicomic flaw, an insufficiently respected genius endowed with too many gifts and too little self-control. At one point Alvan defends the usefulness of "light literature"—by which one assumes he means novels—for their "pictures of our human blood in motion" (XV, 62). This is similar to Meredith's own account of his work in 1887: "My method has been to prepare my readers for a crucial exhibition of the personae, and then to give the scene in the fullest of their blood and brain under stress of a fiery situation."[35] This is the method he used to depict the ordeal of Alvan and his beloved, Clotilde. Years of repression in Meredith burst forth whenever Alvan cries out for personal and literary freedom. The years of writing journalistic hackwork and reading manuscripts for Chapman and Hall found their expression in his outburst of intransigence:

> "Above all things I detest the writing for money. Fiction and verse appeal to a besotted public, that judges of the merit of the work by the standard of its taste:—avaunt! And journalism for money is Egyptian bondage. No slavery is comparable to the chains of hired journalism. My pen is my fountain— the key of me; and I give myself, I do not sell. I write when I have matter in me and in the direction it presses for, otherwise not one word!" [XV, 73].

For all his eloquence, however, Alvan is fatally unaware of the nature of others. "Among Alvan's gifts the understanding of women did not rank high," Meredith bluntly states (XV, 83).

Clotilde, cast as Delilah to Alvan's Samson, is a much less complex figure although in choosing to find strengths in her that do not exist he hastens his downfall. The daughter of a Philistine German family, she has a superficial cleverness that, in the family context, is taken as "force of character." Like Isabel Archer, she believes in the myth of her self-reliance, and she first becomes interested in Alvan when he is described as her mirror image. She idealizes her lover at his own encouragement and imagines that he can indeed "turn rosy visions into facts" (XV, 58), can carry her off with him. The victim of his Olympian rhetoric, he presumes to give her a "soul" and "strength to realize, courage to act" (XV, 61). She seeks refuge in his rhetoric, and he assumes that this is a sign of her intelligence. When the lovers are separated by her parents, who despise him for his Jewish origin, they become the victims of their faith in each other's powers and of their own limited points of view. The "partners in aphorism," as they are early called, end up like the uncomprehending couple in *Modern Love*. Clotilde, who trusts entirely to fate rather than to reason, is betrayed less by what is "false" than by what is weak within. In trusting to the force of her will, which he presumes to have shaped, Alvan succumbs to pride and then regresses to irrational behavior.

Alvan himself projects the curve of his downfall very early in the book, while speaking of the necessity for intelligence: "If we descend to poor brute strength or brutal craft, it is from failing in the brain: we quit the leadership of our forces, and the descent is the beast's confession" (XV, 28). Possessing brilliant intelligence and unruly emotions, Alvan is unable to reconcile brainstuff with blood-instinct. He describes himself as a god, but he becomes instead "a Cyclops hurling rocks" (XV, 111). "He is a Titan, not a god," as a friend describes him, "though god-like he seems in comparison with men" (XV, 149). He is similar to Meredith's idol, Carlyle, "the greatest of the Britons of his time," in his view, who was "Titanic, not Olympian: a heaver of rocks, not a shaper." One may say of Alvan-Lassalle what the exasperated novelist complained of after the publication of "Shooting Niagara": "Spiritual light he has to illuminate a nation. Of practical little or none, and he beats his own brains out with emphasis."[36] One often feels the temptation to extend the comparison to Meredith himself.

Alvan compares himself to an Alp, but he forgets that a mountain touches earth as well as heaven. "He was not heroic, but hugely man," Meredith demonstrates in the novel (XV, 112), and Alvan's "stormy blood made wreck of a splendid intelligence" (XV, 199). Meredith makes a persuasive attempt to attribute the causes of his tragedy and Clotilde's to their inability to attain perspective, to harmonize brain and heart; a comic flaw would seem to occasion a tragic end, whereby "the comic in their natures led by interplay to the tragic issue" (XV, 2). Nevertheless, the novelist cannot help admitting the role of chance in the interplay. Alvan cannot understand Clotilde, but then no one in the book can rightly interpret another's motives. "The facts are seen," Meredith says apropos of Alvan's limited point of view, "and yet the spinning nerves will change their complexion" (XV, 109). It was chance that Lassalle should have fallen in love with a woman from a hostile family; it is chance that the vigorous Alvan-Lassalle, an expert shot, should be killed in a duel by the accidental shot of a poor marksman, himself dying of consumption.

This uncustomary ambiguity on Meredith's part as to the reasons for Alvan's tragedy—implying an inability to find a wholly rational excuse for Alvan's actions—is underlined by the hint that what is unintelligible is a reflection of what is inexpressible. The characters hide themselves under rhetoric, or else escape into what Meredith labels "Dot-and-Dashland": "thinking without language" (XV, 130–131). Yet he himself can scarcely articulate what he means in his passages dealing with his characters' inability to make themselves understood. The failure of the novel to do more than summarize the historical episode in semipoetical analysis is demonstrated through the frequent waste of both psychological analysis and poetry. The potentially magnificent symbol of the "black-draped blighted tree," before which the lovers become pledged and which serves to show the perishability of their union, is presented in a tortuous manner and then forgotten during the remainder of the novel. "That tree stands for Death blooming," Alvan says (XV, 73–77), but it is left almost entirely to the reader's imagination to make such a suggestive image bear its full poetic weight. The blackened tree was obviously meant to stand in contrast to the white, double-blossomed cherry tree in *The Egoist*. The wasted symbol becomes, instead, symbolic of Meredith's weakened resources in *The Tragic Comedians*, a novel, ironically, about inexplicably wasted lives.

Meredith complained in 1881, to the sickly son from his first marriage, of his deteriorating health: "My digestion is entirely deranged, and still I have to write—and for a public that does not care for my work. These were the thoughts that used to give me such alarm at your craving to wield the pen. As for me, I have failed, and I find little to make the end undesirable."[37] The following year, however, he wrote to Leslie Stephen in a happier mood, "I begin rather to feel that I shall write when I try—that is, in a manner to please myself, which has not been in my power for several months of late, though curiously I found no difficulty in verse."[38] Despite the decay of Meredith's novelistic gifts in the 1880's, beginning with *The Tragic Comedians*, his poetic powers found outlet in several of his finest poems. Whereas the novelist began to camouflage his awareness of the historical drift of the period under a bullying rhetoric, the poet could express his mingled hopes and fears in a succession of what one might call public lyrics. In 1883 he published his first volume of poems in over twenty years, *Poems and Lyrics of the Joy of Earth;* two more collections appeared in 1887 and 1888. As the *Annual Register* for 1883 noted of the first collection, "he has the distinction among nineteenth century poets of finding that there is any joy in earth."[39]

The first selection in the 1883 volume is the knotty, and perhaps too insistent, "The Woods of Westermain." It contains Meredith's warning that harmony with nature and self can be achieved only by the willingness to face the fact of the occasional cruelties of nature and of the primitive egoism within oneself. Operative idealism can be constructed only on a sense of reality, a Meredithian theme enunciated in the two preceding novels. More purely successful as poems are "The Lark Ascending" and the revised version of "Love in the Valley," songs of praise to selfless song and humanized earth, both works celebrating what D. H. Lawrence would later call "sap-consciousness." If self is the villain of the group of poems, it is most memorably embodied in the figure of Satan in Meredith's great sonnet "Lucifer in Starlight." Elsewhere, Meredith sings of man as the heir to earth, though he must "burn from Self to Spirit through the lash" ("The State of Age"); that is, he must be subjected to the ordeal of discovery and self-discovery if he is to emerge "a larger self" ("Woods")—the altruist, lover of earth and man. In "Melampus" Meredith depicts the altruist as poet, who sees "nature and song allied." The message here clearly transcends the medium, and one can understand why the historian G. M. Trevelyan, among others, turned to Meredith for philosophical solace. It is unfortunate, however, that Meredith's "healthy and manly outlook," in Chesterton's phrase, should have found expression so often in a "crabbed and perverse style."[40]

Without denying the amorality of Darwin's nature toward man, Meredith affirms the human possibility of reshaping the earth, and of learning lessons of stability and vitality from her if man only chooses to detect them. Man has both a shaping and a defining nature. "Earth was not Earth before her sons appeared" ("Appreciation"), he claims, and, in effect, it is man's poetic ability to articulate nature that produces an image of her sanity. "Life" and "Death" are only what man defines them to be, as he says in "A Ballad of Past Meridian." Meredith implies that man can evolve to the point where he becomes a poet of earth, although such progress can be made only if he accepts the fact of his primitive roots. In *Ballads and Poems of Tragic Life* (1887), a less distinguished collection, Meredith acknowledges that man's fate has hitherto been thwarted by his blind egoism. In the lead poem for that volume, "The Two Masks," he once more notes the importance of the Comic Muse in drawing forth man's potential "Nobleness" by subjecting him to the "stress of action's fire." The theme of the collection, however, is "tragic life"; as in *The Tragic Comedians*, he shows how the comic in men's undisciplined natures leads inevitably to what the world labels a tragic issue.

Between the two volumes of poetry appeared the novel that transformed Meredith into a popular as well as a critical favorite. *Diana of the Crossways* was published in a year that produced as many literary landmarks of the transition from the late Victorian to the modern sensibility as 1859 had boasted of a similarly concentrated number of mid-Victorian documents. One hardly knows which is more depressing to contemplate: the surge of real popularity for Meredith after decades of public indifference toward his finer works, or the matter of Meredith's own admiration for his tarnished achievement.

With his health horribly impaired by now, Meredith produced the novel under conditions which make one want to appreciate it more. But what is written in pain, as Dr. Johnson observed, is rarely read with pleasure. For his heroine's life, Meredith openly exploited incidents from the life of Caroline Norton, who, in 1845, had apparently divulged to the press the secret news of impending repeal of the Corn Laws. Ten years before that, she had been accused by her husband of having an affair with Lord Melborne, the Prime Minister. Mrs. Norton, whom some called the Byron of her sex, took part in attempts to modify the stringent Victorian marriage laws. She was a close friend of Lady Duff Gordon, a close friend of Meredith and the model for the heroine's mother in *Evan Harrington* and for Diana Warwick's friend, Lady Dunstane.

When Meredith utilized a historical event in *The Tragic Comedians*, he did so because of the thematic relevancy to his philosophic interests. But he seems to have borrowed episodes from the life of Mrs. Norton because of his inability to invent fictional materials appropriate to his theme. In consequence, throughout the writing of the novel he was at the mercy of his ambiguous conception of the heroine. To make matters worse, the writing of the novel took much longer than he had expected. These two factors combined to convince him that he was dealing with a live character. In his letters he proudly claimed that he had "a feeble hold of her; none of the novelist's winding-up arts avail; it is she who leads me."[41] He had said as much earlier of Sandra-Vittoria and Beauchamp, but he had put them into an active context that suitably illustrated their characters.

At the mercy of a character who was partly a historical personage and partly a self-projection, Meredith created in Diana a confused rather than a complex woman; instead of presenting a coherent explanation for her action, he tried to bully the reader into accepting her reality. "I never outline my novels before starting on them," he once told a reviewer. "I live day and night with my characters."[42] Balzac and Dickens had also confessed their belief in their characters' reality, but their major creations are nevertheless viewed with firmness of focus and amid lively situations. *Diana of the Crossways* offers misleading proof of sorts to those who feel that Meredith was not really a novelist; it not only breaks the rules of the novel, as his work had done earlier, but it also lacks as compensation any masterly injections of poetry or psychological analysis. If previously he had broken the rules in order to show future novelists what they could do with the form, he now chose instead to regress in theme and method.

Like her author, Diana is a gifted individualist who is forced for economic reasons to become a novelist. Her novels, she admits, are drawn from the people around her: "Authors find their models where they can," she says, "and generally hit on the nearest."[43] Her initial publication is not written for "Public Taste," but her devoted friend Tom Redworth, who fears that its "originality might tell against it," sees to it that the book gets the sort of bullying good reviews that lead to sales. "Genius is good for the public," he rationalizes (XVI, 194–195). A less sympathetic reader may remember Trollope's critical portrait of the authoress, Lady Carbury, in *The Way We Live Now*, who uses similar means to ensure her own success. Diana's book succeeds, however, partly because of the recent scandal involving the married authoress and Lord Dannisburgh. Thus, the novel Meredith is writing has its curious links with Diana's own first effort. In her succeeding novels, she becomes more and more Meredithian in habit. Unable to resolve a character's problems, she chooses to kill her off instead. Meredith, uncertain how to resolve Diana's dilemma, apparently had originally planned to have her commit suicide.

Although Diana feels tempted to indulge in the manner of the French naturalists in her work—that is, to portray "humanity as it is, wallowing, sensual, wicked, behind the mask," as the cynical voice of Ego urges her—she nevertheless keeps to her Meredithian habit of showing "a triumph of the good" and refusing to pander to the low tastes of what Meredith once labeled "Sir Pandarus Public." She seeks refuge, Meredith approvingly notes, in poetic writing:

> Metaphors were her refuge. Metaphorically she could allow
> her mind to distinguish the struggle she was undergoing,
> sinking under it. The banished of Eden had to put on metaphors,
> and the common use of them has helped largely to civilize us.
> The sluggish in intellect detest them, but our civilization is
> not much indebted to that major faction [XVI, 275].

But this is a disturbing form of self-justification to take—both for Diana and for her author. The sight of Meredith so completely out of control in the novel at such times is painful, and there are disarming similarities between Diana's misconceived books and the book which contains Diana. "A fit of angry cynicism," he admits, "now and then set her composing phrases as baits for the critics to quote, condemnatory of the attractiveness of the work" (XVI, 314).

The disaster that results from identification between Meredith and his heroine is similar to that befalling James in his portrait of Hyacinth Robinson. Whereas Hyacinth is one blot in an otherwise lively achievement, *The Princess Casamassima*, Diana is the entire novel. The book must stand or fall on her frail shoulders. In *The Egoist* Meredith had succeeded in his portrait of Clara Middleton without depriving the reader of action or setting. In fact, Clara shines all the more remarkably as a character by means of the opposition established between her and Sir Willoughby Patterne. In *Diana* Meredith attempted to confine the war between egoism and liberated altruism within a single character. "I thank heaven I'm at war with myself," he lets his heroine exclaim (XVI, 48). It is, however, too much to expect that even the most complex character can embody the human struggle and still be able to step aside and be an imperturbable sage, and Meredith expects Diana to do both. Throughout the novel he treats her as an oracle of wisdom, but lets us watch her make mistake after mistake. As Priestley complains, she must serve as both female touchstone, like Clara, and erring egoist, like Willoughby; the result is schizophrenia posing as sanity.

Meredith's failure to present a credible character forces him again and again into the position of demanding that the reader accept her confusion as proof of her reality. She will not show herself to advantage, he declares near the end of the book:

> Only those who read her woman's blood and character with
> the head, will care for Diana of the Crossways now that the
> knot of her history has been unravelled. Some little love they
> must have for her likewise: and how it can be quickened on
> behalf of a woman who never sentimentalizes publicly, and has
> no dolly-dolly compliance, and muses on actual life, and
> fatigues with the exercise of brains, and is in sooth an alien:
> a princess of her kind and time, but a foreign one, speaking a
> language distinct from the mercantile, trafficking in ideas:—
> this is the problem. For to be true to her, one cannot attempt at
> propitiation [XVI, 441].

If Meredith had earlier hinted at the inexpressibility of reality, he attempts in *Diana* to create a being so untrue either to life or to artistic logic that she will be accepted as real. In *The Tragic Comedians* he had dealt with characters whose lives were "fantastical" but also historical; with Diana he tries to bully the reader into accepting her as true to life because fantastical. This is not utterly impossible, but he also demands that his heroine be considered bigger and more rational than life. He may be able to persuade the reader that Diana's most vividly irrational act—the selling of her lover's political secret to the newspapers for the sake of money and vanity—is not beyond the realm of possibility, but he cannot expect the reader to applaud the act for its rational heroism.

The novelist hints that, in her act of treachery, Diana is submitting her lover, Percy Dacier, to an ordeal of sorts. When he marries another woman afterward, Diana concludes, "He could not bear much" (XVI, 437). But Percy has not been presented with the sort of characterization which would persuade the reader to be interested in his ordeal. Instead, Meredith finds himself in the position of being impatient with this uninteresting figure with whom Diana has inexplicably fallen in love and for whom she nearly dies of repentant love, and, at the same time, of demanding that his heroine take him seriously. None of the other men in Diana's life even approximates the disappointing figure of Percy. We see her admirers from her kaleidoscopic point of view, with the result that as readers we have not much to go on. Diana's early "experiences" are hinted at, but not told. Her marriage with the narrow-minded Augustus Warwick, whom we see only briefly, is an irrational act quickly disposed of. The Warwicks separate as the result of the scandal arising from Diana's relations with Lord Dannisburgh—an episode again left entirely to the reader's imagination. After building up the character of Percy Dacier, the rising political leader, to the point where his love for Diana has "ceased to be the lover's hypocrisy" (XVI, 301), Meredith transforms him into "the effigy of a tombstone" gentleman, "a devious filmy sentimentalist" (XVI, 442), who abandons her. Meanwhile, the patient Tom Redworth had grown richer and worthier, like a hero in a comic strip, and Diana is won over to him after watching him play cricket with a group of boys. Presented as the practical Saxon mate for the Celtic heroine, Redworth decides that Diana "would complete him." Their eventual marriage seems more the result of symbolic algebra than of human affection.

Meredith's Marxist admirer, Jack Lindsay, has complained that what spoils *Diana of the Crossways* is the fact that the author's goal is nothing more than a happy marriage.[44] Whatever Meredith's intention with regard to the fate of his heroine, marriage is indeed his way of symbolically affirming the perpetuity of the compromising Victorian world. However uninteresting Redworth may be in the novel, in conception he fills a role similar to that of Knightley in *Emma*. "He appeared to Diana as a fatal power," Meredith notes, "attracting her without sympathy, benevolently overcoming: one

of those good men, strong men, who subdue and do not kindle"
(XVI, 453). Although Diana has affinities with the "New Women"
of the 1880's (becoming, we are told, their favorite heroine for a
time), her ultimate aim is not to achieve the Diana-like independence of her fictional huntress-sister, Isabel Archer, but to face the
world as a Victorian Britomart. Meredith calls Diana "the flecked
heroine of Reality" in opposition to the conventional British
heroine of Romance, rigidly innocent and, from a male point of
view, "guaranteed"—like Percy's "effigy bride," Constance Asper.
In speaking of Trollope's model heroines, James commented on
their "clinging tenderness, a passive sweetness, which is quite in
the old English tradition."[45] With a few exceptions, like Glencora
Palliser or Madame Goesler, Trollope's firmer female protagonists,
or incipient "New Women," are not favorably presented. Women
who will not consent to be hunted along the conventional lines of the
courtship as chase must inevitably be feared as aggressive lionesses, like the overwhelming American Mrs. Hurtle in *The Way
We Live Now*. In *The Egoist* Meredith attacked the Englishman's
habit of treating love as an extension of fox hunting. In *Diana*
he has Lady Dunstane defend the heroine's impulsiveness on the
grounds of women's defective training in life: "It is our education—we have something of the hare in us when the hounds are
full cry" (XVI, 89). If Diana occasionally regresses, the fault is
that of the man responsible; for Diana to advance, she must (like
Clara) be free to love. She is "good under good leading," Meredith
declares (XVI, 399).

The "New Women" of the period, however, were not looking
for "good leading." Although James could satirize the unmanageable and unmarriageable American female reformers in *The Bostonians*, he was never sympathetic to the idea of marriage for his
heroines. The Jamesian hero or heroine is not interested in becoming a perpetuating member of society. He becomes instead an artistic sensibility, of necessity detached and bound only to the laws of
his own perceptive being. If James's characters leap out of their
Victorian context into a dateless and sexless world, Meredith's
heroes are generally at symbolic "crossways," purging themselves
of egoistic personality so that they can accomplish useful work.
If Meredith saw England as a nation of egoists, he turned his lit-

erary resources to the task of encouraging the rise of educated citizens. He could never wholly support the female emancipators because their actions seemed to him more antisocial than profemale. Although the success of *Diana of the Crossways* has been linked to the feminist movement, it is not surprising that a number of women should have seen in Meredith a defense of the male point of view and the status quo. In the last chapter of the novel, he undertakes to show "How a Barely Willing Woman was Led to Bloom with the Nuptial Sentiment," and the book ends with a hint of her pregnancy. A striking example of Meredith's sympathies is the account of his being shocked to discover that *Diana* was being read by teen-age girls. As stories of his daughter's upbringing indicate, he was curiously prudish as a parent.

In the same period when James was disavowing English society as a picturesque ideal, Meredith was defending the limits of society. "Society is the best thing we have," he quotes from Diana, "but it is a crazy vessel worked by a crew that formerly practiced piracy" (XVI, 209). Meredith's aim is to show that the laws governing nature and the laws governing society are interconnected. The taming of the huntress is symbolically required for social perpetuity, but the education of hunted and hunter alike is necessary to instill harmony with nature. This is true not only of individuals but of nations, and in the marriage of convenience between Redworth and Diana, Saxon and Celt, Meredith symbolically tackled the most pressing political problem of the decade—agitation over Irish Home Rule.

As an American in England, James could face the prospect of the gulf between artist and society without uneasiness. Meredith, however, was a novelist of philosophic rather than artistic commitment, and for him the novel existed not merely for showing "felt life" but for prodding progressive action of the sort that would, in time, make the need for novels obsolete. While James's aesthetic theory indicates a detachment from life, Meredith's literary practice betrays a hostility toward art. In *The Tragic Comedians* and *Diana of the Crossways*, Meredith attempted to write novels as a philosopher-historian. He had demanded in *Sandra Belloni* that we accept the reality of his characters because he admitted in advance that they were puppets; our faith in them as people is built upon our awareness of them as fabrications. It is essential to Meredith's plan that we disavow any kind of illusion, and, since he is writing novels, he feels obligated to remind us again and again of the fact of the illusion involved so that, on this basis, we will accept Diana as the real person Meredith obviously felt her to be. But the inability to sustain illusion is the death of art; in Meredith's earnest attempt to infuse his novel with philosophy he symbolically embodies the breakup of the Victorian novel.

The first chapter of *Diana* contains Meredith's most famous call for philosophy in fiction. Deriding fellow-novelists' addiction to "wooden puppetry," he calls on other "gallant pens" to create a public taste for something better. "A great modern writer, of clearest eye and head, now departed," as Meredith notes of Thackeray,

> capable in activity of presenting thoughtful women, thinking men, groaned over his puppetry, that he dared not animate them, flesh though they were, with the fires of positive brainstuff. He could have done it, and he is of the departed! Had he dared, he would (for he was Titan enough) have raised the Art in dignity on a level with History, to an interest surpassing the narrative of public deeds as vividly as man's heart and brain in their union excel his plain lines of action to eruption [XVI, 18].

Meredith was emphatically Victorian with respect to his faith in the value of synthesis, harmony, compromise. "Philosophy bids us to see," he affirms, "that we are not so pretty as rose-pink, not so repulsive as dirty drab; and that instead of everlastingly shifting those barren aspects, the sight of ourselves is wholesome, bearable, fructifying, finally a delight" (XVI, 15). He cautions that the refusal to "embrace Philosophy in fiction" means the extinction of the novel, doomed to remain in some views "the pasture of idiots, a method for idiotizing the entire population which has taken to reading; and which soon discovers that it can write likewise, *that* sort of stuff at least" (XVI, 19). The jaunty Meredithian optimism of the first chapter of *Diana*, however, does not prepare the reader for a book whose very weakness in writing and design and whose facile thematic conclusion could scarcely have convinced perceptive young writers that there was a future in combining old formulas with new subterfuges.

It has been said that the Victorian novel, which at best superbly embodied that complex and divided age, was killed off by various foreign influences—of which James's Americanization of the form was as crucial as Moore's introduction of French naturalist techniques. It may also be demonstrated, however, that the Victorian novel became self-destructive as well through the attempts of George Eliot and Meredith to understand the historical drift and dictate a philosophical answer. The didacticism of the Victorian novel was intrinsic to the form; the novel taught as a matter of course, but it tried never to bully. Holding up a mirror to the Victorian world, the novel demanded a continuing stability of society even while it called for correction of errors within that society. When, in the 1870's and 1880's, the fabric of society began to crumble beyond repair, or when that fabric began to seem incapable of corrective and preservative change, depending on various later views, it became apparent to the last generation of Victorians that they could turn either to desperate polemics or to romantic escapisms of one sort or another. With *Daniel Deronda*, in 1873, George Eliot intuitively realized that the compromised world of Middlemarch was beyond salvation. Meredith, who had been violating the canons of the novel for decades, found himself in the 1870's and 1880's still defending the integrity of the Victorian world. As writer and philosopher alike, he was doomed in his task. His inability to express himself as a novelist kept him from being intelligible to the very readers he courted, just as his earnest call for philosophy in fiction appeared in a novel negligibly fictional. In demanding that the reader accept Diana as real, Meredith ignored his fundamental obligation—perhaps the only novelistic absolute —to give shape to his character. In stridently commanding his readers to accept reality over fiction, he begged them in effect to put down his novel. Moreover, he rejected the creation of "wooden puppetry" only to risk the charge of perpetrating wooden platitudes.

The product of an exhausted man, *Diana of the Crossways* may be said to have exhausted the possibility that fiction could still be written for Victorian readers. Like his heroine, Meredith was at the crossways—of English history and the English novel. It was no longer possible for him to continue portraying English society as comically fixed and seemingly immovable, just as it was impossible to make the old philosophical leaps with his Vernons and Claras into a poetic world seem within reach of human possibility. After a personal ordeal lasting five years after the publication of *Diana*, Meredith made a last attempt at a novel of synthesis and affirmation within Victorian limits. The book, *One of Our Conquerors*, does not succeed in duplicating the achievement of a *Middlemarch*, but it fails in a way fascinating to the student of the novel and in a manner vindicating the vestiges of Meredith's instinctive wisdom and strange genius.

The Limits of Articulation: One of Our Conquerors

> *The internal state of a gentleman who detested intangible metaphors as heartily as the vulgarest of our gobble-gobbets hate it, metaphor only can describe; and for the reason, that he had in him just something more than is within the compass of the language of the meat-markets.*
> (One of Our Conquerors)

In 1885 Meredith, angrily surveying the political dangers of the period, admitted to feeling "the curse of an impotent voice." While his poetry of the 1880's stoically and passionately sang of the need for harmony with nature, Meredith's novels dealt increasingly with the psychological and social discords of the period. In *One of Our Conquerors* (1891), he attempted for the last time in a novel to offer a philosophical prescription for, as he later termed it, "the malady afflicting England."[46] The most ambitious of his works in design, *One of Our Conquerors* analyzes late Victorian society and its individuals on the edge of breakdown and offers as therapy the practice of enlightened, responsible, selfless labor. "As a social and psychological study," Lionel Stevenson declares, the novel "has good claim to be called the richest fulfillment of Meredith's peculiar powers."[47] But it might also be claimed that, in Meredith's last and most heroic and most stylistically strained attempt to salvage the energies and ideals of the Victorian age, he went too far and produced instead a work in which the Victorian novel is seen in the act of committing suicide.

Artistically flawed and philosophically confused, *Diana of the Crossways* became Meredith's most popular novel to date, very largely as a result of public interest in the scarcely veiled references to Mrs. Norton. By the end of 1885 it had gone through three editions, and the popular demand for Meredith had occasioned the first collected edition of his work.* Whatever comfort this might have provided the crippled novelist was dissipated by the death that fall of Meredith's second wife. Marie Vulliamy Meredith was a curiously dependent woman, with little of the spirit of Diana or Clara, as far as one can tell. As she lay dying, Meredith struggled with his grief in a long and frequently moving poem, "A Faith on Trial." The period of stoic mourning for the next few years culminated in one of Meredith's best and most difficult volumes of poetry, *A Reading of Earth*, in 1888. For the moment he had transcended his abstract theories of the comic spirit and his half-scornful dismay at the tragic life into a poetic world of pure nature, in which a description of "Hard Weather" or the "South-West wind" is also an account of human life. Nature and human nature become one, producing an effect at once transcendental and personal. The poet sustains a "blood-thrill" from a "Night of Frost in May," and the song of "The Thrush in February" proclaims "the rapture of the forward view." Perhaps the finest poems in the collection are the "Hymn to Colour," a mystical celebration of love and action, and the two sections of a longer poem, originally published in 1870, here slightly changed and printed separately as "In the Woods" and "Dirge in Woods." The two short poems offer a less tortuous version of the central message of the new volume: the acceptance of life as process combined with a lyric stoicism:

> I am in deep woods,
>   Between the two twilights.
>
> Whatsoever I am and may be,
> Write it down to the light in me;
> I am I, and it is my deed;

* Begun in 1885, ten volumes were ready by 1887. James had already witnessed his first collected edition in 1883.

For I know that paths are dark
  Between the two twilights.
         ("In the Woods")

A wind sways the pines,
      And below
Not a breath of wild air;
Still as the mosses that glow
On the flooring and over the lines
Of the roots here and there.
The pine tree drops its dead;
They are quiet, as under the sea.
Overhead, overhead
Rushes life in a race,
As the clouds the clouds chase;
      And we go,
And we drop like the fruits of the tree,
      Even we,
      Even so.
         ("Dirge in Woods")

"The Thrush in February," published shortly before Mrs. Meredith's death, is an attempt to combine Keats and Darwin—a celebration of the song of the thrush as a portent of spring for the
earth, but also as a symbol of man's enduring thought and service.
Men are the vessels of "the Thought," and if "The vessel splits, the
Thought survives." This poem contains the line "We breathe but
to be sword or block" which so depressed the young E. M. Forster
("I did not want to be either and I knew that I was not a sword").[48]
But the image of the sword suggests the metaphorical strength of
the possibilities of poetry, for example. In "A Faith on Trial"
Meredith uses the occasion of his personal grief as a metaphor
for the need to accept the "harsh wisdom" of nature's continuing
process:

Cry we for permanence fast,
Permanence hangs by the grave;
Sits on the grave green-grassed,
On the roll of the heaved grave-mound.

The only real permanence is death, but "By Death, as by Life, are we fed." Man cannot be blind to the fact of death, but he must continue to see around it, not spending his time contemplating the skull. In human activity, "the Questions that sow not nor spin" are both escaped and answered. Laurence Sterne had argued in *Tristram Shandy* for the necessity of ceaseless human movement as an antidote to thought ("so much of motion, is so much of life"), but, for Meredith, activity and thought are connected. However, he does imply that the achievement of the larger "Thought" is reached through overcoming one's individual questions. Meredith's doubts, in "A Faith on Trial," are first subdued, like Clara's in *The Egoist*, by the sight of a "pure wild-cherry in bloom." The symbolic tree suggests those affirming possibilities in nature which lie beyond the realm of lucid intelligibility.

In the late 1880's Meredith accepted as matter of fact the role of man as a hunted being, in elaboration of the metaphor of Diana the hunted huntress. "We know not how long the hunted bit of life will last," he wrote to Morley of his dying wife.[49] Twenty years later he expressed himself bluntly on the subject: "We are all hunted more or less. Yet Nature is very kind to all her offspring. If you are a fine runner and your blood is up, you don't, in point of fact, feel a half of what you do when lying in bed or sitting in a chair thinking about it."[50] Along with Henley and Robert Louis Stevenson, the crippled Meredith began in the 1880's to hymn the "songs of strength," although poetic strength threatened to turn into merely brutal strength. Metaphorical points are accordingly made more and more by boxing matches than by natural descriptions. And the Meredithian heroes become increasingly less sympathetic. In Vernon Whitford and Tom Redworth, the novelist had devised as ideal mates for his heroines practical and reasonable men, who also hiked and played cricket. In *One of Our Conquerors* he presented as the mate for his heroine a physically energetic man with a bludgeon at his side and little in the way of conspicuous brainstuff. Dartrey Fenellan is a metaphor for manliness in a book which attempts to understand contemporary society more in metaphorical than in straightforward realistic terms. Only with metaphor, the novelist admits, can he still attempt to deal with reality in the novel in an affirmative manner, but the metaphors, when analyzed, suggest more than anything else that life, in the elderly novelist's view, is inexpressible as well as incomprehensible.

In outline, *One of Our Conquerors* has obvious affinities with Meredith's earlier novels. The protagonist and ostensible "conqueror" of the title, Victor Radnor, is a sentimentalist and egoist whose inability to correct himself or understand others is a comic flaw with potentially tragic issue. He is the central figure in a gallery of contrasting men: Dartrey, the unsentimental man of action; Simeon Fenellan, Dartrey's intellectual but inert brother; Colney Durance, Victor's ironic-minded friend; Dudley Sowerby, aristocrat and Victor's choice as suitor for his daughter; Inchling, Victor's cautious, anti-Semitic business partner; Skepsey, his aggressive little factotum. Almost every character in the novel is set against an opposite, although most represent an aspect of, and all contrast in some way with, Victor. But Victor's complexity is not the happy synthesis of the early Meredith heroes; the shift of the author's sympathy toward single-minded men of action like Dartrey indicates a painful change in Meredith's outlook.

As a leader of society and a "merchant prince," Victor presides over an extraordinarily mixed world. Metaphorically and actually, he is conductor of the Radnor circle, which is a semicomic microcosm of English society, united in diversity as an amateur orchestra:

> Dr. Schlesien had his German views, Colney Durance his ironic, Fenellan his fanciful and free-lance. And here was an optimist, there a pessimist; and the rank Radical, the rigid Conservative, were not wanting. All of them were pointedly opposed, extraordinarily for so small an assembly: absurdly, it might be thought: but these provoked a kind warm smile with the exclamation: "They are dears!" They were the dearer for their fads and foibles.
> Music harmonized them.[51]

In its own way, the Radnor circle is as representative and unified as the Middlemarchers, but, if George Eliot's community is itself the controlling force of its inhabitants' destinies, the Radnor circle is under the baton of one man. Victor is no amateur conductor, but altogether an accomplished "leader of musicians, a leader of men," in the world's point of view:

> The halo of the millionaire behind, assures us of a development in the character of England's merchant princes. The homage we pay him flatters us. A delightful overture, masterfully executed; ended too soon; except that the programme forbids the ordinary interpretation of prolonged applause. Mr. Radnor is one of those who do everything consummately [XVII, 237].

Despite opposing views, the people about Victor seem synthesized into a harmonious entity, like Victorian society itself, presumably, and the emblematic conqueror is presented initially as an unshakeable monarch: "He was that man in fifty thousand who despises hostile elements and goes unpunished" (XVII, 12). The permanence of Victorian society is guaranteed by the heroic will and continuing resourcefulness of its complex leader with his appropriate name of "Victor."

Or so it seems, at any rate. Victor apparently controls society and defies natural barriers, but he is actually the most vulnerable character in the novel. As the reader follows the progress of Victor toward his inevitable downfall, he also detects the dissolving fabric of Victorian society. In a novel which ostensibly celebrates once again Meredith's Victorian faith in the powers of synthesis, communication, and progress, the initial sense of harmony turns out to be merely discord not understood. Whatever is, is wrong; once more in Meredith, it is the forces of unreason and triumphant non-communication which make the novel accessible to the modern reader. *One of Our Conquerors* bears comparison with *The Way We Live Now* and *Little Dorrit* as a metaphorical portrait of a doomed society, although Meredith is far less able than his predecessors to embody the doom in a thoroughly concrete setting. As a result of his ill health and his addiction to literary mannerisms, he could only attempt such a portrait through a veil of words that often barely reveals the image sought.

Yet, paradoxically, the Meredithian obscurity often perfectly suits the theme of the novel. Meredith's occasional inability to articulate curiously parallels Victor's inability to comprehend. If it offered nothing else, *One of Our Conquerors* would be of permanent interest to the literary historian as the last major attempt of Victorian genius to reconcile what the twentieth century has recognized to be an incompatible universe. In this novel Meredith sought a solution to the Victorian dilemma beyond the reach of comedy or tragedy alone; instead, he unconsciously created as nihilistic an image of man's possibilities, including his possibilities as a novelist, as the novel can show. Ramon Fernandez has described the successful "struggle for life" of Meredith's heroes as "a struggle for lucidity";[52] in *One of Our Conquerors*, however, it is obscurity which vanquishes both hero and novelist, although in a strangely functional, often compelling manner.

Victor's power and equipoise have been built over his inability to face the fact of an irresponsible, youthful action. As a young man he married an elderly woman for her money; for twenty years he lived with another woman, Nataly, waiting for Mrs. Burman to die. Meredith is not concerned with the lawlessness of Victor's action, but with Victor's inability to face the consequences of his act, to see what he has done to his first wife and what he is doing to Nataly and to his daughter Nesta who is unaware as yet of her illegitimacy. "If we are really for Nature, we are not lawless," Meredith argues at one point (XVII, 121), sanctioning the relationship between Victor and Nataly as a marriage of true minds and hearts. But, ironically, Victor refuses to see the law of nature at work; he is a conventional man in every respect except in his union with Nataly, and he clouds his irregular action with a veil of sentimental rhetoric. Like Sir Willoughby Patterne, he is a "histrionic self-deceiver" (XVII, 55), we discover, who is always willing to be "as deceived as he wished to be" (XVII, 290). When, by accident, Nesta finally discovers the truth of her birth, her first thought is to sympathize with her mother's ordeal, but Victor continues to maintain a rhetorical pose: "Satisfied in being a superficial observer," Meredith notes, "he did not spy to see more than the world would" (XVII, 426). While waiting for Mrs. Burman's death, he sentimentalizes imaginary scenes between them in which she obeys his directorial cue and determines "to end her incomprehensibly lengthened days in reconcilement with him: and he had always been ready to 'forget and forgive.' A truly beautiful old phrase! It thrilled one of the most susceptible of men" (XVII, 47). In the best scene of the novel, Victor, Nataly, and Mrs. Burman finally reassemble after twenty years; the two women sympathize with each other, but Victor misunderstands the nature of the experience involved.

A leader among men, Victor follows Alvan's example in his incomprehension of women. The obligations he owes to the three women in his life are all unsatisfied, and he causes suffering to both wives, ultimately killing the person he loves most dearly. Nesta alone survives and metaphorically conquers; Nataly is destroyed during the course of the novel. In the Victor-Nataly relationship, Meredith expanded the tragedy of the couple in *Modern Love* into a full-scale psychological and sociological study. Having lived a false position for twenty years, Victor relies on "a courageous Nataly to second him" (XVII, 138) in all he does. But she has been under pressure for too long to be able to continue much longer. "We are distracted, perverted, made strangers to ourself by a false position," Meredith notes (XVII, 50). Victor prompts the tragic end by promoting two schemes: the building of a country mansion, Lakelands, in misguided response to Nataly's desire for a small cottage in order to escape from the pressures of London society; and the arranging of a match between the well-meaning, but hopelessly Philistine Dudley Sowerby and Nesta, who is ideally suited for Dartrey. Nataly has hoped only for peace, and, unknown to Victor, has been "living at an intenser strain upon her nature than she or any around her knew" by the time the events of the novel begin (XVII, 117).

In the later Meredith novels the women are generally more intelligent than the men, but they often pay for their fatal insight in the inability to act upon it. The construction of Lakelands reveals to Nataly the commonness of Victor's ambitions, and thenceforth she begins to judge him:

> it was almost as if he had descended to earth from the skies. She now saw his mortality in the miraculous things he did. The reason of it was, that through the perceptible various arts and shifts on her level, an opposing spirit had plainer view of his aim, to judge it. She thought it a mean one [XVII, 173].

Discerning women are Meredith's touchstones. Nataly's discovery is reminiscent of Lady Blandish's painful realization that Sir Austin Feverel's attempt to escape his responsibilities by posing as a god is an admission of his human frailty. When Victor does not find her in complete sympathy with his actions, he momentarily turns his attentions toward the more artfully appreciative Lady Grace. The triangle of *Modern Love* or the Richard-Lucy-Bella relationship in *Richard Feverel* is repeated with a fuller treatment of the problem from all positions involved. Inevitably, Victor and Nataly drift apart emotionally, each taking comfort in his own point of view. While Victor gives way to undue optimism at the situation he thinks he is controlling, Nataly gradually succumbs to alternating emotional hysterics and self-repression. Though her mind remains "rational," Meredith notes, she "had fallen to be one of the solitary who have no companionship save with the wound they nurse, to chafe it rather than try at healing" (XVII, 478).

It is one of the ironies of the book that morbid awareness of the falsity of her position drives Nataly to an ultraconservative view of her daughter's place in society. She fears Dartrey's influence over her, precisely because it would be a liberating one, and she is led to place undue respect in Dudley as a restraining influence. Nataly is one of Meredith's most moving heroines; her regression through the course of the novel, which is halted only during the scene of reconciliation with Mrs. Burman, is as painful to trace as her death is hard to bear. If Victor is a more complex and sympathetic version of Willoughby or Alvan, Nataly is Lucy Feverel grown older and uselessly experienced. A mention of Victor's resorting to the rhetoric of nature leads Meredith to sketch one of his favorite themes: that women are closer to nature because of the suffering they must undergo. "Men call on her for their defence, as a favourable witness: she is a note of their rhetoric. They are not bettered by her sustainment; they have not, as women may have, her enaemic aid at a trying hour. It is not an effort at epigram to say, that whom she scourges most she most supports" (XVII, 139).

Yet Nataly cannot survive the continual self-repression which Victor's incomprehension necessitates, and her death prompts his own collapse and eventual death. In pointed contrast to the catastrophes raised by the inability to face reality or to remain constant to nature is Nesta's triumph at the end of the novel. Nesta Victoria is not only the real victor, as her full name implies, but also Meredith's embodiment of the ideal new Victorian woman, true to Nature and her own nature, selfless and altruistic, and wise in a manner beyond male possibility. The two women are brilliantly juxtaposed, and the decline of the one is balanced by the self-discovery of the other. As the mother cuts herself off from the world and those closest to her, the daughter learns not only of the ambiguity of her position in society but of women's position in general. If *Diana of the Crossways* often reads like a wearisome tract for women's rights, Meredith's subsequent novel vividly embodies the struggles of two generations of women. The younger withstands her ordeal successfully, although the author warns that "sensibilities sharp as Nesta's, are not to be had without their penalties" (XVII, 401). For a moment, like Diana, she feels the desire to escape—with the help of a conventional man like Dudley —the force of "her sex's shudder in the blood" (XVII, 414). But she faces up to her active possibilities in life, evidenced in her championing of the fallen woman, Mrs. Marsett, and by her union with Dartrey. It is Nesta who utters the Meredithian *cri de coeur* in the novel: "There cannot be any goodness unless it is a practiced goodness" (XVII, 341), and it is she who is most fully aware of the humanizing power of laughter. If Clara and Diana have sought for an enlightened, independent role in life, Nesta most entirely embodies the Meredithian "New Woman," although independence is equated with marriage to the proper man. The right man, for Meredith, is the symbolic Dartrey Fenellan, a "manly heart" encased in a "stone figure," as Nataly initially recognizes (XVII, 360).

Nesta succeeds because she is able to channel her energies and imagination:

> This burning Nesta, Victor's daughter, tempered by Nataly's milder blood, was a girl in whom the hard shocks of the knowledge of life, perforce of the hardness upon pure metal, left a strengthening for generous imagination. She did not sit to brood on her injured senses or set them through speculation touching heat; they were taken up and consumed by the fire of her mind. Nor had she leisure for the abhorrences, in a heart all flowing to give aid, and uplift and restore. Self was as urgent in her as in most of the young; but the gift of humour, which had previously diverted it, was now the quick feeling for her sisterhood.

She loves "the lighted world," continues Meredith, and she seeks a balanced nature and an active life. Hers is the discovery of Faust, that through altruistic action one may find peace in the universe:

Far ahead down her journey of the years to come, she did see muffled things she might hope and would strive to do. They were chrysalis shapes. Above all, she flew her blind quickened heart on the wings of an imaginative force; and those of the young who can do that, are in their blood incorruptible by dark knowledge, irradiated under darkness in the mind. Let but the throb be kept for others. This is the one secret, for redemption, if not preservation [XVII, 354–355].

In Nesta, Meredith paid his most affirmative tribute to the powers of youth and womanhood. She is all the more convincing as a character—in contrast to Diana, for example—because of her involvement in a real world and with other characters. Nesta is a Shakespearean heroine, with similarities to Marina or Isabella, above all. While she is suggestive as a poetic symbol of the possibilities of young womanhood, one may argue that, on the modern stage, it is the flawed Claudios or Angelos who make most appeal to credibility. Nesta's victory is a poetic escape from the brooding doubts of such beings. The keynote of her view of nature is contained in her comment to Dudley:

> One day, treating of modern Pessimism, he had draped a cadaverous view of our mortal being in a quotation of the wisdom of the Philosopher Emperor: "To set one's love upon the swallow is a futility." And she, weighing it, nodded and replied: "May not the pleasure for us remain if we set our love upon the beauty of the swallow's flight?" [XVII, 417].

Nesta embodies Meredith's idealism, the idealism built upon a full recognition of reality.

If the young heroine's quest is toward an acceptance of light and useful action, her parents move inevitably toward the domain of darkness, inexpressibility, and impotent endeavor. Nataly finally collapses under the strain. Victor's course in the novel is from incomprehension to incomprehension, although he tries all the while to define an "idea" which inevitably escapes him. Victor's futile search for his lost idea is the central image of the book, and, if he fails because of his inability to see as clearly as his daughter, Meredith's treatment of his blurred point of view is one of the most interesting devices in the novel.

For the first five chapters Meredith chose to introduce the novel through the confused perspective of Victor's mind, beginning with a fall on London Bridge. If Meredith had ever baffled his readers before, he seemed to be doing so with a vengeance in these chapters, containing perhaps the first attempt at an almost continual stream of consciousness in English fiction. (Dujardin had used the method three years earlier in *Les Lauriers sont coupés*.) Meredith justifies his purpose of slowing down the accustomed pace of the novel in order to introduce his main character in this new way, explaining that "if a man's mind is to be taken as a part of him, the likening of it, at an introduction, to an army on the opening march of a great campaign, should plead excuses for tardy forward movements, in consideration of the large amount of matter you have to review before you can at all imagine yourselves to have made his acquaintance." He compares his very different device with that of "the enchanted horse of the Tale, which leaves the man's mind at home while he performs the deeds befitting him" (XVII, 10–11). But Meredith is not aiming at escapist, simpleminded novels for children, he contends, but rather "to the task of the fuller portraiture" of his complex human hero.

The complex presentation of Victor Radnor—seen first of all by means of his mental operations, then from the points of view of everyone around him, including the facile vantage point of the "world"—enables Meredith to create a richly complex individual. Alternately a flat and a rounded character, a sentimental egoist and a well-meaning father, a comic overreacher and a tragic failure, Victor represents, according to Meredith's daughter's account of her father's intention, "a man of a rapid circulation, a prompt assimilation, a benevolent nature, and a loose morality. Such men are sure to conquer and come to naught."[53] Victor typifies the flawed leader of English society—his sexual transgression is brought to light in the period of the Dilke and Parnell scandals—who is successful at executing grandiose schemes but unable to control his private life. His continually "ineffectual catching at the volatile idea" is connected with his inability to recognize his human frailty and hence to conquer himself.[54] The idea is never articulated in Victor's mind, although it is embodied in Nesta's achievement; Victor's career is seen as an unsuccessful attempt at comprehension or articulation.

The maddening obscurity of the first chapters of *One of Our Conquerors* is thus brilliantly functional. The reader is not asked to comprehend what is going on under the rhetoric of evasion, only to see that he is dealing with an uncomprehending individual. The enigmatic first sentence of the novel has been well analyzed by Phyllis Bartlett to show how the novelistic pattern of "paradox, tension, and ambiguity" is set up:[55]

> A GENTLEMAN, noteworthy for a lively countenance and a waistcoat to match it, crossing London Bridge at noon on a gusty April day, was almost magically detached from his conflict with the gale by some sly strip of slipperiness, abounding in that conduit of the markets, which had more or less adroitly performed the trick upon preceding passengers, and now laid this one flat amid the shuffle of feet, peaceful for the moment as the uncomplaining who have gone to Sabrina beneath the tides [XVII, 1].

The mock epic tone perfectly suits the self-styled conqueror who is supremely vulnerable, like the astrologer in La Fontaine who falls into a well. Victor's inability to face elementary facts and his unwillingness to translate rhetoric into articulate sense are both suggested: the "sly strip of slipperiness" is not a Meredithian periphrasis but Victor's own rhetorical substitute for a simple bit of orange peel. It is appropriate that the novel should begin and end with a "fall," and a matter of interest that it should commence and conclude with spring. The fall allows for one of Victor's rare "peaceful" moments, and also a missed chance for moral reflection. He is helped to his feet by a member of the lower class, who dirties the white waistcoat in the process, but Victor is angry for the smudge rather than grateful for the help. Astonished when his anger provokes a rebuke from another man, Victor is described as finding "that enormous beast [the mob] comprehensible only when it applauded him" (XVII, 3). Victor cannot, it seems, make an effective reply to others, and he is "unable to cope" with the other man's charge of his "punctilio." As his mind wanders, he tries to deal with the ensuing "idea in it"—an idea connected with the claims of Nature and of other people—but he is thwarted: "Definition seemed to be an extirpating enemy of this idea, or she was by nature shy" (XVII, 10).

Victor never recovers the idea, although he comes close on occasion. On the first of April, a year later, he and Nataly call upon Mrs. Burman; while the two women pray together, his half-

comprehending mind takes in a sense of the once familiar surroundings amid a dim awareness that he has acted wrongly. The
time on the clock, with a Cupid serving as pendulum ("his own
purchase"), is appropriately off:

> He forgot his estimate of the minutes, he formed a prayer, he
> refused to hear the Cupid swinging, he droned a sound of
> sentences to deaden his ears. Ideas of eternity rolled in semblance
> of enormous clouds. Death was a black bird among them. The
> piano rang to Nataly's young voice and his [Nataly had served
> as companion to Mrs. Burman when Victor met her]. The gold
> and white of the chairs welcomed a youth suddenly enrolled
> among the wealthy by an enamoured old lady on his arm. Cupid
> tick-tocked. —Poor soul! poor woman! How little we mean to
> do harm when we do an injury! An incomprehensible world in-
> deed at the bottom and at the top . . . He heard the cluck of
> a horrible sob coming from him. After a repetition of his short
> form of prayer deeply stressed, he thanked himself with the
> word "sincere," and a queer side-thought on our human suscep-
> tibility to the influence of posture. We are such creatures [XVII,
> 488–489].

Victor has tragically learned nothing. The two women prepare for
death, while the shallow optimist prepares for his triumphant
speech as the first stage of his campaign for Parliament. The
speech is never delivered. While Victor fumbles for his idea, and
an "applausive audience" roars its approval, the news is brought
to him of Nataly's death, and the noise of the audience, which he
has courted all along at the expense of his family, becomes "as
void of human meaning as a sea" (XVII, 505). For Victor, not even
the "tragic hints" gained by the narrator of *Modern Love* are
within reach. He collapses, unable to see Nesta, whose "presence
excites him," and dies without having thought of leaving a will.
The final point of view is that of the unwilling satirist, Colney
Durance, who "considered the shallowness of the abstract Optimist
exposed enough in Victor's history. He was reconciled to it when,
looking on their child, he discerned, that for a cancelling of the
errors chargeable to them, the father and mother had kept faith
with Nature" (XVII, 514).

On a philosophical level, the novel might be described as an
attempt to show the correlation of the laws of nature and society.
At several points in the book, debates are held over the rights of

the individual as opposed to the rights of society—with Victor always on the side of the repression of the individual. By implication, and through the example of Nesta, Meredith argues that the individual needs society for his sphere of activity, just as society needs enlightened individuals for the sake of developing civilization. Meredith provides a bridge between Mill and Lawrence: the full expression of individualism is seen as a social obligation. Dartrey and Nesta continue to live in English society, at any rate —the last such ending in Meredith's fiction for one of his ideally mated couples. His next two pairs escape to Switzerland and Spain, respectively, and the "amazing marriage" of his last novel turns out ultimately to be a brother-sister relationship.

The realization of the complete dissolution of Victorian relationships in the last two Meredith novels does not invalidate his attempt in *One of Our Conquerors* to end the book with a symbolic marriage. It is, nevertheless, the self-destruction of England's symbolic conqueror which sticks longest in the mind—just as it is his inability to attain perspective which makes the tragedy credible and modern. The leader of men and the slave of rhetoric, Victor might easily be a contemporary political figure, and Meredith vividly suggests how personal blindness can also occasion national devastation. Trollope's Melmotte (in *The Way We Live Now*) and Dickens' Merdle (in *Little Dorrit*) are both symbolic leaders of a decaying society, but Victor Radnor succeeds both in his symbolic role and as a complex human figure. Hunter and hunted, conqueror and conquered, he is one of the richest figures in Victorian fiction, despite and often because of the rhetorical veil through which he unconsciously regards life and through which Meredith is semi-consciously led to regard him. Victor's struggle for articulation is as futile as his inability to understand is unshakeable. But Meredith was himself unable to express his theme fully. Thus, the overt theme is the necessity to face the facts: "a frank acceptance of Reality is the firm basis of the Ideal," as Meredith insisted.[56] But the implied theme is that reality is indescribable and probably incomprehensible. Against his will, Meredith unconsciously found himself agreeing with Gissing and the author of the Mark Rutherford novels. The earlier Victorians, in contrast, had believed in an intelligible universe, and, hence, in their abilities to transform it if need be. Nesta's triumph can be demonstrated only in terms of a symbolic marriage to a "stone figure," and Victor's career can be expressed only with a language that is often as obscure as his own point of view.

To a French admirer, Meredith later asked that *One of Our Conquerors* be looked upon "as a kind of literary vengeance" on his uncomprehending critics,[57] but that may have been an effort at self-justification after the fact. Shortly after its publication he complained, "The Novel has been knocked about by reviewers, as I expected. And clearly there is no further chance of peace between us. What they call digressions, is a presentation of the atmosphere of the present time, of which the story issues."[58] It is possible to see Meredith's intention, however, without disguising one's recognition that at times the novel is indeed, in Priestley's phrase, "a charnel-house of slain English," which often amounts to unconscious self-parody. Henley had complained of that tendency in Meredith to be "brilliant to the point of being obscure"; and the last issue of *The Yellow Book*, of all places, contained an attack on Meredith's "preciosity" of language, with the admission of its author that "With the exception of Zola's *La Terre*—hard reading for a different reason—*One of Our Conquerors* was the hardest novel to read that I ever met with."[59]

For a novel about obscurity, it is both fitting and unfortunate that *One of Our Conquerors* should be largely impenetrable, despite the existence of three major characters and the imposing shadow of a fourth, Mrs. Burman. In an interesting comparison of the two manuscripts of the novel in the Yale Library, Fred C. Thomson argues that Meredith's revisions were aimed at providing "a sometimes effective camouflage for what is often mediocre intellectual and psychological content."[60] "Camouflage" is, however, an apt word for describing both the style and theme of the novel, and, if the second manuscript attempts to change the conception of Victor as "a vulgar climber" in the first, it does so only in Victor's own eyes and those of the world. The original title, *A Conqueror in Our Time*, suggests a link with Lermontov's novel of a symbolically flawed self-destructive romantic, *A Hero of Our Time*. The final title, as mentioned earlier, comes from *General Ople and Lady Camper*: "You would not have cared one bit for a caricature," as the chastened General is told, "if you had not nursed the absurd idea of being one of our conquerors." But the horror of Victor's catastrophe is that he is indeed one of the conquerors of society, one of the props of its mercantile foundations, whose blindness has devastating implications. Similarly, Meredith's inability to articulate what he means is a symbolic gesture of the inability of the Victorian novel to continue to deal with a new and incomprehensible world. As long as incomprehension is Meredith's subject, the novel is paradoxically accessible, but, where a symbolic solution is offered (and in the late novels, only symbolic solutions are offered), it can only seem beyond the realm of possibility, just as it is beyond the realm of intelligibility in the accustomed forms of language.

"He writes with the pen of a great artist in his left hand and the razor of a spiritual suicide in his right," quipped Henley.[61] Perhaps the reverse is truer. Meredith was a great spiritual force but an artistic suicide. He often visualized his readers as children but attempted to reach them by appealing to philosophical abstractions. Even the wisest of novelists have made efforts at being accessible, but Meredith in the bulk of his work demands to be taken on his own highly complex level. In works like *Diana of the Crossways* and *One of Our Conquerors*, he became the victim of his own gifts, and in the two succeeding novels, *Lord Ormont and His Aminta* and *The Amazing Marriage*, he created literary abominations. His failure in the 1890's to continue in the Victorian mode, which was the natural accompaniment to his essentially Victorian outlook, resulted in literary hybrids of sporadic interest but overall fatigue. In his earlier work—in *Modern Love, Harry Richmond*, and *The Egoist*, for example—he had managed to utilize and channel his energies effectively and movingly, but it is in a novel like *One of Our Conquerors*, which expresses his multiple talents at their fullest, that his artistic weakness is most cruelly exposed. The expounder of a philosophy of harmony and clarity, he gave way to discord and obfuscation, even if in the process he made an interesting thematic point.

One of Our Conquerors appeared the year after *The Tragic Muse*, James's most Victorian novel in scope and yet his first modern novel in theme. It is interesting to see how a non-Victorian novelist could bring off a neo-Victorian novel—a conscious attempt on James's part to write within the old form—by utilizing a keen visual sense for detail and an acquaintance with the methods of previous Victorian novelists. If Meredith's call was for the novel as philosophy, James chose instead to utilize the art of fiction. If stylistically Meredith stood at the Victorian crossways, he was too committed to Victorian ideas of individual duty and of social law to be able to acquiesce to the necessity for artistic solipsism, which, as was becoming apparent, seemed the only way that art could survive into the modern world. But then Meredith was not devoted to art. Philosophically, he mistrusted it; instinctively, he produced his best works under its accidental guidance. The history of the modern novel begins as an escape not only from Victorian ideas and laws but from ideas of any sort and from laws other than one's own as an artist.

In describing the achievement of Browning and Tennyson, Meredith had argued that "Poets like these must be studied by the light of their own manifested powers. They have subjected their faults, and made them peculiarities or characteristics of their work, springing originally from penetrative insight, from imaginative complexity of perception, or from defective or superabundant energy of expression. They are to themselves 'both law and impulse.' "[62] Victorian individualists, however, were as much Victorian as they were individualistic. Such figures spoke to their times, even if an audience was not always willing to listen or reform. Meredith was a member of this group, whose individual energies contended and combined with the aims of their society. The great Victorians had a tendency to stand apart from their age, to criticize it with a fervor that makes them seem suspiciously modern. Yet the criticism was for the sake of the continuation of that society.

A gifted individualist and a dutiful citizen, Meredith was the last of the age of Carlyle, Mill, Arnold, Ruskin, Tennyson, and George Eliot. With Henry James, the Victorian crossways were finally passed over; for all practical purposes, they had never existed for him. Meredith, on the other hand, can be seen as a representative of the late Victorian world at its best, brilliant but also self-contradictory and, finally, self-destructive. He is himself one of the greatest ruins of an age which he attempted first to enlighten and entertain, and then, unsuccessfully, to salvage. But, if he failed in his philosophical mission, he did create several great novels and a few magnificent poems, and he preached a noble wisdom. Despite his efforts, the Victorian age inevitably collapsed, but in Meredith's best works the best of Victorianism is preserved in such a way that its message seems, at times, startlingly relevant today.

Part III.   Henry James and the Americanization of English Fiction

Introduction

Not long before his death, Meredith described James in the following way:

> His books are hard reading, but I have to read one every year.
> You know the book which he calls *The American Scene*. The
> substance of it all is not a revisiting of America, but a tour of
> James's own inside. He doesn't tell about America, but how he
> felt when he saw this or that in America. Now and then, he goes
> so far as to lead you to a little window in his anatomy, and
> show you a glimpse of landscape that he says is America. But
> taken all in all, it's very little one sees beyond the interior of
> my dear James.[1]

Samuel Butler's contention that every work of art is a portrait of the artist is a distinctly modern idea, a product of the Romantic belief that it is the artist's duty to express his unique individuality in his work. In 1883, in an account of his own artistic views to an admirer, Meredith noted that a novelist, while bound to "present a picture of life," is limited in fact to only "a narrow portion of life." His own aim, therefore, was to "keep my eyes on the larger outlook, as little as possible on myself."[2] One reason Meredith seems suspiciously modern to contemporary readers is that his novels are so personal in style and so revealing in subject matter. His literary battle against egoism was in fact a battle against his own subjective temperament. Meredith attained objectivity by reason of this self-realization and his Stendhalian ability to present his own egoism in perspective—to see it as the laughable and potentially tragic force animating so many of his countrymen in a time of crisis.

Meredith's call for self-awareness and self-discipline derives ultimately from Goethe's warning against the subjectivity of periods (like his own) in decline. "Every healthy effort," Goethe remarked to Eckermann, "is directed from the inward to the outward world."[3] Meredith's witty criticism of *The American Scene*, quoted above, indicates an important source of difference between himself and James, despite their personal friendship, their literary similarities, and their mutual romanticism. Meredith was a Romantic of the variety extending from Goethe to Nietzsche, who argued the need for sublimating the impulses of what in their own cases were intensely individualistic wills for the purpose of serving mankind; James was a Romantic in the manner of Pater, who argued the need for the liberation of the will from all external claims for the sake of feeling aesthetic sensations.

André Malraux has described the nature of Manet's influence on modern painting in words which also describe James's importance for the modern novel: "To realize his *Portrait of Clemenceau* Manet had to dare to be everything in the portrait, and Clemenceau next to nothing." But, like James, Manet related his subject to more than himself; "it was primarily a matter of Clemenceau according to painting as such."[4] James's major difference from Pater lay in his own ability to convert subjective impressions into literature, to relate his aesthetic consciousness of "life" to the enduring realm of "art." James's aesthetic awareness was sufficiently Pateresque so that in his novels he could celebrate those qualities of helpless discrimination in his heroes and heroines which make them connoisseurs of life, very much like himself, rather than active participants. It was James's contribution to fiction that, along with Hardy, Moore, and Gissing, he not only codified the subjective nature of the novelist, but transformed the hero of fiction into a limited, passive observer. In order to relate life to art, the life and the artist first had to be of a special nature; what seemed, to Moore especially, a new freedom of opportunities for the novelist became instead a major restriction to him in terms of choice of subject matter and scope of artistic sensibility.

Even in his early fiction James can be seen as writing for the sake of solving personal, artistic problems and for fiction's own sake. For a time, however, he aspired to objectivity and breadth. Impressed by Goethe as a young man, James for a time tried to assume a classical stance in his critical essays, but by the late 1870's he yielded to the impressionistic methods of Sainte-Beuve. As a novelist, James attempted, until the mid-1880's, to suppress his romantic bent. His familiarity with the French naturalists persuaded his own critics that he was a disciple of realism during much of his writing career. (James's use of passive characters and unhappy endings was ascribed to his adoption of "realism," not to his personal predilection.) James blamed the flourishing of the romance in America on the scarcity of materials suitable for fiction: Hawthorne, for example, was forced to draw upon his own narrow background to make up for the lack of manners and customs in America. By choosing to live in England, James ostensibly turned his back on both the romance as his literary form and romanticism as his philosophy. But in spite of his efforts to utilize the resources of England and English fiction, he found himself depending more and more on his own superior point of view, even as he developed his own advanced fictional system. James's defining impression of England derived from highly colored fictional sources at first. When England did not live up to his aesthetic expectations, he populated his novels and stories with autobiographical projections which do manage (as he says of Hyacinth Robinson) to "keep up the standard."

It is in his fictional work of the 1880's, above all, that the tension between James's early ambitions and his emerging subjectivity is most evident. In an age of transition James first attempted to make use of the literary example of others and then to follow his own inclinations. In *The Portrait of a Lady* he memorably exposed the limitations of the American illusion of self-sufficiency, even though he also memorably articulated the craving for freedom. In *The Bostonians* he satirized the mixture of narrowness of point of view and fanatical devotion to personal causes which characterized his countrymen. In *The Princess Casamassima*, however, he depicted the danger to Jamesian individuals posed by the presumed reformers of society, and in *The Tragic Muse* James advocated the withdrawal from all obligations other than to the practice of art. Art alone is serious, as a character in *The Tragic Muse* declares, while society is "humbug and imbecility." Thereafter, James chose to go his own way, and the English novel, unimpressed by Meredith's warning in opposition, went along with him.

[7] All for Art, or the World Well Lost

He looked at all things from the standpoint of the artist, felt all life as literary material. There are people who will tell me that this is a poor way of feeling it, and I am not concerned to defend my statement—having space merely to remark that there is something to be said for any interest which makes a man feel so much.
(James, "The Author of Beltraffio")

Every novelist's biography reminds us of the extent to which the literary artist is at the mercy of the materials which surround, form, and inform him, but one is often embarrassed at the degree to which the novelist may become (as James called Hawthorne) an "intellectual vampire," preying upon the artistic natural resources at hand. Again and again, James pursued the simple logic of this part of the artist's role; in the figure of Mark Ambient, the author of *Beltraffio*, he indicated that the personal sacrifices made in behalf of one's art are as debilitating in their way as is the sacrifice of one's art to his life, as made by Henry St George in "The Lesson of the Master." If mere living deprives the novelist of artistic strength (which is the Master's lesson), a full artistic life, such as Ambient's, is inextricably connected to sterility and death. Ambient's ambivalence is characteristic of James, for whom the artist was at once the embalmer of life and a man unable to live. Life, for James, characteristically meant the opportunity to see, the capacity to collect impressions, and the working ability to transform impressions into books. "The great thing was to live," as one of his hack-novelist characters perceives, "because that gave you material."[1]

Even if we make allowances for the amount of fictionalizing which he put into them, James's memoirs of his childhood inspire a sense of awe and dismay at the ease with which the future novelist turned his natural passivity into the prerequisite for an artistic career. His amazing memory for the details of his early life only accents the poverty of actual experience. "The truth is doubtless, however, much less in the wealth of my experience," he confides, "than in the tenacity of my impression, the fact that I have lost nothing of what I saw."[2] The fact that he distorted incidents from his youth, and even rewrote letters from his father and William, was part of the process by which the elderly memoirist converted the muddle of life into art. But the same process began early enough, as the earliest surviving (published) letters show. A mock romantic letter survives from James when he was a seventeen-year-old devourer of novels of high life and fashionable romance. Playfully utilizing the coincidence of his last name with G. P. R. James's, he sketched a humorous self-portrait for his friend T. S. Perry: "Born of a race who counted their ancestors far back into the dim ages of chivalry he seemed to have been endowed by the Wizard Nature, both with the fiery indomitable spirit of those times and with their softer attributes of poesy and romance."[3]

If the major conditioning fact of his youth was the instability, the rootlessness, the wanderings of his family circle, which turned him into an observer caught between worlds, another related factor governing his choice of observations was his early absorption in the world of self-indulgence and romance. Left to himself, he improvised reality. Absorbed in books from an early age, James reminds one of Dickens' strangely similar conditioning. It has long been argued that the distinctive point of view in Dickens' novels was partly the result of an imagination fixed in an isolated childhood and overcolored by his reading. As a result, the argument continues, what the mature author saw and felt was controlled and conditioned by the child's reaction.[4] To the qualified degree to which this is true of Dickens, it was also true of James.

James is in the line of the great invalid novelists, although, like Proust's, his invalidism was partly a matter of choice. From an early age, he learned to detach his powers of observation from his body and live by the power of the eyes. His is almost the legend of St. Lucy in reverse: unlike the Saint who plucked out her eyes so that she might consecrate herself entirely to God, James abandoned most other human needs for the sake of visual consciousness. "Impressions were not merely all right," he recalled of his youth, "but were the dearest things in the world; only one would have gone to the stake rather than in the first place confessed to some of them, or in the second announced that one really lived by them and built on them."[5] James gave his father credit for much of his conditioning: the freedom of family life, the primacy of *being* over doing, the injunction that the value of life lay in the conversion of waste into subjective use. Henry James, Sr., did not recognize mistakes or failures since, on the transcendental plane, mere doing was insignificant. Even the act of writing was superfluous for the father since "When a man *lives*, that is lives enough, he can scarcely write." The result in young Henry, as he later explained it, was a "fatalistic philosophy of which the general sense was that almost anything, however disagreeable, had been worth while" so long as an "impressional harvest" was produced.[6]

A dialogue developed, therefore, between Henry and what he saw, a small boy and "others," active life and art, between the actions of his brothers and his own vicarious absorption of their experiences. But if the "liveliest" impression of his youth was the sense "that life and knowledge were simply mutual opposites," there was a compensation for one's impotence in the use of one's consciousness. Such, at least, is the elder novelist's tribute to his youthful ability to convert limitations into victories, to learn to live by the eyes, so that if "one should cease to live in large measure by one's eyes . . . one would have taken the longest step towards not living at all."[7] Meanwhile, he became conscious of fine discriminations.

In "The Lesson of the Master" James was to argue, with mingled rue and irony, the need for the artist—one artist, at least—to abandon his manhood and the desire to live. Nonetheless, for James there was a distinction between mere "living" and "Life," the one connected with experience (such as the artist absorbs vicariously) and the other with artistic sentience (the process of absorption). Lambert Strether's great plea to "live" in *The Ambassadors* is qualified into the injunction to "see" (as Leon Edel points out),[8] and sight was the only one of James's senses—aside, curiously, from taste—to matter to him. It was the one of his faculties which could be put to use and which required the least need for reflection. One has the painful feeling when reading James's minor works—and they appear in all of his phases—that a bit less self-confidence might have been advantageous, that more than a sense of artistic discrimination would have made him a greater writer; without the confidence, however, he could never have continued to write. Planning one of his weakest stories, James argued with himself that thin though the substance of "Two Countries" might be, "It is always enough if the *author* sees substance in it."[9]

With such immense confidence in his powers, it was immeasurably to James's advantage to be, for most of his life, caught between the American and European points of view. If one of his pre-eminently American traits was his faith in his individuality, his freedom as an artist, one of his European features was his awareness of the illusion of freedom, of the necessity for conventions, of the fact of conditioning. As an American-raised artist, he naturally needed, he felt, the artistically useful materials of Europe. The strength of much of his best fiction, especially the work of the 1880's, lies in the tension between opposing worlds, opposing claims, opposing values. The period of James's literary apprenticeship, from the mid-1860's to 1880, was very largely one of trying to choose between such contraries as Europe or America, the novel or the romance, realism or the romantic mode, a public and conventional or a private and artistic life.

At the beginning of his career, James's ambitions were ambitious, eclectic, and objective. The tone of his early reviews is dogmatic, for the most part, although without being consistent. The critic "is in the nature of his function *opposed* to his author," James argued in 1865, and he made a distinction between great criticism, like Goethe's, which is the fruit of ideas and objective standards, and impressionistic criticism, like Sainte-Beuve's, which stems from personal observation and a fine sense for detail. Assuming the mantle of Goethe for the moment, he condemned Whitman's "Drum Taps" on account of the author's egoism: "art requires, above all things," he reminded the poet, "a suppression of one's self, a subordination of one's self to an idea." (He would later on take back his verdict on Whitman and also the grounds for his judgment.) Giving the impression of a sage, James attacked one novel for being "void of human nature and false to actual society," and recommended that its author "study the canons of the so-called realist school." The realism of Trollope irritated him, however, because the characters and events appeared commonplace and the novels devoid of thought. He recommended the study of the French realists to the English, the English moralists to the French, and both as models to the Americans. Eleven years away from writing his first good novel, *Roderick Hudson*, the twenty-one-year-old James professed bitter disappointment to find in a collection of essays on fiction no "canons," no code for the judgment of novels.[10] Twenty years later, in "The Art of Fiction," he would attack Walter Besant for trying to weigh the novel down with rules.

Despite the occasional bullying tone and the pretense of omniscience in affairs of the world and the heart, the early reviews also contain many points central to James's later views on the novel and many issues to be treated in his novels. In 1867 he was already comparing the novelist to the historian, linking the achievement of Balzac with Motley, and declaring that the storytelling might well write with the historian's sense of logic, dealing with "a circle of incidents from which there is no arbitrary issue." In his first long essay, a study of "The Novels of George Eliot," he argued that it is the duty of the critic "to seek out some key" to the artist's method, "some indication of his ruling theory" (a commandment Arnoldian in origin, which James satirized in "The Figure in the Carpet"). Furthermore, it is the duty of the novelist to create a form in which the reader is made to share "quite half the labour," since "the writer makes the reader very much as he makes his characters." The power of the artist is the mark of his freedom, and James opposed to Henry Kingsley's Victorian ideal of duty "a sentiment higher" still—"the sentiment of freedom."[11]

By 1868, with the publication of a dozen fairly slight tales behind him, James realized that he was no Goethe, either in criticism or fiction, and that his affinities were with the more limited, the less moral and philosophical, the more subjective and approachable (and no less judicious) Sainte-Beuve. An important personal remark, inserted in a review of a minor novel, indicated James's directions from 1868 on in the matter of open-mindedness, in the willingness to study and experiment, and in the achievement of the future writer of partial portraits and opposing points of view: "The day of dogmatic criticism is over, and with it the ancient infallibility and tyranny of the critic. No critic lays down the law, because no reader receives the law ready made. The critic is simply a reader like all the others—a reader who prints his impressions. All he claims is, that they are honest; and when they are unfavorable, he esteems it quite as simple a matter that he should publish them as when they are the reverse."[12]

The awareness of his limitations as sage and writer came just before his first unaccompanied trip to Europe in 1869. As an American writer, he had been too much at the mercy of his limited inventive powers and his reading habits; the literary results had been mainly dry romances with ambiguous, vacillating heroines and heroes who die of love. In Europe he discovered that his visual consciousness could serve him in better stead as an artist than it had in America. With his first step on Liverpool soil, he felt that as an artist he had come home from exile.

It should be noted that, from the very beginning, he noticed flaws in his dreams of Europe: he discovered that the lazy, absorbent atmosphere of Italy was fatal to artistic production; that French life was too much a matter of polish and surface, morally insecure; and that England, his eventual adoptive home, was massive, often ugly, and intellectually stultifying. In 1870 he could already enunciate what would be a major part of his critical depiction of England in the 1880's and 1890's. "The English have such a mortal mistrust of anything like criticism or 'keen analysis' (which they seem to regard as a kind of maudlin foreign flummery)," he wrote to William, "that I rarely remember to have heard on English lips any other intellectual verdict (no matter under what provocation) than this broad synthesis—'so immensely clever.' What exasperates you is not that they can't say more, but that they wouldn't if they could." However, he quickly added, "Ah, but they are a great people for all that. . ."[13] He appreciated the English as if they were works of art or the inspiration for such creations (I know them as if I had invented them, he insisted many years later); and so he forgave their lack of inner "character." As he wrote to his mother in 1869, Americans have an abundance of inner resources—was he not himself proof of that?—but they lack artistic finish. Despite the native possession of "energy, capacity and intellectual stuff in ample measure," the American lacks "culture," which is evident in his "poverty of voice, of speech and of physiognomy":

> The pleasantness of the English, on the other side, comes in a great measure from the fact of their each having been dipped into the crucible, which gives them a sort of coating of comely varnish and colour. They have been smoothed and polished by mutual social attrition.[14]

"The tone of things is, somehow, heavier [with the English] than with us," he remarked in an early travel sketch; "manners and modes are more absolute and positive; they seem to swarm and to thicken the atmosphere about you. Morally and physically it is a denser air than ours. We seem loosely hung together at home as compared with the English, every man of whom is a tight fit in his place."[15]

The distinguishing point of his admiration for England reflected not so much an Arnoldian devotion to culture as, thus early in life, a tendency to regard England as material for literary ends. The usual comparison of James and Arnold, in view of their common interest in "culture," is misleading: for Arnold, culture was a means of broadening the outlook of the English; for James, it was a *fait accompli*, which the artist needed for his work. In the sense that he was at the mercy of what his eyes could absorb, he was a man without a commitment to country or ethics, other than what could be used for artistic pigment. He admitted that his interest in London was "chiefly that of an observer in a place where there is most in the world to observe."[16] His impressions of London were, however, preconditioned by his youthful absorption of *Punch* and Thackeray; in 1891 he could still speak of English life as "a big pictured story-book."[17] James is the artist *par excellence* in the sense that Mark Ambient (in the passage quoted at the head of this chapter) is the consummate Jamesian. "His world was all material," James similarly noted of the figurehead of the aesthetic movement, Théophile Gautier,[18] and James projected this image of himself upon the other writers he treated in the 1870's. Hence, Balzac had no other convictions than his devotion to the novel,

James claimed in 1875. Since a "monarchical society is unquestionably more picturesque, more available for the novelist than any other," and since "Bishops, abbés, priests, Jesuits, are invaluable figures in fiction, and the morality of the Catholic Church allows of an infinite *chiaroscuro*," accordingly Balzac was a royalist and a Catholic.[19]

The most extensive elaboration of this fascinating, if somewhat superficial, attitude occurs in the volume on Hawthorne (1879), in which James bade his farewell to America and to the romance for their mutual thinness of atmosphere. If Hawthorne was only a limited romancer, "a valuable moral" may be adduced: "that the flower of art blooms only where the soil is deep, that it takes a great deal of history to produce a little literature, that it needs a complex social machinery to set a writer in motion." Poor Hawthorne—so the thesis proceeds—was guiltless of "theory," had never heard of "Realism," was doomed to attend Bowdoin College rather than Oxford, was simple-minded enough to call a "strolling tailor" a "gentleman" (shades of *Evan Harrington!*), and was trapped within the "cold, bright air of New England" which blew through him and his writings. Yet Hawthorne was an acknowledged master! In a country barren of "paraphernalia," Hawthorne was forced to gather whatever was left and handy to his artistic calling. Therefore, the older novelist decided to transmute the "heavy moral burden" of New England Puritanism into "the light and charming fumes of artistic production":

> Nothing is more curious and interesting [James declares] than
> this almost exclusively *imported* character of the sense of sin
> in Hawthorne's mind; it seems to exist there merely for an
> artistic or literary purpose. He had ample cognizance of the
> Puritan conscience; it was his natural heritage; it was reproduced
> in him; looking into his soul, he found it there. But his relation
> to it was only, as one may say, intellectual; it was not moral
> and theological. He played with it, and used it as a pigment;
> he treated it, as the metaphysicians say, objectively.[20]

This astounding passage should indicate, I think, that James was not as philosophically similar to Hawthorne as has been argued by F. O. Matthiessen, Marius Bewley, F. R. Leavis, and T. S. Eliot. Even James's much quoted tribute to Hawthorne's "deeper psychology" appears in context as another item of usable artistic material:

> The fine thing in Hawthorne is that he cared for the deeper psychology, and that, in his way, he tried to become familiar with it. This natural, yet fanciful, familiarity with it; this air, on the author's part, of being a confirmed *habitué* of a region of mysteries and subtleties, constitutes the originality of his tales.[21]

Taking issue with a French critic who had labeled Hawthorne a pessimist, James blithely argued that, in the instance of "Young Goodman Brown," it "means nothing as regards Hawthorne's own state of mind, his conviction of human depravity and his consequent melancholy [the French critic's contention]; for the simple reason that, if it meant anything, it would mean too much."[22] Yet if (for James) his New England conscience was a given rather than a self-made quality, Hawthorne seemed deeper, nonetheless, than the typical French realist like Flaubert, whose "theory as a novelist . . . is to begin on the outside. Human life, we may imagine his saying, is before all things a spectacle, an occupation and entertainment for the eyes."[23] James denied to Baudelaire any sense of real evil, since "he knew evil not by experience, not as something within himself, but by contemplation and curiosity, as something outside of himself, by which his own intellectual agility was not in the least discomposed . . . A good way to embrace Baudelaire at a glance is to say that he was, in his treatment of evil, exactly what Hawthorne was not—Hawthorne, who felt the thing at its source, deep in the human consciousness."[24] If Hawthorne and Baudelaire were at the mercy of different resources, however, they were still united for James in their ability to turn their conditioned ways of looking at life to artistic advantage. Moral issues as such are never more than artists' pigments. "Morality for James," as Richard Poirier has suggestively remarked, "is a kind of educated cosmopolitanism of the spirit."[25] In "The Art of Fiction" he considered the "moral question" of the novel to be a matter of "the quality of the mind of the producer." The most moral novelist, in this somewhat Pateresque sense, is he upon whom "nothing is lost."

James's determination to treat everything only in the light of art occasioned a peculiar habit of mind indeed. Political or philosophical matters, for example, were treated in the light of aesthetics. In France he was struck by the "picturesque aspect" of politics and by the romantic "spectacle" of a standing army. He even commented on the "high pictorial value" of the English poor, and he could "imagine no spectacle more touching, more thrilling and even dramatic" than the decline of England.[26] In 1877 he wondered whether, to retain her "dramatic epoch," England might " 'take' something": "There is the *Spectator*, who wants her to occupy Egypt: can't she occupy Egypt?" In the same letter (admired by T. S. Eliot) in which he thanked God he had "no *opinions*" with regard to the Dreyfus trial, he also defended the British Empire, which he tended to treat as an artistic creation. Even in 1915, in the midst of his active war effort, he managed to remark that "What is really tragic" about occupied Belgium "is that such an uninteresting little nation should have found itself in such an interesting situation."[27]

In 1874 he wrote to a friend about his addiction "to sentimentalizing . . . the whole *mise en scène* of Italian life" and bade her "pity our poor bare country"—"unendowed, unfurnished, unentertained and unentertaining." He remarked apropos of a picturesque hospital in Warwickshire that such an institution seemed "indeed to exist primarily for the sake of its spectacular effect upon the American tourists." Elsewhere, he suggested, in opposition to the Ruskinian moral view of art, a Pateresque position: "Art is the one corner of human life in which we may take our ease. To justify our presence there the only thing that is demanded of us is that we shall have a passion for representation."[28] Sometimes, when James went too far in taking his artistic ease, he realized that something was wrong. Seeing a picturesque group of Jesuits and their young charges, he gave way to an artificial glow of rhetoric: "We all know the monstrous practices of these people; yet as I watched the group I verily believe I declared that if I had a little son he should go to Mondragone and receive their crooked teachings, for the sake of the other memories—the avenues of cypress and ilex, the view of the Campagna, the atmosphere of antiquity." Thus far, James was giving way to the Gilbert Osmond side of his nature. "But," he continued, "doubtless, when a sense of the picturesque has brought one to this, it is time one should pause." At the sight of Italian poverty, "the tourist can hardly help wondering whether the picture is not half spoiled for pleasure by all that it suggests of the hardness of human life." Surveying the "spectacle" of a young Italian in Genoa ("such a figure had been exactly what was wanted to set off the landscape"), James was startled to discover that up close there was "an unhappy, underfed, unemployed" communist. "This made it very absurd of me," he confessed, "to have looked at him simply as a graceful ornament to the prospect, an harmonious little figure in the middle distance. 'Damn the prospect, damn the middle distance!' would have been all *his* philosophy."[29]

James's most significant comment on the artistic way of life (as he conceived it) occurs in his essay on the hyperaesthetic Gautier:

> He could look every day at a group of beggars sunning them-
> selves on the Spanish Steps at Rome, against their golden wall
> of mouldering travertine, and see nothing but the fine
> brownness of their rags and their flesh-tints—see it and enjoy
> it for ever, without an hour's disenchantment, without a
> chance of one of those irresistible revulsions of mood in which
> the "mellowest" rags are but filth, and filth is poverty, and
> poverty a haunting shadow, and picturesque squalor a mockery.

Yet for James, this "unfaltering robustness of vision—of appetite, one may say—" justified Gautier's disposition and made him "not only strong but enviable."[30] One rather hopes that his enunciation of Gautier's defects was not merely moral rhetoric, but one cannot be sure. Similarly, one cannot be sure whether in *The Princess Casamassima* James was not merely using a squalid environment for scenic effect.

It is one of the wonders of art that, despite such crippling limitations of personality and intelligence, James managed to write so many, and often such intelligent, novels, stories, essays, and travel sketches. Unlike Meredith, who often squandered his magnificent gifts, James put every one of his resources to effective use—much of the time, at any rate. The contact with Europe made a novelist and, for a while, a realist out of him. Aware of the oppositions between and within nations, cultures, individuals, values, James discerned that it was best not to choose one over the other but to utilize the strengths and limitations on both sides. No critical account of *Roderick Hudson* or "The Madonna of the Future," therefore, is adequate which claims to find a resolution to the dualisms involved in those works.

There have been far worse first novels than *Watch and Ward* (1871), and, while James did not take the sort of imaginative chances which Meredith had taken in his first novel (*The Shaving of Shagpat*), he did provide a sense of literary control over his work. In this slight, short Victorian novel about a jilted lover's attempt to bring up a young girl to be his bride, James infused a genuine charm into the character of his heroine. He anticipated the creation of many of his memorable figures when he has Nora warned, prior to her departure for Europe: "Promise me not to lose this blessed bandage of American innocence."[31] A rare event in a James novel, the delicate hero wins his bride at the conclusion. The best of James's early stories, by and large, are laid in Europe and reflect the contrast between "innocent" American travelers or expatriates, hungry for experience and art, and experienced Europeans, like the Signorina in "At Isella" (1871), who desire only simplicity and nature. "I have come on a pilgrimage," the narrator of that story declares: "To understand what I mean, you must have lived, as I have lived, in a land beyond the seas, barren of romance and grace. This Italy of yours . . . is the home of history, of beauty, of the arts—of all that makes life splendid and sweet."[32]

The mixture of naïveté and longing works much better in "At Isella" than in the more famous "A Passionate Pilgrim" (1871), set in England, whose central character is a poor, delicate, sickly American with a "passionate relish for the old, the artificial, and social." "I came into the world an aristocrat," he moans. "I was born with a soul for the picturesque. It condemns me, I confess; but in a measure, too, it absolves me . . . I should have been born here and not there; here my vulgar idleness would have been—don't laugh now!—would have been elegant leisure."[33]

James's first masterpiece dates from 1873. If the artist begins by imitating others, "The Madonna of the Future" is an example of superb pastiche, as good in its way as Balzac's famous parable

"*Le Chef d'oeuvre inconnu,*" its model. Set in Florence, James's story deals with an American expatriate whose romantic dreams have turned to impotent delusions. "I have chosen never to manifest myself by imperfection," Theobald claims; he laments, like James in his study of Hawthorne, the superficiality to which American artists, "excluded from the magic circle," are "condemned." In contrast to Theobald, with his romantic and ill-fated dream of painting a madonna of the future, is a clever, cynical sculptor who specializes in statues which mock human affections and pretensions. Poised somewhere between these extremes of romantic idealism and cynical realism is James's American narrator, who offers his countryman sound advice: "The worthy part is to do something fine! There's no law in our glorious Constitution against that. Invent, create, achieve!"[34] An ambiguity of motive on James's part arises from the fact that the narrator indirectly causes Theobald's death by showing him that he has failed in his goal. The narrator's role in the story would henceforth remain a problem for James, as would the trustworthiness of the predominant point of view.

In a number of works in the mid-1870's, James experimented with various literary models and themes which would reappear later. In "Professor Fargo" (1874), for example, he adapted the Westervelt-Magnetic Lady aspect of *The Blithedale Romance* into a story about "spiritual magnetism" which looks ahead to *The Bostonians,* as well as two works by friends of his: Howells' *The Undiscovered Country* and George du Maurier's *Trilby.* In "Eugene Pickering" (1874) he resorted to the Turgenev pattern of a weak young man caught between a strong, possessive woman and an inexperienced girl. In "Crawford's Consistency" (1876), using an idea suggested by his father, James depicted a peculiarly ambiguous hero whose constancy may be interpreted as either the height of idealism or the gesture of a masochist. The pitiable heroine of "Four Meetings" (1877) may also be the victim of idealism turned to masochism. Having dreamed of Europe as fervently as Theobald, Caroline Spencer is victimized when she finally makes her brief pilgrimage. If Caroline is kept from the "picturesque" Old World by the selfishness of her cousin, Europe comes to Caroline, in the form of her cousin's wife, to be taken care of. The appetite for Europe, for romance, frequently results in a bitter aftertaste.

The two most curious stories of the period, undoubtedly, are "Madame de Mauves" (1874) and "Rose-Agathe" (1878), literary failures for contrary reasons. James's worst efforts were arguably the results either of his inability to keep himself out of his works, as in the first story, or of his attempt to write a completely objective, mechanically well-made story in the French manner. "Rose-Agathe" is the grotesque product of the second desire, a prurient story about an aesthetic young man who falls "passionately" in love with a hairdresser's dummy. If Euphemia de Mauves is an ancestress of Isabel Archer, she is considerably less thought-out and less interesting a character. A naïve American, she marries the dissolute Baron de Mauves "because she had a romantic belief that the best birth is the guaranty of an ideal delicacy of feeling." The force of her addiction to illusions is such that, once she discovers the truth about her husband, she still demands, by "living with closed eyes," to respect her original idealization. James does not make it sufficiently clear whether Euphemia's dreams are to be considered worthy of respect or not. "Illusion of course is illusion, and one must always pay for it," as another character says of her, "but there is something truly tragical in seeing an earthly penalty levied on such divine folly as this." Euphemia is distinctively American, both in her willful reliance upon illusion and in her New England sense of duty in her position. "Whatever befalls you," her mother-in-law counsels, "promise me this: to be yourself."[35] And, whatever her errors, she remains just that—a heroine in James's view, although a potential egoist and sentimentalist by Meredith's reckoning.

James's contradictory feelings toward Madame de Mauves are repeated, to a somewhat less ambiguous effect, in his portrait of Isabel. In both cases it is hard to feel the force of their original illusions—especially when they are so bogus—despite the fact that their romanticism is also James's. Unlike the brilliantly composed novel, the early work is hopelessly confused still more because the story is reflected through the ambivalent eyes of a young American who is not unlike Henry James. Longmore treats moral issues in terms of good and bad aesthetic taste, and he romanticizes Madame de Mauves in a manner which outdoes her idealization of the Baron. If James is ultimately unable to decide what kind of a figure Euphemia is intended to be, he is also much too involved with Longmore, with his mingled timidity and proneness to bursts of rhetorical passion, to present him carefully or clearly. The nature of James's own experience was so ambiguous and limited that he could rarely keep from creating a certain kind of character and situation. The result, in "Madame de Mauves," is a suggestive but indeterminate vision of what he would later do expertly.

The most philosophical—and autobiographical—story of the decade is the allegory "Benvolio" (1875), a trivial treatment of a man with contrary ambitions. Benvolio is torn between the pull of his private life and of the world, between his sense of duty and his craving for pleasure, between the innocent Scholastica and the worldly Countess, in short between America and Europe. He chooses America and fails as a writer. James implies that he has accepted both and gained the double glory. He developed the same basic theme more fully and realistically in that year in *Roderick Hudson*, his first full-length artist fable. Roderick, the sculptor-hero, and Rowland Mallet, his observer and patron, are ostensibly counterparts. "In the novel," Leon Edel declares, "Henry seems to be asking himself an unanswerable question: how can the artist, the painter of life, the recorder, the observer, stand on the outside of things and write about them, and throw himself at the same time into the act of living?"[36] It is the old dilemma posed by James's father: how can one do and be, write and live at the same time? James's decision to write a novel with a romantic hero who destroys himself as a result of unfulfilled energies and thwarted passion has its link with various French novels; the novelty of *Roderick Hudson* lies in the importance with which he treats Rowland, the ancestor of a line of perceptive but meddling narrators in James. As if to prove Pater's contention that the aesthetic observer has more opportunities for success in the modern world than the artist, James shifts his attention in the course of writing the novel from Roderick to Rowland; yet he manages to make both protagonists more complex in attitude and function than critics have allowed for. Eventually he would unite the observer and the man of action in the figure of the Jamesian artist—above all in the portrait of Miriam Rooth in *The Tragic Muse*. The two halves are still disconnected in *Roderick Hudson*, but James suggests that there is more in each figure than meets the eye.

Rowland's own romantic aspirations are evidenced when he climbs an alp in order to pick a flower for Mary Garland; in his adoption of the young American sculptor he hopes to live vicariously through him. Rowland plays the villain in the novel, curiously enough, in the sense that he first introduces Roderick to the "world" (always a risky undertaking in James) and later he provokes his protégé's death by belaboring the fact of the artist's egoism and willfulness. Yet these qualities are partly what helped to make an artist of Roderick to begin with. Rowland is both patron and patronizing throughout, trying to exert power stealthily in imitation of his author. The very name of "Mallet" suggests grim possibilities, as well as the nature of Rowland's own artistic function in his manipulation of his ward. Curiously, it is Rowland, and not the romantic hero, who argues against the idea that the human will is "destined" in any way: "The will is destiny itself," he tells Roderick, who has argued the reverse. Rowland represents the American belief (illusion?) of self-sufficiency. Asked to define his faith to Christina Light, whose Catholicism enforces her sense of fatalism, he admits only that his is a personal religion—"One's religion," he says, "takes on the colour of one's general disposition."[37]

The major success of the book is neither Rowland nor Roderick but Christina, half madonna and half ballerina (as James describes her), half innocent American girl and half corrupting, Europeanized *femme fatale*. Christina proved too much for the limited frame of the novel, and James called upon her again as the Princess Casamassima. He also revived the stoical and wise Madame Grandoni and the mannerist sculptor Gloriani, who somewhat resembles the cynical sculptor in "The Madonna of the Future." By the time of *The Ambassadors*, where Gloriani reappears respected and influential, James realized that the earthly race was not to the romancer or the realist but to the opportunist. As a study of a cluster of American artists in Rome, James's novel superficially resembles *The Marble Faun*. While Hawthorne used his figures to illustrate a fable about the nature of sin, James directed his attention to the problems of the artist, particularly his own. Hawthorne's major legacy to James was the creation of a figure like Miles Coverdale (in *The Blithedale Romance*), an ironical observer who is, for the sake of describing the scene around him objectively to the reader, necessarily but also tragically detached from life. As realists with thwarted romantic drives and limited active abilities, Coverdale and Rowland Mallet anticipate James's subsequent observer-narrators, from Ralph Touchett to Lambert Strether, who are first conceived as invalids but later as heroes.

James's skepticism as to the efficacy of taking an active role in life can already be seen in *The American* (1877). For all his rugged and sometimes comical heroism, Christopher Newman learns to obey a Jamesian code of nonaction. Newman is, after Christina, James's first major character, and he is a distinctly Jamesian type of character. Speaking of the distinguishing quality of one of his later heroes, James would note, "It all comes back in the last analysis to the individual vision of decency, the critical as well as the passionate judgment of it under sharp stress."[38] Hence, Newman, who has already shown his distaste for vengeance before coming to Paris, repeats himself with regard to punishing the Bellegardes' treachery toward him. For all of his possessiveness and innocent vanity, it is his "remarkable good nature" which at once distinguishes him and allows him to be defeated in his wish to marry Claire de Cintré. "I have a very good opinion of myself," he announces very early,[39] and he lives up to the sense of decency under pressure that the novelist has exacted of him. In this sense, he is not a free character, despite his claims to the contrary. Speaking of the English, James noted that they are responsible and free, that their awareness of certain limitations makes them more free than Americans, who flounder about wastefully because they have no sense of boundaries.[40] The American is less free precisely because he is bound to an illusion of his own limitless capacities, an illusion of freedom. The paradox is central to an understanding of *The American and The Portrait of a Lady.*

Thus, while on the surface the conflict in *The American* seems like that between a realistic, "free" American (the embodiment of free enterprise) and a melodramatic, fixed world of corrupt Europeans, it is the Europeans who are free to hold back from Newman what he is powerless to take. When Claire is locked up in a convent, Newman feels himself confronted by something "too strange and too mocking to be real; it was like a page torn out of a romance, with no context in his own experience." But Claire has told him at the beginning of their acquaintance that she is "not a heroine." In a parody of the Victorian readers' expectations of the novel, Claire has just finished reading to her niece a fairy tale which points ahead to the impossibility of her marriage to Newman: " 'But in the end the young prince married the beautiful Florabella,' said Madame de Cintré, 'and carried her off to live with him in the Land of the Pink Sky. There she was so happy that she forgot all her troubles, and went out to drive every day of her life in an ivory coach drawn by five hundred white mice. Poor Florabella,' she explained to Newman, 'had suffered terribly.' "[41]

James defended the unhappy ending of *The American* to Howells on the grounds that the conditioning on both sides had made any other conclusion realistically impossible (though James had, of course, chosen precisely the circumstances he wished). Where would they have lived? he demanded, adding that "the interest of the subject was, for me, (without my being at all a pessimist) its exemplification of one of those insuperable difficulties which present themselves in people's lives and from which the only issue is by forfeiture—by losing something." James was calmly and confidently fixed on the matter:

> We are each the product of circumstances and there are tall stone walls which fatally divide us. I have written my story from Newman's side of the wall, and I understand so well how Mme de Cintré couldn't really scramble over from *her* side! If I had represented her as doing so I should have made a prettier ending, certainly; but I should have felt as if I were throwing a rather vulgar sop to readers who don't really know the world and who don't measure the merit of a novel by its correspondence to the same.[42]

James's friend Edmund Gosse claimed in 1890 that James had introduced realism to England, and had thus "inaugurated the experimental novel in the English language," with the writing of *The American*.[43] But what seemed realistic because of the absence of a happy ending now seems romantic, on James's part, because of his determination to end his novel in accordance with his own fatalistic views. Nevertheless, he promised Howells, at that time the editor of the *Atlantic*, many happy endings for his next novel.

James's attitude toward the novel seems both fixed and romantic, rather than realistic and open-minded as he himself felt. The continuing charm of *The American* probably depends very heavily on the romantic assumptions of readers that what they are reading will turn out happily despite the warning signs along the way. Yet whether *The American* is a novel colored by romance or the reverse, it is still a work with an inner logic set up by the author. The characters act as they do because the author has set up no alternatives; their paths (to borrow a metaphor from *The Portrait*) are "very straight." Theirs is a world deliberately novelistic, and James puts into each world an inner novelist, or group of novelists, whose only role is to provoke the main actor's actions. Mrs. Tristram performs this function in *The American*:

> "I am a highly civilized man," said Newman [very early in the novel]. "I stick to that. If you don't believe it, I should like to prove it to you."
> Mrs. Tristram was silent a while. "I should like to make you prove it," she said, at last. "I should like to put you in a difficult place."[44]

This novelistic prerogative is undertaken later by both Dr. Sloper (in *Washington Square*) and Ralph Touchett (in *The Portrait*). A thin line, as we have already seen in the figure of Rowland Mallet, separates patronage from meddling. If the using of other people is the Hawthornian sin of sins, for James it is the artist's necessity, but the degree to which one is a successful artist in life—the life of the James novel, that is—depends on the breadth of one's point of view, the degree to which one imagines oneself related to other people and other people to oneself. The problematic figures in James, whatever his own intention (and one thinks especially of Maggie Verver in *The Golden Bowl*), are those who consider things only in relation to themselves and thus blind themselves to anything other than subjective reality. But James himself, as is all too evident, was prone to do that.

It was the handling of the international theme in his fiction which gave James his initial popularity. In an unsigned review in the *Nation* for May 1878, James considered the implications in a mediocre English novel about an American girl in Europe. "His story suggests this reflection," James wrote, "that it is possible, after all, to write tales of 'American society.' We are reminded that there *are* types—that there is a good deal of local color—that there is a considerable field for satire." He noted that the field is more open to a knowing American novelist than the biased English novelist before him: "It has been affirmed hitherto that it is next to impossible to write novels about American society on account of the absence of 'types.' But it appears that there is an element in our population that has attained to the typic dignity—the class of young ladies whose chief object in life is to capture an English 'swell.' "[45]

A month later, "Daisy Miller" appeared in the *Cornhill Magazine*, followed shortly afterward by *The Europeans* and "An International Episode." It is noteworthy that the American heroines of these works do not marry European "swells." Daisy dies in Rome, her innocence unperceived by a Europeanized American; Gertrude Wentworth settles for a Europeanized Bohemian; Bessie Alden gives up her English conquest, Lord Lambeth, for inscrutable reasons. Only the brash Mrs. Headway in "The Siege of London" (1883) is true to type; yet her success is a warning that English society is hardly worth fighting for.

"Daisy Miller: A Study" is one of James's most deservedly famous stories. The point of view of the story is that of the Europeanized Winterbourne, who has succumbed to the ironic way of looking at life. His is the tragedy of the detached life, and Daisy's is a death by irony rather than malaria. In a story almost as good, if far less known, "The Pension Beaurepas" (1879), James employed a first-person narrator whose faculties of observation keep him at a necessary and a poignant distance. This nameless character is among the best of James's adaptations of Hawthorne's Coverdale, whose detached vision in his tragedy. He pities the unfortunate, Europeanized American girl, Aurora Church, who is being dragged through Europe in search of a respectable marriage. One evening, as he talks to her through the grille of an iron gate, he is momentarily tempted to help her. "It seemed to me, for a moment, that to pass out of that gate with this yearning, straining young creature would be to pass into some mysterious felicity. If I were only a hero of romance, I would offer, myself, to take her to

America."[46] But the moment passes, and he is left alone with himself—and his ironic vision—once again.

One of the highlights of "The Pension Beaurepas" is the portrait of the Ruck family with their own limitations. The unfortunate Mr. Ruck, declares the narrator, "has spent his whole life in buying and selling; he knows how to do nothing else. His wife and daughter have spent their lives, not in selling, but in buying; and they, on their side, know how to do nothing else. To get something in a shop that they can put on their backs—that is their one idea; they haven't another in their heads."[47] The study of manners can often touch at a moral nerve, and at times like this James is both amusing and moving. A genial counterpart to Mr. Ruck is the businessman Mr. Westgate in "An International Episode." Teasing the two stolid Englishmen who are visiting America, he warns them away from Boston in August, with a wit that cuts both ways by saying that "Boston in this weather would be very trying; it's not the temperature for intellectual exertion. At Boston, you know, you have to pass an examination at the city limits; and when you come away they give you a kind of degree."[48]

The Europeans (1878) begins in Boston and then moves to the suburbs. Although it is short on local color (other than in the opening pages), it is rich in its dissection of a kind of New England sensibility which wears its inhibitions on its sleeve. "You are all so afraid here, of being selfish," the European-born American hero tells Gertrude Wentworth, the heroine. The "Europeans" of the title are both really Europeanized Americans, Felix and his sister the Baroness, who have come to America to find rich mates. Felix is accommodating and basically innocent and thus he both succeeds and to some degree becomes re-Americanized. The Baroness, however, is too fastidious and too demanding. Like one of Meredith's comical liars, she is a danger if not a nuisance to the Wentworth circle. In a story in which James is straining not to become involved, not to provide anything more than the happy endings promised to Howells, the Baroness becomes a distraction to the genial flow of the story. Another potential "inner novelist" (she would manipulate the Wentworths and America for her own ends), she finds herself among immovable material. "She found her chief happiness in the sense of exerting a certain power and making a certain impression," James states flatly, but he immediately afterward creates an unwarranted sympathy for her through the use of a runaway metaphor: "and now she felt the annoyance of a rather wearied swimmer who, on nearing shore, to land, finds a smooth straight wall of rock when he had counted upon a clean firm beach."[49]

The imagery of the novel is elsewhere more appropriately selected. Mr. Wentworth "looks as if he were undergoing martyrdom, not by fire, but by freezing"; and he greets Felix's request for his daughter's hand "with a light in his face that might have flashed back from an iceberg" (James generally associated icy imagery with New Englanders, most notably with Olive Chancellor in *The Bostonians*). The Wentworth sisters are well-drawn counterparts: Gertrude dreams of romance and rebels against the family sense of duty; Charlotte is humorously prim. "I don't think one should ever try to look pretty," she says with a straight face.* The most curious figure in the novel, however, is the cosmopolitan New Englander (almost a contradiction in terms for James), Robert Acton, another version of Rowland Mallet or the narrator of "The Pension Beaurepas." "He was addicted to taking the humorous view of things, and he had discovered that even in the narrowest circles such a disposition may find frequent opportunities," James remarks.[50] The counterpart of the Baroness, he plays with her in the same way she plays with the Wentworths, but he is as much at the mercy of irony as she is of romance. James concluded *The Europeans* with four weddings in what may have been an act of calculated triviality—a sop to the demands of his editor and readers —or else a real desire to please, a motive increasingly strong through the next decade.

Confidence (1879), the dreadful book which followed *The Europeans*, may have originated as an earnest attempt to write a conventional Victorian novel. The theme is Jane Austen's—the danger of first impressions—but the style is alternately lethargic and melodramatic, with a happy ending that grotesquely parodies what James considered to be the Victorian model. Perhaps the one note-

---

* Curiously, it is the Charlottes whom James will later respond to in the guise of Laura Wing in "A London Life" or Adela Chart in "The Marriages" or Fleda Vetch in *The Spoils of Poynton*.

worthy thing about *Confidence* is the admission, for the first time in James, that the observations of a Rowland-like character ("Bernard liked to feel his intelligence at play; this is, perhaps, the highest luxury of a clever man")[51] may be entirely mistaken. James repeated this idea more successfully, the same year, in "The Diary of a Man of Fifty." The narrator, who has thought himself deceived by a fickle Italian Countess, tries to warn a young man who resembles him at his age against marrying the Countess' daughter. In the sketch for the story in his notebook, James planned to make the symmetrical analogy real, but in writing the story he switched his emphasis to the blindness of his narrator. "My instinct had warned me," the older man boasts of his escape, "and I had trusted my instinct." But the younger man is more clear-sighted. "You couldn't have been much in love with her," he retorts. And he is right. Not only does the analogy turn out to be false, but the original supposition was wrong too. "Was I too cautious—too suspicious—too logical?" the narrator moans at the end.[52]

James may well have been at a moment of crisis. If the intelligent, detached observers of his stories can be limited in view, can be blind on occasions, what of their creator? Instead of giving way to skepticism, he began to explore the possibilities of playing off different points of view in his fiction in order to approximate an atmosphere of collective truth. He had already written an essay in dialogue form ("*Daniel Deronda:* A Conversation") in which opposing views of George Eliot were balanced by the Jamesian mouthpiece Constantius. In late 1879 he wrote "A Bundle of Letters," which is about the inability of any of the characters involved to see beyond his own angle of vision. The most interesting figure, from the biographical point of view, is the sickly aesthete, who is the first and most deadly of James's occasional exercises in self-parody. "What is there in Louis Leverett except the accent, the emphasis, that differentiates him from Henry James?" asks Joseph Warren Beach.[53] James gave Leverett his own opinions on life, art, England, New England, and French literature, but he considerably exaggerated the tone:

> The great thing is to *live*, you know—to feel, to be conscious of one's possibilities; not to pass through life mechanically and insensibly, like a letter through the post-office.

I don't think that in Boston there is any real sympathy with
the artistic temperament; we tend to make everything a matter
of right and wrong. And in Boston one can't live—*on ne peut
pas vivre*, as they say here. I don't mean one can't reside—
for a great many people manage that; but one can't live,
aesthetically—I may almost venture to say, sensuously.

Art should never be didactic; and what is life but an art?
Pater has said that so well, somewhere.

If James is intimating that he may have been mistaken in his point
of view thus far, he is also showing how he has been misunder-
stood by his brother William and others. Leverett presumes to do
what James is in fact doing in the story: "I am much interested,"
Leverett boasts, "in the study of national types; in comparing,
contrasting, seizing the strong points, the weak points, the point
of view of each. It is interesting to shift one's point of view—to
enter into strange, exotic ways of looking at life."[54] Yet for James
the various points of view, including the Pateresque, are limited;
the author alone sees what is really happening. Louis Leverett will
never have James's ability to transform consciousness into works
of art; just as, for that matter, Isabel Archer, for all her Jamesian
self-confidence, will never reach the position of her creator. Only
the wise artist of sufficient genius, as he implies in his essay on
Delacroix in 1880, can realize and make use of "other points of
view, other ways of looking at things, than one's own."[55]

James emerged from his bout of self-questioning with a heightened confidence in his powers rather than skepticism. In 1880 he
reached his full stride with the writing of *Washington Square*.
James had now pared his literary models (or coequals) down to
George Eliot and Turgenev, whose combined influence contributed
much to *The Portrait of a Lady*. His critical model was now un-
abashedly Sainte-Beuve, no literary lawgiver but a creator of
"Partial Portraits." "He valued life and literature equally for the
light they threw upon each other," James declared. Above all,
Sainte-Beuve was an active observer, "the very genius of observation, discretion, and taste."[56] Perhaps at no other period of his life
could James have created such a perfect novel as *Washington
Square*: a well-made story filled with authorial feeling. Only in a
mood of complete self-assurance could he have chosen for his

materials a limited heroine, a Europeanized American suitor, and an ironical, Jamesian father and still have decided to make of Catherine Sloper one of his most appealing characters.

Catherine is rare among the novelist's heroines in being neither clever nor beautiful (for Jamesian heroes and heroines, at the mercy of their eyes, can fall in love only with beautiful people), yet she attains enough wisdom in the course of her development to cut herself adrift from the world in what will be the characteristic Jamesian manner. A useful comparison might be made between her and such literary ancestresses as Eugénie Grandet and Florence Dombey. Eugénie is shuttled between a miserly father and a dandyish fortune hunter, both united, despite the differences in background and manners, in an absorption in greed and selfishness; yet Eugénie exemplifies for Balzac a superior Christian selflessness which manages to make itself felt on earth. Florence Dombey is ignored or hated by a selfish parent, who learns in time the values of love and community. Thus, the values of a Eugénie or Florence are the values of a higher providence and a potential communal selflessness. Catherine, at the end of *Washington Square*, exemplifies nobody but herself, voluntarily shut up in an old house, with her embroidery, "for life, as it were."

In the scheme of the novel, she had no other choice; the recognition of the fact is a part of her real triumph. In one of his saddest sentences, James characterizes the nature of her tragedy and her realization of it: "From her own point of view the great facts of her career were that Morris Townsend had trifled with her affection, and that her father had broken its spring." Catherine's development in *Washington Square* is from the typical clinging Victorian heroine of Trollope ("In reality, she was the softest creature in the world") to a Jamesian intelligence, aware of the limitations of the world and thereby freed from illusions to the contrary. The other characters in the novel are developed in a contrary direction: exemplars of the world to Catherine, they fit more and more into stereotypes. For the young girl, with a "secret passion for the theatre," Morris first seems like a young man in a play, "yet Mr. Townsend was not like an actor; he seemed so sincere, so natural." At the close of the novel, however, Morris is entirely rhetorical, and the parting scene (chapter twenty-nine) is superbly poignant, with its juxtaposition of Catherine's natural emotion and Morris' calculated cruelties. The final letter he sends her is a brilliant example of that contrast, which is another form of the aesthetic-minded opposition between life and art: "The letter was beautifully written, and Catherine, who kept it for many years after this, was able, when her sense of the bitterness of its meaning and the hollowness of its tone had grown less acute, to admire its grace of expression."[57]

Washington Square is, for that matter, a novel about writing a novel, a work of art which contains within it a warning against judging life as an artistic spectacle. One wonders if James realized that fact, even as he dismissed the book in later years for specious reasons: its lack of "paraphernalia" or of any expansive development. Schematically, the novel contains a developing heroine stalked by three "inner novelists," who would attempt to manipulate her for artistic effect. Morris is the most obvious of the three, in terms of plot action, but her aunt and her father represent the same opposition of point of view that James had been shaking off since "The Madonna of the Future." Mrs. Penniman is a romantic manipulator, distorting reality to fit a romantic-melodramatic pattern. Dr. Sloper, on the other hand, is an ironist and cynical realist, with absolute confidence in his own point of view and a correspondingly limited awareness: James warns us very early that "with all his irony," the doctor can be misled. "Don't undervalue irony," is his password throughout, but he is as blind about his daughter at the end of his life as he is when we first meet him. Throughout the book he cherishes the sense of "entertainment" that can be derived from watching his daughter try to retain his approval and Morris' affection, neither of which, of course, she has ever really had. At times, he plays with and torments her for the sake of amusement, to see if she will "stick." In this respect, he is a caricature of a Jamesian artist, testing the integrity of his characters under sharp stress. But Dr. Sloper protests his realistic-minded attitude too much. He argues that he is "not a father in an old-fashioned novel," but, like the sculptor in "The Madonna of the Future," he carries his scorn of romantic stereotypes too far. Like a French naturalist (Sloper is conveniently a doctor by profession), he becomes the victim of what his eyes—and his eyes only—can reveal to him. For Sloper, as for Zola and the Goncourts (in James's view), realism becomes mannerism; in his old age, "he visited only those patients in whose symptoms he recognized a certain originality."[58]

Washington Square is not only James's best work of the 1870's but one of the great late Victorian novels. A reader of nineteenth-century novels may be interested in James's attempt to refashion literary models, to come to terms with, and keep a safe distance from, the conventions of romance and realism, to fuse the French belief in conditioning with the American faith in one's freedom of choice. The resultant novel is more, however, than an exercise in literary synthesis. By the time of *Washington Square*, James was the heir to three traditions: he was an American who admired the French naturalists, but who lived in England. In his fusion of three traditions, he brought the novel to a climax of sorts, but, in his subversion of literary conventions later on and in his desire to go his own way if necessary, he demonstrated his modernity. From 1864 to 1879 he pursued his literary apprenticeship, writing hundreds of critical and travel essays, a great many short stories, and five novels. In 1880 he published only three essays and *Washington Square*, but he had reached undoubted maturity and had, incidentally, depicted a major truth. A novel about literary conventions encases a study of the nature of convention itself.

In her resistance against being manipulated by others, Catherine gains a sort of victory inconceivable in terms of the structure of the Victorian novel. Trollope's Lily Dale was unique among the great Victorian heroines in disappointing the Victorian readers' desire for the happy ending: the marriage that would symbolize the unity of the Victorian world itself. The only permissible alternative was death, or, as in *Wuthering Heights*, a marriage literally made in heaven. James's heroes and heroines generally testify to a break from the Victorian mould. Symbolically, they are, or, like Catherine, they become, orphans, who must learn to live with the law of their being. In this respect they follow their author's example. They are conditioned by the world, and they are conditioned by the logic of the world of their novels; realization of the fact frees them from false illusions and enables them to maintain a personal, inviolable independence. Like James, they are solipsists;

without his ability to convert impressions into art, however, they are rarely contented solipsists.

In 1873 James wrote to Charles Eliot Norton, with full artistic confidence: "I regard the march of history very much as a man placed astride of a locomotive, without knowledge or help, would regard the progress of that vehicle. To stick on, somehow, and even to enjoy the scenery as we pass, is the sum of my aspirations."[59] For James, solipsism was an untroubling faith. "Subjective consciousness," which his father had denounced as the pre-eminent "evil of human nature"[60] and which Victorians and New Englanders alike had battled as a major threat to their way of life, such was James's highest good. Hawthorne had suggested that the life of the artist is in its extreme form the life of the damned, and Meredith had called on the Comic Spirit to laugh away man's egoism. James had neither intellectual nor moral roots of any real depth, and one may cynically contend that he was supremely lucky in this respect in a singularly disruptive period of English history. To "stick on, somehow, and even to enjoy the scenery," to transform the accumulated deposits of observation and reading into novels was his ambition—and his success—at a relatively early age. His most successful artist-figure, Miriam Rooth, lives by the rule James learned: to succeed as an artist, "you must forage and ravage and leave a track behind you; you must live upon the country you traverse."[61] As James's major works of the 1870's and, above all, of the 1880's show, despite human and artistic limitations he still managed to find extremely rich materials at hand.

[8] Points of View and Pointed Views: James in the 1880's

The Two Freedoms in The Portrait of a Lady

> The word "freedom" sounds so fine that one
> could not do without it, even though its
> meaning should be nothing but an illusion.
> (Goethe)

In no other of their novels do Meredith and James reveal basic differences from one another, as well as their greatest respective literary strengths, more than in *The Egoist* and *The Portrait of a Lady*. Written within a year or so of each other, the two novels strike me as being the finest, wisest, and most rewarding products of two very distinctive sensibilities. The plot of each book involves a charming and inexperienced heroine's discovery of life as a result of her relationship with an egoist, but, while Clara Middleton uses her discovery to withdraw from her fiancé and from the egoism latent in her own personality, Isabel Archer's discovery, after marrying Gilbert Osmond, *is* her freedom, which enables her to withdraw into her own individuality. For Clara, the awareness and scourging of egoism precedes the freedom to love, to become involved with others; for Isabel, the freedom to be—to be aware of the unfreedom of others—is victory enough.

In Sir Willoughby Patterne Meredith drew a comic portrait of the egoist as poseur, the slave of the applause of others; if Sir Willoughby's egoism represents a social danger, it can be vanquished simply by exposure to laughter. By contrast, Gilbert Osmond is the egoist of romantic melodrama in his machinations and in his exposure, and his allure depends precisely on the human need for illusions in order to sustain life. Both men represent aspects of their respective authors—Meredith's histrionic manner and James's Pateresque sensibility—but where Meredith saw the social need for voluntary self-discipline, James was, during the 1880's, in the process of yielding to the charm of a life of aesthetic detachment from society. In the figure of Ralph Touchett, he presented a better version of Osmond—a finer consciousness, if a similarly amoral conscience—who is untroubled by the pressures of the world. Although Meredith realized that the "cast" of *The Egoist* was "against the modern style," at least one reviewer of *The Portrait of a Lady* recognized that as a "representative" of "a new epoch," James's novel "has its own virtues."[1]

Not only in style is *The Portrait of a Lady* perhaps the best-written novel produced by an American; in subject matter, also, it presents one of the most pertinent analyses of the American character ever undertaken. It may well be the most important American novel to the degree that it makes the fullest tribute to the idealism of the "American Dream," the American myth of self-reliance and self-importance, while, at the same time, revealing the sharpest awareness of its limitations. Isabel Archer is created on Emersonian lines, and her actions dismay and disappoint readers who approach her on the literal level alone. It is pointless to wonder of her why she acts as she does, being attracted to Gilbert Osmond in the first place and returning to him at the end. Given the logic of the novel, she has no choice; she has been created in such a way as to provoke no other possible action. To demand that she be a "free" character is to fall prey to Isabel's own delusion. On American terms, only an illusion of freedom is possible; true freedom comes only with the recognition of limitations. We are all limited, as Madame Merle harshly observes at one point,[2] and the novel may be read as a dialogue between Isabel Archer's romantic American and Madame Merle's cynical European ways of looking at life.

Thus, the major Jamesian themes of the 1870's converge in *The Portrait*; if the themes are familiar, however, the treatment is on the highest level. Writing ten years later of a minor artist, James described his own position by the time of *The Portrait:* he had "reached that happy period of life when a worker is in full possession of his means, when he has done for his chosen instrument everything he can do in the way of forming it and rendering it complete and flexible, and has therefore only to apply it with freedom, confidence and success." Perhaps prompted by the memory of his own experience prior to 1880, James went on to claim that "These, to our sense, are the golden hours of an artist's life; happier even than the younger time when the future seemed infinite in the light of the first rays of glory, the first palpable hits."[3] *The Portrait of a Lady* was written in those golden hours of deserved self-confidence. It is ironic, of course, that in his moment of artistic triumph he should have created a heroine who fails in her material goals. Isabel is another would-be novelist who would try to make her own fate; her road to ruin, as Richard Poirier observes, "is paved with James's good intentions as well as her own." Poirier's analysis of the Isabel-James relationship is astute: "Isabel's ambition is James's achievement, and the position she desires from which to see life most knowledgeably and compassionately is, by the testimony of the novel itself, the one which James has attained."[4] Yet, by the end of the novel, Isabel manages a curious sort of success.

The book seems to have been written at a period of great freedom for James. It was begun in Florence in 1879 and had very little else to compete with it. (While he had been writing earlier novels, he had been forced, for economic reasons, to churn out scores of essays and stories.) It was serialized in England and America simultaneously and was guaranteed a respectable audience. Critics were already speaking of a new American school at work, headed by Howells and James, and there was widespread interest in what the head of the "analytical school" (as it was sometimes called), the author of the popular "Daisy Miller," would publish next.

That segment of the public which may have worried James most, however, was his family, and especially William, who was needling him to produce "fatness and bigness" in his next work.[5] "I don't at all despair, yet, of doing something fat," he wrote William in 1878, following the latter's disparagement of *The Europeans;* to his mother, not long after, he confessed that he now found "people in general very vulgar-minded and superficial—and it is only by a pious fiction, to keep myself going, and keep on the social harness, that I succeed in postulating them as anything else or better."[6] The mixture of ambition and fastidiousness seeped into the formation of his curious lovers, Isabel and Osmond, who are comically similar to each other (like Thackerayan foils), but also tragically separate. In one way, James was conforming to the patterns of the Victorian novel: the story of a girl deceived by villains is standard enough; as a girl self-deceived, Isabel draws upon predecessors in George Eliot and Jane Austen. But it was soon apparent that he was doing something new with his materials.

Horace Scudder, the future editor of the *Atlantic*, which had just serialized the novel, commented on Isabel in the magazine "as representative of womanly life today"—showing the extent to which she could be read as a late Victorian American heroine:

> The fine purpose of her freedom, the resolution with which
> she seeks to be the maker of her destiny, the subtle weakness
> into which all this betrays her, the apparent helplessness of her
> ultimate position, and the conjectured escape only through
> patient forbearance,—what are these, if not attributes of
> womanly life expended under current conditions?

Scudder also discerned that the novelist had made of Isabel something different from early heroines: she and the other characters in the novel live in "isolation"; they are developed with a distinctively Jamesian "method," so that they are true to the artistic logic of their situation, although not necessarily true to the reader's expectations. They are also true to literature, if not necessarily true to life. "This self-consistency," Scudder shrewdly noted, "is a separate thing from any consistency with the world of reality. The characters, the situations, the incidents, are all true to the law of their own being, but that law runs parallel with the law which governs life, instead of being identical with it."[7] In this respect, Isabel contrasts with George Eliot's self-denying heroines, who exist in and for a social context. James was often compared by contemporaries to George Eliot, as a novelist of analysis of character and motive rather than of action, but James's artistic modernity contrasts interestingly with her Victorian moral allegiance.

"These novelists are more alike than any others in their processes," Howells declared, "but with George Eliot an ethical purpose is dominant, and with Mr. James an artistic purpose. I do not know just how it should be stated of two such noble and generous types of characters as Dorothea and Isabel Archer, but I think that we sympathize with the former in grand aims that chiefly concern others, and with the latter in beautiful dreams that primarily concern herself."[8] The extent to which James broke away from the influence of George Eliot is symptomatic of the way he broke away from the Victorian novel. His first long essay, which was also his first signed article, was on "The Novels of George Eliot" (1866), and he reviewed all of her later fiction, as well as her poems, as they were published. The review of *Middlemarch*, in 1873, centers upon her avoidance of artistic unity. *Middlemarch* is "a treasure-house of detail, but it is an indifferent whole," he declared; as crucial evidence for his charge, he cites her refusal to allow her main characters to play other than "a subordinate part." Dorothea Brooke, after all, "is of more consequence than the action of which she is the nominal center," and her marriage to Casaubon is never described to "its full capacity."[9] James inherited George Eliot's interest in the motivations of character, and in a notebook entry he bemoaned the "want of action" in his novel up to the point of Isabel's marriage: "the weakness of the whole story," he confided to himself, "is that it is too exclusively psychological."[10] Given the nature of his undertaking, there was little choice, and, in the attempt to resort to more action, James may even be criticized for resorting to the crudely melodramatic scenes between Isabel, Osmond, and Madame Merle in the latter part of the novel.

By the mid-1870's James had turned to praise of George Eliot, along with Turgenev, as a novelist of fullness of outline and breadth of sympathy. (They replaced Balzac and George Sand as his novelistic models.) A novel he returned to again and again was *Daniel Deronda*, the neglect of which in France occasioned him to attack the French naturalists. A great deal has been written of the similarity between Isabel and Gwendolen Harleth, but James did not borrow George Eliot's heroine so much as he chose to interpret her in the light of his conception of Isabel: "Gwendolen is a perfect picture of youthfulness—its eagerness, its presumption, its preoccupation with itself, its vanity and silliness, its sense of its own absoluteness. But she is extremely intelligent and clever, and there-fore tragedy *can* have a hold upon her." James declared of Gwen-dolen that "It is the tragedy that makes her conscience, which then reacts upon it," and he claimed to "think of nothing more power-ful than the way in which the growth of her conscience is traced, nothing more touching than the picture of its helpless maturity." James noted a split between George Eliot the Victorian novelist and George Eliot the proto-Jamesian artist, between an "artificial" and a "spontaneous" side to her: "There is what she is by inspira-tion and what she is because it is expected of her."[11] It was typical of James to regard the artistic impulse as the more natural one. The Victorian George Eliot had discerned the necessity for Daniel Deronda in the scheme of the novel, as well as the need for Doro-thea Brooke to be subordinated to the microcosmic world of Middlemarch.

James conceived of Isabel, as he declared in the preface to the New York edition of the novel, before he knew what to do with her. He had an image of her and needed only to determine the sort of situation or "ado" that she would logically lend herself to. No doubt he drew upon mingled reminiscences of George Eliot heroines—and upon his transmuted memory of his cousin Minny Temple, full of the capacity for life but doomed at an early age—but the resultant protagonist was a very new kind of heroine for Victorian readers. "I am not in the least conventional," Isabel her-self warns very early in the novel (p. 48), and James's description of her in the preface—"a certain young woman affronting her destiny"—is additionally disconcerting.[12] Only the Brontë sisters could have conceived of a Victorian heroine *affronting* her destiny. More typical were the efforts of Jane Austen or George Eliot to create heroines confronting their destinies, accepting their pre-ordained places in the English system. And what else was "destiny" —as even Diana of the Crossways or Clara Middleton discovers— but, symbolically, love and marriage? Poirier has engagingly lab-eled Isabel "an Emersonian Becky Sharp,"[13] but for the Victorians, especially Thackeray, Becky was a metaphorical threat to social well-being. It is typical of James's continuing spell that we can approach his heroine by easily detaching her from her social milieu. In our desire to see her free from Osmond, for example, we tend to forget that the popular feeling toward divorce in 1881 was on a par with its views on free love.[14] The mere suspicion of adultery was enough to destroy Sir Charles Dilke's political career later in the decade; in Parnell's case personal scandal occasioned the defeat of Irish Home Rule legislation.

It is one of Isabel's triumphs, in fact, that, as a character, she is conceived in terms of art, not history. Fifty years ago it was common practice to reprove James for his escape from history. H. G. Wells, in a famous attack on James, noted the tendency of his characters to stand apart from the needs of body and time: "cleared for artistic treatment," they "never in any way *date*."[15] James's treatment of history in *The Portrait* provides a direct way of comparing the ageless, independent figure of Isabel with the heroine of *Middlemarch*. Both Dorothea and Isabel marry unhappily, and for both of them the ruins of Rome loom prominently in the background at the moment they realize their errors. Yet Rome means little *as* Rome to Dorothea. She senses "the oppressive masquerade of ages, in which her own life too seemed to become a masque with enigmatical costumes," but she refuses to give way to self-pity. Casaubon, on the other hand, feels remote from Rome and is tragically unaware of what Ladislaw calls the "vital connection" between periods of history.[16] To the critics of *Romola* who have charged that George Eliot merely transposed the problems of her day into the Renaissance, one might reply that this was precisely her purpose: to note the vital connections between the two periods even while showing the dangerous force of personality, as represented by Tito Melema or Savonarola. "Vital connection" was not an article of faith to Henry James, who stressed, on the contrary, the importance of the detached individual point of view. In describing Isabel among the ruins of Rome at the moment she discovers that her marriage was not a free act on her part but the result of Madame Merle's manipulation, James paints in the background more emphatically than George Eliot:

> Isabel took a drive, alone, that afternoon; she wished to be
> far away, under the sky, where she could descend from her
> carriage and tread upon the daisies. She had long before this
> taken old Rome into her confidence, for in a world of ruins the
> ruin of her happiness seemed a less unnatural catastrophe.
> She rested her weariness upon things that had crumbled for
> centuries and yet still were upright; she dropped her secret sad-

ness into the silence of lonely places, where its very modern quality detached itself and grew objective, so that as she sat in a sun-warmed angle on a winter's day, or stood in a mouldy church to which no one came, she could almost smile at it and think of its smallness. Small it was, in the large Roman record, and her haunting sense of the continuity of the human lot easily carried her from the less to the greater. She had become deeply, tenderly acquainted with Rome; it interfused and moderated her passion. But she had grown to think of it chiefly as the place where people had suffered [p. 454].

It is one of Dorothea's moral triumphs that she does not make of Rome an objective correlative for her suffering. Despite the declaration of "continuity" between Isabel and the human lot, the reader senses that the ruins form a highly colored backdrop for her suffering, rather than the reverse. "Small" though she objectively sees it to be, her "secret sadness" stands in relief, and her consciousness of the scene puts her into the position of the novelist or the reader. As long as Isabel has the consciousness of a Jamesian artist, she remains free of suffering, free of change, and free of any social connection. Isabel's connection to her fate runs along the tracks of artistic necessity rather than social or historical conditioning.

With her desire for freedom and her ability to appropriate Rome to her consciousness, Isabel is typically American, and much of the texture of the novel involves the alignment of the self-reliant American with the fixed portrait of a "Lady." Since much has been written on the Emersonian qualities of Isabel, one might quote from James's own, somewhat patronizing, account of Emerson, written about the time of the conception of *The Portrait:*

He insisted upon sincerity and independence and spontaneity, upon acting in harmony with one's nature, and not conforming and compromising for the sake of being more comfortable . . . The doctrine of the supremacy of the individual to himself, of his originality, and, as regards his own character, *unique* quality, must have had a great charm for people living in a society in which introspection—thanks to the want of other entertainment—played almost the part of a social resource.[17]

Isabel's self-reliance is her dominant trait, and her belief in her independence hinges upon it. Arnold Kettle has identified the theme of *The Portrait* as "the revelation of the inadequacy of Isabel's view of freedom"[18] but it is necessary to study the roots of her delusion in the nature of her character. She acts in perfect harmony with her nature, combining philosophical with artistic logic.

At the first mention of Isabel in the novel, it is noted, in her aunt's telegram, that she is "quite independent." This leads her cousin, Ralph Touchett, to wonder "in what sense is the term used?"—"in a moral or in a financial sense?"—before he informs the reader of his mother's sardonically similar "independence": "She likes to do everything for herself, and has no belief in any one's power to help her" (p. 9). Mrs. Touchett's form of independence, however, is ultimately synonymous with lack of purpose and sterility of existence. "I like my liberty too much," Isabel tells her rejected American suitor, Caspar Goodwood. "If there is a thing in the world that I am fond of, . . . it is my personal independence." If Caspar is disconcerted, so must Victorian readers have been. "It is to make you independent that I want to marry you," he argues, with a logic which might have appealed to the author of *Emma* (or to the hero of James's next novel, Basil Ransom). "An unmarried woman—a girl of your age—is not independent. There are all sorts of things she can't do. She is hampered at every step."

> "That's as she looks at the question," Isabel answered, with much spirit. "I am not in my first youth—I can do what I choose—I belong quite to the independent class. I have neither father nor mother; I am poor; I am of a serious disposition, and not pretty. I therefore am not bound to be timid and conventional; indeed I can't afford such luxuries. Besides, I try to judge things for myself; to judge wrong, I think, is more honourable than not to judge at all. I don't wish to be a mere sheep in the flock; I wish to choose my fate and know something of human affairs beyond what other people think it compatible with propriety to tell me" [pp. 139–140].

The force of her doomed idealism makes Isabel one of the most vital characters in fiction. What in an American transcendentalist context seems the height of courage, however, is out of place in a conventional English context. Isabel's aim is curiously reminiscent of Richard III's at the close of the *Henry VI* plays:

I have no brother, I am like no brother;
And this word "love," which greybeards call divine,
Be resident in men like one another
And not in me: I am myself alone.

When Caspar charges that she sounds as if she "were going to commit a crime," she proudly replies, "Perhaps I am. I wish to be free even to do that, if the fancy takes me" (p. 141).

The criminal—the socially "free" man—has long played a sympathetic part in American folklore, but James knew that there is no really gratuitous act. James had long before praised the "elevated morality" of *Romola*: the idea that we are determined by our deeds. "Can any argument be more plain. Can any lesson be more salutary?" he asked.[19] In *The Portrait*, however, James is less interested in the moral question of nemesis than in the matter of the artistic logic. Isabel does what she does because she thinks she is free; she then accepts the outcome of her action because she is what she has always been. Her great act of independence in the book is to accept Osmond's proposal. "It was impossible to pretend that she had not acted with her eyes open," she tells herself afterward; "if ever a girl was a free agent she had been" (p. 355). When she finally confesses her mistake to her friend Henrietta (before, however, she learns how she has been manipulated by Madame Merle), she reveals how fundamentally little she has been changed by suffering. She repudiates Henrietta's suggestion that she leave her husband with the refusal to "publish [her] mistake":

> "I don't know what great unhappiness might bring me to;
> but it seems to me I shall always be ashamed. One must accept
> one's deeds. I married him before all the world; I was perfectly
> free; it was impossible to do anything more deliberate. One
> can't change, that way," Isabel repeated.
> "You have changed, in spite of the impossibility. I hope
> you don't mean to say that you like him."
> Isabel hesitated a moment. "No, I don't like him. I can tell
> you, because I am weary of my secret. But that's enough;
> I can't tell all the world."
> Henrietta gave a rich laugh. "Don't you think you are rather
> too considerate?"
> "It's not of him that I am considerate—it's of myself!" Isabel
> answered [pp. 427–428].

James later praised the proud humility of Mrs. Frances Kemble. "The greatest pride of all," he maintained, "is to be proud of nothing, the pride not of pretension but of renunciation."[20]

Isabel remains proud throughout *The Portrait,* although she does manage to learn the delusive nature of what she once considered her freedom. On the eve of her great mistake (in the chapter directly before the introduction of Osmond into the novel), Isabel considers herself free of all ties: "it was in her disposition at all times to lose faith in the reality of absent things . . . The past was apt to look dead" (p. 196). She discovers, of course, that one must accept human responsibilities; on a human scale, she emerges more sympathetically at the end than Mrs. Touchett. She also discovers—or rather, we discover—that she is subject to the system of the novel. With characteristic irony, James lets his "unconventional" heroine succumb to a man who describes himself as "convention itself." In a sense, Isabel does succeed in the novelist's prerogative of making her own fate. In the sense that she demands to act out her character, Isabel is permitted some show of will. But it is James, of course, who has really shaped her character and he has put her into a novel filled with inner novelists who take advantage, through malice or mistaken kindness, of the nature of her character.

Isabel would not be so vulnerable if James had not made her so romantic to begin (though not to end) with. Richard Chase has suggestively argued that the novel is about "the limits of romance." "Isabel," he notes, "tends to see things as a romancer does, whereas the author sees things with the firmer, more comprehensive, and more disillusioned vision of the novelist."[21] It might be added that Isabel is set among other characters who resemble, to some degree, Jamesian novelists. Isabel herself curiously resembles the romantic American side of the author, which he managed more or less successfully to subdue by 1880. Her rootless family life, her early trips to Europe, here eccentric and self-guided education, strikingly resemble James's. The Archer daughters, we are told, "had had no regular education and no permanent home; they had been at once spoiled and neglected . . . Her father had a large way of looking at life, of which his restlessness and even his occasional incoherency of conduct had been only a proof." Left to her own resources, Isabel "had had the best of everything," had never come in contact with anything "disagreeable," and had been sustained by an extraordinary imagination. At moments, James warns us (and himself) that "she paid the penalty of having given undue encouragement to the faculty of seeing without judging" (pp. 26–27).

As a child, we discover, Isabel has learned to impose romance upon reality. An unopened door in her grandmother's house provides the most vivid proof we have of Isabel's willful romanticizing:

> She knew that this silent, motionless portal opened into the street; if the sidelights had not been filled with green paper, she might have looked out upon the little brown stoop and the well-worn brick pavement. But she had no wish to look out, for this would have interfered with her theory that there was a strange, unseen place on the other side—a place which became, to the child's imagination, according to its different moods, a region of delight or of terror [p. 19].

Thenceforth, she will continue to impose her imagination upon what she sees. After meeting Osmond and hearing his "dry" and self-pitying account of himself, her imagination, James assures us, "supplied the human element which she was sure had not been wanting" (p. 232). Earlier in a similarly "generous error" she has idealized Madame Merle: "if Madame Merle had not the merits she attributed to her, so much the worse for Madame Merle" (p. 163).

Despite the extravagant posture James sometimes ascribes to Henrietta, it is she who most clearly and promptly realizes that Isabel is drifting to a mistake through romantic willfulness. "The peril for you," she warns, "is that you live too much in the world of your own dreams":

> "—you are not enough in contact with reality—with the toiling, striving, suffering, I may even say sinning, world that surrounds you. You are too fastidious; you have too many graceful illusions. Your newly-acquired thousands will shut you up more and more to the society of a few selfish and heartless people, who will be interested in keeping up those illusions."

> Isabel's eyes expanded as she gazed upon this vivid but
> dusky picture of her future. "What are my illusions?" she
> asked. "I try so hard not to have any."

Isabel has the romantic belief that she can do whatever she wants and still please other people. The time will come, Henrietta warns, when she must displease herself and others, despite her fondness for "admiration" and being "thought well of. You think we can escape disagreeable duties by taking romantic views—that is your great illusion, my dear. But we can't. You must be prepared on many occasions in life to please no one at all—not even yourself" (pp. 189–190). The essential theme of the novel, as opposed to the romance, has always been that of "Lost Illusions," although James, working between the two forms, neither himself surrendered nor lets his heroine surrender the illusion of the self. It is as true of *The Portrait* as of *Washington Square* before it that romantic views come to grief, but so do realistic views. At the end of the novel, Isabel's dreams and Madame Merle's plans have alike been shipwrecked, but James finds, for Isabel, a personal way out.

Isabel is the center of *The Portrait of a Lady* (virtually everyone and everything else in the novel exist for her sake), but her way of looking at life is only half of the dialectic involved. The novel might be subtitled, in imitation of James's memoirs, "An American Girl and Others"; but since Isabel is not a future novelist, her detachment from others, her youthful subjectivity, is not convertible for artistic use. In the first half of the book, she engagingly conquers the novel she is in; much of the second half, she is conquered by it and put into her proper place. The prerequisite for her initial conquest is that she be firm, active, and uncomprehending. In this she anticipates Mona Brigstock in *The Spoils of Poynton*, "who is *all* will" but without judgment or taste—hence, for James, one of the successful ones of this earth.[22]

For all her weaknesses, Isabel impresses and misleads everyone. Her mind, Lord Warburton remarks bitterly, "looks down on us all; it despises us," and there is an amount of truth to this and to his subsequent protest: " 'You judge only from the outside— you don't care,' he said presently. 'You only care to amuse yourself!' " (p. 68). Part of the appeal of Madame Merle, thenceforth, lies in her judicious aloofness from others, which Isabel sees as "simply the essence of the aristocratic situation." It has its connection, of course, with the artistic situation, too. For Isabel, Madame Merle has "the great thing"; she has the good fortune "to be in a better position for appreciating people than they are for appreciating you" (pp. 165–166). Madame Merle makes her first appearance in the novel when Ralph's kindly father is dying; his death, of course, makes an heiress of Isabel and turns her from being Madame Merle's friend to somebody to be used by her. Compassion is momentarily in abeyance, and Isabel's model is now ominously a worldly woman, whose "pleasure was now to judge rather than to feel" (p. 163). *Tout comprendre c'est tout épater* is Madame Merle's cynical philosophy, but Isabel is not alarmed, "for she had never supposed that, as one saw more of the world, the sentiment of respect became the most active of one's emotions" (p. 214).

If Isabel represents a side of James outgrown, or at least outdistanced, Madame Merle represents much of the lure of Europe he had learned to see through. In one of the autobiographical sections in his notebooks, entered in 1881, James recalled "the vision of those untried years," his youthful eagerness for "life" and "success" and the desire "to see something of the world."[23] In the novel it is Mrs. Touchett who decides to introduce Isabel "to the world" (p. 35); Madame Merle, as Ralph points out, "is the world itself" (p. 220). One of the crucial thematic scenes in *The Portrait* involves a comparison between Emersonian American and worldly European views of life. The passage, which is often cited in discussions of the novel (although Madame Merle's argument is generally minimized), reaches its climax when Isabel refuses to consider any potential suitor—Caspar, for example—in terms of his house. Madame Merle retorts,

> "That is very crude of you. When you have lived as long as I, you will see that every human being has his shell, and that you must take the shell into account. By the shell, I mean the whole envelope of circumstances. There is no such thing as an isolated man or woman; we are each of us made up of a cluster of appurtenances. What do you call one's self? Where does it begin? Where does it end? It overflows into everything that belongs to us—and then it flows back again. I know that a large part of myself is in the dresses I choose to wear. I have a great respect for *things!* One's self—for other people

—is one's expression of one's self; and one's house, one's
clothes, the book one reads, the company one keeps—
these things are all expressive."

Isabel disagrees:

"I don't know whether I succeed in expressing myself, but
I know that nothing else expresses me. Nothing that belongs
to me is any measure of me; on the contrary; it's a limit,
a barrier, and a perfectly arbitrary one. Certainly, the clothes
which, as you say, I choose to wear, don't express me; and
heaven forbid they should!" [pp. 175–176].

Isabel adopts William James's distinction between the inner "I"
and the socially influenced "me." James compressed into this passage the dialogue between free will and determinism that had
already appeared in *Roderick Hudson* and *The American*. To judge
from the evidence of his letters, one would tend to place James
personally on Madame Merle's side of the argument, although as
an artist he cherished his own freedom. It is part of the mastery
of his art that Isabel should make us wish to see her at freedom,
despite her bondage to her character and, hence, her fate.

Madame Merle is the most ambiguously characterized figure in
the book. One tends to think of her as a melodramatic villainess
because of her later scenes in the novel with Isabel and Osmond.
Initially, however, she charms everyone. Ralph calls her the "clev-
erest woman" he knows, and "the one person in the world whom
[Mrs. Touchett] very much admires" (p. 153). Isabel considers her
the image of success, the consummate "great lady," with the single
flaw of not being "natural" in Rousseauvian terms:

by which the girl meant, not that she was affected or pretentious;
for from these vulgar vices no woman could have been more
exempt; but that her nature had been too much overlaid by
custom and her angles too much smoothed. She had become
too flexible, too supple; she was too finished, too civilised.
She was, in a word, too perfectly the social animal that man and
woman are supposed to have been intended to be; and she had
rid herself of every remnant of that tonic wildness which
we may assume to have belonged even to the most amiable
persons in the ages before country-house life was the fashion.

As a consequence, Isabel realizes, Madame Merle cannot be considered "as an isolated figure; she existed only in her relations with
her fellow-mortals" (p. 167)—unlike a romantic, detached, Ameri-

can girl. Both Isabel and James take delight, at this point, in Madame Merle as a "charming surface," an elaborate artifact, who seems to exist only for the sake of being admired by American observers. Later in the novel the flaws are pointed out. Madame Merle is the quintessential "lady" of the novel; and Oscar Cargill is, therefore, undoubtedly right in his surmise that the title of the book is ironic.[24] Her villainy is that of an artist *manqué:* unsuccessful at making her own fate, she attempts to manipulate others. But in doing so, she passes, in the reader's mind, from a fine portrait of a lady to a crude agent of melodrama.*

Gilbert Osmond, by contrast, may strike readers as the greater or the lesser villain because of the passive nature of his role in the conspiracy. Whether or not he is "James's first notable study in modern perversity," as F. W. Dupee says, he does resemble a "stock conspirator of melodrama," and his egotism is fully a match for Isabel's.[25] He, too, is an amateur artist: along with his slim talent as a watercolorist, he is a successful inner novelist manipulating his daughter. "This kind of thing doesn't find me unprepared," he says when he hears of Pansy's infatuation for Ned Rosier. "It's what I educated her for. It was all for this—that when such a case should come up she should do what I prefer" (p. 327). With Isabel he is not so fortunate. After she marries him, she does worse than defy him; she sees through him. What she sees is a pseudoartistic temperament such as James exposed, comically, in the figure of Louis Leverett. Osmond's appeal lies mainly in his pretense of living only for the sake of good taste and for himself. At their first meeting, she expresses "considerable sympathy for the success with which he had preserved his independence. 'That's a very pleasant life,' she said, 'to renounce everything but Correggio!' " (p. 232) There is a certain amount of irony in Osmond's deluded appraisal of Isabel, and, were James not identified to a

---

* There is the following interchange with Isabel, for example, in which the effect is overly theatrical:

"What have you to do with me?" Isabel went on.

Madame Merle slowly got up, stroking her muff, but not removing her eyes from Isabel's face.

"Everything!" she answered [p. 453].

And there is the rhetoric in her speeches to Osmond: "It was precisely my devilry that stupefied her. I couldn't help it; I was full of something bad. Perhaps it was something good; I don't know. You have not only dried up my tears; you have dried up my soul" (p. 458).

point with Osmond, one might even find an unintentional humor in his Pateresque appeal to her: "Don't you remember my telling you that one ought to make one's life a work of art? You looked rather shocked at first; but then I told you that it was exactly what you seemed to me to be trying to do with your own life." (p. 269).

It is characteristic of James's heroes to become precisely that: artists at life. Osmond's failure, to some extent, lies not in his aesthetic attitude but in his mediocrity and hypocrisy. Rather than live for himself, "this base, ignoble world, it appeared, was after all what one was to live for." Isabel does not, after all, disbelieve in what Osmond has hypocritically argued, for he had "pointed out to her so much of the baseness and shabbiness of life, opened her eyes so wide to the stupidity, the depravity, the ignorance of mankind, that she had been properly impressed with the infinite vulgarity of things, and of the virtue of keeping one's self unspotted by it." Osmond's defect, thus, is not that what he preaches is wrong, but that he does not practice what he preaches. The lure of Osmond as an *image* is as strong to Isabel as the image of Madame Merle: "She was to think of him as he thought of himself—as the first gentleman in Europe. So it was that she had thought of him at first, and that indeed was the reason she had married him" (p. 376). It is natural, perhaps, that some recent critics have pitied Osmond for being as much mistaken in Isabel as she with him. James's moral distinction is not altogether clear.

The "immoral" nature of the subsidiary characters in *The Portrait* depends, very largely, upon the parts they play as inner novelists, taking over James's function for him. Mrs. Touchett sets the chain of events in motion by introducing Isabel to the "world"; Madame Merle unites Isabel with Osmond (in a manner curiously unspecified in the novel—thereby forcing the reader to become an inner novelist, too); Osmond attempts, unsuccessfully, to tyrannize his wife. It is striking how these manipulators of Isabel appeal to elements basic in her, and thus cannot be said really to have diverted her from a way of life not essentially of her own choosing. It is Isabel's true admirers who cause unwarranted mishap, precisely because they appeal to elements in her (such as intellectual prowess, or femininity) which simply do not exist or else leave her free to her own willfulness. In a real sense, Ralph Touchett is the greatest "villain" of *The Portrait*, because he is the least aware of Isabel's limitations and because he is the most Jamesian figure in the book.

In James's fiction Ralph is the culminating figure of the tragedy of ironic detachment, and after Lambert Strether he bears the closest resemblance to James. His sense of irony, his intelligence, and his artistic good taste are all James's, to a degree that almost dims the likeness between James and Osmond. Isabel in time comes to see Ralph as Osmond's superior in three respects: she wonders whether Osmond's "sense of humour were by chance defective" (p. 341); she realizes that Ralph is "much more intelligent" ("quite apart from his being better") than her husband (p. 380); and, quite early and without then realizing the significance of the distinction, she notes differences in taste: "Ralph had something of this same quality, this appearance of thinking that life was a matter of connoisseurship; but in Ralph it was an anomaly, a kind of humorous excrescence, whereas in Mr. Osmond it was the keynote, and everything was in harmony with it" (p. 229).

James reiterated this distinction in his comparison of Fleda and Mrs. Gereth in *The Spoils of Poynton*. "Almost as much as Mrs. Gereth's her taste was her life, but her life was somehow the larger for it." Ralph is for James an autobiographical projection of the superiority of the defective organism. James had written, while a young man, that "To call a man healthy nowadays is almost an insult—invalids learn so many secrets. But the health of the intellect is often promoted by physical disability."[26]

James clearly intended Ralph to represent the spirit of good sense. A keynote occurs when he attempts to settle a dispute between his mother and Henrietta. "Ralph," says James, "with his experimental geniality, suggested, by way of healing the breach, that the truth lay between the two extremes" (p. 81). James boasted of his own "habit (so insufferable to some of my friends) of ever and again readjusting the balance after I have given it an honest tip."[27] The most pertinent passage linking the two men is the description of Ralph's freedom:

His outward conformity to the manners that surrounded him was none the less the mask of a mind that greatly enjoyed its independence, on which nothing long imposed itself, and which, naturally inclined to jocosity and irony, indulged in a boundless liberty of appreciation [p. 30].

Ralph is, hence, the most Jamesian of the inner novelists at work settling Isabel's fate. He confesses, in language which reminds us of Dr. Sloper's, that he lives for the "spectacle" which she affords him. "I shall have the entertainment of seeing what a young lady does who won't marry Lord Warburton," he tells her very early, and he asks his dying father to leave Isabel a fortune for the sake of his "entertainment," to indulge his imagination (pp. 129, 160–162).

In this, he is, of course, living vicariously through her; seeing her gratify her imagination, he will gratify his, and, as long as there is something for him to see, he has something to live for. Isabel's failure hastens his death. "It was for you that I wanted— that I wanted to live," he confesses. "But I am of no use to you" (p. 441). In a sense, he has never really been of use to her; he has neither understood nor served her satisfactorily. Ralph plays the "apostle of freedom" (as Osmond savagely thinks) (p. 404) to a heroine ignorant and willful. Old Mr. Touchett had noticed something "immoral" in his son's plan for Isabel, and there is something definitely questionable in Ralph's advice to the new heiress:

> "Don't ask yourself so much whether this or that is good for you. Don't question your conscience so much—it will get out of tune, like a strummed piano. Keep it for great occasions. Don't try so much to form your character—it's like trying to pull open a rosebud. Live as you like best, and your character will form itself . . . Spread your wings; rise above the ground. It's never wrong to do that" [p. 194].

No wonder, then, that Isabel should feel that Ralph cannot help approving of her marriage with Osmond—"for he knows that whatever I do I do with reason," she tells a horrified Mrs. Touchett (p. 294).

This is by no means to suggest that Ralph is an immoral villain. Rather, he is an artist and an artistic necessity. Madame Merle's cruel words contain much truth: "He imparted to you that extra lustre [the inheritance] which was required to make you a brilliant match. At bottom, it is him that you have to thank" (p. 490). This echoes Isabel's own exasperated rebuke to Ralph, when he tries to stop the marriage: "You say you amused yourself with planning out my future—I don't understand that. Don't amuse yourself too much, or I shall think you are doing it at my expense" (p. 302).

The moral danger of James's artist-heroes is that they move on a plane where conscience is replaced by artistic propriety. Their watchword is not what is right or wrong but what is suitable or unsuitable for the occasion. Much has been written on James's sense of evil and its similarity with Hawthorne's, but it is fairly obvious, I think, that James merely utilizes where Hawthorne felt. F. O. Matthiessen has linked Osmond with Hawthorne's villains; for James too, he argues, "the evil nature was the cold egoist who used or preyed upon other people."[28] This may be an apt enough description of Osmond, but for James there is no moral opprobrium involved. The ego using or preying upon other egos is not, after all, markedly different from the Jamesian artist. Connect this type of artist with living matter, however, and he is potentially dangerous, as Ralph Touchett is dangerous.

It might seem the Jamesian artist's mission to destroy what he has created, to fix into place what has seemed free. And yet, with extraordinary novelty, James really does nothing of the sort in *The Portrait of a Lady*. The title is doubly ironic because all of the Jamesian inner artists created free enough to manipulate her end up in a fixed posture of melodrama (like Osmond or Madame Merle) or romantic rhetoric (like Ralph). Yet Isabel is deliberately left up in the air. Despite the amount of critical blood spilt over the question of the ending of the novel—"Why does Isabel return to Osmond, and what will happen to her?"—and despite the number of attractive theories put forward, one might do worse than suggest that, while James considered the novel to be artistically "complete," he did not by any means consider Isabel to be finished. "The obvious criticism," he admitted to himself, "of course will be that it is not finished—that I have not seen the heroine to the end of her situation—that I have left her *en l'air.*—This is both true and false. The *whole* of anything is never told; you can only take what groups together. What I have done has that unity—it groups together. It is complete in itself—and the rest may be taken up or not, later."[29]

The novel understandably bothered many early reviewers, who decided that no (or unhappy) endings were part of the "new school" of novelists.* In Howells' important study of James, pub-

* A number of reviewers, however, were scandalized by what they assumed was an ending in which an adulterous union between Isabel and Caspar is predicted.

lished the next year, the lack of an ending was seen as an integral part of James's new view of the novel. "If we take him at all," Howells pointed out, "we must take him on his own ground, for clearly he will not come to ours." Among the "concessions" which Howells noted that the reader must make while reading James is the willingness to be left "to our own conjectures in regard to the fate of the people in whom he has interested us."[30]

It is James's purpose to make artists of us, his readers; for this purpose he has given us a novel which is at once carefully patterned and open to outside construction. In this dual method of approach, James plays with the reader's expectations and often leads him astray. For example, two-thirds of the way through the novel, after several years of Isabel's married life have passed unreported, he begins a subplot involving Ned Rosier's attempt to marry Pansy Osmond. In this parody of the main plot (where the keynote is that the lovers are severely "limited"), Rosier is a slight, genial, aesthetic collector of bibelots, and it is from his defective point of view that James reintroduces us to Isabel: "framed in the gilded doorway, she struck our young man as the picture of a gracious lady (p. 321). If this passage occurred at the end of the novel—and if Rosier's point of view were wholly reliable—one might well agree with the critical thesis of Poirier and others that James has "fixed" his heroine firmly in place. He has not.

Isabel tries to assume the mask Osmond wishes her to wear; in the last third of the novel we see that she not only has retained her own independent point of view, but she also has come to accept the complexity of a world where things are not as they seemed to her once simple, picture-making gaze. She now praises Lord Warburton for being able to put himself in Rosier's place, noting that "it shows imagination" (p. 389). Moreover, with the triumph of inner maturity, she accepts the fact of complexity: "Deep in her soul—deeper than any appetite for renunciation—was the sense that life would be her business for a long time to come" (p. 492). One thinks of James's comment on the effect upon the new American of the Civil War; it provoked an awareness of "proportion and relation, of the world being a more complicated place than it had hitherto seemed, the future more treacherous, success more difficult."[31] To accept the truth of this means that, ironically, we cannot presume to demand a finished portrait of Isabel. She has developed, at the end of the novel, into a character with a lively sense of complexity, scarcely more fathomable than Henry James. As a character in a James short story puts it, "The proper time for the [portrait] likeness was at the last, when the whole man was there—you got the totality of his experience."[32] At the end of *The Portrait*, hence, we have our last view of Isabel, but James means us to understand that we do not at all know the last of her. "The *whole* of anything is never told; you can only take what groups together."

James's evasion of the finished portrait, consequently, is in keeping with his artistic philosophy at this period of his career. The Victorian novel demanded stability of characterization, a firm focus, and an ending which, if not necessarily happy, at least ended something. Marriage and children were preferred because they represented a society in which unity (however precarious) and perpetuity were political and philosophical necessities. But the 1880's was a time of considerable social unrest, and James was hardly a Victorian moralist by ambition or in background. Amid the flux of historical and human change, only works of art seemed fixed values to him. At the end of *The Portrait*, the heroine returns to the English country house where her adventures started, and James allows her to "complete" an imaginary cycle:

Nothing was changed; she recognized everything that she had seen years before; it might have been only yesterday that she stood there. She reflected that things change but little, while people change so much, and she became aware that she was walking about as her aunt had done on the day she came to see her in Albany. She was changed enough since then—that had been the beginning. It suddenly struck her that if her Aunt Lydia had not come that day in just that way and found her alone, everything might have been different. She might have had another life, and to-day she might have been a happier woman. She stopped in the gallery in front of a small picture— a beautiful and valuable Bonington—upon which her eye rested for a long time. But she was not looking at the picture; she was wondering whether if her aunt had not come that day in Albany she would have married Caspar Goodwood [p. 499].

The circle seems to come to an extraordinary close with the appearance of Goodwood at that moment with his renewed appeal, but the grounds for his argument, for anyone who has read the novel, are specious. "We can do absolutely as we please," he declares, echoing Isabel's original illusion; "to whom under the sun do we owe anything? . . . The world is all before us—and the world is very large" (p. 518). By now Isabel has learned just how false that clinging to self and freedom is, and, by turning into the "very straight path" before her, she displays the fullest extent of her freedom, in Jamesian terms. One need only turn to the parenthetical aside in *Portraits of Places* where James describes the paradoxical freedom of the English: "Every one is free and every one is responsible . . . With us there is infinitely less responsibility; but there is also, I think, less freedom."[33]

James's definition of freedom may be singular—and of more use to the artist than the philosopher—but it enabled him to maintain an artistic confidence and equilibrium, and to write, even after sustained residence in England, the most distinctly American novel of his time. Upon its publication, however, much of the basis for his confidence would be undermined by the combination of hostile criticism and the death of a number of people dear to him. Hereafter, the history of James in the 1880's is one of uncertainty—a search for literary forms acceptable to the public that might also serve as memorials to the dead.

The Art of Fiction and the Act of Fiction

> "Now what is your point of view?" she asked of her aunt. "When you criticize everything here, you should have a point of view. Yours doesn't seem to be American—you thought everything over there so disagreeable. When I criticize, I have mine; it's thoroughly American."
> "My dear young lady," said Mrs. Touchett, "there are as many points of view in the world as there are people of sense. You may say that doesn't make them very numerous! American? Never in the world; that's shockingly narrow. My point of view, thank God, is personal!"
> (The Portrait of a Lady)

In October 1880, with the work on *The Egoist* and *The Tragic Comedians* behind him, Meredith complained that he felt "next to useless, except to admire the performances of certain . . . Fairy Princes." With the serials of *Washington Square* and *The Portrait of a Lady* running simultaneously, Meredith compared James's literary prowess to "the ease of a spangled circus-master."[34] But it was in the early 1880's that James, despite such major achievements as the two preceding novels and *The Bostonians* to come, began to exhibit symptoms of withdrawal from his social life and in his literary work. Introduced to James in 1882, Edmund Gosse was to remember that he seemed "a little formal and frightened, which seemed strange in a man living in constant communication with the world." Later in the decade, William James would characterize his brother as being, despite all the "protective resemblances" of "strange heavy alien manners and customs," the "same dear old, good, innocent and at bottom very powerless-feeling Harry . . . , caring for little but his writing, and full of dutifulness and affection for all gentle things."[35] In a decade marked by the deaths of major figures of the relatively stable past, James mourned the passing of both his literary mentors and his parents, and in an age of profound changes he began to experiment with the form and theory of fiction. Increasingly falling under the attacks of critics and learning to give up any hope for popular success as a novelist, James turned defensively to his art; his themes reflect, as a result, the need for withdrawal from, and for independence in, a world which had come to seem dangerous and even predatory.

The Portrait of a Lady was written during the "golden hours" of James's career, with a masterful combination of purpose, wit, and confidence which, for various reasons, was never to be fully regained. The novel, without having a sensational sale, went through at least ten printings in America and England following publication in late 1881. Much critical attention was paid to it, both in homage to James's talent and in response to the literary gossip about what the *National Review*, for example, was billing as "The New School of Fiction." A collected edition of James's fiction was promised for 1883, and success seemed assured. There were also disclaimers, however. An anonymous critic for *The Quarterly Review,* in an essay on "American Novels" printed in January 1883, was considerably less friendly than most. "Dull unspeakably dull," he charged, sneering at what he labeled "the Transatlantic aesthetic reformers."[36]

The *Quarterly's* animus was directed not so much against James's recent novel as against William Dean Howells' eulogy of the author in the November 1882 issue of the *Century.* As Donald Murray has shown in his study of James's English reviewers during the 1880's, the extravagant claims of the Howells essay had a damaging effect upon James's reputation.[37] James's longtime friend could not restrain a partial lament that the novelist who had early in his career "stood at the dividing ways of the novel and the romance" had chosen the former. "His best efforts," he remarked, "seem to me those of romance," but he admitted that romance was now perhaps an "outworn form." The eulogy of James is tempered somewhat by an implied elegy for the romance—which James had attacked, despite Howell's protests, in his *Hawthorne*—and for the old-fashioned novel. James's triumph, he noted, is that of a new subjectivism in which the artist is more important than his material:

> It is, after all, what a writer has to say rather than what he
> has to tell that we care for nowadays. In one manner or other
> the stories were all told long ago; and now we want merely
> to know what the novelist thinks about persons and situations.
> Mr. James gratifies this philosophic desire.

Howells' defense of James's unconventional methods was underlined by an unfortunate artistic chauvinism: "The art of fiction," he maintained, "has, in fact, become a finer art in our day than it was with Dickens and Thackeray." Novelists of the "new school," while influenced by George Eliot and Hawthorne in this respect, are even more interested in the subtlest workings of "human nature" than they, and in "form," the new writers are somewhat subdued followers of the French realists.

> This school, which is so largely of the future as well as the
> present, finds its chief exemplar in Mr. James; it is he who
> is shaping and directing American fiction, at least. It is the
> ambition of the younger contributors to write like him; he has
> his following more distinctly recognizable than that of any
> other English-writing novelist.[38]

If pride goeth before a fall, it is certainly a pity that James's reputation should have toppled with the aid of another's pride in him.

Rebecca West, in her impressionistic study of James (1916),
declared that his popularity had been very real roughly between
1875 and 1885. In 1872, while trying to answer one of William's
periodic requests that he broaden his appeal, James asserted an
independent-minded wish not to be bound by public taste: "The
multitude, I am more and more convinced, has absolutely no taste
—none at least that a thinking man is bound to defer to. To write
for the few who have is doubtless to lose money—but I am not
afraid of starving."[39] But this was before he had written anything
of distinct literary merit. By 1881 he had several great works behind him, plus a considerable social position and literary reputation. Howells' essay had a damaging influence upon the reputation
during a time of intense self-questioning for James. He was considered important enough now, ironically, to be disposed of with
a volley of critical clichés—as the member of the "analytical
school," the novelist without endings, the neo-French "realist"—
which resounded through the following decade. Henceforth, a defensive tone can be observed in James's writings in the eighties.
For a time, a constant need to explain, without drawing attention
to, himself and a fruitless desire to become popular by turning to
the writing of topical books in a conventional style with real endings were evident.

James's confidence was not substantially tested until after publication of *The Bostonians* and *The Princess Casamassima,* and it
is certainly true to say that he lost confidence in the English public
more than in himself. In late 1881, before the critical storm broke,
James returned to America, and his notebooks testify that he was
aware of a turning point in his career. For one thing, he was to
utilize his notebooks from now on as a real literary aid, which
meant that he was cautiously accepting the methods of the new
French writers whom he had been criticizing up to now for their
limitation of subject matter and for their empirical rather than
moral point of view. "I have lost too much," he warned himself,
"by losing, or rather by not having acquired, the note-taking habit."

> It might be of great profit to me; and now that I am older,
> that I have more time, that the labour of writing is less onerous
> to me, and I can work more at my leisure, I ought to endeavour

to keep, to a certain extent, a record of passing impressions,
of all that comes, that goes, that I see, and feel, and observe.
To catch and keep something of life—that's what I mean.
Here I am back in America, for instance, after six years of
absence, and likely while here to see and learn a great deal that
ought not to become mere waste material.

Instead of filling the notebook with impressions of America, however, James proceeded to sketch an autobiographical fragment and
regard himself in perspective. He had returned to New England
to see his family ("to revive my relations with them, and my sense
of the consequences that these relations entail," he curiously declared), but he felt his time "terribly wasted here!" The word
"waste" reverberates through the passage: James realized that he
had made his choice to live in England, and that, in middle age,
he had "no time to waste" as a collector of usable impressions—
as an artist.[40]

If he felt himself necessarily cut off from his American background ("Boston is absolutely nothing to me—I don't even dislike
it," he would write a year later, and his impressions of New York
are only slightly more genial), he compensated for this loss by
clinging to London. Feeling a "ferocious homesickness" for London, he reflected upon what he deemed to be his "anchorage for
life":

> I have *lived* much there, felt much, thought much, learned
> much, produced much; the little shabby furnished apartment
> ought to be sacred to me. I came to London as a complete
> stranger, and today I know much too many people. *J'y suis
> absolument comme chez moi.* Such an experience is an education
> —it fortifies the character and embellishes the mind.

Continuing his reflections, James reminded himself that "magnificent" as London was, it was also damp, dirty, ugly, oversized,
inhuman, and even vulgar. But for the Jamesian artist, for whom
London meant materials rather than a participant way of life:

> London is on the whole the most possible form of life. I take
> it as an artist and as a bachelor; as one who has the passion
> of observation and whose business is the study of human life.
> It is the biggest aggregation of human life—the most complete
> compendium of the world. The human race is better represented
> there than anywhere else, and if you learn to know your
> London you learn a great many things.[41]

It is ironic that James's next novel should have been conceived as "an attempt to show that I *can* write an American story," but in the interval between late 1881 and the spring of 1883 a number of events managed to shake his faith in the security of his London "anchorage" and made him want, almost to the point of exasperation, to come to terms with America.

In February 1882 his mother died, occasioning in his notebook a strangely operatic rhetoric of grief and a sense of consolation "that certain supreme impressions remain!"[42] He returned to London with a sense of relief; America had seemed "on the whole a poor world this time." He was grateful to be in London at a time when he could return to work. The London season was over for the summer, and a curious new note appeared in James's journal: "I know too many people—I have gone in too much for society."[43] This new theme which would reverberate more and more in future writings and declarations emerged: to be an artist, one must be as careful as possible to avoid overly personal relations—precisely because of the "sense of the consequences that these relations entail." One of the major incidental themes in the novels, from *The Bostonians* to *The Tragic Muse,* is the need for the main character to detach himself from family, friends, society, conventions if he is to survive as an artistic or just an independent consciousness. One of James's overt intentions, in these very novels, was to relate himself to the conventions of the Victorian novel; and the sense of cross-purposes involved provides for the reader an interesting tension and a consequent ambiguity.

The immediate result of his return to America was a short story, which picked up an idea he had jotted down in 1879: "Description of a situation, or incident, in an alternation of letters, written from an aristocratic, and a democratic, point of view;—both enlightened and sincere."[44] In "The Point of View" (1882), James utilized the impressions from his trip, but the seven points of view of America in the tale reflect a deliberate mixture of apperception and blindness. James might have taken his cue from Alexander Pope:

> 'Tis with our judgments as our watches, none
> Go just alike, yet each believes his own.

James accepted his brother's pluralism in this respect; yet the position of artist enabled him to combine various points of view, to take into consideration both the diversity of reality and the reality of diversity.

"The Point of View" reveals James's willingness, for the time being, to accommodate himself to other points of view, and in this it points toward much of his best work in the decade. As in *The Bostonians*, the clash of opposing points of view makes for comedy, but the connection of half-truths also equals a sort of cumulative truth. The story has been cited to show James's revulsion against America; actually, however, James paid tribute to his father's and brother's patriotism. The angle of vision most scathingly anti-American, aside from that of the French Academician, is that of a character James has used before and treated unsympathetically. Aurora Church's bullying mother—from "The Pension Beaurepas" —makes a charge sometimes cited as James's own: "In this country the people have rights, but the person has none." Yet in 1882 James had written from America, "it is pleasant to be in one's native land, where one is someone and something"; in the *Haw-thorne* he had stressed "the importance of the individual in the American world."[45] The personal anguish recorded in the notebooks is put into the letter of Louis Leverett, the sickly aesthete from "A Bundle of Letters":

> I am a stranger here, and I find it hard to believe that I ever was a native . . . There is no form here . . . I feel as if I were sitting in the centre of a mighty "reflector." A terrible crude glare is over everything, the earth looks peeled and excoriated; the raw heavens seem to bleed with the quick, hard light.

Meanwhile, an English M.P. is impressed by the lack of interest of the best people in politics, as well as by the high material standards and the great emphasis placed on education ("My leading impression is that the children in this country are better educated than the adults").[46]

The Frenchman, however, finds nothing in America but a plenitude of deficiencies. In a condemnatory passage which archly parodies James's famous list in his *Hawthorne* of the "paraphernalia" lacking to an American artist, Lejaune notes the absence of amenities, manners, salons, society, conversation, imagination, sensibility, nuns, beggars, cocottes, architecture, art, literature, theater, political movements, officials, authority, functionaries, doorkeepers, officers, uniforms, badges, and restrictions. "As for the people," he complains, "they are the English *minus* the conventions. You can fancy what remains." The American novel, he observes, is lacking in form, matter, style, and "general ideas." A proof of the Frenchman's limitations is afforded by his jaundiced comment on Henry James himself:

> They have a novelist with pretensions to literature, who writes about the chase for the husband [another of the letter-writers of this story is doing exactly that] and the adventures of the rich Americans in our corrupt old Europe, where their primeval candor puts the Europeans to shame. *C'est proprement écrit;* but it's terribly pale.[47]

Of the remaining points of view, that of the American expatriate Miss Sturdy is probably closest to James's own. America is delightfully good-natured, he says through her, but it does not have the basic material needed for the novelist of manners; there are no manners.

The American patriot, Marcellus Cockerel, the last of the seven to be heard from, has clearly absorbed the faith of Henry James, Sr., in democracy and in "America as the land of the future."[48] Despite a tendency toward caricature, Cockerel is allowed to hit back at James's English critics and to utter one of the author's best epigrams: Americans "are more analytic, more discriminating, more familiar with realities. As for manners, there are bad manners everywhere, but an aristocracy is bad manners organized." He is also given the chance to turn the pointed view back toward Europe:

> They revile us for our party politics; but what are all the European jealousies and rivalries, their armaments and their wars, their rapacities and their mutual lies, but the intensity of the spirit of party? what question, what interest, what idea, what need of mankind, is involved in any of these things? Their big, pompous armies, drawn up in great silly rows, their gold lace, their salaams, their hierarchies, seem a pastime for children; there's a sense of humor and of reality over here that laughs at all that.

"Yes we are nearer the reality—we are nearer what they will all have to come to," he continues, in a strain very dear to James's father's heart. "The questions of the future are social questions."[49]

One wonders what Henry James, Sr., would have thought about the form of his son's tribute to him. In late 1882, however, he gave up the will to live without his wife. By the time James hurried home from Europe again, his father was dead. And now he was really as well as figuratively an orphan, a man without a home in his native country. The next years were for James ones of intense dissatisfaction and searching, as Leon Edel's biography abundantly documents. In this sense of dislocation James was at one with the decade. Any late Victorian who sensed that he was living in a transitional period needed only to consult the obituary columns. In 1880 James's two exemplars of the French and English approach to the novel, Flaubert and George Eliot, the empirical and the moral realist, died. Within two years, such major political and philosophical leaders of the age as Disraeli, Carlyle, Darwin, and Pusey followed them. More important, in terms of James's career, were Emerson and Trollope, but, most important of all the writers close to him, Turgenev died in 1883. James elegized George Eliot, Emerson, Trollope, and Turgenev in noteworthy essays, which later comprised part of the volume of *Partial Portraits* (1888), his best single book of criticism. It was characteristic of James to wax eloquent over the altar of his memory of the dead. One senses, in retrospect, that he was laying his younger, more optimistic self to rest as well.

The first new piece of fiction after "The Point of View" was "The Siege of London" (1883), and it is characteristic of the change in mood. For a story of its length, very little happens. While two American observers look on, Nancy Headway, a self-reliant and disreputable Californian, tries to get into English society and succeeds. As one of the Americans cynically observes, "English society was always looking out for amusement and . . . its transactions were conducted on a cash basis." "I have gone in too much for society," James had written in his notebook, and he now began to separate himself from the setting he had once idealized. He continued, delicately, to prey upon society for the sake of collecting materials for his fiction, but he began to realize more and more that society was also preying upon him and upon itself. Through the writing of *The Awkward Age*, James still found merit in a social world which, however decadent, maintained a veneer of wit and manner; with the depiction of the utterly predatory world of *The Wings of the Dove*, James retreated from even that delusion. In "The Siege of London," the vulgar Mrs. Headway is more than a match for the undesirable society she aims at. Littlemore and Waterville, the two fastidious American onlookers, are considerably better-mannered, as it appears, than any of the English, and, at one point, the latter affirms the necessity of at least keeping up one's own standards: "One ought to assume that one is in society—that one *is* society—and to hold that if one has good manners, one has, from the social point of view, achieved the great thing."[50]

In this story about an independent American woman's attempt to get into society, James chronicled almost the reverse of his own goal: to keep his independence even while continuing to use society. The success of the Western divorcée may be read as a symbolic representation of the breakdown of social standards, but James needed that society as surely as he was an artist. George Painter's comment on Proust's similar need for society is surely relevant with regard to James: "A drawing room, it seemed to Proust, was itself a work of art, of which its habitués were both the performers and the creators, devising the formal movements of the mysterious ballet they danced, inventing the words of the frivolous but portentous drama they played."[51] On the heels of "The Siege of London" came a blunter statement of James's mixed feelings. In a study of "Du Maurier and London Society," he indicated the nature of the cleft between the artist and his materials— intimating that perhaps only the caricaturist could take full advantage of the decline of manners. In point of fact, the English could not be called "an aesthetic people":

> They have not a spontaneous artistic life; their taste is a matter of conscience, reflection, duty, and the writer who in our time has appealed to them most eloquently on behalf of art [Ruskin] has rested his plea on moral standards—has talked exclusively of right and wrong. It is impossible to live much among them, to be a spectator of their habits, their manners, their arrangements, without perceiving that the artistic point of view is the last that they naturally take.[52]

James's dialogue between what he considered the Ruskinian and the "artistic point of view" (a French import with a dash of Pater) continued through the decade, appearing notably in "The Author of *Beltraffio*" and "The Art of Fiction."

Of the other stories written or conceived between 1883 and 1884, only two have literary merit: "Pandora" and "The Author of *Beltraffio*." The other stories all give considerable evidence of James's difficulty in finding a subject or a style suitable to the short story. "The Impressions of a Cousin" (1883), "Lady Barberina" (1884), and "Georgina's Reasons" (1884) are much too long and much too uneven to merit praise, but they deal with vital artistic materials. In a sense, they are stories about the unsuccessful writing of stories. In "The Impressions of a Cousin," James returned to the first-person narrative form after a four-year lapse, and to an unprecedented degree (though in this it anticipates subsequent first-person narratives) the narrator becomes so involved with the story as to thwart any possible ensuing objectivity for the reader. Instead of seeing what is going on, we only see, and even that not very well, the efforts of the narrator to see what is going on and to control the action of the story.

"Lady Barberina" was perhaps intended as a comic version of the Lydgate-Rosamond section of *Middlemarch*. The hero is a doctor and an egoist, and his English highborn bride is distinguished for nothing but "the look of race." Barberina Centerville is married to Jackson Lemon for his money, while he is attracted to her for eugenic reasons: "it had taken a great social outlay to produce such a mixture." Lemon considers himself, for that matter, an American "heir of all the ages."[53] James only accentuated the obvious when he changed Barberina to Barbarina for the New York edition—in case anyone had missed the barbed reference to Arnold's Barbarian class. The hero of "Georgina's Reasons" is representative of a new type in James's fiction: "I am not master of anything," says Captain Benyon. "There is not a man in the world less free. I am a slave. I am a victim." A cross between Christopher Newman and Fleda Vetch, he is represented as an honorable man who must necessarily suffer in a dishonorable world. "Dishonor was in everything but renunciation"[54] is the sincere, if slightly glib, moral of his life.

"A New England Winter" (1884) contains another Jamesian self-parody in the figure of Florimond Daintry, an expatriated aesthete who returns to Boston. Florimond is a broadly comic version of James's Pateresque side: an impressionist with a "great deal of eye," an egoist with the tiniest of backbones. "He believed himself to know everything about art, and almost everything about life" —especially as regards "the character of the French, the works of Zola, the theory of art for art, the American type," and so on. One of the objects of Florimond's sight, however, James considered to be the most salient feature of American life:

> He felt at moments that he was in a city of women, in a country of women . . . The talk, the social life, were so completely in the hands of the ladies, the masculine note was so subordinate, that on certain occasions he could have believed himself (putting the brightness aside) in a country stricken by a war, where the men had all gone to the army, or in a seaport half depopulated by the absence of its vessels.[55]

Felix had noticed as much in *The Europeans*, and it would be one of the major refrains of *The American Scene*: since the Civil War, and because of the omnivorousness of the demands of business, America had ceased to have a masculine-oriented society. In *The Bostonians*, James attempted a full-scale treatment of the problem. In "Pandora" (1884) he created an amusing pendant to Daisy Miller in the figure of a willful and successful young American. Pandora Day is the "self-made girl," making the most of America now that Europe "had less and less prestige" for the would-be traveler. In the story James indulges in a parody of his "international theme." Count Vogelstein, the Teutonic point of view, has gotten his mistaken notion of Americans from reading "Daisy Miller," and he knows from secondhand experience about the "constant danger of marrying the American girl."[56]

"The Author of *Beltraffio*" (1884) was James's first work of fiction with a novelist as protagonist, although other themes of the period were incorporated into the story. Between the hyperaesthetic novelist, Mark Ambient, and his devoutly Protestant wife is waged an implied struggle for the possession of their seven-year-old son. Dolcino is characterized in a manner which anticipates all the future Jamesian innocents to come: "There was something touching, almost alarming, in his beauty, which seemed to be composed of elements too fine and pure for the breath of this world." The reader is asked to believe that the child is allowed to die by his mother, who fears that he will someday read Ambient's books; yet after Dolcino's death Mrs. Ambient gives way and, before dying, peruses her husband's books. One wonders if a streak of morbidity is required in order to appreciate *Beltraffio*; indeed, because of the ambiguous nature of the narrator of the story, one cannot be fully sure whether Ambient is a creditable devotee of "the gospel of art" or something of an immoralist (an ambiguity further compounded by the fact that James modeled Ambient on John Addington Symonds).[57]

Ambient is made bafflingly all-inclusive and elusive. He speaks one moment of being as true to life as possible; a moment later he is talking of the necessity to polish his "plate," to arrive at a "firm and bright" purpose. Before long, he is discussing what might either be the conflict between the novelist and the moral apriorist, between the pagan and the Protestant points of view, or else between the surveyor of "things as they are" and the lover of illusion. The contradictions are apparently meant to be answered by the narrator's claim that Ambient "looked at all things from the standpoint of the artist, felt all life as literary material." He represents a composite artist, one assumes, and combines contradictory artistic points of view. Ambient might get away with this if James's narrator were not so ambiguous a figure himself. "You Americans are very sharp," Ambient tells him at one point. "You notice more things than we do." Yet the narrator is even more an aesthete than Ambient. "It was not the picture, the poem, the fictive page, that seemed to me a copy," he intones at one point apropos of the novelist's home, "these things were the originals, and the life of happy and distinguished people were fashioned in their image." The view is that of Whistler and Wilde in the eighties: that life is of value only to the extent that it copies art. Like the narrator of "The Madonna of the Future" before him, he helps precipitate the tragedy by tactlessly showing Mrs. Ambient her husband's new novel. When he sees the child's corpse, at the end, he savors a last aesthetic *frisson*: "Poor little Dolcino was more exquisitely beautiful in death than he had been in life."[58]

One striking thing about "The Author of *Beltraffio*" is the fact that it anticipates "The Art of Fiction," James's greatest critical essay. In his first published essay, James had deplored the absence of a study of the canons of fiction; thereafter, his thesis was that the art of fiction precluded rules. After Howells' 1882 essay on James touched off a controversy over the "new" or "analytical" school of fiction, James became increasingly defensive. He began to create what often seem like conscious self-parodies with the aim of showing the discrepancy between the critical and the real image of himself. When the novelist Walter Besant delivered his lecture on "Fiction as One of the Fine Arts" in April 1884, James undoubtedly saw himself used as a target once more. Defending the emphasis on "story," Besant made an obvious allusion to the Howells' piece: "We have all along been training ourselves how to tell the story, and here is this new school which steps in, like the needy knife-grinder, to explain that there is no story left at all to tell."[59]

Besant's lecture, printed immediately afterward, stressed various points which were by then anathema to James: that the novel is "governed and directed by general laws" that "may be laid down and taught," that the novel must be "the result of personal experience and observation," and that it "almost always starts with a conscious moral purpose."[60] It was about this time that James was writing "The Author of *Beltraffio*"; by way of preparing his rejoinder to Besant, he tried out some of his ideas in the story. "There's a hatred of art—there's a hatred of literature!" Ambient exclaims of the Philistinism around him, and James re-echoes this in the essay: " 'Art,' in our Protestant communities, where so many things have got so strangely twisted about, is supposed in certain circles to have some vaguely injurious effect upon those who make it an important consideration, who let it weigh in the balance."[61] The importance of the novel, both men agree, is that it can give "an impression of life itself," but Ambient laments, "When I see the kind of things that Life does, I despair of ever catching her peculiar trick." Or, as James puts it, "catching the very note and trick, the strange irregular rhythm of life, that is the attempt whose strenuous force keeps Fiction upon her feet."[62]

The tone of "The Art of Fiction" is defensive throughout. James defers to Besant's contention that fiction is one of the fine arts; otherwise, he disavows Besant's or any other critic's list of aprioristic rules. The novel, to be taken as seriously as James wishes, must be above any limiting criteria. The artist's individual point of view must be kept free if the novel is to develop and change along with the development and change of history. "Art lives upon discussion," he states at the beginning of the essay, "upon experiment, upon curiosity, upon variety of attempt, upon the exchange of views and the comparison of standpoints." In such a free atmosphere the standard categories—the novel versus the romance, the "modern" versus the old-fashioned novel, the novel of character versus the novel of action—are pointless. James indicates, for example, "no obligation to which the 'romancer' would not be held equally with the novelist"; one must grant each the choice of his *donnée* and expect him to conform only to the same sort of working logic as applies to the painter or the historian: the depiction of life. In reply to the charge of having developed the "modern novel," James counters, "One writes the novel, one paints the picture, of one's language and of one's time, and calling it modern English will not, alas! make the difficult task any easier."[63]

James also denies Besant's insistence upon the need for "personal experience." With the idea already in mind for *The Princess Casamassima*, he makes an eloquent defense of the power of the artistic imagination:

> The power to guess the unseen from the seen, to trace the
> implication of things, to judge the whole piece by the pattern,
> the condition of feeling life in general so completely that you
> are well on your way to knowing any particular corner
> of it—this cluster of gifts may almost be said to constitute
> experience, and they occur in country and in town, and in the
> most differing stages of education. If experience consists of
> impressions, it may be said that impressions *are* experience,
> just as (have we not seen it?) they are the very air we breathe.

"Impressions *are* experience": James's artistic lesson can be summed up in the three words. The advice he offered to the novice was the recommendation to be like himself: "Try to be one of the people on whom nothing is lost."[64]

For such a person (and James described George Eliot and Hyacinth Robinson, as well as himself, as such), the question of the "conscious moral purpose of the novel" is nonsense. "We are by no means sure that art is very intimately connected with a moral mission," he had already written in 1874.[65] For James, the imposition of a moral purpose went hand in hand with a refusal to face life. Although linked in this respect with the French realists, he would criticize Zola and Maupassant for looking only at the side of life from which the English looked away. "How can a portrait be painted (in any way to be recognizable) of half a face?" he had asked in his review of Nana, which turned into a critique of the English and French limitations of point of view. "It is not in one eye, but in the two eyes together that the expression resides, and it is the combination of features that constitutes the human identity."[66]

"The essence of moral energy is to survey the whole field," he reiterated in "The Art of Fiction," and thus morality hinges upon the whole conception of the artist's point of view. The quality and the quantity of one's impressions, one's experience, go hand in hand with the amount of "moral sense" found in one's works. James's argument (which he repeated in the preface to the New York edition of The Portrait) is both rhetorically brilliant and deliberately evasive:

> There is one point at which the moral sense and the artistic
> sense lie very near together; that is in the light of the very
> obvious truth that the deepest quality of a work of art will
> always be the quality of the mind of the producer. In proportion
> as that intelligence is rich and noble [changed to "fine"
> from the magazine to the book publication of the essay] will
> the novel, the picture, the statue partake of the substance of
> beauty and truth. To be constituted of such elements is,
> to my vision, to have purpose enough. No good novel will
> ever proceed from a superficial mind; that seems to me an
> axiom which, for the artist in fiction, will cover all needful
> moral ground.[67]

Despite his parodies of Pateresque young men, James successfully transformed the message of the "Conclusion" to the Renaissance from an injunction to passive observers to an appeal for the active production of fiction. Where Meredith had stressed the need for fiction to encourage civilized social behavior, for James the writing of fiction was activity enough. James's essay is a superb admission of the elasticity of the novel form, with no other intent behind it than "a plea for liberty," as he observed to Robert Louis Stevenson. Stevenson had written an immediate rejoinder, "A Humble Remonstrance," arguing that the secret of the novel is that it is different from, more ordered than, life.* Stevenson's is a less persuasive essay to read now, but it does have a controlling idea, whereas James's essay seems in many ways a collection of brilliantly worded cautions.

If the overt theme of "The Art of Fiction" is that the novelist must be free to do as he wishes, the implied corollary is that James himself must be left at liberty. "The writer in the *Pall Mall*," James coyly interjects (amid a defense of the novelist's right to choose whatever subjects he wants), "opposes the delightful (as I suppose) novel of *Margot la Balafrée* to certain tales in which 'Bostonian nymphs' appear to have 'rejected English dukes for psychological reasons.'" As in "The Point of View" and "Pandora," James is wrily calling attention to himself (to "An International Episode" in particular); and, continuing his defense of artistic prerogative, he professes to see within the scope of his own tale "dramas within dramas . . . , and innumerable points of view."[68] James underlined the personal nature of the essay by publishing it as the climactic section of his carefully named volume, *Partial Portraits*.

Four other essays in that volume were written about this time, the best of which is the affectionate study of Trollope, whom James had long read and liked. In a tribute to the recently deceased master of the usual in fiction, as he characterized Trollope, James con-

* Stevenson's essay did have the result, one presumes, of occasioning a number of changes between the *Longman's* version of "The Art of Fiction" (1884) and the revised version in *Partial Portraits* (1888). Most important was the change from "The only reason for the existence of a novel is that it *does* compete with life" to "The only reason for the existence of a novel is that it does attempt to represent life." Much of the paragraph in which the line occurs was rewritten. One wonders if James bowed to the position in Stevenson's "Remonstrance" that "no art does 'compete with life.' Man's one method, whether he reasons or creates, is to half-shut his eyes against the dazzle and confusion of reality." James also changed the tenor of his remarks on *Treasure Island*.

trasted him favorably with his French contemporaries: "In spite of his want of doctrinal richness I think he tells us, on the whole, more about life than the 'naturalists' in our sister republic." James's praise follows, to be sure, an appalled examination of such literary Victorianisms in Trollope as "slaps at credulity," the lack of a desire to appear a historian. "It is impossible to imagine what a novelist takes himself to be," James declared, echoing a sentiment he had expressed as early as 1867 and was to repeat in "The Art of Fiction," "unless he regard himself as an historian and his narrative as a history":

> It is only as an historian that he has the smallest *locus standi.*
> As a narrator of fictitious events he is nowhere; to insert
> into his attempt a back-bone of logic, he must relate events
> that are assumed to be real.

James was not altogether remote from Trollope in some respects. Although he berated Trollope's use of "fantastic names," James was not averse to names like Headway or Wingrave (the latter for a pacifist soldier). James was also sympathetic to Trollope's artistic achievement: "He accepted all the common restrictions, and found that even within the barriers there was plenty of material." Unlike even the least objectionable of the naturalists, Daudet, Trollope exemplified the English writer, "at home in the moral world." "So much of the life of his time is reflected in his novels," he noted, "that we must believe a part of the record will be saved."[69] In *The Tragic Muse,* James would eulogize art for preserving history, for defying historical change, and he would do so in a book which echoes something of Trollope's political novels and which contains perhaps his most Trollopian heroine, Biddy Dormer.

The three other essays are personal tributes to Alphonse Daudet, who had just provided James a clue for *The Bostonians,* to George Eliot, and to Turgenev. The publication of J. W. Cross's *Life and Letters* occasioned praise of a writer who was, for James, a limited woman* with compensating powers of imagination, who has "made

---

* She had no "aesthetic life," that is. "We feel in her, always," James declared, "that she proceeds from the abstract to the concrete" (as opposed to Turgenev, who began with his characters) and "that her figures and situations are evolved, as the phrase is, from her moral consciousness, and are only indirectly the products of observation" (*Partial Portraits*, pp. 50–51).

us believe that nothing in the world was alien to her."[70] The loss of Turgenev was even more strongly felt. In addition to being his personal friend, Turgenev had been the only living novelist with a sufficiently wide range of artistic point of view: "He felt and understood the opposite sides of life." James had early identified himself with Turgenev in terms of their poetic separation from their native lands, their artistic methods and subject matter, and their stoical philosophy. Though he realized how pale a shadow he was in comparison with the great Russian, he sensed that with his death had also passed away the old-fashioned prerogative of the finest novelists—their ability to imagine other points of view than their own. James candidly recalled that the great Russian "cared, more than anything else, for the air of reality, and my reality was not to the purpose. I do not think my stories struck him as quite meat for men."[71] In the conception of *The Princess Casamassima*, James attempted a full-scale homage to Turgenev.

The mid-1880's was, for James, very much a period of tribute making and leave-taking. Accompanying the elegiac essays just mentioned were the two long novels of the period, fictional hails and farewells (with an emphasis on the latter) to the style and subject matter of Hawthorne, Dickens, and Daudet in the first, and of Turgenev, Zola, and early James in the second. He was to lay to rest the ideals of his native land in *The Bostonians* and his father's political ideas in *The Princess Casamassima*. In 1884 he wrote a strangely cool essay on the man he once described as his youthful idol, Matthew Arnold. "When there is a question of his efficacy, his influence," James remarks by way of concluding, "it seems to me enough to ask one's self what we should have done without him, to think how much we should have missed him, and how he has salted and seasoned our public conversation."[72] In 1886 he wrote a study of Howells, who had been his literary adviser and friend and who had praised and publicized him in many essays, which adopts an extremely patronizing tone. "He is animated by a love of the common, the immediate, the familiar and vulgar elements of life," James pointed out, harping again and again on Howell's naïveté and artistic faultiness and emphasizing those elements in him which critics had (largely because of the 1882 Howells essay on James) attributed to James himself.[73] Of Emerson, James wrote in 1887 that his "personal history is condensed into the single word Concord, and all the condensation in the world will not make it look rich."[74] Emerson had no conception of passion, no sense of evil, no notion of wrong, and no literary form. Decidedly, James had come to patronize all his former patrons.

The shorter fiction of the late 1880's by and large takes up themes James had used earlier, but the emphasis is different, the tone considerably more ambiguous. The characters become more and more representative than real, and they very often represent various kinds of derangement and unspecified evil. A new theme which appears is the menace of one's parents, one's elders, one's relatives, one's friends. "Mrs. Temperly" (1887), his first published story in three years, is a grotesque comedy about the destructive strength of a mother's will. In another story probably written at this time, though published several years later, "The Marriages," James describes the torments wrought upon her father and brother by a self-righteous girl determined to keep the father from remarrying. Again, however, there is an ambiguity involved in the interpretation of Adela Chart. James does not make it clear enough whether we are to blame her for meddling, or to sympathize with her desire to keep the memory of her dead mother alive. In both respects she has affinities with James's artists.

The short novel of the period, *The Reverberator* (1888), is indicative of James's feelings of the hazards of his present, indeterminate position. In "Louisa Pallant" (1888) he had reverted to his international theme, discarded for several years, probably in the hope of regaining the popularity undermined by the last two novels. In his notebook sketch for the work, he reminded himself of Howells' recent letter claiming that he did "the 'international' far better than anything else." The occasion for *The Reverberator* was to be an attack upon the newspapers as symptomatic of the "democratization of the world," but James revealed his own defensiveness in the act of beginning a historically oriented novel about "the invasion, the impudence and shamelessness, of the newspaper and the interviewer, the devouring *publicity* of life, the extinction of all sense between public and private."[75] The novel can be enjoyed as a deliberate parody of James's earlier treatments of the international theme: the Parisian hero Gaston, of American extraction, has a brother-in-law named Alphonse (naturally) and a sister named Madame de Cliché; while the American Dossons, father and daughters, whom Gaston meets, are scarcely more believable when introduced. That Gaston and Francie Dosson can marry happily would have been impossible in James during the period of *The American* or "Lady Barberina." "It is simply impossible for us to live with vulgar people," Gaston's sister exclaims,[76] resorting to James's former belief in conditioning to account for the impossibility of an alliance between a democratic American and an aristocratic Frenchman. Probably as he felt his own connections with family and country weaken, James changed his mind on the matter.

The importance of this short novel in his development is as a gauge to James's feelings of independence, emphasizing the need to cut off interfering ties, familial or otherwise. When Gaston's family tries to tear him away from Francie, an artist-friend enters with a successful plea that he preserve himself: "To rescue from destruction the last remnant of your independence. That's a much more important matter even than not treating her shabbily. They are doing their best to kill you morally—to render you incapable of individual life."[77] Even in so slight a work James could not resist arguing the most essential of his articles of faith: keep yourself free. Such an attitude is crucial to the history of the novel, which had previously depended upon the commitment of the novelist and his characters to their world.

"A London Life" (1888) was begun as another "episode in that 'international' series which," James considered, "really, without forcing the matter or riding the horse to death, strikes me as an inexhaustible mine."[78] Whatever his illusions on that point, the finished, rather lengthy story is his most vivid proof during the decade that he had given up on English society—and perhaps had lost faith in the appeal of American innocence as well. Laura Wing, his American heroine, is quite possibly his most unpleasant character: a virago of self-righteousness, she eclipses in his respect even Meredith's impossible Rhoda Fleming. Meredith showed the evil effects caused by fundamentalist self-righteousness; James, on the other hand, is fatally ambiguous with regard to the nature of his heroine. He included "A London Life" in the same New York edition volume that contains *The Spoils of Poynton,* and he pays tribute there to Laura's "high lucidity" which lends importance to her action. Like Fleda Vetch, he claims, she has "acuteness and intensity, reflexion and passion, has above all a contributive and participant view of her situation."[79] If this is supposed to be so, then James was rarely so self-deluded as in his creation of her. As the reflector of a thoroughly immoral and, equally bad, an uninteresting modern society, Laura is fine. Her view of her stupid brother-in-law, Lionel Berrington, vividly testifies to James's repudiation of his original idealization of the English gentry. The English are "the great race," he had written Charles Eliot Norton in 1880: "it takes more to make an Englishman, on the whole, than to make anyone else."[80] In 1888 he could write: Laura "marvelled at the waste involved in some human institutions (the English country gentry for instance) when she perceived that it had taken so much to produce so little." The cherished traditions have left no trace "in poor Lionel's stable-stamped composition," and the human inhabitants are a disgrace to their fine old house:

> The contrast was before her again, the sense of the same curious duplicity (in the literal meaning of the word) that she felt at Plash—the way the genius of such an old house was all peace and decorum and the spirit that prevailed there, outside of the schoolroom, was contentious and impure. She had often been struck with it before—with that perfection of machinery which can still at certain times make English life go on of itself with a stately rhythm long after there is corruption within it.[81]

James's outrage is aesthetic rather than moral, but the motivation he allows his heroine is flawed in both respects. It is not the immorality of her sister's and brother-in-law's life that worries her; it is the personal horror that everything will be reflected back upon herself since "nothing so disagreeable had ever befallen her or was likely to befall her as the odious possibility of her sister's making a scandal." To prevent the impending divorce, Laura tries unsuccessfully to thwart the inevitable, to maintain an impossible appearance of familial decorum. "My poor child," one of the more experienced characters, Lady Davenant, asks her, "how long do you expect to make believe?" And to Laura's somewhat stolid suitor,

Wendover, the older woman declares, "She exaggerates the badness of it, the stigma of her relationship. Good heavens, at that rate where would some of us be?"[82] The social depravity within London life of the period makes itself vividly felt in the figure of the promiscuous, and outrageously named, Lady Ringnose, but James's focus throughout is blurred because of the shrillness and ineffectiveness of his principal reflector. James's failure to control what he is doing allows too often for the menacing nature of the "innocent" characters he creates.

The presence of a flawed point of view by no means lessens the merit of two other tales of the period. "The Liar" has provoked justifiable critical annoyance at James's selection of a reflector, the painter Lyon, who may be correct in his judgment of Colonel Capadoce, the ostensible liar of the story, but who pursues his self-righteousness to the point of sadism.[83] The Colonel's deceit has its compensating artistic side: "it is art for art and he is prompted by the love of beauty," Lyon admits at one point.[84] James's greatest piece of fiction of the period, and perhaps his best tale, is an extraordinary parable of an artistic sensibility like Lyon's severing its human connections. "The Aspern Papers" (1888) is his most terrifying artist fable, although he may not have been aware of all the implications involved. In his notebook citations for the story, he stressed the comic nature of the model for his narrator, a "Shelley fanatic," who was given the chance to possess some Shelley letters if he agreed to marry the old maid who owned them.[85] The story contains an extraordinarily rich deposit of Jamesian themes: the private versus the public life; the danger of overvaluing art to the point of forgetting its roots in life; the tragedy of detachment, by an ironical point of view, from life; the comedy and tragedy caused by uncomprehending egoism. "In life without art you can find your account," he had written ten years earlier, "but art without life is a poor affair."[86]

It is a brilliant central irony that the narrator and main character of "The Aspern Papers," who plots fruitlessly to get at lost love letters of the great American poet, should remain nameless for the reader. And Jeffrey Aspern, dead for many years, manages to dominate the story as an artistic symbol of a lost age. "There is no more poetry in the world," his aged former mistress, Juliana Bordereau, declares with justification.[87] Rarely was James so successfully romantic in his writings as in his attempt to preserve the mysteries that his narrator would try to expose. Aspern is described as the American Shakespeare, and James sees to it that one can no more discover the mystery of his life than solve the riddle of the sonnets. It is the sonnets that matter, he implies, not the man. "Know him only by what's best in him," by his work, as one of James's later characters is cautioned when she attempts to meet her literary idol.[88]

In revising "The Aspern Papers" for the New York edition, James toned down the comic implications of the story and stressed the melodramatic elements. The narrator becomes more outspokenly a villain than in the earlier version. Leon Edel has observed that initially the narrator "seems an artist *manqué*,"[89] but, to some degree, he remains aesthetic throughout—to the point of denying art itself. In this he is an even more ambiguous descendant of the narrator of "The Author of *Beltraffio*." James's main problem in the story was how to present an objective drama through the eyes of a flawed sensibility. At one point, in a manner both aesthetic and revolting, he imagines Juliana with the letters: "I believed that she would cling to them till then and I think I had an idea that she read Aspern's letters over every night or at least pressed them to her withered lips. I would have given a good deal to have a glimpse of the latter spectacle." But, a few moments later, we are undoubtedly meant to share the force of his delight in the American Shakespeare, who, like Hawthorne, had triumphed against all odds as an artist in America (contrary also to the thesis of James's *Hawthorne*):

> His own country after all had had most of his life, and his
> muse, as they said at that time, was essentially American.
> That was originally what I had loved him for: that at a period
> when our native land was nude and crude and provincial, when
> the famous 'atmosphere' it is supposed to lack was not even
> missed, when literature was lonely there and art and form
> almost impossible, he had found means to live and write
> like one of the first; to be free and general and not at all
> afraid; to feel, understand and express, everything.[90]

Set in Venice, the story forces the reader to become a romanticist, if not a romantic, and to accept the impossible fact of the existence of an American Shakespeare. It is interesting that James's archpoet should have been born in his own hometown, New York. The poet and the observant narrator represent the two sides of James set forth earlier in *Roderick Hudson*, but both men are now actively artists, the one a transmitter of impressions and the other a collector of them.

James's best stories for another decade would be, directly or indirectly, artist fables, and "The Aspern Papers" is the most memorable of them all. Here he is the master, not a victim, of ambiguity; the story is by far the most complex and humanly perceptive member of a group, which consists too often of variations on the theme of the sensitive artist stunted or ignored by a despicable world. "The Lesson of the Master" (1888) is in theme a curious counterpart to "The Author of *Beltraffio*." In the earlier story, James had stressed the all-encompassing nature of the artist—Ambient stands for anything and everything—while the "lesson" of the Master is that for the artist to succeed at perfection he must live as a "disenfranchised monk." Ambient's unfortunate marriage did not forbid the production of, one presumes, masterpieces—neither did Hardy's—but St George claims that the economic demands of marriage forbid the creation of "some sort of little perfection." The misery of the Reardons in Gissing's *New Grub Street* is a grim confirmation of his thesis, but it is not certain whether James is stressing celibacy for the sake of art or for the sake of self. One must work, St George urges, for one's self: "one's conscience, one's idea, the singleness of one's aim." His disciple, therefore, undergoes the longest journey of the celibate artist, keeps his Jamesian "independence," and emerges inviolate but only arguably triumphant. In our last view of Paul Overt, he is seen standing "in the small, inexpensive, empty street" where he lives, unsure whether he has chosen wisely: "He lingered, questioning himself still, before going in, with nothing around and above him but moonless blackness, a bad lamp or two and a few far-away dim stars."[91] The loneliness of the artist has rarely been so movingly suggested.

Two other stories of a slightly later period, "The Pupil" and "Brooksmith" (1891), may be mentioned in this context as autobiographical indications of James's mood. Morgan Moreen, shuttled through Europe as part of an unstable ménage, represents an extreme view of James's own childhood experiences, as well as his discontent with the "worldly" ambitions which had once caused him to idealize society. "Brooksmith" is as much James's allegorical autobiography of this period as "Benvolio" was earlier, but the emphasis has changed from the artist's possibilities to his limitations, and the artist's material is considerably less alluring. Brooksmith is the butler who has arranged the perfect, small society of his master, but there is now no more material worthy of his use. Such "society had become a necessity of Brooksmith's nature"; using this material, he had unobtrusively managed to put "the right people *with* the right people." With his master's death, the lack of a usable society elsewhere is pointed up. "The question for him to have asked before accepting the position," the narrator conjectures, "would have been not, 'How many footmen are kept?' but 'How much imagination?' "[92]

The other short fiction of the period is uninviting, except as indications of James's attack on society. In his earlier works the villains were individuals put into the novel for that express purpose—evil was an artistic necessity for the machinery of the plot. But now evil is elusive and pervasive and beyond one's ability to confine or overcome. James's critical essays of this time are marred to a considerable extent by vagueness and personal defensiveness. The essay on Trollope had said something about Trollope as well as James, but the study of Maupassant (1888) is of interest mainly for James. It is here that he makes the astonishingly calm reflection, apropos of Maupassant's theory that every writer is bound by a personal illusion of the world, that it hardly matters whether the artist's "impression" is an "illusion" so long as he expresses that impression with clarity. From now on, James would annoyingly refer to writers as various "cases," and would find it impossible not to be entirely subjective. As, by his own admission, he read less and less, his literary essays were now devoted to the works of friends (like Stevenson or Mrs. Ward), to exotics (like Kipling or Pierre Loti), or to authors he had written on before.

James had opened the decade of the 1880's with a confident belief in the power of a great writer to have and to express an awareness of various points of view. "There are as many points of view in the world as there are people of sense," as Mrs. Touchett declares in *The Portrait of a Lady* (pp. 49–50), and the author of "The Point of View" could take in and juxtapose various contradictory truths. Isabel Archer must learn, in the course of *The Portrait*, that there are other ways of looking at life than her own, that truth exists more in juxtaposition than in singularity of point of view; when she does this, she gives up the illusion of her independence, but is thereby free of illusions.

In his novels of the 1880's, James attempted to accommodate himself to various ways of seeing life and writing besides his own; although he was not a popular success as a result, he presented in these works an extraordinary richness of texture and subject-matter. In thematic design, the novels of the eighties still resemble the great nineteenth-century novels that deal with the interrelation of society and the individual. In James's hands, however, the individual seeks to extricate himself from that society, and the artist is becoming more and more a singular case. At the end of the decade, James was emphasizing the individuality rather than the typicality of the artist. Kipling's merit, for example, was the possession of a highly colored point of view. In 1891 he referred to that author's "identity as marked as a window-frame"—adding that it was the particularity of Kipling's point of view that gives it value: "It is the blessing of the art he practises that it is made up of experience conditioned, infinitely, in this personal way—the sum of the feeling of life as reproduced by innumerable natures; natures that feel through all their differences, testify through their diversities."[93] Meanwhile, James was relying more and more upon single points of view in his stories, with increasing ambiguity of perspective. And with the publication of *The Tragic Muse*, he bade farewell, once and for all, to the attempt to write within a Victorian framework.

An American Comedy: The Bostonians

> *It is a better subject than I have ever had before,*
> *and I think will be much the best thing I have*
> *done yet. It is called* The Bostonians. *I shall be*
> *much abused for the title, but it exactly and*
> *literally fits the story, and is much the best,*
> *simplest and most dignified I could have chosen.*
> *(Henry James, writing to his brother*
> *William, 1884)*

Edmund Wilson has observed of James's three long novels of the 1880's, *The Bostonians, The Princess Casamassima,* and *The Tragic Muse,* that they exhibit signs of "a will to participate in life, to play a responsible role, quite different from the passive ones of the traveler who merely observes or the victim who merely suffers" so typical in James.[1] While the novels also show an increasing tendency to back away from history and to assert the right to freedom of the detached individual, it is true that James applied himself in these works to a Victorian conception of the novel form—which seems suspiciously closer to Meredith than to early and late James. *The Bostonians* is the most "American" of the three in subject matter, but James, writing in England, sought to take advantage of the outcries against "Americanization" which he heard in London and Paris, as well as immediate advantage of the topicality of feminist agitation, in order to achieve popular success. To his American critics he triumphantly showed that he could handle an important American subject; to his English critics he showed himself adept in the writing of a Victorian style.

Whatever the similarities to Meredith demonstrated in *The Bostonians*, they are, once again, superficial. Where Meredith was championing the rights of the New Woman to belong actively in society in *Diana of the Crossways*, James at the same time chose to ridicule the operations of feminists—of all social and political groups, for that matter, which encroach upon the private lives of cultured, single individuals. Where Meredith had displayed the tragedy of the futile efforts of Nevil Beauchamp to reform society, James treated the aspirations of Basil Ransom and Olive Chancellor alike as the stuff of comedy. Two potential Meredithian idealists, with devotions to Carlyle and Goethe, are shown up as cranks, and an American girl whose passivity seems derived from Trollope's heroines is presented as a dummy. It is understandable that feminist readers tend to dislike *The Bostonians* (although James's biases are not against women but organizations), but it is ironic that in a book attacking political causes James is making an implicit defense of the need for personal inviolability—a theme which American radicals and reactionaries alike seem to believe in, too. If Meredith was a radical novelist, albeit in the Victorian manner, James shows himself to be, in *The Bostonians* and the novels which followed it, a subversive novelist—although, in the case of *The Bostonians*, a subversive with a brilliant sense of humor.

The Portrait of a Lady had been the culmination of James's literary resources till then, but a novel in the same manner was out of the question. The trip to America about that time had shown James that he could no longer be happy at home. And, with the deaths of both parents, he was left, almost symbolically, without a home. Uneasily approaching his fortieth birthday, he confided to his notebook the literary uncertainty he now felt:

> If I can only *concentrate* myself: this is the great lesson of life.
> I have hours of unspeakable reaction against my smallness of
> production; my wretched habits of work—or of un-work;
> my levity, my vagueness of mind, my perpetual failure to
> focus my attention, to absorb myself, to look things in the
> face, to invent, to produce, in a word. I shall be 40 years old in

April next: it's a horrible fact! I believe however that I have learned how to work and that it is in moments of forced idleness, almost alone, that these melancholy reflections seize me. When I am really at work, I'm happy, I feel strong, I see many opportunities ahead. It is the only thing that makes life endurable. I must make some great efforts during the next few years, however, if I wish not to have been on the whole a failure. I shall have been a failure unless I do something *great!*

The desire to "do something *great*" coalesced with the plan "to write a very *American* tale," as James notified his Boston publisher and his notebook one week before his fortieth birthday. He had declared, just before writing the above passage, that Boston meant absolutely nothing to him. He had consoled himself with the number of impressions he had received in New York the year before, but in general he had felt his stay "terribly wasted." Yet in April 1883, he seemed very much determined to attempt a "strong and good" subject "with a large rich interest . . . The whole thing as local, as American, as possible, and as full of Boston: an attempt to show that I *can* write an American story."[2]

The defensive nature of his claim seems very likely to have been occasioned by the adverse publicity he had recently received. The hostile critic in the *Quarterly Review* (January 1883) had insultingly charged that the new American school offered very little distinctly American, that in James "the women are all flirts, so far as they are anything," while "the men are very like the conventional American of the stage."[3] In the April 1883 issue of the *Atlantic Monthly* (which carried the first installment of James's terrible dramatic adaptation of "Daisy Miller"), Charles Dudley Warner's essay on "Modern Fiction" contained a sober defense of the older novelists who had offered idealizations of nature rather than naturalism, and a rebuke of the new analytical, psychology- and realism-oriented, storyless, and endingless (especially happy-endingless) novels. "It is constantly said that the conditions in America are unfavorable to the higher fiction," Warner declared:

that our society is unformed, without centre, without the definition of classes, which give the light and shade that Heine speaks of in Don Quixote; that it lacks types and customs that can be widely recognized and accepted as national and characteristic; that we have no past; that we want both romantic and historic background; that we are in a shifting, flowing, forming period which fiction cannot seize on; that we are in diversity and confusion that baffle artistic treatment; in short, that American life is too vast, varied, and crude for the purpose of the novelist.

That James read this essay we know by an allusion to it in his Daudet study of the same year. One can speculate that he had not missed the point of Warner's conclusion: that there were subjects for the American novelist, and that out of such material Hawthorne had been able, with the use of "creative imagination" (with imagination what could one not accomplish, as James himself replied to Walter Besant in "The Art of Fiction"), to weave "those tragedies of interior life, those novels of our provincial New England, which rank among the great masterpieces of the novelist's art. The master artist," concludes Warner, "can idealize even our crude material, and make it serve."[4] It is ironic, however, that James should have intended in his next novel to do something of the sort, but instead he accomplished the reverse: to show up the highest idealisms of America as so much crude material.

Perhaps the most suggestive of the essays directed toward the new "analytical school" was James Herbert Morse's study in the *Century* for July 1883. Morse echoed Warner's chauvinism in his claim that American life offered material aplenty "to meet the largest demands of the novelist," and he insisted that "When our Thackeray or Scott comes, with the right grasp, he will certainly find character in individual and group, variety in social life, and that change and ferment which give the largest scope to the novelist." Combined with this (the sort of statement that the young Henry James had used to make when he envisaged himself an American Balzac) was Morse's implicit, taunting contention that James was not a novelist of this caliber, and that James's mastery lay "in his analysis of externals, not in sympathetic reproduction of heroic qualities." For an American, James "never gets into the spirit of our American homelife." His talents are limited, his style too patterned and clever, and, perhaps above all, his works are entirely too subjective. Morse very adroitly points out how James has written himself into all his books, and the resultant image is "one of fine intellectual powers, incapable of meanness; of fastidious tastes, and of limited sympathies; a man, in short, of passions refined away by the intellect." The essay closes with an appeal to James to show "that he has a genuine sympathy with the chief underlying motive of American institutions, which is, as we understand it, not to make life lovely for the few, but to make generous action and honest growth possible for the many—even at the expense, if necessary, of some self-sacrifice on the part of the few."[5]

Morse's essay appeared three months after the first sketch for *The Bostonians*, and nearly a year before James began to write it (for serialization, as it turned out, in the *Century*), but the somewhat patronizing tone must have annoyed and helped spur him to show that he could write not only "an American story" but also a strikingly objective work, a masterly invasion into the stylistic domain of Thackeray and Dickens when need be. He sent off a plan of the novel to his publisher while spending the spring of 1883 in America (after his father's death). The novel would relate, topically, "an episode connected with the so-called 'woman's movement' "—which James had already appraised in its social aspect. The heroine, he went on, would be the "clever and 'gifted' " progeny of "old abolitionists, spiritualists, transcendentalists, etc." who had to choose between the proddings of a female reformist friend and the conservative young man she loves.[6] James had several immediate precedents for dealing with spiritualist-reformist groups: Hawthorne's *The Blithedale Romance*, which had dealt with the Brook Farm experiment and also with a similar struggle for possession; the Mrs. Jellyby sections of *Bleak House*; Howells' *The Undiscovered Country* (1880), which had considered the recent occultist fad in Boston; and Daudet's recently published *L'Évangéliste*. In his first sketch for *The Bostonians*, James revealed that Daudet's novel had given him "the idea of the thing"—probably in terms of the character of a young girl under the spell of a religious fanatic, and the notion, attacked by Daudet, of an "apostleship of woman" in whom "no indication of their sex" can be seen.[7]

James had long been interested, in his fiction, in the new woman, the self-made girl, the domineering feminist. He came back again and again to George Sand, for example, whom he deemed one of the first modern women because she had looked at life like a man:

"She reached him, she surpassed him, and she showed how, with native dispositions, the thing could be done," James noted in his 1899 essay on her. In private, he expressed himself wittily and bluntly: "She was a man: a woman can transform herself into a man, but never into a gentleman!" he told a friend in 1914.[8] The comic implications of women stepping into men's roles had been memorably handled by writers before James; for him, however, this inversion was indicative of a historical fact of modern American (as well as European) life. De Tocqueville had earlier noted the absence of "manly candor" from American political life, and the preponderance of women had been observed by Felix in *The Europeans* and by Florimond in "A New England Winter." The men are devoted to business, so the women see to everything else, as James gloomily echoed throughout *The American Scene*. By 1883 James had come to this conclusion through personal observation: seeing life as so much material for the artist, he had noted very little distinctly masculine life on his return to America. The Civil War had, of course, depleted much of the male population of New England. Consequently, the subject for the new novel would be "very national, very typical": "I wished to write a very *American* tale, a tale very characteristic of our social conditions, and I asked myself what was the most salient and peculiar point in our social life. The answer was: the situation of women, the decline of the sentiment of sex, the agitation on their behalf."[9]

As noteworthy as his turn to an American subject and a historical topicality was James's attempt in *The Bostonians* to remove the critical image of his style. Coming from a novelist noted for character analysis, as the reviewers said, the new novel is as much of interest for what the characters *do* as for what they are. Joseph Warren Beach has given a fair enough account of James's usual descriptive methods: "If you are to use the word story at all in connection with these novels, the story is not what the characters do, nor how the situation works out. The story is rather the process by which the characters and the situation are revealed to us."[10] Thus, Beach concludes, we do not really know a Jamesian character until the end of the novel (and then, one might add, not entirely). But in *The Bostonians* James gives very elaborate descriptions of his characters as he introduces them, in the manner of earlier Victorian novelists, and the descriptions stick. We see very little of Isabel Archer when she makes her first appearance in *The Portrait of a Lady* (instead, characteristically, we first see her looking at the other characters), but we have an unusually elaborate "portrait" of Basil Ransom: tall, thin, poor in dress but imposing in appearance, distinctively Southern.

After a page of minute description James becomes aware of the unusualness of his resorting to such a practice, and he interrupts the passage with a defiantly patronizing authorial interjection, harking back to the methods of Dickens and even Sterne:

> It is not in my power to reproduce by any combination of characters this charming [Southern] dialect; but the initiated reader will have no difficulty in evoking the sound, which is to be associated in the present instance with nothing vulgar or vain. This lean, pale, sallow, shabby, striking young man, with his superior head, his sedentary shoulders, his expression of bright grimness and hard enthusiasm, his provincial, distinguished appearance, is, as a representative of his sex, the most important personage in my narrative; he played a very active part in the events I have undertaken in some degree to set forth.

Not only does James set up an ironic distance from his characters by so fixing them in place in advance, but he also barely conceals his dislike of a reading public which has forced him into this stylistic straitjacket. After the aside just cited, the testimony of an omniscient narrator, he half sneers, "And yet the reader who likes a complete image, who desires to read with the senses as well as with the reason, is entreated not to forget that he prolonged his consonants and swallowed his vowels" and so on. No wonder that the other figure in the first scene, taking in the measure of the hero, should see much less—as one would in life rather than in a novel: "Mrs. Luna looked up at all this, but saw only a part of it."[11] And here we realize that James's unusually detailed description has achieved a brilliant counterpoint to the guiding principle of the novel: that real people are limited to narrow points of view.

In *The Portrait* James pursued the implications of the limitations of point of view of a self-reliant American girl to their logical and tragic conclusion. He achieved this, however, at the risk of confusing his readers, and in his next novel he transformed the theme into a comic mode by pointing up the unchangeable limitations of point of view both in his characters and in his readers. *The Portrait of a Lady* and *The Bostonians* are the tragic and comic sides of a truth made later by Yeats, "that tragedy must always be a drowning and breaking of the dykes that separate man from man, and that it is upon these dykes comedy keeps house."[12] At the end of *The Portrait* Isabel enters the enlightened realm of uncertainty and complexity of life, but Basil, his bride Verena, and the antagonist Olive are all trapped within the limitations of artistic being.

James invented, for his purposes, a Victorian narrator, who almost becomes, by the sheer number of his intrusions into the novel, a character in his own right, one very different from the Jamesian novelist noted by Morse. The narrator is omniscient or unknowing as the occasion demands. At one point in the novel, he calls himself (p. 267) a "historian who has gathered these documents together"—less in literal obedience to James's idea of the novelist as historian than to the convention of Fielding. The narrator actively keeps us from being misled: "in reality," he says at another point, Verena's father is not interested in morality but in publicity (p. 101). He can be mock-apologetic as to a character's views: "I am but the reporter of his angry *formulae*" (p. 50), he says of Ransom's outrage at a proposed attempt at prohibition. Sometimes he is confidential, as when he says of Olive: "it shall be confided to the reader that in reality she never knew, by any sense of her own, whether Verena were a flirt or not" (p. 119). He can be sententious, in the manner of George Eliot, as in this later passage on Olive: "If she had been less afraid, she would have read things more clearly; she would have seen that we don't run away from people unless we fear them and that we don't fear them unless we know that we are unarmed" (p. 375). A moment later, while trying to describe the elusiveness of Verena, he presents an image of helplessness: "I despair of presenting it [Verena's situation] to the reader with the air of reality" (p. 380).

By a persistent logic, the narrator is most active, and the distance between the characters is most felt, in the more comic sections of the novel, while the sections that slip into tragedy draw from the narrator an admission of real helplessness. In the great scene between Verena and Olive in the darkened house at Marmion (chapter thirty-nine), James eliminates the distance between himself and the narrator; they are both unable to deal with the haunted presence of Olive, who has finally begun to sense the truth about Verena. "These are mysteries into which I shall not attempt to enter," he breaks in, after asking rhetorical questions as to what Olive is feeling at the moment, "speculations with which I have no concern; it is sufficient for us to know that all human effort had never seemed so barren and thankless as on that fatal afternoon" (p. 409). The narrative tone changes here, emphasizing a difference in the accustomed tone of the book—between the comedy attempted and the poignancy that accidentally breaks into the novel. It is undeniable that one feels very sorry for Olive at this point, although elsewhere she has been presented in a humorous frame of reference. The fact is that James's customary interest in character rather than plot has gotten out of hand in his portrait of Olive. The slip is not fatal, however; the chapter in which it occurs is the most memorable in the book. We are reminded at such moments, even as we are reminded of the fact in Meredith's best novels, that the line between comedy and tragedy is slight, that every comedian is a tragic hero when seen from within (the point of comedy is to see him only from outside), and that tragedy seen in perspective inclines toward comedy.

Elsewhere, however, the narrator insures a distance between the characters and us which keeps us from sympathizing unduly with either of the warring factions. Although Olive becomes almost a tragic figure, she is originally defined in comic terms: "There are women who are unmarried by accident, and others who are unmarried by option," the narrator declares, "but Olive Chancellor was unmarried by every implication of her being. She was a spinster as Shelley was a lyric poet, or as the month of August is sultry" (pp. 17–18). And later, while noting that Verena was momentarily under her charm, the narrator adds: "The idea of Olive's charm will perhaps make the reader smile; but I use the word not in its derived, but in its literal sense" (p. 167).

James's ironic distance from Ransom should be just as evident to a careful reader. "I shall not attempt a complete description of

Ransom's ill-starred views," the narrator confides, "being convinced that the reader will guess them as he goes, for they had a frolicsome, ingenious way of peeping out of the young man's conversation" (p. 189). Speaking of the shame of his poverty which keeps Ransom from proposing to Verena, the narrator interjects, "His scruples were doubtless begotten of a false pride, a sentiment in which there was a thread of moral tinsel, as there was in the Southern idea of chivalry" (p. 320). When Ransom confesses the basic articles of his faith to Verena (principles of which James shared one or two), the narrator becomes momentarily and coyly apologetic: "The poor fellow delivered himself of these narrow notions (the rejection of which by leading periodicals was certainly not a matter for surprise), with low, soft earnestness, bending towards her so as to give out his whole idea, yet apparently forgetting for the moment how offensive it must be to her now that it was articulated in that calm, severe way, in which no allowance was to be made for hyperbole." The last part of the passage seems scarcely true, nor does Verena's admission that he has spoken in "a distinct, lucid way" (p. 334). The contradiction between the truth of what Ransom is often saying (according to James) and the manner in which he is saying it—plus, of course, the manner of person he is—is symptomatic of one of the weaknesses of the novel: given James's mistrust of ideology and especially political opinions, and given the ease with which characters shed entire ideologies in James, the reader may with reason mistrust any of the very real ideas put forth in the novel.

If the ideas are often valid enough outside the boundaries of the novel, James's characters fit very tightly into the texture of the book. *The Bostonians* is one of James's best-written as well as best-constructed novels. Despite critical objections that after a dazzling opening section the novel goes to pieces (a charge more true of the two long novels that followed it), it is inconceivable that James could have matched the icy perfection of the first part or, for structural and thematic reasons, have wanted to do so. On examination, the novel appears carefully planned, and even some of the brilliant excesses can be justified thematically. Book One justifies the choice of title, which in turn accompanies the choice of theme: the comic limitations of point of view. The book was not originally to be about Boston, but about an outsider's limited conception of it, although James went on to characterize his Bostonians as extremely shortsighted themselves. "I hadn't a dream of generalizing—but thought the title simple and handy," James told his brother after the tepid reception of the book, "and meant only to designate Olive and Verena by it, as they appeared to the mind of Ransom, the southerner and outsider looking at them from New York. I didn't even *mean* it to cover Miss Birdseye and the others, though it might very well. I shall write another: *The Other Bostonians.*"[13] The first half of the book deals with Ransom's obviously biased point of view, and the juxtaposition of his narrow angle of vision with the reformers' idealistic fantasies makes for inevitable comedy. The second half deals with the reformers, Olive and Verena at any rate, as seen by themselves, preparing for their feminist "crusade." Ransom's chivalric pretensions are neatly balanced by their crusading instincts; each side will speak loftily, as the novel proceeds, of the sacredness of its cause.

Book Two shifts from Boston to New York (and briefly back again), and we are allowed to cast the same cold eye upon Ransom that he directs toward Olive and the "Female Convention." At the end of the second book, Verena is attracted to and shaken by Ransom, but begs Olive to rescue her—a parallel for her turn to Ransom for assistance at the very end. Book Three takes up the "war to the knife" between Olive and Ransom for possession of Verena. However, since that reduces itself to "a question of which should pull hardest" (p. 383) there is no real contest. Ransom is physically stronger and also a war veteran; by his winning of Verena, James provided with a vengeance the "happy ending" demanded by his critics. The end of *The Bostonians* is unsettling in its assertion of brute might to bring off the denouement and in its intimation that the couple will not live happily ever after beyond the happy ending.

Because of the nature of an outside point of view making slanted judgments and the confused nature of the groups and persons being surveyed, almost everything in *The Bostonians* is presented as a contradiction in terms. The aggressive fullness of description provides for the juxtaposition of contradictory traits, and everything is described as it is and as it seems to be. Thus, James says, Ransom has a "first-rate intelligence" but is "conscious of the narrow range, as yet, of his experience. He was on his guard against generalisations which might be hasty; but he had arrived at two or three that were of value to a gentleman lately admitted to the New York bar and looking out for clients"—and then Ransom proceeds to make a generalization of platitudinous inanity, "that the simplest division it is possible to make of the human race is into the people who take things hard and the people who take them easy" (pp. 10–11). Ransom is a Southerner who has disapproved of the Civil War as a "national fiasco," yet is determined to keep women in the prewar, if not prefall, condition of subordination. With a touch of Gilbert Osmond, he likes women "not to think too much" (p. 11), although for a while he is almost sucked into the orbit of Olive's sister, Mrs. Luna, who adroitly pays homage to and parodies his views. Wondering about Olive's views, "he felt . . . that if she had the religion of humanity— Basil Ransom had read Comte, he had read everything—she would never understand him" (p. 19), but soon enough we learn that the "first-rate intelligence" and reading knowledge of "everything" in Ransom narrows down to a wholesale allegiance to the Victorian sage, Carlyle. "It's an age of unspeakable shams, as Carlyle says," Ransom echoes approvingly (p. 334). Elsewhere, James notes that he is at once "stoic" and "reactionary" ("We are born to suffer—and to bear it, like decent people" [p. 232]) yet not at all averse to public success ("He had always had a desire for public life; to cause one's ideas to be embodied in national conduct appeared to him the highest form of human enjoyment" [p. 188]). His wish to be personally and dogmatically independent, but also free to encroach upon others at will, has similarity with James's idea of the artist, but the political implications of this are at once comical and familiar. Don't tread on me, he says in effect, so that I may with ease step on you—a slogan cherished throughout parts of America to this day.

Similar contradictions occur within Olive. If Ransom, serving a public career as lawyer, should fight for the sake of privacy, it is appropriate that the most morbidly fastidious and shy character in the novel should sacrifice herself to a public career. It is inevitable, in the logic of the book, that if Olive should be horrified by the reporter Matthias Pardon's suggestion that the two of them "run" Verena at the Music Hall, then at the end of the novel she will be doing precisely that. In another paradoxical situation, the young woman for whom Olive and Ransom are fighting maintains an overbearing passivity. Verena's pliancy and lack of personality make her singularly desirable. Ransom is struck by her "naturally theatrical" manner, and Olive wonders how she can be so unaffected by the despicable background in which she has been raised. In a novel in which each major character is assigned an elaborately described, unique environment, each remains isolated and untouched, circumscribed only by the novelistic role James has assigned him.

Such paradoxes of being make for an amusing clash of contrasts in the novel, but their essential contradictoriness (and isolation) puts the characters at home in a world distinctly American. Only in America, James implies, can such bizarre phenomena occur. When, at the beginning of the book, Olive hints to Ransom of the nature of the reformist meeting they will be attending, James plays with the comic implications of what will follow:

> "If, as you say, there is to be a discussion [says Ransom], there will be different sides, and of course one can't sympathise with both."
> "Yes, but everyone will, in his way—or in her way—plead the cause of the new truths. If you don't care for them, you won't go with us."
> "I tell you I haven't the least idea what they are! I have never yet encountered in the world any but old truths—as old as the sun and moon. How can I know? But *do* take me; it's such a chance to see Boston."
> "It isn't Boston—it's humanity!" Miss Chancellor, as she made this remark, rose from her chair, and her movement seemed to say that she consented [p. 21].

James's description of the "Bostonians" in the first book is marvelously funny. For Olive, it is "a company of heroes" (p. 37), while Ransom sees only "mediums, communists, vegetarians" (p. 31). The mixed crowd also includes the veteran reformer Miss Birdseye, the domineering Mrs. Farrinder (and her anonymous husband), the skeptical Dr. Prance, the fraudulent Selah Tarrant with his wife and daughter, and the newspaperman Pardon.

From Olive's point of view, Miss Birdseye "was heroic, she was sublime, the whole moral history of Boston was reflected in her displaced spectacles" (p. 34), but James dwells lovingly on the significance of the old lady's dimness of sight (it will be Miss Birdseye who, on mistaken evidence, gives Ransom Verena's address in Cambridge and later blesses their union, thinking that he has been converted to the cause of women's rights). James's wit is never more lethally brilliant than in his portrait of Miss Birdseye, although his hostility toward the New England heroic tradition is clearly evident in his manner of description. "The long practice of philanthropy," he observes, had succeeded in depriving her of distinctive features, as well as a personal life, and, without a personal identity, she turned into "a confused, entangled, inconsequent, discursive old woman, whose charity began at home and ended nowhere, whose credulity kept pace with it, and who knew less about her fellow-creatures, if possible, after fifty years of humanitary zeal, than on the day she had gone into the field to testify against the iniquity of most arrangements."

> Since the Civil War much of her occupation was gone; for before that her best hours had been spent in fancying that she was helping some Southern slave to escape. It would have been a nice question whether, in her heart of hearts, for the sake of this excitement, she did not sometimes wish the blacks back in bondage. She had suffered in the same way by the relaxation of many European despotisms, for in former years much of the romance of her life had been in smoothing the pillow of exile for banished conspirators. Her refugees had been very precious to her; she was always trying to raise money for some cadaverous Pole, to obtain lessons for some shirtless Italian. There was a legend that an Hungarian had once possessed himself of her affections, and had disappeared after robbing her of everything she possessed. This, however, was very apocryphal, for she had never possessed anything, and it was open to grave doubt that she could have entertained a sentiment so personal. She was in love, even in those days, only with causes, and she languished only for emancipations. But they had been the happiest days, for when causes were embodied in foreigners (what else were the Africans?), they were certainly more appealing [pp. 26–28].

The amount of ridicule poured upon such a character is interesting in light of James's claim that she was meant to represent "an old survivor of the New England Reform period."[14] William was horrified by what he thought his brother had intended as a malicious portrait of Elizabeth Peabody, Hawthorne's sister-in-law, but it is probably truer to say that in her embodied impotence James was laughing at the entire New England heritage.

Some of Miss Birdseye's limitations are curiously akin to Emerson's. As James said of Emerson in 1887, "he was altogether passionless . . . He had no personal, just as he had almost no physical wants." The two figures share alike an ignorance of artistic taste and of evil. In 1883 James played off Emerson and Carlyle in a review of their published correspondence,[15] and the opposing nature of their philosophical beliefs is echoed in *The Bostonians*. If the reformist spirit was embodied in such forms as Brook Farm, James could note in the Emerson essay how futile such critical experiments were in practice. "Nothing is more perceptible to-day," he wrote (while also recalling Emerson's detachment from such endeavors), "than that their criticism produced no fruit—that it was little else than a very decent and innocent recreation—a kind of Puritan carnival."[16] James may have felt, especially under the pressure of his brother's criticism, that he had gone too far in his characterization of Miss Birdseye. It is interesting to see how she is adjudged a "poor little humanity hack" early in the book (p. 37), while she dies "a battered, immemorial monument" (p. 395) to the late heroic age. But as with his portrait of Olive, James's caricature had turned into something deeper.

Whatever her ridiculous appearance in the early sections of the book, Miss Birdseye is treated much more gently than the new reformers, the practitioners of the newest truths. Mrs. Farrinder is the professional among reformers; she knows exactly what she wants ("to give the ballot to every woman in the country and to take the flowing bowl from every man" [p. 30]), and how to go about getting it. When Olive asks her what she can contribute to the feminist cause, Mrs. Farrinder is ruthlessly practical: " 'What *have* you got?' Mrs. Farrinder inquired, looking at her interlocutress, up and down, with the eye of business, in which there was a certain chill. 'Have you got money?' " (p. 36). The cold practicality of an earlier James character comes to mind: " 'I don't pretend to know what people are meant for,' said Madame Merle. 'I only know what I can do with them.' "[17] Also present at the scene at Miss Birdseye's are the newspaperman and the mesmeric healer and his family. They are all (except for Verena) Dickensian regulars. Matthias Pardon is the publicist of the new and the private (one of the titles James had considered for the novel was *The Revealer*), a familiar target for James, but one reminiscent to readers of the American chapters of *Martin Chuzzlewit*. "He had a sort of enamel of good humour," James observes later, "which showed that his indelicacy was his profession; and he asked for revelations of the *vie intime* of his victims with the bland confidence of a fashionable physician inquiring about symptoms" (p. 140). It is characteristic of Verena's vacuity that she should find his proposal of marriage and a "run" on the lecture platforms "rather dazzling."

James's caricature is rather too broad in Pardon's case, but his Selah Tarrant is a perfect successor to Dickens' Chadband. A "moralist without moral sense" (p. 109), he represents the dregs of the radical movement. Married to the confused daughter of a famous abolitionist, Selah "had begun life as an itinerant vendor of lead-pencils (he had called at Mr. Greenstreet's in the exercise of this function), had afterwards been for a while a member of the celebrated Cayuga community,* where there were no wives, or no husbands, or something of that sort (Mrs. Tarrant could never remember), and had still later (though before the development of the healing faculty) achieved distinction in the spiritualistic world" (p. 71). "He look like the priest of a religion that was passing through the stage of miracles," James remarks, adding that his real idol was the newspapers and that his eye was always directed toward "receipts" (pp. 100–102). One of James's modest triumphs of Dickensian characterization is Mrs. Tarrant, whose brain succumbs to "vapors of social ambition" as a result of Olive's interest in her daughter. At the end of the novel, she alone among the disappointed reformers manages to gain some advantage by heaving "herself into the arms of Mrs. Burrage [the wealthy social-

---

* In 1875 James had reviewed Charles Nordhoff's study of various such communistic communities, declaring the amorality of such places as Oneida to be "simply hideous," and somberly concluding: "The whole scene, and all that it rested on, is an attempt to organize and glorify the detestable tendency toward the complete effacement of privacy in life and thought everywhere so rampant with us nowadays" (*Literary Reviews and Essays*, p. 266).

ite], who [Ransom] was sure, would, within the minute, loom upon her attractively through her tears, and supply her with a reminiscence, destined to be valuable, of aristocratic support and clever composure" (p. 449).

Such characters might be said to pre-exist, in the manner of Dickensian characters, rather than to develop in the manner of James's more typical creations. Another atypical characteristic of *The Bostonians* is the length to which James goes to paint in distinctively American backgrounds for the main characters—even though it is typical of Olive, Basil, and Verena that they live in isolation, like figures of American romance. Boston and Cambridge are pictorially vivid, as is New York. Describing Ransom's New York neighborhood with an almost vengeful minuteness, James breaks in to remind us that such a concession to the believers in environmental conditioning is not really viable as in French fiction (if even there):

> I mention it not on account of any particular influence it may have had on the life or the thoughts of Basil Ransom, but for old acquaintance sake and that of local colour; besides which, a figure is nothing without a setting, and our young man came and went every day, with rather an indifferent, unperceiving step, it is true, among the objects I have briefly designated [p. 186].

Ransom no more fits into his adoptive home than Verena or Olive have fitted in among their backgrounds. The brilliance of James's description of his native New York has not always been pointed out. Besides the images of Washington Square (so curiously missing in the novel of that name) or Central Park or a Tenth Street boarding house, there is the great scene in Mrs. Burrage's house in preparation for Verena's performance there. Society must be amused, even if, as a socialite remarks, "you must be pretty desperate when you have got to go to Boston for your entertainment" (p. 249). James uses Ransom's point of view with great success here:

> It was certainly the fashionable world, for there was no one there whom he had ever seen before. The walls of the room were covered with pictures—the very ceiling was painted and framed. The people pushed each other a little, edged about,

advanced and retreated, looking at each other with differing faces—sometimes blandly, unperceivingly, sometimes with a harshness of contemplation, a kind of cruelty, Ransom thought; sometimes with sudden nods and grimaces, inarticulate murmurs, followed by a quick reaction, a sort of gloom. He was now absolutely certain that he was in the best society [p. 248].

"Differing faces" is, of course, a keynote of the pluralistic world of the novel. An amusing use of differing points of view of the same scene is provided when Verena describes to Ransom the "Female Convention": "The heat was intense, the weather magnificent, and great thoughts and brilliant sayings flew round like darting fireflies . . . we consumed quantities of ice-cream!" However, he has his own ideas: "Her description of the convention put the scene before him vividly; he seemed to see the crowded, overheated hall, which he was sure was filled with carpet-baggers, to hear flushed women, with loosened bonnet-strings, forcing thin voices into ineffectual shrillness" (pp. 236–237). Characters doomed to pass through life seeing things only through a limited point of view have always been the proper subjects for comedy. It is the prerogative of the artist, however, to avoid such human limitations, to collect differing attitudes into his works. Art is the reconciler of what in the world are petty oppositions. In one of the most moving passages in the novel, Ransom waives his Southern prejudices as he stands before the monument to the Civil War dead in Harvard Memorial Hall:

> For Ransom these things were not a challenge nor a taunt; they touched him with respect, with the sentiment of beauty. He was capable of being a generous foeman, and he forgot, now, the whole question of sides and parties; the simple emotion of the old fighting-time came back to him, and the monument around him seemed an embodiment of that memory; it arched over friends as well as enemies, the victims of defeat as well as the sons of triumph [p. 242].

It is the value of art, as James points out in *The Princess Casmassima* and *The Tragic Muse*, that it lasts, that it provides relief and joy long after the "howling" of the sides and parties of the world has passed away.

The ceremony at the altar of the dead is the only passage in the book, however, where art is celebrated even indirectly. It is characteristic of James's heroes that they are artists at life, and this allows them (after so much is denied them) a breadth of point of view and a measure of freedom unknown to the people around them. The major figures in *The Bostonians,* on the contrary, are limited in action and point of view. Rather than making them one-dimensional figures, this defect curiously makes them all the more suitable for playing the American and novelistic roles they are assigned. Problems arise, however, when James begins to overanalyze a figure like Olive to the point that she begins, embarrassingly, to round out, or when he assigns to a character like Ransom his own impressions of the "womanised" nature of modern America:

> "The whole generation is womanised, the masculine tone is passing out of the world; it's a feminine, a nervous, hysterical, chattering, canting age, an age of hollow phrases and false delicacy and exaggerated solicitudes and coddled sensibilities, which, if we don't soon look out, will usher in the reign of mediocrity, of the feeblest and flattest and the most pretentious that has ever been. The masculine character, the ability to dare and endure, to know and yet not fear reality, to look the world in the face and take it for what it is—a very queer and partly very base mixture—that is what I want to preserve, or rather, as I may say, to recover; and I must tell you that I don't in the least care what becomes of you ladies while I make the attempt!" [pp. 333–334].

Of course, James would never have adopted Ransom's aggressive tone or his political solution. For James, the crisis of the period, in England and America, meant materials for fiction. Ransom's impressions, so much admired by Lionel Trilling and other critics,[18] are shared by Olive. She has a different answer to the problem, however:

> Olive had a standing quarrel with the levity, the good-nature, of the judgments of the day; many of them seemed to her weak to imbecility, losing sight of all measures and standards, lavishing superlatives, delighted to be fooled. The age seemed to her relaxed and demoralised, and I believe she looked to the influx of the great feminine element to make it feel and speak more sharply [p. 125].

In his *Atlantic* review of the novel, Horace Scudder shrewdly noted that it "is not in the least a contribution to the study of the woman question, so called" (as a good many English reviewers had taken it, assuming that James was on Ransom's side). "It is rather a study of the particular woman question in this book."[19] The novel is not about "the sacred mothers refusing their commission";[20] rather, it concerns the purely novelistic question of who is to win Verena Tarrant. James needed for this purpose a man of iron will, a proven veteran, "of a hard-headed and conservative disposition," as he wrote in his notebook.[21] The ironic distance set up between the reader and Ransom has already been mentioned, and in virtually every descriptive passage the Southern-born, unsuccessful lawyer ("He had had none but small jobs, and he had made a mess of more than one of them" [p. 187]) is amusingly lambasted. The political essays he writes are unpublished because "his doctrines were about three hundred years behind the age" (Ransom naturally thinks otherwise); and his critique of the age is as shrill as Olive's, just as his chivalric pretensions are as absurd as her desire for a crusade. "I know not exactly how these queer heresies had planted themselves," the narrator conjectures,

> but he had a longish pedigree (it had flowered at one time with English royalists and cavaliers), and he seemed at moments to be inhabited by some transmitted spirit of a robust but narrow ancestor, some broad-faced wig-bearer or sword-bearer, with a more primitive conception of manhood than our modern temperament appears to require, and a programme of human felicity much less varied. He liked his pedigree, he revered his forefathers, and he rather pitied those who might come after him [pp. 189–190].

The comic climax of Ransom's illusions comes when one of his articles is accepted for publication by *The Rational Review*, "a journal," as Irving Howe acidly notes, "of which the title sufficiently suggests both its circulation and influence."[22] It is obviously no accident that the title of Verena's never-to-be-delivered lecture at the Music Hall has the similarly ironic title of "A Woman's Reason."

Ransom is a romantic bully with comic illusions which humanize him, within the scope of the novel, and which allow for his feat of chivalry: to wrest Verena at the end of the novel from what he deems the "mighty multitude" (p. 428). Earlier, he feels secure that "however she might turn and twist in his grasp he held her fast"; metaphorically, he regards his future bride as an animal to be tamed and assumes that she is indulging in "instinctive contortions" and "that a good many more would probably occur before she would be quiet" (p. 402). The brutality behind the chivalric pose is undeniable. For the sake of providing his readers with a conventionally happy ending, James lets Ransom have his way. Although he approves of some of his convictions, however, James is hostile to the figure. In light of Ransom's adoration of Carlyle, it is pertinent to remember the feelings of the James family toward the Victorian sage. James's father, who had met Carlyle, had attacked him in 1881 as a "hardened declaimer." "He who best denounced a canting age," he noted, "became himself its most signal illustration, since even his denunciation of the vice succumbed to the prevalent usage, and announced itself at length a shameless cant." Especially interesting is the charge of Henry James, Sr., that Carlyle's sin was that of the artist—making the same point about him that James had made of Hawthorne and Gautier: "It always appeared to me that Carlyle valued truth and good as a painter does his pigments, not for what they are in themselves, but for the effects they lend themselves to in the sphere of production."[23] William, on the other hand, had an obvious admiration for Carlyle's force of will, and it seems no accident that William should have admired Basil Ransom as well. In 1886 Henry James characterized Carlyle, Meredith's philosophical idol, in a letter to Norton, as "the most disagreeable in character of men of genius of equal magnificence."[24]

It is fitting that the object of Ransom's chivalric attentions should be so questionable a prize as Verena Tarrant. He is nonplussed by the ideas she has swallowed, but he readily sees that she is pliable to any superior will. Both Olive and Basil provide her with a negative education; yet the one easily passes through her, and the other may apparently do likewise. She is essentially untouchable: "Though she had grown up among people who took for granted all sorts of queer laxities," the narrator observes, "she had kept the consummate innocence of the American girl" (p. 121). But it is an American innocence, as James reminds us through the decade, kept alive by ignorance. There is an Emersonian appeal in Verena's simple faith and her instinctively democratic feelings. "There were so many things that she hadn't yet learned to dislike," we read of her divergence from Olive, "in spite of her friend's earnest efforts to teach her. She had the idea vividly (that was the marvel) of the cruelty of man, of his immemorial injustice; but it remained abstract, platonic; she didn't detest him in consequence" (pp. 120–121).

On the subject of the "Question of Women," Verena speaks with rhetorical effect throughout the novel, but one is never sure of her full sincerity. When Olive begins to worry about Verena's interest in Ransom, the girl retorts, "I thought you had discovered by this time that I am serious; that I have dedicated my life; that there is something unspeakably dear to me," and so on, but the narrator reminds us of the theatricality of her sincerity: "The habit of public speaking, the training, the practice, in which she had been immersed, enabled Verena to enroll a coil of propositions dedicated even to a private interest with the most touching, most cumulative effect" (pp. 300–301). The lure of rhetoric is, however, one from which very few James characters are immune, with the result that we occasionally doubt their sincerity. Early in their relationship, Verena admits, "Do you know, Olive, I sometimes wonder whether, if it wasn't for you, I should feel it so very much!" (p. 155). Olive, ironically, takes this as a compliment.

It is no surprise, then, that with the pressure exerted by Basil's will and attractiveness, Verena should come over to his view. "It was simply that the truth had changed sides," James archly notes, although he adds that Verena's nature is the same. "It was always passion, in fact" (whether to renounce for Olive or to submit to him), "but now the object was other" (pp. 384–385). As the prize of an ideological debate, surely Verena is not to be taken seriously. In terms of the philosophical battle between Ransom and Olive, Carlyle and Emerson, the object is ludicrous. For an exasperated Scudder, the innocent heroine of *The Bostonians* seemed "this impossible Verena"; stressing her "innate vulgarity," he called her a "cheap imitation of spiritual beauty."[25] In terms of the chivalric pattern (or mock pattern?) of the novel, one can also consider her an "exquisite Andromeda," as Van Wyck Brooks does, and hers "the feminine virtue of passive receptivity," in F. W. Dupee's phrase.[26] She is a deliberate mixture of innocence and vulgarity (James stresses the badness of her taste again and again), and James characterizes her in the phrase: "It is to be feared, indeed, that Verena was easily satisfied" (p. 390). Even Ransom is struck by the ease with which she gives up her belief in her gifts as a reformist speaker: "He was indeed quite appalled at the facility with which she threw it over, gave up the idea that it was useful and precious" (p. 388).

James had Daudet very much in his mind as he prepared *The Bostonians*. "Daudet's *Évangéliste* has given me the idea of this thing," he confided to his notebook, with respect to the theme of the victimization of the private life by a public, religious cause.[27] In his 1883 essay on Daudet he complained of the lack of analysis in the characters of Madame Autheman, the strong-minded fanatic, and Eline Ebsen, her pliant victim:

> The fact is that M. Daudet has not (to my belief) any natural understanding of the religious passion; he has a quick perception of many things, but that province of the human mind cannot be *fait de chic*—experience, there, is the only explorer. Madame Autheman is not a real bigot; she is simply a dusky effigy, she is undemonstrated. Eline Ebsen is not a victim, inasmuch as she is but half alive, and victims are victims only in virtue of being thoroughly sentient.[28]

It is hard for the reader of *The Bostonians*, however, to detect the "spiritual joints" in Verena that James found lacking in Eline. It might be argued, for that matter, that spiritual joints would be out of place in the light of Verena's role in the novel. For the sake of a conventional action with predictable characters, psychological analysis is hardly necessary for a Victorian heroine with the "clinging tenderness" and "passive sweetness" that James commemorated in Trollope's heroines. James's characteristic interest, as Scudder noted in his review, is in every possible psychological aspect of his character. From this critical commonplace of the time, Scudder went on to make a provocative observation: "It is when this interest leads Mr. James to push his characters too near the brink of nature that we step back and decline to follow." The relations between Olive and Verena, he charged in 1886, sometimes proceed "to dangerous lengths, and we hesitate about accepting the relation between them as either natural or reasonable." In the scene at the end of the novel, for example, with "its almost indecent exposure of Miss Chancellor's mind," James "allows the story just to tumble down" by contrast.[29]

Scudder's uneasiness is understandable. James had intended a very American tale in theme and a distinctly Victorian novel in style, and the two do not always fit well together (hence, James's need to put his own views in a character he is ironically detached from). But he could not resist resorting to an analysis of Olive Chancellor which threatens, part of the time, to force a situation drawn from comedy into a tragic mode. The relations between Olive and Verena have been extensively studied. Indeed, what is praised as James's pre-Freudian "daring" in this respect has accounted for some share of the revival of interest in the novel in the past two decades. Is Olive Chancellor a Lesbian? In James's conscious mind, of course not, although it has become the prerogative of recent literary critics to ransack James's unconscious mind. Intense female friendships were common enough in New England and Victorian England, with one woman very often worshipping another.* Hawthorne says of such a friendship between Priscilla and Zenobia in *The Blithedale Romance:* "We men are too gross to comprehend it."[30] Or as Olive puts it, defending the relationship, "it only proves how little such an association as ours is understood" (p. 311). It is characteristic of the all-inclusiveness of the novel form that readers should feel encouraged to become psychiatrists and study a literary creation like Olive as a case study; one can as easily determine how many psychoses Olive has as how many children Lady Macbeth had. For purposes of the novelistic action in which she takes part, it is essential that Olive fight Ransom for Verena. James may have drawn on the relationship between his invalid sister Alice and her strong-willed friend Katherine Loring for personal details. And there is a measure of similarity between James and Olive in terms of their fastidious taste and personal shyness.

Olive is a synthesis drawn from various literary sources in

* The strange case of Edith Simcox, who prostrated herself before George Eliot on occasion, has been documented in a book by K. A. McKenzie (*Edith Simcox and George Eliot*, London: Oxford University Press, 1961).

James and others. The most obvious parallel, perhaps, is with Zenobia in *The Blithedale Romance*, a type of woman who appears frequently in James's fiction of the 1880's, the "New Woman" with a cause: "the woman of 'sympathies,'" as James called Zenobia in a short essay on Hawthorne in 1879, "the passionate patroness of 'causes,' who plays as it were with revolution, and only encounters embarrassment."[31] Olive is thereby linked with a considerably more attractive woman, the Princess Casamassima. She is described in images of cold reminiscent of James's portrait of the staunch Bostonian Mr. Wentworth in *The Europeans*. Her role in the novel is to "take up" Verena, in a manner that echoes Roger's adoption of Nora in *Watch and Ward* or Rowland's patronage of Roderick Hudson. She is the only character in the novel with taste, which is necessarily insulted by her contact with the reformers. She is another echo of George Eliot's heroines, or Isabel Archer as the latter might have become if she had never left Albany: "The most secret, the most sacred hope of her nature," as James notes of Olive, "was that she might some day have such a chance, that she might be a martyr and die for something" (p. 13). Olive is all these characters but more so—to the point of satire. Unlike them, she is a "woman without laughter" (p. 18), and, hence, subject to our own laughter. Her dreams of a female crusade are misguided illusions, noble in intent but impossible: "The world was full of evil, but she was glad to have been born before it had been swept away, while it was still there to face, to give one a task and a reward" (p. 156). She is described as being "in the nature of things, entangled in contradictions," and with a mingled intelligence and simplicity distinctly Bostonian she misreads history through a feminist point of view, she develops grandiose schemes for changing history, and she naïvely selects Verena Tarrant as her Joan of Arc. In an aside, the narrator comments on her inconsistency: "It may therefore be imagined how sharp her vision would have been could she only have taken the situation more simply; for she was intelligent enough not to have needed to be morbid, even for purposes of self-defence" (p. 152).

The note of personal morbidity is developed and analyzed to the point where the comic situation she is in becomes almost fatally blurred. Olive believes, like a naturalistic novelist, in the determining influence of one's personal background: "It is always supposed that revolutionists have been goaded, and the goading would have been rather deficient here were it not for such happy accidents in Verena's past." But the "happy accident" that Olive dwells on is the possibility "that Verena, in her childhood, had known almost the extremity of poverty, and there was a kind of ferocity in the joy with which she reflected that there had been moments when this delicate creature came near (if the pinch had only lasted a little longer) to literally going without food" (pp. 109–110).

If James is satirizing Olive's naïveté in this respect (she feels that the memory of poverty will make Verena more dedicated to their cause), he also accidentally suggests a psychological aberration as well. Elsewhere, he shows that Olive's obsessive social concern, which he has treated comically earlier, is an attempt to compensate for intense personal loneliness. In the extraordinary scene (from which I will quote only the closing lines) in which she realizes that she has lost Verena to Ransom, James turns Olive into a tragic heroine:

> She would just sit there and hold her hand; that was all she
> could do; they were beyond each other's help in any other way
> now. Verena leaned her head back and closed her eyes, and
> for an hour, as nightfall settled in the room, neither of the young
> women spoke. Distinctly, it was a kind of shame. After a while
> the parlour-maid, very casual, in the manner of the servants
> at Marmion, appeared on the threshold with a lamp; but
> Olive motioned her frantically away. She wished to
> keep the darkness. It was a kind of shame [pp. 412–413].

The entire scene is worthy of D. H. Lawrence at his best, but the apparently ambiguous nature of the women's relationship must have perplexed many contemporary readers much as it did Scudder.

Olive is presented for the most part, however, as a deluded, humorless, sexless figure—but then, one might add, so is Miss Birdseye. By implication, James seems to be satirizing the entire tradition of New England reformers. The combination of high ideals, social criticism, and lack of achievement from an artistic point of view puts Olive among distinguished company. In at least one detail, Olive models herself upon Henry James, Sr. If the elder

James's "best known remark is that, 'to a right-minded man,' a crowded horse-car is 'the nearest approach to heaven upon earth,'"[32] perhaps that partly explains the tenacity of Olive's "theory" of the necessity to ride in such conveyances: "Boston was full of poor girls who had to walk about at night and to squeeze into horse-cars in which every sense was displeased; and why should she hold herself superior to these?" (p. 23).

In the same year that saw the serial publication of *The Bostonians*, James also produced the following eulogy of George Eliot:

> To her own sex her memory, her example, will remain of the
> highest value; those of them for whom the "development"
> of woman is the hope of the future ought to erect a monument
> to George Eliot. She helped on the cause more than any one,
> in proving how few limitations are of necessity implied in the
> feminine organism. She went so far that such a distance seems
> enough, and in her effort she sacrificed no tenderness, no grace.
> There is much talk to-day about things being "open to
> women"; but George Eliot showed that there is nothing that
> is closed.[33]

Such a moving tribute should indicate how little James was on the "side" of either warrior in his novel. Women have a right to be heard, he argues, especially if they are George Eliots. With regard to feminist agitation, James could not have entered into the philosophical argument of a John Stuart Mill ("All the selfish propensities, the self-worship, the unjust self-preference, which exists among mankind, have their source and root in, and derive their principal nourishment from, the present constitution of the relation between men and women").[34] He could not create a philosophically conscious "New Woman," like those of Meredith and Lawrence. Still, he could justifiably argue that he had detected as an artist one of the major truths of his time. In 1895 he noted of a recent study that "The idea of his little book is the Revolution in English society by the *avènement* of the women, which he sees everywhere and in everything. I saw it long ago—and I saw in it a big subject for the Novelist."[35] Olive Chancellor is the first public-minded woman in James's fiction, and she is immediately followed by the Princess Casamassima and Julia Dallow (in *The Tragic Muse*). If in

"The Art of Fiction," James argued for the idea of the novel as history, in his novels of the 1880's he brilliantly established the validity of that criterion.

The Bostonians is a great novel despite the various confusions of purpose, and partly because of them. James succeeded in his desire for an American subject, even if it meant subjecting American illusions, and particular regional illusions, to deadly satire. The success of the Victorian style is manifest in the brilliance of the many characters described, from Basil to Miss Birdseye. James even attached a happy ending, although with such a vengeance that one might well prefer the open ending of *The Portrait of a Lady*. The critical reception of the book was as infuriatingly dense, by and large, as the reviews of *The Portrait* had been. While writing the novel James declared, "It is a better subject than I have ever had before, and I think will be much the best thing I have done yet." When it was published, he turned upon it with undue severity: "The whole thing is too long and dawdling," he wrote William:

> This came from the fact (partly) that I had the sense of knowing terribly little about the kind of life I had attempted to describe—and felt a constant pressure to make the picture substantial by thinking it out—pencilling and "shading." I was afraid of the reproach (having *seen* so little of the whole business treated of,) of being superficial and cheap—and in short I should have been much more rapid, and had a lighter hand, with a subject concerned with people and things of a nature more near to my experience.[36]

It is curious to find James apologizing, in the manner of Walter Besant on the need for relying on "personal experience," after having produced a major English novel. James's temporary willingness, in the mid-1880's, to handle major themes of a nature outside his immediate experience indicates that the evolution of his later manner was a loss as well as a gain. The tension between the Victorian and the American, the conventional and the independent-minded Henry James resulted in a hybrid masterpiece devoted to the idea behind comedy and the comedy behind idealism.

Politics versus the Empire of Things:
The Princess Casamassima

> *"Illusion of course is illusion, and*
> *one must always pay for it."*
> *("Madame de Mauves")*

If *The Princess Casamassima* seems the least Jamesian of novels in its scope and intentions, it is an archetypal James novel in its ultimate theme and choice of hero. In his review of the book R. H. Hutton noted James's love of presenting "character adrift from all its natural moorings."[37] While the novelist appeared to be describing several of the major social issues of the day—the sense of drift in the air, and the fear of and agitations toward a socialist revolution—he came instead to articulate a major personal theme of his subsequent works: the need for the Jamesian individual to cut himself adrift from the perilous world, to treat life in the spirit of art as a passive, albeit self-reliant, observer. As Gissing was doing in *Demos*, James treated the economic crisis of the period as a theme for art.

The mid-1880's was marked by a severe depression, by chronic unemployment, and by the constant threat of rioting and even revolution on the part of the working classes. On February 8, 1886, a mob gathered in Trafalgar Square to hear H. M. Hyndman and other socialist leaders promise the imminence of revolution; in the preceding year Émile Zola ended *Germinal* with a dream of socialist solutions to the class wars of the period. In *The Princess Casamassima* James captured enough vivid social details, drawn from his observations of the working classes and from his readings in the London *Times* and of Zola and Dickens, to guarantee the book the status of a major historical novel of the 1880's; in the one of his novels to depict the history of his time with abundance of detail, however, he also indicated the dangers of history for the Jamesian individual. The book resembles one of Pater's "Imaginary Portraits" in this respect: the overly sensitive hero lives in a transitional period, and, in the attempt to deal with the pressures of the age, they destroy him. James modeled his protagonist upon the self-divided heroes of Turgenev, but, where the Russian novelist exposed both the irony of their situation and the fatal weaknesses in their character, James treats Hyacinth Robinson without irony as a romantic hero filled with beautiful illusions. The trouble with *The Princess Casamassima*, which is otherwise a rich and fascinating book with an assortment of finely drawn characters, is Hyacinth Robinson; the trouble with Hyacinth Robinson is Henry James.

January 1885 found James in a rare "beastly political" mood. In a letter addressed to Grace Norton at this time, he commented on the recent destructive acts of Irish dynamiters at home and on the general chaos abroad. Watching the "decline" of "old England" provided a "thrilling" and "dramatic" entertainment, at least;[38] with his eyes fixed on England struggling not to collapse, James professed to derive as much aesthetic enjoyment as, in his fiction, Dr. Sloper had received from surveying his daughter under pressure or Ralph Touchett from observing Isabel. The letter indicates why James would capitalize, in his new novel, on the spectacle of England in the midst of change, and the tone of his remarks foreshadows why *The Princess Casamassima* would fail as a novel of ideas. James's habit of seeing everything as so much potential material for the novelist inevitably kept him from forming any other views than the necessity for history keeping itself on the side of the Jamesian artist. Political issues of every kind seemed meaningless to him when compared to works of art. James demanded that history itself be a work of art, fixed and beautiful.

James had written in 1879, apropos of the English theater, "The world is being steadily democratized and vulgarized, and literature and art give their testimony to the fact. The fact is better for the world perhaps, but I question greatly whether it is better for art and literature."[39] James's penchant for the status quo had long kept him from having a political opinion that was not basically aesthetic. In an early travel sketch, he had remarked of England that "conservatism here has all the charm and leaves dissent and democracy and other vulgar variations nothing but their bald logic. Conservatism has the cathedrals, the colleges, the castles, the gardens, the traditions, the associations, the fine names, the better manners, the poetry; Dissent has the dusky brick chapels in provincial by-streets, the names out of Dickens, the uncertain tenure of the *h*, and the poor *mens sibi conscia recti.*"[40]

In an essay on Rheims in 1877 he again set off and combined politics, religion, and aesthetics, as he considered the conflict "between the actively, practically liberal instinct and what one may call the historic, aesthetic sense, the sense upon which old cathedrals lay a certain palpable obligation. How far should a lover of old cathedrals let his hands be tied by the sanctity of their traditions? How far should he let his imagination bribe him, as it were, from action?"[41] The latter question has an especially significant ring with respect to James's theme in *The Princess.*

W. H. Tilley has amply shown the historical background for *The Princess Casamassima*, especially James's reading of *The Times*'s articles on Irish and socialist agitators in the early and middle 1880's. It seemed to James "an age of politics," as Tilley suggests. In September 1884 he wrote to a friend:

> Nothing *lives* in England to-day but politics. They are all-devouring, & their mental uproar crowds everything out. This is more & more the case; we are evidently on the edge of an enormous political cycle, which will last heaven knows how long. I should hate it more if I didn't also find it interesting. The present political drama can't help being so, in spite of the imbecility of so many of the actors. The air is full of events, of changes, of movement (some people wld. say of revolution, but I don't think that).[42]

In February 1884 James announced to the *Atlantic* editor that he could begin a new novel for him next year (although he had yet to begin writing *The Bostonians* for the *Century*), "a very good *sujet de roman.*" He anticipated "the enjoyment of a popularity"—expecting no doubt that *The Bostonians* would be a popular success as a result of his capitulations in style and subject matter—and he indicated that the example of the French naturalists was very much on his mind.[43] In the same month, he wrote to Howells that "there is nothing more interesting to me now than the effort and experiments of this little group [Zola, Daudet, the Goncourts, and others], with its truly infernal intelligence of art, form, manner—its intense artistic life." Insisting that theirs was "the only kind of work, to-day," that he respected,[44] James prepared a novel which would benefit from the taking of notes, and which would show the effects of environment and heredity upon his protagonist.

A marked difference in mood separates *The Bostonians* from *The Princess:* in the former James may be said to have erected an ironical barrier between America and himself; in the latter there seems to be a barrier between himself and everything else much of the time. A notebook entry for August 1885 shows that he was acutely self-defensive as he prepared his novel of "ideas": "One does nothing of value in art or literature unless one has some general ideas, and if one has a few such, constituting a motive and a support, those flippancies and vulgarities (abusive reviews in newspapers) are the last thing one troubles about." Alone in the world and having sent off for serialization a book which created no popular reverberations, as hoped, James turned for philosophical support to the actual writing of *The Princess.* He complained in the notebook (his only existing notebook reference to the novel) of the vagueness of what he had just begun to write, but he also complimented himself on the strength of the idea:

> The subject of the *Princess* is magnificent, and if I can only
> give up my mind to it properly—generously and trustfully
> —the form will shape itself as successfully as the idea deserves.
> I have plunged in rather blindly, and got a good many characters
> on my hands; but these will fall into their places if I keep
> cool and think it out. Oh art, art, what difficulties are like thine;
> but, at the same time, what consolation and encouragements,
> also, are like thine? Without thee, for me, the world would be,
> indeed, a howling desert. The *Princess* will give me hard,
> continuous work for many months to come; but she will also
> give me joys too sacred to prate about.[45]

One may deduce from this why a novel originally scheduled to be on a political subject turned, as James wrote, into a defense of art and the Jamesian individual. He had begun it with a rich, historical subject in mind, but with vagueness of detail and purpose; the finished novel indicates alternating moods of euphoria and personal despair in James which prevented him from repeating the substantial objectivity of *The Bostonians.*

The novel was drawn from a variety of personal sources, which combined with the accounts of unrest in *The Times.* For example, there were the ideas of Henry James, Sr., who had long disliked the entrenched conservatism of England, and who believed "in the imminence of a transformation-scene in human affairs": a liberal political change for the better, at least at home. In his transcendental-political essays, the elder James sought to reconcile "Socialism" with "Civilization," Fourierism with conservatism, to produce a religious form of socialism.[46] A conscious desire may be detected, on James's part, to show up the impossibility of his father's idealism in *The Princess.* Two major sources of opposition to his father's views came from the example of the French Revolution, especially as interpreted by Taine, and from the disenchanted last novel of Turgenev, *Virgin Soil.*

Turgenev had been dead for a year when James sent off his plan for *The Princess,* but, since James had identified himself so closely with Turgenev in outlook and choice of subject matter, it seems no surprise that his novel should have appeared an act of homage. Critics of the period were quick to point out the resemblances between *The Princess* and *Virgin Soil.* One need only look at James's essays on Turgenev to see the extent of his conscious identification:

> M. Turgénieff [he wrote in 1874] gives us a peculiar sense of being out of harmony with his native land—of his having what one may call a poet's quarrel with it. He loves the old, and he is unable to see where the new is drifting. American readers will peculiarly appreciate this state of mind; if they had a native novelist of a large pattern, it would probably be, in a degree, his own.

James described *Fathers and Sons* as dealing with the opposition between the forces of tradition and innovation, and he observed that, despite the tragic nature of this conflict, "in all that poets and philosophers tell us of it the clearest fact is still its perpetual necessity."[47] Turgenev's Bazarov with his allegiance to nihilism and the new science anticipates the Princess's swearing "by Darwin and Spencer as well as by the revolutionary spirit."[48]

James's review of *Virgin Soil,* as has been often pointed out, sounds in part like a rough draft for *The Princess.* The Russian novel, James notes, capitalizes on "certain 'secret societies' " known vaguely to the outside world; its hero Nezhdanov is "a particularly good subject for irony," sharing with Turgenev's other heroes the function "to be conspicuous as failures, interesting but impotent persons who are losers at the game of life." James characterizes this Russian "subjective" type (which Turgenev in his essay on "Don Quixote and Hamlet" had called the Hamlet figure) in a manner which clearly points toward Hyacinth Robinson:

> His central figure is usually a person in a false position, generally not of his own making, which, according to the peculiar perversity of fate, is only aggravated by his effort to right himself. Such eminently is the case with young Neshdanoff, who is the natural son of a nobleman, not recognized by his father's family, and who, drifting through irritation and smothered rage and vague aspiration into the stream of occult radicalism, finds himself fatally fastidious and sceptical and "aesthetic"—more essentially an aristocrat, in a word, than any of the aristocrats he has agreed to conspire against. He has not the gift of faith, and he is most uncomfortably at odds with his companions, who have it in a high degree— these types of "faith" which surround Neshdanoff being most vividly portrayed.[49]

The plots of the novels are similar enough, and James's radicals likewise prate about the sacredness of their cause. But James apparently forgot, or failed to notice, just how vulnerable to irony his own hero was.

James's interest in a political novel with an "aesthetic" hero was somewhat confused by his highly colored views of the French Revolution. In the fall of 1882 he made a trip through the French provinces to collect notes for the travel volume *A Little Tour in France*. At a period of dislocation in his life he especially noticed the ravages of the Revolution, as well as the current menace of syndicalist agitators. "Wherever one goes, in France," he wrote, "one meets, looking backward a little, the spectre of the great Revolution; and one meets it always in the shape of the destruction of something beautiful and precious." Revolutionists thus became invariably connected in his mind with "image-breakers," and he attacked Victor Hugo's *1793* for its homage to "the hideous sediment of blood and error." The *ancien régime*, on the other hand, was treated with the respect worthy of such an aesthetic spectacle. "It produced a great deal of vaporous sentimentality,"

James wrote of the *ancien régime,* "but it sometimes gave a very delicate point to the feelings."[50]

The lure of material glamour—and the thrill of watching a doomed spectacle—provided James with an aesthetic argument which he confused with political ideology and hardened into an aesthetic dogma. In 1875 he succumbed to rhetoric in an essay on one of the minor figures at the French court:

> A part of our kindness for the eighteenth century rests on the fact that it paid so completely the price of both corruptions and enthusiasms. As we move to and fro in it we see something that our companions do not see—we see the sequel, the consummation, the last act of the drama. The French Revolution rounds off the spectacle and renders it a picturesque service which has also something besides picturesqueness. It casts backward a sort of supernatural light, in the midst of which, at times, we seem to see a stage full of actors performing fantastic antics for our entertainment. But retroactively, too, it seems to exonerate the generations that preceded it, to make them irresponsible and give them the right to say that, since the penalty was to be exorbitant, a little pleasure more or less would not signify. There is nothing in all history which, to borrow a term from the painters, "composes" better than the opposition, from 1600 to 1800, of the audacity of the game and the certainty of the reckoning. We all know the idiom which speaks of such reckonings as "paying the piper." The piper here is the People. We see the great body of society executing its many-figured dance on its vast polished parquet; and in a dusky corner, behind the door, we see the lean, gaunt, ragged Orpheus filling his hollow reed with tunes in which every breath is an agony.[51]

The passage, with its concern more for color than accuracy, for effect rather than point, is typical of the writing (and attitudinizing) that fills much of *The Princess Casamassima.* It is curious that, on the heels of a novel in which an admirer of Carlyle is treated ironically, James should have succumbed to the Carlylean habit, much deplored by the elder James, of using rhetoric for its own sake.

The tendency to put half-formed views to rhetorical use has a crippling effect on the style of *The Princess Casamassima,* where romantically inflated prose does not combine effectively with naturalistic details. The novel begins in a brilliant effort to graft the deterministic theories of Zola onto the style of Dickens; the treatment of the lower-class world of Lomax Square and the description of the visit to Newgate Prison demonstrate mingled human sympathy and ironic distance, not found often enough elsewhere. Hyacinth Robinson at ten years old, the illegitimate son of a French milliner and (probably) the English lord she has murdered, is well characterized; like David Copperfield, however, he becomes increasingly bothersome the more he ages into a pallid replica of his creator. The first sections of the novel, however, have an objective descriptive force and a melodramatic usefulness. Newgate Prison is described in the hybrid manner of Dickensian detail and Jamesian theme which worked so well together in *The Bostonians*. Miss Pynsent's visit to Newgate, to see Hyacinth's dying mother, conveys a vividly claustrophobic feeling: "She never had felt so immured, so made sure of; there were walls within walls and galleries on top of galleries; even the daylight lost its colour, and you couldn't imagine what o'clock it was" (p. 35).

The first book of *The Princess* is arguably too long and overly detailed in light of what follows it. Nevertheless, it contains an admirable objectivity never recaptured. James, in the manner of a French naturalist, took notes for the prison scene on a visit to Millbank Prison. The resultant rhetoric is at once appropriate and effective. Elsewhere in the novel he gave way to descriptive passages that seem merely rhetorical in the sense of being calculated and artificial. A character's propensity to rhetorize may be used effectively as a means of showing his inability to deal with reality so long as the novelist knows that his character is indulging in rhetoric (Meredith's Sir Willoughby Patterne is an outstanding example). James was not always as perceptive in this respect as he was in *The Bostonians*. The hero of *The Princess* is weighted down by naturalist theories of determinism and also by a cargo of illusions, some of which are James's own. When Hyacinth discovers the irregularity of his birth, he tries to reconcile the republicanism inherited from his mother's plebeian stock with the attitudes inherited from his aristocratic father. His "article of faith" is in his inherited sensibility: "the reflection that he was a bastard involved in a remarkable manner the reflection that he was a gentleman" (p. 128). (Richmond Roy's similar reflection provides a good deal of the comedy of Meredith's *Harry Richmond*.) In trying to create a hero with dual instincts, James fashioned a character with a tendency toward opposing rhetorics: "Decidedly, he cried to himself at times, he was with the people and every possible vengeance of the people, as against such shameless egoism as that [being ignored by his father's relatives]; but all the same he was happy to feel that he had blood in his veins which would account for the finest sensibilities" (p. 130).

In his articles for the *Nation* and various magazines in the late 1870's, James got into the habit of describing the London poor in phrases like "the hard prose of misery," and of finding "a high pictorial value" in the slum dwellers.[52] Likewise, Hyacinth's senses vibrate to "the deep perpetual groan of London misery" in a manner altogether too self-conscious and aesthetic. It is not misery but the spectacle of misery that he observes, in a passage close in style to the opening of Gissing's *Workers in the Dawn*:

> Hyacinth had roamed through the great city since he was an urchin, but his imagination had never ceased to be stirred by the preparations for Sunday that went on in the evening among the toilers and spinners, his brothers and sisters, and he lost himself in all the quickened crowding and pushing and staring at lighted windows and chaffering at the stalls of fishmongers and hucksters . . . He liked the reflection of the lamps on the wet pavements, the feeling and smell of the carboniferous London damp; the way the winter fog blurred and suffused the whole place, made it seem bigger and more crowded, produced halos and dim radiations, trickles and evaporations, on the plates of glass [pp. 60–61].

Immediately before Hyacinth succumbs to theatrical heroics, and pledges himself to serve the mysterious anarchist leader Hoffendahl, he gives way to a burst of inflated attitudinizing:

> The puddles glittered roundabout, and the silent vista of the street, bordered with low black houses, stretched away, in the wintry drizzle, to right and left, losing itself in the huge tragic city, where unmeasured misery lurked beneath the dirty night, ominously, monstrously, still, only howling, in its pain, in the heated human cockpit behind him. Ah, what could he do? What opportunity would rise? [p. 267].

It is conceivable that James originally planned to treat Hyacinth as a subject for irony, in the manner of Turgenev's Nezhdanov; but any such intention clashes with his appeals throughout the novel that his reflector is to be taken very seriously. What Hyacinth sees is what James saw as he prepared for the novel, and what he feels is only a slightly exaggerated form of Jamesian romanticism. In contrast to the flashy prose of misery, Hyacinth also dreams of the aristocratic heaven on earth (his half birthright): "the vision of societies in which, in splendid rooms, with smiles and soft voices, distinguished men, with women who were both proud and gentle, talked about art, literature and history" (p. 104). There is a naïveté in the visions of both low and high life, but it is impossible to be sure that James is being ironical in either view. In any case, he used a flawed point of view to reflect the already flawed historical argument in defense of the status quo: the view that the upper classes and lower classes must be left untouched so that they can resemble tableaux in the style of Watteau and Hogarth, respectively, for the sensations of a James-Hyacinth.

With some element of distance between himself and his main character, James might have effectively used Hyacinth's addiction to rhetoric to bolster one of the major themes of the novel: the paralyzing nature of one's illusions. The secondary characters are presented with considerable success because of James's refusal to succumb to their various limitations of point of view, but Hyacinth is fatally burdened by James's claims for "the sentient faculty of a youth on whom nothing was lost" (p. 125). In the preface to the New York edition of the novel, James went woefully (and with undue self-congratulations) out of his way to link Hyacinth with Shakespeare's heroes on the basis of their being "finely aware" of everything around them: "It is those moved in this latter fashion who 'get most' out of all that happens to them and who in so doing enable us, as readers of their record, as participators by a fond attention, also to get most. Their being finely aware—as Hamlet or Lear, say, are finely aware—*makes* absolutely the intensity of their adventures, gives the maximum of sense to what befalls them."[53]

By this curious reading, Hamlet and Lear become Pateresque figures, heroic on account of their consciousness, not their actions.

This view has obvious literary affinities with the Romantics' interpretation of *Hamlet* as a tragedy of the "superfluous activity of mind" (in Coleridge's phrase), as the modern tragedy of subjectivity. If one has the choice between being a Hamlet or a Don Quixote—intelligent and impotent or foolish and active—Turgenev urged that Quixote was the better political model. In *The Princess Casamassima* James opted for the figure of Hamlet, as Turgenev had done in *Virgin Soil*, but his main character is so much the victim of rhetoric, political or aesthetic, that he turns into a deluded Quixote. James's concept of heroism made it necessary that his heroes be sentient victims: "the person capable of feeling in the given case more than another of what is to be felt for it, and so serving in the highest degree to *record* it dramatically and objectively, is the only sort of person on whom we can count not to betray, to cheapen or, as we say, give away, the value and beauty of the thing."[54] In short, it may be deduced from James's preface that the finer one is the more he suffers, and the more one suffers the more he is worthy of the novel he is in.

D. H. Lawrence would have called such a protagonist a "murderee," but James's term for such a character is "aristocrat," aristocratic aloofness and aesthetic detachment being very often interchangeable in his vocabulary. For Isabel Archer the essence of the aristocratic temperament meant the ability to see and judge others from a high pedestal. In *The Portrait of a Lady* James showed the speciousness of such a desire, but elsewhere he characterized the aristocrat in terms of superior sensibility. The hero of George Eliot's *The Spanish Gypsy*, James wrote in an early review, "exhibits the highest reach, the broadest range, of the aristocratic character. This is the real tragedy. Silva is tortured and racked—even if he be finally redeemed—by his deep and exquisite sensibilities."[55] In Hyacinth Robinson, James attempted a character who would both see and feel as an aristocrat, and who would also feel the contrary pull of inherited democratic sympathies. However, instead of creating a semblance of a human being, James presented an endlessly vibrating organism, almost a parody, in many respects, of the protagonists of Pater or the literary determinists. James may have suspected as much when he referred, in the preface to the New York edition of *What Maisie Knew*, to "our portentous little Hyacinth . . . tainted to the core, as we have seen him, with the trick of mental reaction on the things about him and fairly staggering under the appropriations, as I have called them, that he owes to the critical spirit. He collapses, poor Hyacinth, like a thief at night, overcharged with treasures of reflexion and spoils of passion of which he can give, in his poverty and obscurity, no honest account."[56]

It would be a fruitless task to show where James's characterization of Hyacinth goes astray were it not for the fact that the problem with Hyacinth is also the problem with James. Hyacinth represents *in extremis* the Jamesian sensibility who lives entirely by what his senses (especially his eyes) take in and according to what his romantic imagination palpitates. Our first view of him as a child, "planted in front of the little sweet-shop," foreshadows the way he will develop: "He used to stand there for half an hour at a time, spelling out the first page of the romances in the *Family Herald* and the *London Journal,* and admiring the obligatory illustration in which the noble characters (they were always of the highest birth) were presented to the carnal eye" (p. 4). It is from reading romances in the *Family Herald* that Kate Ede, the passive heroine of Moore's *A Mummer's Wife,* receives a distorted view of life. Hyacinth's youthful illusions are a throwback to those of the nobility-loving Madame de Mauves; but as an adult he is still presented in terms of sweetshop windows. As the Princess remarks, "Fancy the strange, the bitter fate: to be constituted as you are constituted, to feel the capacity that you must feel, and yet to look at the good things of life only through the glass of the pastry-cook's window!" (pp. 316–317). In *A Small Boy and Others* James characterized his childhood feelings of detachment from "others" by speaking of his "view of them as only through the confectioner's hard glass."[57]

James informs us quite early of Hyacinth's "quick perception as well as a great credulity," but he bluntly adds that "he was altogether, in his innocent smallness, a refined and interesting figure" (p. 13). We read that "even at the age of ten Hyacinth Robinson was ironical" (p. 12); yet long after his apparent conversion to the Jamesian side of the politico-aesthetic argument, he is being described in a manner that shows his incapacity for self-irony:

The reader will doubtless smile at his mental debates and oscil-
lations, and not understand why a little bastard bookbinder
should attach importance to his conclusions. They were not important for either cause, but they were important for himself,
if only because they would rescue him from the torment of his
present life, the perpetual laceration of the rebound. There was
no peace for him between the two currents that flowed in his
nature, the blood of his passionate, plebeian mother and that of
his long-descended, supercivilised sire. They continued to toss
him from one side to the other; they arrayed him in intolerable
defiances and revenges against himself. He had a high ambition:
he wanted neither more nor less than to get hold of the truth
and wear it in his heart [p. 471].

The Perils of Hyacinth seem never to end, and James subjects him
to continual stresses.

It is irritating, thus, to be told of Hyacinth's objectivity, of his
unlimited perspective, "of the rather helpless sense that, whatever
he saw, he saw (and this was always the case), so many other
things beside. He saw the immeasurable misery of the people, and
yet he saw all that had been, as it were, rescued and redeemed
from it; the treasures, the felicities, the splendours, the successes,
of the world" (p. 434). The treasures, however, when specified,
range from fine bindings to exquisite bibelots; the felicities include
eating a marquise at Tortoni's; the spendors are the Bulwer and
Feuillet novels come to life; and success is gauged only in terms
of materials. "The glossy butler at Medley had had a hundred more
of the signs of success in life" than the shabby but good-natured
Mr. Vetch, as Hyacinth notices at one point (p. 340). Sensuous
apperception is dearly bought at the price of human sympathy.

It is very hard to believe that Hyacinth's boasted sense of complexity of perspective is not another of his many illusions. The
novel might be subtitled "Hyacinth the Epicurean," or "The Sensuous Education of Hyacinth Robinson," or, perhaps, "*L'Éduca-
tion très sentimentale.*" The more the hero "knows," however,
the less he seems to learn. Very early in the book, when the
child is ten and Miss Pynsent is wondering whether or not to take
him to the deathbed of his mother in prison, Mr. Vetch offers the
following advice: "don't stuff him with any more illusions than
are necessary to keep him alive; he will be sure to pick up enough

on the way. On the contrary, give him a good stiff dose of the truth at the start" (p. 27). The advice is sound, even if Mr. Vetch is misguided enough at the time to think that the discovery of the stigma of his birth will turn Hyacinth into a radical like himself (just as Olive Chancellor, for similar reasons, thinks that Verena's poverty will result in reformist fervor). Instead of a good stiff dose of the truth, Hyacinth gets a double dose of illusions: he grows up with a highly colored view of himself as half radical, half aristocrat, altogether an actor treading the boards of fate. Hyacinth swathes himself in the language of a modern Hamlet: "he wished to go through life in his own character; but he checked himself, with the reflection that this was exactly what, apparently, he was destined not to do. His own character? He was to cover that up as carefully as possible; he was to go through life in a mask, in a borrowed mantle; he was to be, every day and every hour, an actor" (p. 64). Hyacinth enters the novel in a melodramatic, neo-Dickensian situation, and he leaves it with an act of purest melodrama.

If Hyacinth learns to spell by means of the romances of high life in the *Family Herald*, he develops the habit of looking at life through the rose-colored glasses of certain books. "Reading was his happiness," James says, trying to assign some reason for Hyacinth's fabulous inbred powers of intellection, "and the absence of any direct contact with a library his principal source of discontent" (p. 74; this was changed to "the hard shock of the real" in the New York revision). Both he and the people he encounters characteristically take on a literary air. Upon meeting the Princess, he feels himself in the situation of a hero in a French novel; when he knows her better, she seems the "incarnation of the heroine of M. Feuillet's novel, in which he had instantly become immersed" (p. 284). Captain Sholto seems to have stepped out of Bulwer's novels and the low-life characters obligingly step out of Dickens for Hyacinth's delectation. In his memory, the time spent at the Princess's residence at Medley becomes transmuted into "a kind of fable, the echo of a song; he could read it over like a story, gaze at it as he would have gazed at some exquisite picture" (p. 366). Whether he is picture painting the "toilers and spinners" or idealizing the aristocracy—"fancying himself stretched in the shadow of an ancestral beech, reading the last number of the *Review des Deux Mondes*" (p. 120)—Hyacinth is too literary for his own good.

It is scarcely surprising that Hyacinth should be as much attached to the theater as James himself; it "was full of sweet deception for him. His imagination projected itself lovingly across the footlights, gilded and coloured the shabby canvas and battered accessories, and lost itself so effectually in the fictive world that the end of the piece, however long, or however short, brought with it a kind of alarm, like a stoppage of his personal life. It was impossible to be more friendly to the dramatic illusion" (p. 140).

Dramatic or novelistic illusion colors his way of life; it is characteristic of his credulity in maturity that he should see his political role in a literary guise: "it could not fail to be agreeable to him to perceive that ["like some famous novel," James inserted here in the revised text] he was thrilling" (p. 214). Hyacinth is prepared for his political vows to Hoffendahl and to the anarchist cause by first imagining "the particular part he was to play" and determining "to play it with brilliancy, to offer an example—an example, even, that might survive him—of pure youthful, almost juvenile, consecration" (pp. 256–257). His volunteering for the heroic role is characteristically a passive act ("he found he had sprung up"), a yielding to rhetorical impulse. The only political act he can undertake is to kill himself, half aristocrat that he is. It is of course ironic that he should seem useful to the anarchist leader precisely because he can pass as a gentleman.

Hyacinth treats life as a spectacle for the artist, specifically the Jamesian artist, and the political or philosophical message of the book is relevant only in terms of so personal a point of view. Whereas James can transform his impressions into works of art, Hyacinth is necessarily unable to do the same (although as a bookbinder he utilizes his artistic impulse for a while). For Hyacinth, the choice in life is not so much between the lower and upper classes as between the two rhetorics he is prone to indulge in, between patronizing the "toilers and spinners" or idealizing the world of brilliant conversation and Parisian cafés. If the Jamesian artist must needs be a passive collector of impressions, Hyacinth quivers with a sensibility that parodies the Pateresque, while lacking the intelligence of one of Pater's heroes. "For this unfortunate but remarkably organised youth," James declares, "every displeasure or gratification of the visual sense coloured his whole mind, and though he lived in Pentonville and worked in Soho, though he was poor and obscure and cramped and full of unattainable desires, it may be said of him that what was most important in life for him was simply his impressions [James added "and reflections" to the revision]. They came from everything he touched, they kept him thrilling and throbbing during a considerable part of his waking consciousness, and they constituted, as yet, the principal events and stages of his career" [p. 117]. Paris becomes for him, thereby, the welcome source of "a thousand palpitations," a "Great Good Place" for the sensations: "it came over him that the most brilliant city in the world was also the most blood-stained; but the great sense that he understood and sympathised was preponderant, and his comprehension gave him wings—appeared to transport him to still wider fields of knowledge, still higher sensations" (pp. 362–363).

The lack of distance between James and his protagonist has the damaging effect of making the author's own view of art appear rarefied if not simple-minded. James feared that historical changes would mean the elimination of the society he depended on as material for his novels, and that revolutions would endanger the practice of the artist to gather beautiful impressions. A revolution, he intimates, will necessarily mean the destruction of the fabric of existent beauty, as well as the elimination of the "high pictorial value" of the poor. Once in power, Hoffendahl "would cut up the ceilings of the Veronese into strips," Hyacinth writes from Venice, "so that every one might have a little piece of anything and I have a great horror of that kind of invidious jealousy which is at the bottom of the idea of a redistribution" (p. 380). In *Twilight of the Idols*, Nietzsche also insists that the guiding motive of socialists (and Christians) is revenge, "a means for besmirching *this* world."[58] But where Nietzsche saw the danger to civilization, Hyacinth (with James) sees only a potential loss for himself. James might have considered Gissing's fear that the real danger to works of art may result from their being ignored by future, materialistic generations.

One does not expect political acumen of a novelist, but one may legitimately demand a tenable picture of civilized values from one ostensibly defending them. Art seems to matter only for the sake of provoking exquisite thrills in the bosom of Hyacinth Robinson; history becomes a museum and must remain so. The poor will always be with us, but thank goodness they exhibit such magnificent facial types! Hyacinth's letter to the Princess from Venice takes on considerably less force in the immediate context of the novel. What he has learned is the beauty of denial and the facile conclusion "that want and toil and suffering are the constant lot of the immense majority of the human race."

> I have found them everywhere, but I haven't minded them. Excuse the cynical confession. What has struck me is the great achievements of which man has been capable in spite of them— the splendid accumulations of the happier few, to which, doubtless, the miserable many have also in their degree contributed . . . The monuments and treasures of art, the great palaces and properties, the conquests of learning and taste, the general fabric of civilisation as we know it, based, if you will, upon all the despotisms, the cruelties, the exclusions, the monopolies and the rapacities of the past, but thanks to which, all the same, the world is less impracticable and life more tolerable —our friend Hoffendahl seems to me to hold them too cheap and to wish to substitute for them something in which I can't somehow believe as I do in things with which the aspirations and the tears of generations have been mixed [p. 380].

Art, for Hyacinth, becomes a matter of collection rather than production; and the defense of art is uneasily based more on rhetoric than on reasoning.

Hyacinth's discovery of the lesson of art prompts him to make a series of observations which seem no less limited than his earlier views but which are meant to ring with undeniable truth:

> Everywhere, everywhere, he saw the ulcer of envy—the passion of a party which hung together for the purpose of despoiling another to its advantage [p. 390].

> "I think there can't be too many pictures and statues and works of art," Hyacinth broke out. "The more the better, whether people are hungry or not. In the way of ameliorating influences, are not those the most definite?" [p. 399].

In spite of the example Eustache Poupin gave him of the reconcilement of disparities, he was afraid the democracy wouldn't
care for perfect bindings or for the finest sort of conversation.
The Princess gave up these things in proportion as she advanced
in the direction she had so audaciously chosen; and if the Princess could give them up it would take very transcendent natures
to stick to them [p. 471].

"Culture, no less than politics, can harden into ideology," as
Irving Howe remarks.[59] In the place of political rhetoric Hyacinth
learns to substitute an aesthetic rhetoric, disarming in its subjectivity. Hyacinth's early political vocabulary is aptly enough described by the despicable but shrewd Paul Muniment as "silly bits
of catchwords" (p. 110), but it is essential to the fabric of his
political reversal that Hyacinth should end up sagely conversing
on "the danger of too much coddling legislation on behalf of the
working classes" (p. 540).

If James is short on ideas and Hyacinth overlong on rhetoric,
the novel still carries sufficient force on account of the subsidiary
characters drawn about the hero. If James was too close to Hyacinth personally to be aware of his limitations as a character, he is
distant enough from the others to present them and their milieu
in an objective and convincing light. The secondary characters are
drawn from either the upper or lower classes—Disraeli's "two
nations"—between which James saw an impassable gulf. "The
upper classes are too refined, and the lower classes are too miser-
able," James had written in 1877, although he deemed the continued "aristocratic constitution of society" necessary for the sake
of aesthetic observers.[60] Fortunately, as he pointed out in his 1888
essay on London, the lower classes too can derive pleasure by
watching their superiors. This is restated by Rosy Muniment: " 'If
everyone was equal,' she asked, 'where would be the gratification
I feel in getting a visit from a grandee?' " (p. 400). With her mixture of egoistic calculation and grotesquerie, she is a fascinating
figure. Hyacinth first sees her as a victim of society, but later
considers her a witch. A cripple who maneuvers others, she seems
not so much a borrowing from Dickens (as has been suggested)
as a strangely cruel reflection on James's part of his invalid sister.
More genuinely helpless and more Dickensian is Miss Pynsent,

Hyacinth's adoptive mother, who stuffs the boy with gentlemanly illusions and encourages him to take a patronizing stance in life. As James notes at one point, Hyacinth always found "an odd, perverse, unholy satisfaction" in the look in her face that "seemed to say that she prostrated herself, that she did penance in the dust, that she was his to trample upon, to spit upon" (p. 56). Thus encouraged, he patronizes the "people," especially, and inexcusably, the vital and vulgar Millicent Henning.

For Hyacinth, Millicent is "magnificently plebeian," and sums up the "sociable, humorous, ignorant chatter of the masses, their capacity for offensive and defensive passion, their instinctive perception of their strength on the day they should really exercise it" (p. 120), and so on. When he finally gets around to appreciating her qualities as a woman, it is to meet with (convenient) betrayal; despite the tendency of the hero to see her for most of the novel as a type, James manages to convey through her a sense of healthy vigor lacking in the other characters. She is the "muse of Cockneyism," a respectable Nana. Another figure patronized by Hyacinth is the shabby fiddler Mr. Vetch, who introduces him to the theater and to the socialistic circle of the Poupins, French radical émigrés. Vetch outlives what the author calls the "democratic glow," however, and settles into the easy stoicism which all too often passes for wisdom in James. In general, the lower-class radical types, like Schinkel or Paul Muniment, are presented with clarity and force. Mysteriously above them, although never seen in the novel, is the anarchist leader Hoffendahl, described always in religious terms, the object of a dangerous cult.

Representing the upper classes are the Prince and Princess Casamassima, Madame Grandoni, Lady Aurora, and Captain Sholto. Sholto is the enigmatic figure who introduces Hyacinth to the Princess for her collection of democrats, as he calls it. He also introduces him to what James in *The Ambassadors*, with great seriousness, calls the "empire of 'things.' "[61] Sholto's apartment, "from the low-voiced, inexpressive valet who, after he had poured brandy into tall tumblers, gave dignity to the popping of soda-water corks, to the quaint little silver receptacle in which he was invited to deposit the ashes of his cigar, was such a revelation for our appreciative hero that he felt himself hushed and made sad, so poignant was the thought that it took thousands of things which he, then, should never possess nor know to make an accomplished man" (p. 196; changed to "a civilized being" in the revision). Somehow the Veronese and the silver ash tray become confused together as part of the empire of things for James. Lady Aurora is the anomaly among the radicals in the book; in her quiet, eccentric way she does good work among the poor. Madame Grandoni is the upper-class counterpart to Mr. Vetch: a stoical, trustworthy old woman who warns Hyacinth not to part with his individuality. "Do not give up *yourself*," she urges, and adds: "I like people to bear their troubles as one has done one's self" (p. 211). She and Vetch are the resigned good angels of the Princess and Hyacinth, respectively, and she professes to derive "entertainment" by watching her friend behave in a difficult situation. It is another of the accidental ironies in the book that Hyacinth alone has the aesthetic good taste to applaud "a certain quality of breeding" (p. 512) in so otherwise negative a figure as Prince Casamassima, the stolid, suspicious, ignorant nobleman whom Christina Light was forced to marry in *Roderick Hudson*. But if Hyacinth alone can sufficiently appreciate the Prince, most readers of the novel have no trouble esteeming James's portrait of the Princess.

With very few exceptions, James's male victims are not among his better characters, but his *femmes fatales* are generally successful (in this respect, James is similar to Hardy). The Princess Casamassima may be said to play the flame to Hyacinth's moth, and James redeemed much of the novel by trying to come to terms with this elusive woman who had refused to be confined to *Roderick Hudson*. Contradictoriness of impulse and confusion of background combine to make Hyacinth merely weak, but they make of Christina a character vitally feminine. She considers, as Madame Grandoni relates, "that in the darkest hour of her life she sold herself for a title and a fortune." Consequently, "she regards her doing so as such a horrible piece of frivolity that she can never, for the rest of her days, be serious enough to make up for it." She is "modern," as her estranged husband is reminded, and she is bluntly honest ("There are things it is better to conceal," he replies [p. 229]).

Frustrated personally, she turns to revolutionary politics. Christina is a considerably more sympathetic character than Olive

Chancellor, whom she resembles in the desire to take up a cause and a protégé, as well as in her endeavor to escape from personal problems in the process. Contemporary critics found her politically and sexually immoral (James keeps the Christina-Paul relationship obscure by having it viewed through the defective vision of the Prince), but modern readers can admire James's skill in showing the intellectual aspirations and frustrations, as well as the willful attempts at depersonalization of the new—late Victorian—woman. If Hyacinth is a less interesting Jude, Christina is a more dynamic Sue Bridehead. In the poignant and ironic last scene in the novel between her and Hyacinth—she thinking herself in the thick of the political battle, while regarding him as "out of it"—she becomes vividly impersonal before his eyes. If he had originally thought of her as a character in a Feuillet novel, he now responds to her personal charm, but she refuses his homage, turning away from him (as James added in the revised version, one of the few really effective changes) "as with a beat of great white wings that raised her straight out of the bad air of the personal."[62] "It expressed [to return to the 1886 text] an indifference to what it might interest him to think about her to-day, and even a contempt for it, which brought tears to his eyes" (p. 577).

The most frighteningly depersonalized figure in the novel, and one of James's finest characterizations, is Paul Muniment. "You ought to remember that, in the line you have chosen," he tells the Princess, "our affections, our natural ties, our timidities, our shrinkings . . . All those things are as nothing, and must never weigh a feather beside our service" (p. 498). As with Gilbert Osmond, James pushes his character to the brink of melodrama without sacrificing credibility. Muniment is a mixture of selfishness, self-sufficiency, and rigid personal detachment. Like Madame Merle, he regards people only in their capacity to be used. Burke memorably warned of the dehumanization of the political theoretician: "They have perverted in themselves, and in those that attend to them, all the well-placed sympathies of the human breast," he cautioned in the *Reflections on the Revolution in France,* and we have seen all too often how radicals and reactionaries alike have been willing to sacrifice individuals to their theories (in James's opposition of art to politics, the individual counts for everything —the Jamesian individual, that is). Muniment's unlikeness to

Hyacinth accounts for part of his sinister appeal: "He was tremendously reasonable, which was largely why Hyacinth admired him, having a desire to be so himself but finding it terribly difficult":

> Muniment's absence of passion, his fresh-coloured coolness, his easy, exact knowledge, the way he kept himself clean (except for the chemical stains on his hands), in circumstances of foul contact, constituted a group of qualities that had always appeared to Hyacinth singularly enviable. Most enviable of all was the force that enabled him to sink personal sentiment where a great public good was to be attempted and yet keep up the form of caring for that minor interest [pp. 374–375].

In perhaps the most chilling passage in the book, Paul and his sister congratulate each other upon their superior ability in using others ("I don't care what happens," she purrs, "for I know I shall be looked after" [p. 488]). "He would make society bankrupt, but he would be paid," James says when he introduces him into the novel (p. 84). Almost alone among the main characters in The Princess, Paul has no illusions of any sort. He and not Hyacinth has the faculty of irony: he "seemed capable of turning revolutionists themselves into ridicule, even for the entertainment of the revolutionised" (p. 97). Deluded as usual, Hyacinth decides that "This man he could entreat, pray to, go on his knees to, without a sense of humiliation" (p. 110). In the revision, James stresses Paul's conscious villainy in coercing Hyacinth to become Hoffendahl's needed victim. As he is led away, Paul passes "his arm round him, as if by way of a tacit expression of indebtedness" (p. 271). In the New York edition, this was changed to the following: Paul passed "a strong arm round him, holding him all the way as if for a tacit sign of indebtedness. This gave Hyacinth pleasure till he began to wonder if it mightn't represent also the instinct to make sure of him as against possible weak afterthoughts."[63] It is Hyacinth's unconscious willingness to let himself be destroyed that makes him a natural cat's-paw, a Lawrentian murderee, but hardly a Hamlet.

As a young man, James had once professed "doubt whether the central object of a novel may successfully be a passionless creature," and he had attacked Epictetus' stoicism on the grounds that it denied to man the possibility of freedom of action: "The great defect of the system, is that it discourages all responsibility to anything but one's own soul."[64] By the time of *The Princess* James had repudiated his—and the Victorian Age's—earnest optimism. "Let your soul live—it's the only life that isn't, on the whole, a sell," he would later write to a friend.[65] There are no political solutions and no active heroes. In this respect James follows the example of Dickens, who stressed human disjunction and created Arthur Clennam in *Little Dorrit*, perhaps the first notably passive hero in English fiction. James's easy helplessness is in contrast to Dickens' anguished resignation in *Hard Times*. In the figure of Mr. Vetch he echoes Stephen Blackpool in Dickens' novel: there is no way to reform society that will not "make a bigger mess than the actual muddle of human affairs, which, by the time one had reached sixty-five, had mostly ceased to exasperate . . . The idea of great changes . . . took its place among the dreams of his youth; for what was any possible change in the relations of men and women but a new combination of the same elements" (pp. 348–349). However ineffectual, and even uninteresting, Hyacinth often becomes in James's characterization, he is an important prefiguration of the modern image of man as helpless before limiting political or psychologically deterministic factors. Where others would despair, however, James maintained a reassuringly fixed belief in the sacredness of art and the private life.

Schopenhauer, early in the century, had predicted the trend in the 1880's and 1890's of men seeking relief from the horrors of modern life by enjoying or creating works of art:

> The pleasure we receive from all beauty, the consolation which art affords, the enthusiasm of the artist, which enables him to forget the cares of life,—the latter an advantage of the man of genius over other men, which alone repays him for the suffering that increases in proportion to the clearness of consciousness, and for the desert loneliness among men of a different race, —all this rests on the fact that the in-itself of life, the will, existence itself is . . . a constant sorrow, partly miserable, partly terrible; while, on the contrary, as idea alone, purely contemplated, or copied by art, free from pain, it presents to us a drama full of significance. This purely knowable side of the world, and the copy of it in any art, is the element of the artist.[66]

If James may in any way be called a Schopenhauerian novelist (as has been suggested),[67] it is only by reason of a passage like that. But James was scarcely a doctrinaire pessimist. Speaking of Gissing, the most pessimistic of his contemporaries, James noted that it is in the artist's power to "offer us another world, another consciousness, an experience that, as effective as the dentist's ether, muffles the ache of the actual and, by helping us to an interval, tides us over and makes us face, in the return to the inevitable, a combination that may at least have changed."[68] For James the materials that the artist uses are considerably less important than the artist's manner of handling them. It hardly matters whether the artist's subject is "lamentable," he suggests in an essay on Daudet: "The success of a work of art, to my mind, may be measured by the degree to which it produces a certain illusion; that illusion makes it appear to us for the time that we have lived another life—that we have had a miraculous enlargement of experience."[69] Art is an illusion which lasts, while history is a reality which passes—such is the underlying idea behind *The Princess Casamassima* and *The Tragic Muse.*

Even with flaws in the argument and central character, *The Princess Casamassima* is one of the few works of lasting merit which used the unrest of the 1880's as its starting-off point. It may be that James's insensitivity to the realities of economic distress in the period curiously worked in his favor. Choosing as artistic material the items from *The Times* that the nation was trying not to come to terms with, James provided an evocative enough glimpse of discontented, generally confused, and inarticulate workers; he played on the public fear of the various secret societies. In the New York preface, he contended "that the value I wished most to render and the effect I wished most to produce were precisely those of our not knowing, of society's not knowing, but only guessing and suspecting and trying to ignore, what 'goes on' irreconcileably, subversively, beneath the vast smug surface."[70] The appeal to the reader of 1886 was unsuccessful, one suspects, partly because of the very prominence of the dangers that the public did not want to face, but, in the light of modern history, many readers have been understandably swept aside by "the degree of realism" (as Yvor Winters puts it) extracted from a plot, "essentially, so inane."[71] With a splash of rhetoric, Hyacinth hints to the Princess of the existence of "an immense underworld, peopled with a thousand forms of revolutionary passion and devotion . . . In silence, in darkness, but under the feet of each one of us, the revolution lives and works. It is a wonderful, immeasurable trap, on the lid of which society performs its antics" (p. 308). One has come to look with less amusement at the "conspiracy" theory of history, but James is echoing his passage on the *ancien régime*, quoted earlier.

After the publication of *The Princess*, James addressed to Charles Eliot Norton a rhetorical warning to the English aristocracy:

> The condition of that body seems to me to be in many ways very much the same rotten and *collapsible* one as that of the French aristocracy before the revolution—minus cleverness and conversation; or perhaps it's more like the heavy, congested and depraved Roman world upon which the barbarians came down. In England the Huns and Vandals will have to come *up*—from the black depths of the (in the people) enormous misery, though I don't think the Attila is quite yet found—in the person of Mr. Hyndman.

This is the very warning that Burckhardt had made to his students at Basel (and that Ortega y Gasset was to make in *The Revolt of the Masses*). Several months earlier, James had written to William, "Every one here is growing poorer—from causes which, I fear, will continue."[72] In the face of economic distresses thirty years earlier, Dickens had cautioned in *Hard Times* that if the poor would always be with us, it was a good idea to cultivate in them "the utmost graces of the fancies and affections, to adorn their lives so much in need of ornament." Considerably less liberal than Dickens, James emphasized the necessity for the cultivation of aesthetic sensations—although scarcely for everyone. Only Hyacinth can appreciate the most important lesson of art: that it lasts. The Princess's rented estate, Medley, offers a striking contrast to the world of Lomax Place:

> The spectacle of long duration unassociated with some sordid infirmity or poverty was new to [Hyacinth]; he had lived with people among whom old age meant, for the most part, a grudged

and degraded survival. In the majestic preservation of Medley there was a serenity of success, an accumulation of dignity and honour [p. 278].

In *The Princess Casamassima*, James took another—crucial—step in the direction of modern fictional attitudes. Despite the use of recent historical materials, his theme became the need for escape from history; history is presented as a nightmare from which his heroes must awake if they are to survive. As he wrote the novel, his attempt at chronicling the historical changes of the period turned gradually into a desire to affirm artistic permanence, just as his wish to portray a modern Hamlet became the need to construct a vicarious autobiography. In the last and most ambitious of his long novels of the 1880's, *The Tragic Muse* (conceived about the same time as its two predecessors), James tried to piece together the conscious and unconscious aims of his earlier novels of the decade. In writing what he assumed would be his last novel for some time, he produced the most curious of his neo-Victorian hybrids of the period, at once his most personal and most novelistically conventional book.

Apologia pro vita sua: The Tragic Muse

> *Each of the masterpieces is a purification of the world, but their common message is that of their existence, and the victory of each individual artist over his servitude, spreading like ripples on the sea of time, implements art's eternal victory over the human situation. All art is a revolt against man's fate.*
> (*André Malraux,* The Voices of Silence)

At the end of the 1880's, while Meredith, in the most stylistically demanding of his novels, was desperately arguing for the last time the need for self-discipline if Victorian society was to survive, James produced the most stylistically conventional of his novels, which is also his first modern novel in its celebration of artistic self-assertion. *One of Our Conquerors* reveals the full extent of Meredith's Victorianism; afterward he regressed in style and theme. But *The Tragic Muse*, despite some resemblance to one of Trollope's political novels, "inaugurated the new era" (as a contemporary reflected in 1903)[73] of the later Jamesian manner in fiction. A recent critic has called it James's "last Victorian novel, as we generally use the term,"[74] but that is to confuse the style of the book with its theme. Meredith's novels are considerably more advanced than James's technically, but remain Victorian because of the author's viewpoint. For all his absorption in the details and styles of Victorian (and continental) fiction, James remained uniquely himself. In a novel devoted to the conflict between "art" and the "world," James not only chose art, he chose art on his own terms. *One of Our Conquerors* and *The Tragic Muse* are both ambitious, testimonial novels, and both testify to the fact that the writing of Victorian novels was no longer possible. Where Meredith wrote for the sake of a world which, by 1891, had largely disappeared, James addressed himself to the glorification of himself as an artist and a liberated consciousness.

The 1880's marks the period of James's most ambitious work in fiction, the time he most fully immersed himself in the mainstream of English fiction while also experimenting with the form and theory of the novel most suitable to his own needs. In an age of intense change in the subject matter and style—and public—of the novel, he tried to align himself with the tried methods of Dickens and George Eliot and Turgenev, as well as with the newer views of Zola and Pater. Moreover, in a bid to attain popularity, as well as to combat the criticisms which followed him after the publication of Howells' tributary essay, James resorted to a number of devices: he applied conventional fictional practices, such as the use of fixed characters and a happy (that is, wedded) ending in *The Bostonians*; he exploited the topicality of social unrest in *The Princess Casamassima*; and he even returned in *The Reverberator* and "A London Life," to the "international subject" which had provided him with a measure of popularity in the 1870's. In every case, however, he received generally imperceptive critical responses, continued attacks on moral and chauvinistic grounds, and fairly modest sales—miniscule in comparison with the popular successes of Hall Caine or Mrs. Humphry Ward in the same period. Although none of the three long novels which followed *The Portrait of a Lady* had bad sales, as was Gissing's experience at the same time, and all three went through at least two editions, it is significant that James's English publisher reduced the order for the first one-volume edition of each work from five thousand copies in the case of *The Bostonians* to two thousand copies in the case of *The Tragic Muse*.[75]

In October 1888, three months before *The Tragic Muse* made its first serial appearance, Howells reviewed a group of recent James stories and commented incredulously that "It is in a way discreditable to our time that a writer of such quality should ever have grudging welcome; the fact impeaches not only our intelligence, but our sense of the artistic. It will certainly amaze a future day that such things as his could be done in ours and meet only a feeble and conditional acceptance from the 'best' criticism, with something little short of ribald insult from the common cry of literary paragraphers."[76] James's reaction to the gradual erosion of his reputation varied from an acid repudiation of the public taste to Miltonic outbursts to Howells of having "entered upon evil days." "It sounds portentous," he wrote to Howells in January 1888, "but it only means that I am still staggering a good deal under the mysterious and (to me) inexplicable injury wrought —apparently—upon my situation by my last two novels, the *Bostonians* and the *Princess*, from which I expected so much and derived so little. They have reduced the desire, and the demand, for my productions to zero—as I judge from the fact that though I have for a good while past been writing a number of good short things, I remain irremediably unpublished. Editors keep them back, for months and years, as if they were ashamed of them, and I am condemned apparently to eternal silence."[77] In one of the most personal of his artist fables, "The Next Time" (1895), James would wryly comment on the neglect of Ray Limbert despite his desperate attempts to produce a popular success:

> Several persons admired his books—nothing was less contestable; but they appeared to have a mortal objection to acquiring them by subscription or by purchase: they begged or borrowed or stole, they delegated one of the party perhaps to commit the

volumes to memory and repeat them, like the bards of old, to listening multitudes. Some ingenious theory was required at any rate to account for the inexorable limits of his circulation.[78]

Although the work of his friend and devotee Mrs. Ward, *Robert Elsmere*, had exceptionally good sales in the year of its publication (1888), James found himself venerated by a small cult but completely ignored by the public at large.

Despite his depression, James still found comfort in what as a young man, in his first published essay (1864), he had described as the novelist's "salvation": "work."[79] James's feeling that art consists of concrete products rather than personal impressions or witty conversation differentiates him from the circle of aesthetes of the period. Even the most excessively Pateresque of his heroes, Hyacinth Robinson, has dreams of publication. Characteristically, James spoke of the artist's aligning "feminine observation" with "masculine conclusion," aesthetic passivity with artistic creation. For James, the act of literary creation was a "sacred cause" with real standards. In an age without sufficient taste, as he says of Hyacinth, "he, at least, among the disinherited, would keep up the standard" (p. 124). The failure of the public to respond would not ruffle his confidence, in the long run. If his books did not sell or his plays did not run, he would assume that the failure lay in the mediocrity of public taste.

In 1887 he began what he thought would be his last novel, at least for some time, and the act of artistic production became his major theme. "Here I sit," James confided to his notebook in March 1888, "impatient to work":

> only wanting to concentrate myself, to keep at it: full of ideas, full of ambition, full of capacity—as I believe. Sometimes the discouragements, however, seem greater than anything else—the delays, the interruptions, the *éparpillement*, etc. But courage, courage, and forward, forward. If one must generalize, that is the only generalization. There is an immensity to be done, and without vain presumption—I shall at the worst do a part of it. But all one's manhood must be at one's side.[80]

Despite setbacks from public and critics alike, James had embarked upon his longest and most complex novel to date with continued faith in his powers and purpose. In July he confided to Robert Louis

Stevenson his intention "to leave a multitude of pictures of my time, . . . having a certain value as observation and testimony." By October James was calling attention to his chosen form of "saturation" with life in a famous letter to William in which he also boasted of his desire "to write in such a way that it would be impossible to an outsider to say whether I am at a given moment an American writing about England or an Englishman writing about America (dealing as I do with both countries,) and so far from being ashamed of such an ambiguity I should be exceedingly proud of it, for it would be highly civilized."[81] Everything that James had learned as a novelist was to find a place in The Tragic Muse, and he poured into it as much of life as his powers of observation and intuition permitted him.

The Tragic Muse is unquestionably James's most venturesome novel—at once more expansive and concrete, panoramic and intimate, than anything he had yet attempted or was ever to consider duplicating. Everything that he felt he knew about art and politics, society and the theater, Paris and London and the English countryside, public and private life converged into what he had originally planned as a novel half the size of The Princess. Instead of having one hero torn between political and artistic ideals, he presented two in that position. For the first time he resisted the temptation to include an American (aside from the unseen tenant of the Dormer country estate) in a novel of his. Instead of having a plot and a group of characters subordinate to a central figure, he depicted a social world to which most of his characters relate. In the New York preface to the novel, he compared his design to that of one of his favorite painters, Tintoretto, in the San Rocco Crucifixion; he also attempted to combine variety of detail with strictness of composition. This would imply an embarrassment of riches, but The Tragic Muse is not a masterpiece. It is perhaps symptomatic of James's limitations that all the resources which he could put to use could not save the novel from going to pieces, despite some excellent characterization, considerable wit, and an adequate plot. Too much of the book seems a fictional essay on the subject of art and the artist's life. However, the book has its interest for readers of James who might also be interested in his personal views of art, and for historians of the novel who can trace in the book the emergence of the modern literary sensibility.

James professed, in the preface to the novel, to have been motivated by the desire "to 'do something about art'—art, that is, as a human complication and a social stumbling-block"—as if, somehow, most of his work had not always concealed this basic theme. The "conflict between art and 'the world,' " he continues, had struck him "as one of the half-dozen great primary motives."[82] What he does not add is that the four main characters of the novel are all exercises in self-portraiture, while the conflict is between James's own, sometimes vague, concept of "art" and his even vaguer prefiguration of the "world." In outline, the book has certain affinities with the political novels of Trollope: two somewhat helpless young members of the upper class are asked to choose between a public career and a private, independent life. In Trollope, the hero would have certainly decided upon the public career, and Peter Sherringham thereby chooses the conventional solution by settling down to a diplomatic career and an appreciative, passive wife. Precisely because his course is so obvious (there is never any question, for example, that he will give up his career to marry the actress Miriam Rooth), his part in the novel reflects the predictable quality of a Trollope protagonist, but without having any of that master's redeeming sense of humanity in compensation. James's other hero, Nick Dormer, is caught between political devotions to his dead father, his elderly mentor Mr. Carteret, and the possessive Julia Dallow,* and the aesthetic pull, on the other side, of Gabriel Nash, who explains the artist's role, and Miriam Rooth, who embodies it. With Nick there is at least some sense of choice, and, consequently, one is interested in following his development until he chooses the artist's way. Thereafter, his career is both predictable and of necessity low-key. Fortunately, among the major characters, Miriam and Nash offer vital contrasts, and the minor figures are drawn with considerable care and appeal.

Peter Sherringham is the least successful of the major characters; considering the role he is forced to play, however, he comes off better than might be expected. He is an enlightened late Victorian

---

* The elder Dormer suggests Trollope's Plantagenet Palliser, Mr. Carteret echoes the Duke of St. Bungay, and Julia Dallow's ambitions resemble Laura Kennedy's in the Phineas Finn novels. It should be noted, however, that in his generally favorable essay on Trollope written in 1883 James wrote: "His political novels are distinctly dull, and I confess I have not been able to read them" (*Partial Portraits*, p. 131).

with a passion for the theater and a devotion to his diplomatic duties. Sherringham is fatally conventional; James, accordingly, describes him with a fictional amplitude which he had earlier reserved for figures like Basil Ransom. Despite the look of "foreignness of cast" in his features, he is assuredly a representative of his time, his class, and his country.[83] Circumspect and skeptical, he cherishes the possession of at least one illusion: the theater. James sympathetically allows "that Sherringham, though the child of a skeptical age and the votary of a cynical science, was still candid enough to take the serious, the religious view of that establishment" (I, 237). He is deluded enough in the author's view, however, to think that he can combine art and public duties and that he can keep his aesthetics separate from his life. The enjoyment, as well as the practice, of art is a full-time job, according to James.

Because of his limitations, Peter's role in the novel is basically one of mechanical necessity. He is the propagandist of the theater and consequently the patron of Miriam. He encourages others to an independent artistic life, but, without any artistic talent, his own life is doomed to public service. To Miriam he speaks of the "standard" of her calling and the value of her effect. "Be beautiful—be only that," he tells her: "Be only what you can be so well—something that one may turn to for a glimpse of perfection, to lift one out of all the vulgarities of the day" (I, 377). For Peter, as for James, "the representation of life" is better than "the real thing," and the practice of the artist makes possible a form of negative capability, a loss of one's social self, at any rate. "It's an amusement like another [Peter says of the theater]: I don't pretend to call it by any exalted name; but in this vale of friction it will serve. One can lose one's self in it, and it has this recommendation (in common, I suppose, with the study of the other arts), that the further you go in it the more you find" (I, 86–87). At times, he threatens to become a walking essay on the drama, but it is necessary that he be trustworthy in this respect so that the reader will see, through his point of view, the nature of Miriam's triumph as an actress. It is his discriminating taste that also makes his praise of Nick's portraits relieve our suspicions as to whether the painter has talent or not.

To the degree that the four principles are touchstones for one another, they are also Jamesian types. Sherringham is a descendant of Rowland Mallet in his adoption of an artist-ward, of Basil Ransom in his insistence that his wife play the subordinate role to him, of Madame Merle in his determination to suppress his private feelings under a mask of social decorum. To the extent that he successfully remains conventional, it might be argued that his is a histrionic victory of sorts. When he speaks of his determination to be an ambassador (even of a shaky Central American republic), Miriam retorts: "And they call *us* mountebanks!" (II, 639). Sherringham may represent James's worldly ambitions (as Leon Edel claims),[84] but a faith in the world requires considerably more illusions than a faith in art as far as James is concerned. When Peter begs Miriam to forego her theatrical career and become an ambassador's wife, she bluntly informs him of the misguided nature of his worldly goals. "Miriam's histrionic hardness flung him back against a fifth-rate world, against a bedimmed, star-punctured nature which had no consolation—the bleared, irresponsive eyes of the London heaven" (II, 790).

Peter is introduced into the novel as a fixed portrait, and he never has a real freedom of choice afterward. His cousin and counterpart, Nick Dormer, is also initially presented (I, 2) as part of a *tableau vivant* of Britons in Paris ("finished productions, in their way"), but he is allowed to break out of the frame in order to assert his independence as an artist. Whatever James's former views of conditioning, he now presents the successful artist as a self-creation. Aside from the fact of his friendship with the aesthetic Nash, Nick is at a loss to explain his anomalous artistic bent: "There has never been anything of the sort among us," he protests to Nash; "we are all Philistines to the core, with about as much aesthetic sense as that hat. It's excellent soil—I don't complain of it—but not a soil to grow that flower. From where the devil, then, has the seed been dropped?" (I, 198). It is possible that James's feeling of estrangement—in aesthetic terms, at least —from his family had led to the idea that the artist (he, himself) was alone and unique in the world. If his rejection of Sherringham may signify a repudiation of the worldly life, James almost goes too far in the opposite direction with Nick, whose lonely eminence he implicitly compares with his own. As Miriam notes late in the book, "You'll do things that will hand on your name when my screeching is happily over. Only you do seem to me, I confess, rather high and dry here—I speak from the point of view of your comfort and of my personal interest in you. You strike me as kind of lonely, as the Americans say—rather cut off and isolated in your grandeur" (II, 830). Nick tends to dissolve as a character when, like James, he suspends for himself the possibility of human relationships and settles down to the task of creation. He

> had become aware of a certain social tightness, of the fact
> that life is crowded and passion restless, accident frequent
> and community inevitable. Everybody with whom one had
> relations had other relations too, and even optimism was a
> mixture and peace an embroilment. The only chance was to let
> everything be embroiled but one's temper and everything
> spoiled but one's work [II, 697].

In this understated manner, Nick achieves a modest success of sorts. Occasionally, however, James threatens to endanger his credibility to the reader by burdening him with a sensibility loaded to excess. In the New York preface, James congratulates Nick and Miriam for having postponed "the 'world' to their conception of other and finer decencies."[85]

In the novel Nick is so little given to rhetorical outbursts that what similarity he has with Hyacinth Robinson works in his favor. James stresses Nick's "certainty of eye," but he allows him an upper-class background to account for his ability to travel to Paris and put his eyes to use: "the place had always had the power of quickening sensibly the life of reflection and of observation within him" (I, 19, 21). Like Hyacinth, he sees with an imaginative complexity of point of view. "He had the gift," James notes, "so embarrassing when it is a question of consistent action, of seeing in an imaginative, interesting light anything that illustrated forcibly the life of another" (I, 276). Also, like his predecessor, he is in effect two men, with a political and an artistic, a public and a private life.* "He was conscious of a double nature; there were two men in him, quite separate, whose leading features had little in common and each of whom insisted on having an independent turn at life"

* It is characteristic of James that in the decade of *Dr. Jekyll and Mr. Hyde* and *The Picture of Dorian Gray* he was never to consider the moral possibilities of the *Doppelgänger* theme; the dichotomy was never other than the private versus the public man, and in his ghost story of the theme, "The Private Life," he treated it as a subject for comedy.

(I, 284–285). Like Verena Tarrant, Nick has a gift for words that assures him of political success:

"I speak beautifully. I've got the cursed humbugging trick of it.
I can turn it on, a fine flood of it, at the shortest notice.
The better it is the worse it is, the kind is so inferior. It has
nothing to do with the truth or the search for it; nothing
to do with intelligence, or candor, or honor. It's an appeal to
everything that for one's self one despises," the young man
went on—"to stupidity, to ignorance, to density, to the love of
names and phrases, the love of hollow, idiotic words, of
shutting the eyes tight and making a noise" [I, 113].

To judge by the evidence in James's fiction, such as "The Path of Duty" and *The Tragic Muse*, the only requirements for a political career are personal good looks and a flair for rhetoric. But to be a member of Parliament is not to be free in the sense that the artist is free, and Nick loves his freedom. (It is here that James's American nature is evident, even in the midst of an English setting.) In following Julia Dallow's desire that he run for Parliament, "he had let others choose for him" (I, 287); in accepting Mr. Carteret's patronage, he construes this to mean that apparently "he was not fated to go in for independence" (I, 334). It is noteworthy, however, that when he breaks away from his political "part" (which, like Peter's career, is made to seem more histrionic and less natural than the actor's role), Nick feels the need to proclaim his independence to both mentors with a vengeance that seems excessively cruel.

Nick prefers the satisfaction of representing his constituents upon canvas to representing them in Parliament; he would rather have them sit for him than have to sit for them. His idealization of his calling puts him in an ambivalent position with regard to other people. He speaks of his constituency in an aesthetic manner: "what does *it* represent, poor stupid little borough, with its smell of meal and its curiously fat-faced inhabitants? Did you ever see such a collection of fat faces, turned up at the hustings? They looked like an enormous sofa, with the cheeks for the gathers and the eyes for the buttons" (I, 266). Yet, despite his sneer at "a parcel of cheese-eating burgesses" (II, 607), Nick presents his artistic ambition as follows to Nash:

"There it is," said Nick at last—"there's the naked, preposterous truth: that if I were to do exactly as I liked I should spend my years copying the more or less vacuous countenances of my fellow-mortals. I should find peace and pleasure and wisdom and worth, I should find fascination and a measure of success in it—out of the din and the dust and the scramble, the world of party labels, party cries, party bargains and party treacheries —of humbuggery, hypocrisy and cant. The cleanness and quietness of it, the independent effort to do something, to leave something which shall give joy to man long after the howling has died away to the last ghost of an echo—such a vision solicits me at certain hours with an almost irresistible force" [II, 437–438].

The triumph of the artistic way of life lies as much in its detachment from as in its depiction of the world, and for James the successful artist was almost an anarchist with standards.

Nick learns to please himself, in the course of the novel, but in one of the best and most curiously worded passages he is seen in the dim light of an ambiguous triumph, like Paul Overt in "The Lesson of the Master." Nash has been comforting him, but Nick now faces his loneliness. "He had felt a good deal, before, as if he were in Nash's hands," James has earlier noted, "but now that he had made his final choice he seemed to himself to be altogether in his own. Gabriel was wonderful, but no Gabriel could assist him much henceforth" (II, 611–612).

When he had gone Nick threw himself back on the cushions of the divan and, with his hands locked above his head, sat a long time lost in thought. He had sent his servant to bed; he was unmolested. He gazed before him into the gloom produced by the unheeded burning out of the last candle. The vague outer light came in through the tall studio window, and the painted images, ranged about, looked confused in the dusk. If his mother had seen him she might have thought he was staring at his father's ghost [II, 615–616].

Nick's friend and sometime mentor, Gabriel Nash, is one of the delights of the novel, even if he seems to play only a tangential role in the context of the plot. It is Nash who first encourages the member of Parliament to become a painter, and Nick feels that if he "was an ambiguous being, . . . he was an excellent touchstone" (II, 431). It is a measure of James's relative objectivity and good humor in the novel that he felt he could once again resort to conscious self-parody in his depiction of Nash. Just as the young painter represents James alone and at work, his slightly older friend resembles James physically and aesthetically. While Nick echoes the serious side of Hyacinth Robinson, Nash echoes his slightly ridiculous addiction to sensations. His business, he claims, is "the spectacle of the world," but, when pressed, he adds that he looks "in preference at what is charming in it." Nash is an exaggeration of Hyacinth, but with money:

> "I accomplish my happiness—it seems to me that's something. I have feelings, I have sensations: let me tell you that's not so common. It's rare to have them; and if you chance to have them it's rare not to be ashamed of them. I go after them—when I judge they won't hurt any one."
> "You're luck to have money for your traveling-expenses," said Nick [I, 193–194].

Like James, Nash is prone to judge everything in terms of "fine shades" (the topic of mockery, by the way, in Meredith's *Sandra Belloni*), and they share the Arnoldian amusement at blunt Anglo-Saxon names.

A more important source of similarity between author and creation is their common refusal to be pinned down by formulas or generalizations. But Nash is a literary creation, and, in a sense, he is limited by his reiterated emphases on freedom and feeling. In time, the attacks upon generalization become clichés, and the advocate of "personal experiments" turns into "the great explainer," in Miriam's phrase. Ultimately, Nick grows impatient with the aesthete's unchangeability:

> He had grown used to Nash—had a sense that he had heard all he had to say. That was one's penalty with persons whose main gift was for talk, however irrigating; talk engendered a sense of sameness much sooner than action. The things a man did were necessarily more different from each other than the things he said, even if he went in for surprising you. Nick felt Nash could never surprise him any more save by doing something [II, 612].

The portrait of Nash derives in part from James's memory of his father.[86] The aesthete prefers being to doing, and refuses to write again (he has written a novel) on the grounds that literature, since it is written "for the convenience of others," "requires the most abject concessions" and "plays such mischief with one's style" (I, 36). In *Notes of a Son and Brother*, James remembered his father's uneasiness at William's abortive decision to become a painter: "What we were to do instead was just to *be* something, something unconnected with specific doing, something free and uncommitted . . ." James recalled his father once saying that "When a man *lives*, that is lives enough, he can scarcely write."[87] The dialogue between reflection and action runs through James's earlier fiction, and Nash is a comic descendant of the transcendentalist American expatriate Theobald in "The Madonna of the Future." He is a composite, all in all, of James, the elder James, Walter Pater, an old acquaintance named Herbert Pratt, and possibly Oscar Wilde. James had met Wilde during his visit to America in 1882 and was not impressed. When James mentioned his homesickness for London, Wilde replied, "Really! You care for *places*? The world is my home."[88]

"Where there's anything to feel I try to be there!" (I, 28) is Nash's password. Because of his ambiguous nature, he is a combined source of Jamesian advice (the commands to encourage the beautiful and to maintain one's integrity, for example) and symbolic warning. He is an example of singularity of point of view, to which James was in the process of succumbing. When Nash looks forward to the prospect of Miriam's yielding to the vulgarities of the age, he brings to the surface the sadism that is part of the detached life of aesthetic observation: "In the end [he predicts] her divine voice would crack, screaming to foreign ears and antipodal barbarians, and her clever manner would lose all quality, simplified to a few unmistakable knock-down dodges. Then she would be at the fine climax of life and glory, still young and insatiate, but already coarse, hard and raddled, with nothing left to do and nothing left to do it with, the remaining years all before her and the *raison d'être* all behind. It would be curious and magnificent and grotesque" (II, 620).

Nash's eager anticipation of the "spectacle" is reminiscent of James's artistic satisfaction at watching the spectacle of England in decline. But Nash is not an artist and is therefore subject to the limitations of his role in the novel. He cannot bear to be painted by Nick, since "he was so accustomed to living upon irony and the interpretation of things that it was strange to him to be himself interpreted, and (as a gentleman who sits for his portrait is always liable to be) interpreted ironically" (II, 848). He makes his exit from the novel, sardonically, as an unfinished portrait, "jammed . . . back into its corner, with its face against the wall" (II, 861)— James's customary metaphorical designation of death. As the descendant of a long line of Jamesian artistic manipulators and ironic narrators, Nash is himself symbolically fixed in place.

With his eccentric nature, Nash tends to provide more interest for the reader of *The Tragic Muse* than either of the two heroes. An even greater advantage to the book is the presence of the Muse herself. For James, art entailed action, not merely an apperception but a concrete representation of life. In the section of the novel in which Nick and Gabriel exchange comments on art while strolling through Paris, the young painter momentarily silences the aesthete by declaring, "Ah, the beautiful—there it stands, over there! . . . I am not so sure about yours—I don't know what I've got hold of. But Notre Dame *is* solid; Notre Dame *is* wise; on Notre Dame the distracted mind can rest. Come over and look at her!" (I, 189–190). Aptly enough, another great lady is preparing to show up Nash's ineffectuality: Miriam Rooth. James's first notebook citation for the novel was made in June 1884, while he was also preparing *The Bostonians* and *The Princess*. It would be "a study of the histrionic character": "a confirmation of Mrs. Kemble's theory that the dramatic gift is a thing by itself—implying of necessity no *general* superiority of mind."[89] In the character he developed, James drew upon his memories of actresses he had seen at the Comédie Française, upon his friendship with Mrs. Kemble, and possibly upon his own defensive feelings that he had become an artist without a philosophy or general ideas. Miriam's methods as an actress have strong affinities with James's concept of the novelist, and, despite her initial limitations, she is the most successful of the four main characters, for the audience inside and outside the novel, in terms of what she does and what she represents.

Miriam is introduced in a manner reminiscent of Isabel Archer's entrance in *The Portrait of a Lady*; she is vaguely described, as compared with the fixed portraits of the other characters, but she is prominent for her "largely-gazing eyes" (I, 24). Even more than Isabel, she is one on whom nothing is lost, and, considerably more than Hyacinth, she puts her observations to practical use. Determined to become an actress, she makes a very bad initial showing of her talents. By dint of work (which includes extensive observation) and the acquiring of an "idea" (about which James is vague), however, she becomes a major actress. Peter Sherringham undertakes to expose her to those parts of life she has missed, and he is struck by "the queer jumble of her taste, her mixture of intelligence and puerility. He saw that she never read what he gave her, though she sometimes would have liked him to suppose so; but in the presence of famous pictures and statues she had remarkable flashes of perception. She felt these things, she liked them, though it was always because she had an idea she could use them. The idea was often fantastic, but it showed what an eye she had to her business." Peter maintains a sense of superiority to her which is echoed and undercut by the Nash-Nick relationship: "He had fine ideas, but she was to do the acting, that is the application of them, and not he; and application was always of necessity [thinks Peter] a sort of vulgarization, a smaller thing than theory" (I, 248–249).

"The great thing was that from the first she had abundantly lived," James later wrote in tribute to Mrs. Kemble, "and, in more than one meaning of the word, acted—felt, observed, imagined, reflected, reasoned, gathered in her passage the abiding impression, the sense and suggestion of things."[90] Similarly, James links Miriam to his own view that the artist's most valuable gift is his ability to accumulate and transform impressions:

> She was delighted to find that seeing more of the world
> suggested things to her; they came straight from the fact,
> from nature, if you could call it nature: so that she was
> convinced more than ever that the artist ought to *live*, to get
> on with his business, gather ideas, lights from experience—ought
> to welcome any experience that would give him lights. But
> work, of course, *was* experience, and everything in one's life
> that was good was work. That was the jolly thing in the
> actor's trade—it made up for other elements that were odious:
> if you only kept your eyes open nothing could happen to you
> that wouldn't be food for observation and grist to your mill,

showing you how people looked and moved and spoke,
cried and grimaced, or writhed and dissimulated, in given
situations. She saw all round her things she wanted to "do"—
London was full of them, if you had eyes to see [II, 551].

The opposition between art and life, observation and action, which
James had depicted in his first novel about artists, *Roderick Hudson*, is resolved in the figure of Miriam Rooth, the observer as
actress.

In Miriam is embodied better than anywhere else in James the
conception of the artist as predator. "Genius is only the art of
getting your experience fast, of stealing it, as it were; and in this
sense Miss Rooth's a regular brigand," as Peter humorously puts it
(II, 545). When he takes her into the foyer of the Comédie Française—the great "scene" of the novel—he speaks of the conditions
of the artist: "the need to take its ease, to take up space, to make
itself at home in the world, to square its elbows and knock others
about. That's large and free; it's the good-nature you speak of.
You must forage and ravage and leave a track behind you; you
must live upon the country you traverse" (I, 392).

In compensation for the artist's triumph over the world, he must
give up his human birthright—such, at least, was the theme of
"The Lesson of the Master," and it is repeated in *The Tragic Muse*.
Vasari recounts how, when the son of Luca Signorelli died, the
great painter, "with extraordinary fortitude," felt the artistic need
to paint the dead child, "so that he might always behold in this
work of his hands what Nature had given him and cruel Fortune
taken away." In Zola's novel about the French Impressionists,
L'Oeuvre, an analogue of sorts to James's novel, the painter-hero
does the same thing with his dead son—but more out of dedication
to his art than from personal grief. Claude Monet is supposed to
have caught himself, at his wife's deathbed, studying her changing
flesh tones. Such cases are extreme examples of what are otherwise, for many artists, simply the necessary facts of artistic life.
Henry James is one of the more extreme cases of the novelist as
artist, and the intensity of his belief in his calling and the intensity
of his characters' faith in their own powers lift them above the
artists and aesthetic heroes of modern literature. It is an article of
faith for James and a character like Miriam that if art is a personal

transmutation of nature, then at its best it is more real than the real thing. "Miriam's effort was to make the fictive true," as Peter observes at one point, and in her theatrical triumph he reflects that her negative capability (the "idea of her having no character of her own" [I, 242]) is transformed into theatrical truth. Her private life "was not worth speaking of. These things were the fictions and shadows; the representation was the deep substance" (II, 534). The end of art is to achieve a Platonic idea of truth (as Schopenhauer had argued), but the artist risks becoming, in the process, personally shallow and addicted to rhetoric offstage. In her private life, Miriam remains rather vulgar and speaks in a stagy manner. "She uttered the things she felt as if they were snatches of old play-books," James remarks, "and really felt them the more because they sounded so well" (II, 680). But, in what is obviously James's own *cri de coeur* in the novel, Miriam exclaims, "The world be hanged; the stage, or anything of that sort (I mean one's faith), comes first" (II, 453).

If the keynote of the creative artist is, for James, his immense personal freedom of choice, it is typical of the worldly person to be sharply circumscribed by conventions. If Miriam is able to be a hundred persons rather than one, as Peter notes, her political opposite, the rising liberal leader Mr. Macgeorge, is considered by Nick "a being almost grotesquely limited" (I, 414). Julia Dallow's political opinions seem to boil down to the desire to keep Tories out of Parliament and to put Nick in, and Mr. Carteret's ideas have been frozen in place since 1830. "The good old man had almost a vocabulary of his own," Nick reflects, "made up of old-fashioned political phrases and quite untainted with the new terms, mostly borrowed from America; indeed, his language and his tone made those of almost any one who might be talking with him appear by contrast rather American" (I, 323). Curiously, the political figures in the novel are characterized to great effect, while the artists are often so close to being Jamesian mouthpieces that they suffer from a deficiency of fictional identity. *The Tragic Muse* opens and closes within a conventional Victorian framework, but, under the placid surface with its typed figures and omniscient narrator and happy ending, is a theme essentially subversive to the Victorian novel and the society it reflects. It is James's aim, as much as

Miriam's and Nick's, to forage on the conventional materials of life and fiction. In transmuting life into art and then back again, however, he presents us with a society that is essentially artificial as compared to artifice which is made to seem natural. James's conception of the artist, eloquently stated though it often is, has disturbing elements in it, in the light of later literary history: the idea of appearance versus reality is completely overturned, and the balance between the artist and the world he represents is subjectively upset. For Keats, the artist (with Shakespeare as his model) could lead a life of allegory as a representative, composite man; for James, man is of value only to the degree that he leads a metaphorical life as artist. Thus, the artist becomes, more and more, specialist and solipsist.

"Don't talk to me about politics," Joyce is supposed to have replied when asked his opinion of fascism in 1920: "I'm only interested in style." In *The Tragic Muse* the notion of public service, in the conventional sense, is beneath consideration. The ideals of a member of Parliament, which Trollope had considered the highest possible position open to an Englishman and which Meredith's Beauchamp struggled in vain to become, are dismissed as histrionic in a pejorative sense. Politics deals with transitory matters; as James notes, Nick had been elected before on the basis of "the fresh cleverness of his speeches, tinted with young idealism and yet sticking sufficiently to the question (the burning question, it has since burned out)" (I, 93). James's knowledge of politics was fairly vague, drawn largely, one would guess, from casual conversations with such figures as Gladstone and John Bright at clubs or dinner parties, and especially from dinner-party gossip. His incompetence in matters political is amply illustrated by the occasional reports on Parliament which he submitted to the *Nation* in the late 1870's. While priding himself on his impartiality as to sides and parties, he sneered at Disraeli on racial grounds and deplored England's decline on aesthetic grounds. He could never shake off the idea that the British Empire was an artistic creation, for example, and in the famous letter in which he thanked God he had no political opinions, he treated the imperial question as sacrosanct. Alluding to "Politics" to Stevenson in 1893, he smugly announced: "When you say that you always 'believed' them beastly I am tempted to become superior and say that I always knew them so."[91] (It is only fair to mention, in passing, that in 1915, when James became a British subject, one of his sponsors was Prime Minister Asquith, who remarked in private that "the bonds of friendship were strained to cracking when I had to subscribe to the proposition that he could both talk and write English.")[92]

It is typical of the Jamesian artist to insure his sense of personal distance by composing or fixing others into place. Julia becomes "a composed picture" for Nick, and Mr. Carteret on his deathbed presents himself "to Nick's picture-seeking vision as a figure in a clever composition or a novel" (II, 579). Similarly, he disposes of his relations with Gabriel by beginning a portrait of him; it is left undetermined at the end of the novel whether Julia's resumption of friendship with and her decision to sit for her portrait for Nick mean that they will ultimately be married. James leaves the novel open enough for Victorian readers to supply a happy ending if they wish to do so, but it is by no means sure, from the logic of the book, that a woman who is unworthy in Nick's view, of the bibelots left her by her late husband could also be his wife. The members of Nick's family are also drawn with a precision that makes them memorable but fixed: the matronly Lady Agnes, with her fear of poverty; and Nick's sisters, the appealing Biddy, whose gentle firmness reminds one of Trollope's heroines and who marries Peter, and the unappealing Grace.

The worldly characters have value only for the artist who portrays them; they are circumscribed by the inner artists of the novel as well as by James. To the artists, however, he allows a freedom of choice evident to all but nonartists. Thus, the men with power are not those who sit in Parliament, but those with artistic resources. In his essay on Daumier (1893), James re-emphasized the theme that "Art is an embalmer, a magician, whom we can never speak too fair":

> People duly impressed with this truth are sometimes laughed at for their superstitious tone, which is pronounced, according to the fancy of the critic, mawkish, maudlin or hysterical. But it is really difficult to see how any reiteration of the importance of art can overstate the plain facts. It prolongs, it preserves,

it consecrates, it raises from the dead. It conciliates, charms, bribes posterity; and it murmurs to mortals, as the old French poet sang to his mistress," you will be fair only so far as I have said so." When it whispers even to the great, "You depend upon me, and I can do more for you, in the long-run, than any one else," it is scarcely too proud.[93]

It is of course ironic that so poor a subject matter in James's view should be redeemed by so great an art. Although by the late 1880's he had ceased to believe in the English as the most brilliant race in the world if the portraits of Lady Barberina or Lionel Berrington are indications, he still felt an aesthetic appeal in them. Likewise, Nick treats his constituents with disdain, but wishes to devote his life to "copying the more or less vacuous countenances of [his] fellow-mortals"; and Miriam gives herself up to "the great childish audience, gaping at her points, expanded there before her like a lap to catch flowers" (II, 870).

Ultimately, the novel is a defense of the artist, whether actress, painter, or novelist. "All art is one," as Nick remarks (I, 13), and James draws a number of parallels between the various arts. In his eulogy of Miriam's achievement he reminds us that Shakespeare's tribute to those who hold "the mirror up to nature" is directed to actors, as representatives of the artist. Through the 1880's James made various tributes to the portrait (*The Portrait of a Lady, Portraits of Places, Partial Portraits*), emphasizing, in the manner of Sainte-Beuve, the subjective nature of his descriptions. Nick Dormer's portraits seem close in spirit to John Singer Sargent's work, which James admired. "There is no greater work of art than a great portrait," he wrote in an essay on Sargent,[94] and in *The Tragic Muse* Gabriel Nash describes portrait painting as "a revelation of two realities, the man whom it was the artist's conscious effort to reveal and the man (the interpreter) expressed in the very quality and temper of that effort." The modern artist, following in Pater's footsteps, is more aware of the second reality, but, as Gabriel continues, ideally the portrait offers "a double vision, the strongest dose of life that art [can] give, the strongest dose of art that life [can] give" (II, 461). Nash is unwilling to be portrayed himself, however, although he is pinned down by both Nick and James.

If the novelist has an advantage over the painter and actor (or dramatist), it is precisely in his ability to combine a pictorial and a dramatic method. It is curious that James should not have heeded the advice of Gabriel, who argues that in an age of complexity the novel is the most elastic of forms:

> To-day we are so infinitely more reflective and complicated and diffuse that it makes all the difference. What can you do with a character, with an idea, with a feeling, between dinner and the suburban trains? You can give a gross, rough sketch of them, but how little you touch them, how bald you leave them! What crudity compared with what the novelist does! [I, 73].

James was unable to follow this advice; even as he was finishing the novel, he was planning his assault upon the theater and a "childish public," as he assumed.

It is a further pity that James overlooked the possibilities of the novel form when he wrote *The Tragic Muse*. The best parts of the book (qua novel) are the most conventional, the most heavily borrowed portions, but too much of the remainder is a long, animated conversation on, and defense of, art. The subject of the novel seems promising in advance—Peter's debate between love and duty, Nick's struggle between art and politics, and Miriam's triumph despite the odds against her—but halfway through the novel the subject is resolved, the choices are made, and the triumph is inevitable. Hereafter, the novel is swamped by James's self-indulgent appeals for artistic freedom, and advertisements for the glories of art. Along the way, he presents at least one good rhetorical passage on Nick's stroll among the portraits in the National Gallery:

> These were the things that were the most inspiring, in the sense that they were the things that, while generations, while worlds had come and gone, seemed most to survive and testify. As he stood before them sometimes the perfection of their survival struck him as the supreme eloquence, the reason that included all others, thanks to the language of art, the richest and most universal. Empires and systems and conquests had rolled over the globe and every kind of greatness had risen and passed away, but the beauty of the great pictures had known nothing of death or change, and the ages had only sweetened their freshness. The same faces, the same figures looked out at different centuries, knowing a deal the century didn't, and when they joined hands they made the indestructible thread on which the pearls of history were strung [II, 827–828].

The eloquence of statement and the rolling cadences here effectively conceal a fairly simple idea, perhaps the one artistic idea, as such, in James's novels: art lasts. With a few more ideas, however, James might have noticed that not all art lasts—or is allowed to last. The most eloquent defense of art on these lines was made by André Malraux in *The Voices of Silence:* "All art is a revolt against man's fate." But while Malraux included notable illustrations to prove his point, James was forced to turn to his own achievement for confirmation.

To Stevenson, James claimed that *The Tragic Muse* was "the longest and most careful novel" he had ever written.[95] It is certainly his longest novel, at any rate. To his brother William, he was considerably more realistic, but characteristically self-confident:

> I have no illusions of any kind about the book, and least of all about its circulation and "popularity." From these things I am quite divorced and never was happier than since the dissolution has been consecrated by (what seems to me) the highest authorities. One must go one's way and know what one's about and have a general plan and a private religion—in short have made up one's mind as to *ce qui on est* with a public the draggling after which simply leads one in the gutter. One has always a "public" enough if one has an audible vibration—even if it should only come from one's self.[96]

"With that work, your *Tragic Muse*," William had just exuberantly written, "and last *but by no means least*, my *Psychology*, all appearing in it, the year 1890 will be known as the great epochal year in American literature."[97] Despite his brother's intransigence, William James was right—partly because of his brother's intransigence. The origin of the modern novel was marked by the repudiation of society and the glorification of self. Hence, the archetypal modern novel is a work concerning the artist or, better yet, the writing of the novel one is reading.

In *The Tragic Muse* James wrote a *Bildungsroman* in reverse. If Goethe treats Wilhelm Meister's apprenticeship in art as a necessary step to prepare him for life, James characteristically puts his characters through a training in life (a life similar to his own) so that they can become artists like himself. Where Meredith, no less a subjective writer in conception than James, had looked to the writing of fiction as a form of therapy whereby he objectively exposed his comic weaknesses and warned against their social danger, James treated the novel as a form of advertisement for himself in which even his weaknesses were made to appear strengths. James's celebration of art is a celebration of solipsist art like his own— related not to life but to literature, with rules of behavior no less rigorous for being subjective. Beginning with *The Tragic Muse,* James went his own way with a vengeance.

> *The art of writing novels is to present a picture*
> *of life, but novel-writing embraces only a*
> *narrow portion of life. I trust that I keep*
> *my eyes on the larger outlook, as little as*
> *possible on myself.*
> *(Meredith to an admirer, 1883)*

> *One must go one's way and know what one's*
> *about and have a general plan and a private*
> *religion . . . One has always a "public" enough*
> *if one has an audible vibration—even if it should*
> *only come from one's self.*
> *(Henry to William James, 1890)*

"The death of George Meredith," G. K. Chesterton mourned, "was the real end of the Nineteenth Century, not that empty date that came at the end of 1899. The last bond was broken between us and the pride and peace of the Victorian age. Our fathers were all dead."[1] Meredith outlived Queen Victoria by eight years, but both were figureheads in their last years, venerable and often pompous relics in a world which did disservice to them both, first by mistaking their weaknesses for strengths and then, gradually, forgetting that they had had strengths. After *One of Our Conquerors* Meredith disintegrated as a novelist and thinker of importance; ironically, it was in his later years that he was most revered in both capacities. Of his last two novels, *Lord Ormont and His Aminta* (1894) is a fatiguing tribute to muscularity, and *The Amazing Marriage* (1895), despite an interesting plot, is tiresome in its simulated high spirits. In both books he treated the theme of loveless marriage more explicitly than would have been permitted in his early work. In each case the heroine, for justifiable reasons, leaves her husband; but the reader is apt to leave off reading long before that rupture occurs. The style in each work is considerably simpler than that of *One of Our Conquerors*. However, in abandoning the great themes of his past work, Meredith found himself at the mercy of a flawed novelistic manner which no longer, in his case, provided the rewards of psychology, philosophy, and comedy as compensation for his usual weaknesses. *The Amazing Marriage* ends with an infuriating announcement—which had been bad enough when made in *Sandra Belloni* and *Diana of the Crossways*—that the incredibility of what has come before is to be explained by the fact that in real life "Character must ever be a mystery, only to be explained in some degree by conduct; and that is very dependent upon accident: and unless we have a perpetual whipping of the tender part of the reader's mind, interest in invisible persons must needs flag."[2]

After *The Tragic Muse*, which he was perceptive enough to realize was not headed for commercial or critical success, James turned to the writing of plays in a bizarre and futile attempt to enlarge his income and widen his popularity. The trauma created by his failure in this enterprise, abundantly documented by Leon Edel, resulted in a further withdrawal of James from the real world into a world of subjective values. In the novels and stories of the 1890's he clung to the image and point of view of a child or childish adult (his artists often fall into this category), maintaining his uncontaminated but watchful innocence in a corrupt society. What from one point of view represents psychological, not to mention social, regression, from another represents poetic advance—and, for James, artistic necessity. The child became father to the man, and then grew up to become Milly Theale and Lambert Strether.

In the course of the 1880's James shifted his personal allegiance from the world as picturesque material for the novelist to the artist's own world of consciousness, which can transform any impressions into the stuff of art. By the time of "A London Life" (1888) James indicated that the point of view of the Jamesian individual is superior to anything the world offers. In the figures of Louis Leverett and Florimond Daintry, he had mocked his own Pateresque sensibility; in Dr. Sloper, Gilbert Osmond, and Ralph Touchett, he showed the harm that such sensibilities cause others whom they treat in the light of an aesthetic spectacle. But for Hyacinth Robinson, as well as Miriam Rooth, the formula that

James submits is one of "The world be hanged; the stage, or any-thing of that sort (I mean one's faith), comes first." If *Washington Square*, *The Portrait of a Lady*, and *The Bostonians* (in my view, three of James's four best novels, along with *The Wings of the Dove*) all showed the limitations of the individual point of view left to itself, James's later novels reversed that lesson. It is pre-cisely the consciousness of a Lambert Strether or a Maggie Verver —as well as the insane narrator of *The Sacred Fount*, whose in-sanity is part of his aesthetic self-righteousness, or the deluded telegraph operator of "In the Cage," who also gloats in the sense of power she thinks she has over others simply by knowing what they do not—which is superior to the standards of the world. Strether's consciousness, in particular, turns everything and everyone that it sees "into visions" (according to Richard Poirier), detaching "them from time and from the demands of nature," and providing them with "the composition of *objets d'art*."[3] Poirier links James with Emerson in this ability to find refuge in a personal world of style, but the similarity is closer to Pater, who had concluded the *Renaissance*, after all, with a plea for individuals to make the most "of a quickened, multiplied consciousness."[4]

James differed from both Emerson and Pater in his ability to convert subjective impressions into concrete works of art, but the heroism of a Strether, like Hyacinth Robinson before him, consists in his ability to make a work of art of his own consciousness. Strether's progress can be observed in his admiring discovery of "the empire of 'things' "—the bric-a-brac collected in Maria Gos-trey's "shrine"—and then in his even more appreciative initiation into Madame de Vionnet's superior temple. Her apartment is su-perior to Maria Gostrey's because it came to her without any effort on her part: "Chad and Miss Gostrey had rummaged and pur-chased and picked up and exchanged, sifting, selecting, comparing; whereas the mistress of the scene before him, beautifully passive under the spell of transmission . . . had only received, accepted and been quiet." Even better than Madame de Vionnet's inherited world or Maria Gostrey's purchased one is Strether's own created world; his greatest triumph comes at the moment when he trans-forms the French country scene he visits, late in the novel, "into a composition," into the Lambinet painting he had wanted long before. When Madame de Vionnet and Chad Newsome drift down the river into his composition, he is less shocked by the discovery of their illicit union than determined to fix them in place on the canvas of his mind forever. What do such beings matter, after all, unless they serve to provide a beautiful "performance" (as he applauds it)[5] for him? The beauty of histrionics, for James as well as Strether, is that, like all art, it provides the illusion of long duration, that, as far as the Jamesian individual is concerned, it lifts him out of the transitory world into the fixed world of one's own mind.

Such an aesthetic view of life necessitates a subjective standard of the individual's own making. James's importance for the modern novel lies in the way he transformed Pater's dictum that the world exists at best as an aesthetic spectacle, not something the individual can or should actively exert himself in, into a formula for both the author of novels and the hero of fiction. "The privilege the reader is offered," as Stephen Spender observes, "is to become Henry James,"[6] and it is ironic that Pater's appeal to court as many impressions as possible in order to keep from ending up the prisoner of one's dream of a world should have been transformed into the limiting and singular possibility that James made of it. James's hold upon the Bloomsbury circle, for example, can be evidenced in an ecstatic study of his work which appeared in the *Independent* in 1904. The novelist is praised for his "acute and restless sense both of the intricacy and of the value of human relations," and he is compared favorably to Tolstoy in his account of the helplessness of the "individual will" to do anything other than maintain a superior sense of awareness.[7] George Moore had already noted in the 1880's that James habitually places his characters "in a calm, sad, and very polite twilight of volition";[8] for Moore this seemed a literary weakness. For sensitive readers after the turn of the century, and especially after the First World War, James's tribute to the life of passive withdrawal seemed more suitable than Tolstoy's insisting on the need for intelligent action. The Jamesian ethic of noble helplessness can be observed in figures as remote from each other as the protagonist of Ford Madox Ford's *Parade's End* and the heroes of F. Scott Fitzgerald, Ernest Hemingway, and Saul Bellow.

The difference between James and Tolstoy noted by the writer for the *Independent* is much the same as the distinction between James and Meredith that I have been making in this book. Where the American novelist evolved an ethic of helpless discrimination, albeit in novels conceived as finished artifacts which compete with and triumph over life, Meredith, in his novels, promoted an ideal of active, selfless service to society which stands in opposition to the lure of purely subjective or aesthetic values. Meredith's "villains" are artists in life, whose villainy and artistry alike consist in their escape from reality. For Meredith a workable idealism could be achieved only if men kept their eyes on the real world and the laws of society; even in his novels, he insisted upon reminding his readers that they were in the midst of an illusion, a form of escapism, which had value only to the extent that it exposed illusions and forced the reader to cast a hard look at the world preparatory to changing it for the better. Meredith's most famous line of poetry—"We are betrayed by what is false within"—is a reminder that subjective illusions are the cause of all weakness, personal and social, and that it is our duty therefore to realize and expel what is false within for the sake of understanding and removing what is false without also. E. M. Forster's declaration, in *Aspects of the Novel*, that Meredith "will never be the spiritual power he was about the year 1900"[9] may be true enough, but there is something uncomfortably smug in Forster's sense of relief that the individual has no other responsibilities than to personal relations. (It is one of the ironies of literary history that the personal relations of the Bloomsbury group should have been so strained and unsatisfactory.)

If Meredith, for all his gifts as poet and philosopher, psychologist and humorist, could not always succeed in fusing his resources satisfactorily, and if his message appears hollow in many quarters today, he did successfully provide aid for other novelists, both in his failures and in his continuing willingness to experiment. The issue of the *Kenyon Review* (Autumn 1943) devoted to critical essays on James contains an editorial note on Forster which mentions the importance to Forster of Meredith, whose "chief greatness" is defined "to have been the cause that greatness might be in other writers." While the editorial overlooks the fact that in such works as *The Egoist* and *Harry Richmond* Meredith achieved an eminence matched by few English novelists before or after him, it does accurately account for Meredith's notable contribution to younger writers: "It was Meredith who conceived of a fiction that might have such a scope, such a pyrotechnic, as drama had in the hands of Shakespeare." Forster learned from him to produce his own "refreshing collocation of wit and poetry . . . Nevertheless he is a purified Meredithian, like the second and improved generation of a stock. Forster has a grace where Meredith has an excess, and is surely the wiser for Meredith's lumbering."[10]

The suspicion of literary kinship between Meredith and Joyce has been confirmed by Stanislaus Joyce and Richard Ellmann, and one finds in Meredith's novels a number of experiments with the use of myth, symbolism, poetic lyricism, and even stream of consciousness (in the opening chapter of *One of Our Conquerors*) that points toward Joyce.[11] If Meredith affected Joyce in matters of style and technique, he anticipated D. H. Lawrence in terms of subject matter. He was a crucial link between Carlyle and Lawrence, although he was considerably more humane and cultivated than Carlyle. In his poetry and fiction Meredith celebrated the "blood-thrill" (the phrase is from "Night of Frost in May") of man in nature who discovers that the power of nature is within himself as well. Meredith's "Earth" was the most sensuous and hopeful version of nature to be hymned in the late nineteenth century, and, after the publication of *Origin of Species*, he was the single eminent Victorian to accept as well as to praise nature—a lonely model in this respect for Lawrence. Moreover, the Lawrentian themes of the battle of the sexes, of the necessity for women's educational and emotional development, and of the possibility of marriage as a state of "star-equilibrium" rather than loveless servitude, were all articulated in fiction and poetry by Meredith. There is an obvious Meredithian strain in Lawrence's friend Aldous Huxley, and the latter's ultimate incarnation as a California sage curiously parodies Meredith's own last years as the Grand Guru of Box Hill. At the present time, Anthony Burgess seems the most Meredithian of novelists in terms of his prodigious literary gifts and his curious use of them.

Meredith cannot be said to be entirely forgotten by modern novelists, even if they have profited only indirectly by his influence. The nature of James's influence upon the modern novel is a considerably more pervasive and acknowledged matter: as a master of literary craftsmanship; as the developer of the detached, ironical point of view in the novel; as the creator of the hero as victim, superior in sensitivity to the forces which overcome him. What separates Meredith as a Victorian from James as a modern novelist is not their literary methods, which, as in their extensive analysis of character, are alike in many cases, but their literary philosophies. For Meredith the novel existed for the sake of the world, while for James the world existed for the sake of the novel. Where Meredith devoted himself in the 1880's to works which cautioned his age against the dangers that threatened to destroy it, James took advantage of the dissolution of the Victorian world to make of it a subject for fiction. In 1895, while deploring the "Americanization" of England, James nevertheless considered it a "great broad, rich theme" for a novel if it could capitalize "on the great modern collapse of all the forms and 'superstitions' and respects, good and bad, and restraints and mysteries—a vivid and mere showy general hit at the decadences and vulgarities and confusions and masculinizations and feminizations—the materializations and abdications and intrusions, and Americanizations, the lost sense, the brutalized manner—the publicity, the newspapers, the general revolution, the failure of fastidiousness. *Ah, que de choses, que de choses!*"[12]

James and Meredith produced their best work at the beginning of the 1880's, the decade in which the Victorian world collapsed and the modern age inched into being. But where Meredith went to pieces in the effort to save the best of the Victorian world from dissolution, James, by shifting his values from the world to his own inner world and his own artistic standards, successfully salvaged the writing of fiction—and the need for fiction—for the modern world.

Appendix, Notes, Index

[*Appendix*] *A Selected List of Novels, Other Important Publications, and Historical Events of the 1880's*

Year	Novels Published	Other Books	Historical Events
1875	Trollope: *The Way We Live Now*		Disraeli buys Suez shares
1876	George Eliot: *Daniel Deronda* James: *Roderick Hudson* Meredith: *Beauchamp's Career* Trollope: *The Prime Minister*	Bradley: *Ethical Studies*	
1877	James: *The American* Meredith: *The Case of General Ople and Lady Camper* Tolstoy: *Anna Karenina* Turgenev: *Virgin Soil* Zola: *L'Assommoir*	Mallock: *The New Republic* Meredith: "The Idea of Comedy"	Grosvenor Gallery opens
1878	Hardy: *The Return of the Native* James: "Daisy Miller" and *The Europeans*	Gilbert and Sullivan: *H. M. S. Pinafore* James: *French Poets and Novelists* Pater: "The Child in the House" English Men of Letters series	Congress of Berlin Whistler vs. Ruskin
1879	James: *Confidence* (English publication) Meredith: *The Egoist, The Tale of Chloe*	George: *Progress and Poverty* Ibsen: *A Doll's House* James: *Hawthorne*	Parnell founds Irish Land League Zulu War Birth of Einstein, E. M. Forster, Paul Klee, and Wallace Stevens
1880	Dostoevsky: *The Brothers Karamazov*	Ruskin: *Fiction, Fair and Foul* Zola: *Le Roman expérimental*	Gladstone became Prime Minister Death of George Eliot and Flaubert

Year	Novels Published	Other Books	Historical Events
	Gissing: *Workers in the Dawn* Hardy: *The Trumpet-Major* Howells: *The Undiscovered Country* James: *Washington Square* Meredith: *The Tragic Comedians* Shorthouse: *John Inglesant* Trollope: *The Duke's Children* Zola: *Nana*		
1881	Flaubert: *Bouvard et Pecuchet* Hardy: *A Laodicean* James: *The Portrait of a Lady* Trollope: *Dr. Wortle's School* White: *The Autobiography of Mark Rutherford*	Carlyle: *Reminiscences* Darwin: *Autobiography* Gilbert and Sullivan: *Patience* Ibsen: *Ghosts* Rossetti: *Poems and Ballads* Wilde: *Poems*	Irish Land Bill Hyndman founds Social Democratic Federation Majuba Birth of Picasso and Bartok Death of Carlyle, Disraeli, and Dostoevsky
1882	Besant: *All Sorts and Conditions of Men* Hardy: *Two on a Tower* Howells: *A Modern Instance* Stevenson: *New Arabian Nights*	Arnold: "Literature and Science" Ibsen: *An Enemy of the People* Trollope: *Lord Palmerston*	Invasion of Egypt Married Women's Property Act Phoenix Park murders Birth of Braque, Joyce, Stravinsky, and Virginia Woolf Death of Darwin, Emerson, Pusey, Rossetti, and Trollope
1883	Maupassant: *Une vie* Moore: *A Modern Lover* Schreiner: *The Story of an African Farm* Stevenson: *Treasure Island*	Jefferies: *The Story of My Heart* Meredith: *Poems and Lyrics of the Joy of Earth* Nietzsche: *Thus Spoke Zarathustra*	Fabian Society founded Birth of Jaspers, Kafka, Ortega y Gasset, and Webern Death of Colenso, Fitzgerald, Manet,

Year	Novels Published	Other Books	Historical Events
	Trollope: *The Fixed Period, Mr. Scarborough's Family,* and *The Land Leaguers*	Seeley: *The Expansion of England* Trollope: *Autobiography*	Marx, Turgenev, and Wagner
1884	Gissing: *The Unclassed* Huysmans: *A Rebours* Jefferies: *The Dewy Morn* Tolstoy: *The Death of Ivan Ilych* Trollope: *An Old Man's Love* Twain: *Huckleberry Finn*	Froude: *Carlyle in London* Ibsen: *The Wild Duck* James vs. Besant: "The Art of Fiction" Ruskin: *The Storm-Cloud of the Nineteenth Century* Spencer: *The Man versus the State*	Franchise extended Salon des Indépendants Imperial Federation League formed Death of Reade
1885	Butler: *The Way of All Flesh* (manuscript completed) Haggard: *King Solomon's Mines* Howells: *The Rise of Silas Lapham* Meredith: *Diana of the Crossways* Moore: *A Mummer's Wife* Pater: *Marius the Epicurean* Stevenson: *Prince Otto* White: *Mark Rutherford's Deliverance* Zola: *Germinal*	Arnold: *Discourses in America* Burton, translator: *Arabian Nights* Gilbert and Sullivan: *The Mikado* Moore: "Literature at Nurse" Ruskin: *Praeterita* Whistler: "The 10 O'Clock" Revised edition of Old and New Testament	Gordon at Khartoum Dynamite explosions Birth of Alban Berg, Lawrence, and Pound Death of Victor Hugo
1886	Gissing: *Demos* Hardy: *The Mayor of Casterbridge* James: *The Bostonians* and *The Princess Casamassima* Moore: *A Drama in Muslin*	Ibsen: *Rosmersholm* Kipling: *Departmental Ditties* Mach: *Analysis of Sensations* First English translation of Marx: *Capital*	Home Rule Bill (defeated) Lord Salisbury became Prime Minister Dilke case Death of Liszt

Year	Novels Published	Other Books	Historical Events
	Stevenson: *Kidnapped* and *Dr. Jekyll and Mr. Hyde* Zola: *L'Oeuvre*	Tennyson: "Locksley Hall Sixty Years After"	
1887	Hall Caine: *The Deemster* Dujardin: *Les Lauriers sont coupés* Gissing: *Thyrza* Haggard: *She* and *Allan Quatermain* Hardy: *The Woodlanders* Jefferies: *Amaryllis at the Fair* Maupassant: *Pierre et Jean* Moore: *A Mere Accident* White: *The Revolution in Tanner's Lane* Zola: *La Terre*	Dewey: *Psychology* Kipling: *Plain Tales from the Hills* Mallarmé: *Poésies* Meredith: *Ballads and Poems of Tragic Life* Pater: *Imaginary Portraits* Rimbaud: *Illuminations* Sardou: *Tosca* Stevenson: *The Merry Men*	Golden Jubilee Trafalgar Square riots Independent Labor Party formed Birth of Chagall Death of Jefferies
1888	Bellamy: *Looking Backward* Doyle: *A Study in Scarlet* Glassing: *A Life's Morning* James: *The Reverberator* and "The Aspern Papers" Pater: *Gaston de la Tour* Stevenson: *The Master of Ballantrae* Mrs. Ward: *Robert Elsmere*	Arnold: *Essays in Criticism*, second series Chekhov: *Ivanov* Doughty: *Arabia Deserta* James: *Partial Portraits* Meredith: *A Reading of Earth* Moore: *Confessions of a Young Man* Nietzsche: *Twilight of the Idols* Strindberg: *Miss Julie*	Birth of T. S. Eliot Death of Arnold and Lear
1889	Doyle: *The Sign of Four* Gissing: *The Nether World* Howells: *A Hazard of New Fortunes* Tolstoy: *The Kreutzer Sonata*	Bergson: *Essai sur les données immédiates de la conscience* Browning: *Asolando* *Fabian Essays* Pater: *Appreciations*	Dock strike Vizetelly conviction Birth of Heidegger, Marcel, and Wittgenstein Death of Bright, Browning, Collins, and Hopkins

Year	Novels Published	Other Books	Historical Events
1890	Gissing: *The Emancipated* James: *The Tragic Muse* Zola: *La Bête humaine*	Booth: *In Darkest England* Frazer: *The Golden Bough* Ibsen: *Hedda Gabler* W. James: *Principles of Psychology* Stanley: *In Darkest Africa* Whistler: *The Gentle Art of Making Enemies*	Bismarck out of power Parnell suit Death of Newman and Van Gogh
1891	Gissing: *New Grub Street* Hardy: *Tess of the d'Urbervilles* Melville: *Billy Budd* Meredith: *One of Our Conquerors* Wilde: *The Picture of Dorian Gray*	Doyle: *Sherlock Holmes* Howells: *Criticism and Fiction* Morris: *News from Nowhere* Wilde: *Intentions*	Death of Melville and Parnell
1892	Gissing: *Born in Exile* Zola: *La Débâcle*		Gladstone became Prime Minister Death of Tennyson
1893	James: "The Middle Years"	Bradley: *Appearance and Reality*	Gladstone's second Home Rule Bill defeated
1894	Meredith: *Lord Ormont and His Aminta* Moore: *Esther Waters*	*The Yellow Book*	Death of Pater and Stevenson
1895	Meredith: *The Amazing Marriage*	James: *Guy Domville* Wilde: *The Importance of Being Earnest*	
1896	Hardy: *Jude the Obscure* Stevenson: *Weir of Hermiston*		Death of Morris

[Notes]

For convenience, the following abbreviations will be used.

Gissing, *Letters to Family*	George Gissing, *Letters to Members of His Family*, eds. Algernon and Ellen Gissing (London: Constable, 1927).
James, *Collected Tales*	Henry James, *Collected Tales*, 12 vols., ed. Leon Edel (Philadelphia: Lippincott, 1961–1964).
James, *French Poets and Novelists*	Henry James, *French Poets and Novelists* (London, 1878).
James, *Letters*	Henry James, *Letters*, 2 vols., ed. Percy Lubbock (New York: Scribner's, 1920).
James, *Notebooks*	Henry James, *Notebooks*, eds. F. O. Matthiessen and Kenneth B. Murdock New York: Oxford University Press, 1947).
James, *Partial Portraits*	Henry James, *Partial Portraits* (London, 1888).
James, *Selected Letters*	Henry James, *Selected Letters*, ed. Leon Edel (New York: Farrar, Straus and Cudahy, 1955).
James: The Critical Heritage	*Henry James: The Critical Heritage*, ed. Roger Gard (London: Routledge and Kegan Paul, 1968).
Matthiessen, *The James Family*	F. O. Matthiessen, *The James Family* (New York: Knopf, 1947).
Meredith, *Letters*	George Meredith, *Letters*, 3 vols., ed. C. L. Cline (London: Oxford University Press, 1970).
Meredith, *Works*	George Meredith, *Works*, Memorial Ed., 27 vols. (London: Constable, 1909–1911).
Moore, *Works*	George Moore, *Works*, Carra Ed., 21 vols. (New York: Boni and Liveright, 1922).
Pater, *Works*	Walter Pater, *Works*, Library Ed., 10 vols. (London: Macmillan, 1910).

[1] Introduction: Two Novelists

[1] Henry James, "Dumas the Younger," in *The Scenic Art*, ed. Allan Wade (New York: Hill and Wang, 1957), p. 267.

[2] Mrs. Humphry Ward, *Robert Elsmere* (London: Nelson, 1952), p. 474 (first published, 1888).

[3] James, *Letters*, I, 72.

[4] James, *Notebooks*, p. 28.

[5] James, *Letters*, I, 58, 114.

[6] Gissing, *Letters to Family*, p. 139.

[7] James, *Letters*, II, 252.

[8] C. L. Cline, "Introduction," in Meredith, *Letters*, I, xxix.

[9] Meredith, *Letters*, II, 858.

[10] James, *Letters*, II, 257.

[11] Meredith, *Letters*, I, 160–161; III, 1619.

[12] Stanislaus Joyce, *The Dublin Diary*, ed. George Harris Healey (Ithaca, N.Y.: Cornell University Press, 1962), pp. 84, 93.

[13] Meredith, *Letters*, II, 632.

Part I. The English Novel in the 1880's

[2] The Old Order Changes

[1] Gissing, *Letters to Family*, pp. 92, 172.

[2] Meredith, *Letters*, II, 768.

[3] Philip Magnus, *Gladstone* (London: John Murray, 1954), pp. 274, 161.

[4] Gissing, *Letters to Family*, p. 136.

[5] John Ruskin, *The Storm-Cloud of the Nineteenth Century*, in *Works*, Library Ed., 39 vols., eds. E. T. Cook and Alexander Wedderburn (London: Allen, 1903–1912), XXXIV, 78–79.

[6] G. Kitson Clark, *The Making of Victorian England* (Cambridge, Mass.: Harvard University Press, 1962), p. 31.

[7] Jacob Burckhardt, *Judgments on History and Historians*, tr. Harry Zohn (Boston: Beacon Press, 1958), p. 224.

[8] W. L. Burn, *The Age of Equipoise* (New York: Norton, 1964); David Thomson, *England in the Nineteenth Century* (London: Penguin Books, 1950), p. 234.

[9] H. V. Routh, *Towards the Twentieth Century* (New York: Macmillan, 1937), p. 9.

[10] Matthew Arnold, "Numbers," in *Discourses in America* (London, 1885); Thomas Carlyle, "Shooting Niagara: and After?" in *Works*, Centenary Ed., 30 vols. (London: Chapman and Hall, 1888–1901), XXX, 45–46.

[11] George Gissing, *Thyrza* (New York: Dutton, n.d.), p. 92 (first published, 1887).

Asa Briggs, *Victorian People* (London: Odhams Press, 1954), p. 102. Harry Levin, *Refractions* (London: Oxford University Press, 1966), ...8.

Anthony Trollope, *Autobiography*, ed. Bradford Booth (Berkeley: ...versity of California Press, 1947), pp. 29, 28 (first published, 1883). Robert M. Polhemus, *The Changing World of Anthony Trollope* (...keley: University of California Press, 1968), pp. 187, 2–3.

Anthony Trollope, *Dr. Wortle's School* (London: Oxford World's ...ssics, 1928), p. 242 (first published, 1881).

Anthony Trollope, *The Land Leaguers* (New York, 1883), p. 3.

Anthony Trollope, *Lord Palmerston* (London, 1883), p. 104. Briggs, *Victorian People*, p. 113.

Anthony Trollope, *Thackeray* (London: Macmillan, 1925), p. 57 ...rst published, 1879); Trollope, *Autobiography*, pp. 100–101.

Moore, *Confessions of a Young Man* and *Avowals* (in same vol.), *Works*, IX, 455, 88.

[3] The Freeing of the Ego

[1] Jean Jacques Rousseau, *Confessions* (New York: Modern Library, ...d.), p. 3; John Bunyan, *Grace Abounding to the Chief of Sinners* (in ...ame vol. with *The Pilgrim's Progress*) (Boston: Houghton Mifflin, ...969), p. 7; Pater, "Pascal," in *Miscellaneous Studies*, *Works*, VIII, 80; George Moore, *A Mere Accident* (London, 1887), p. 86.

[2] Walter Pater, *Letters*, ed. Lawrence Evans (London: Oxford University Press, 1970), p. 52.

[3] Dostoevsky, *The Brothers Karamazov*, tr. Constance Garnett (New York: Modern Library, 1937), pp. 317–318.

[4] Harry Levin, *The Gates of Horn* (New York: Oxford University Press, 1963), p. 127.

[5] See Jerome Hamilton Buckley on the Victorian "Passion of the Past," in his *The Triumph of Time*, ch. vi (Cambridge, Mass.: Harvard University Press, 1966).

[6] Anthony Trollope, *Autobiography*, ed. Bradford Booth (Berkeley: University of California Press, 1947), p. 1.

[7] G. K. Chesterton, *Heretics* (New York: John Lane, 1905), p. 132; Friedrich Nietzsche, *Beyond Good and Evil*, tr. Walter Kaufmann (New York: Vintage Books, 1966), p. 92.

[8] Samuel Butler, *The Way of All Flesh*, in *Works*, Shrewsbury Ed., 20 vols. (London: Jonathan Cape, 1925), XVII, 62.

[9] U. C. Knoepflmacher, *Religious Humanism and the Victorian Novel* (Princeton, N.J.: Princeton University Press, 1965), p. 255.

[10] Butler, *The Way of All Flesh*, p. 387.

[11] John Ruskin, *Praeterita*, in *Works*, Library Ed., 39 vols., eds., E. T. Cook and Alexander Wedderburn (London: Allen, 1903–1912), XXXV, 166, 279, 119, 220.

[12] George Gissing, *Demos* (London: Dent, n.d.), p. 312 (first published, 1886); Gissing, *Thyrza*, p. 14.

[13] Carlton J. H. Hayes, *A Generation of Materialism: 1871–1900* (New York: Harper and Brothers, 1941), pp. 175–176.

[14] Henry George, *Progress and Poverty* (New York: Modern Library, n.d.), p. 10 (first published in America, 1879).

[15] Helen Merrill Lynd, *England in the Eighteen-Eighties* (London: Oxford University Press, 1945), p. 9.

[16] Herman Ausubel, *In Hard Times: Reformers Among the Late Victorians* (New York: Columbia University Press, 1960), pp. 170, 149.

[17] *Annual Register* for 1887 (London, 1888), Pt. I, 190.

[18] Meredith, *Letters*, II, 964.

[19] *Annual Register* for 1883 (London, 1884), Pt. I, 69.

[20] See Clark, *The Making of Victorian England*, ch. vi; Hayes, *A Generation of Materialism*, pp. 135–136; Walter E. Houghton, *The Victorian Frame of Mind* (New Haven, Conn.: Yale University Press, 1957), see esp. chs. iv, vii, and x.

[21] Quoted in the *Annual Register* for 1880 (London, 1881), Pt. I, 75.

[22] Gissing, *Thyrza*, p. 93.

[23] *Journal of the Statistical Society, 1880–1890*, Vols. 44–54 (London, 1881–1891); Thomas Hardy, "The Profitable Reading of Fiction," in *Life and Art*, ed. Ernest Brennecke, Jr. (New York: Greenberg, 1925), p. 62.

[24] Edward Bellamy, *Looking Backward* (New York: Modern Library, 1951), p. 36.

[25] John Morley, *On Compromise* (London: Macmillan, 1903), p. 217 (first published, 1874); James, "Ivan Turgénieff," in *French Poets and Novelists*, p. 233.

[26] Alfred North Whitehead, *Science and the Modern World* (New York: Macmillan, 1925), p. 143.

[27] G. K. Chesterton, *The Victorian Age in Literature* (London: Oxford University Press, 1966), p. 93.

[28] J. A. Froude, *Thomas Carlyle: A History of His Life in London*, 2 vols. (New York, 1884), I, 248.

[29] See U. C. Knoepflmacher, *Religious Humanism and the Victorian Novel* (Princeton, N.J.: Princeton University Press, 1965).

[30] Friedrich Nietzsche, *Twilight of the Idols*, in *The Portable Nietzsche*, tr. and ed. Walter Kaufmann (New York: Viking Press, 1954), pp. 521, 530.

[31] Walter Kaufmann, *Nietzsche: Philosopher, Psychologist, Antichrist* (Princeton, N.J.: Princeton University Press, 1968), p. 418.

[32] Friedrich Nietzsche, *The Will to Power*, tr. and ed. Walter Kaufmann, assisted by R. J. Hollingdale (New York: Random House, 1967), p. 452; Pater, "Style," in *Appreciations*, *Works*, V. 18.

33 Pater, "Coleridge," in *Appreciations, Works,* V. 66.

34 Burckhardt, *Judgments on History and Historians,* p. 218.

35 H. Stuart Hughes, *Consciousness and Society* (New York: Knopf, 1958), ch. ii; Moore, *Confessions of a Young Man,* in *Works,* IX, 464 (first published, 1888; revised, 1916).

36 Johann Eckermann, *Conversations with Goethe,* tr. John Oxenford (London: Dent, 1930), pp. 126, 313–314.

37 Erich Heller, *The Artist's Journey into the Interior and Other Essays* (London: Secker and Warburg, 1966), pp. 84, 132–133.

38 William James, *The Varieties of Religious Experience* (London: Longmans, Green, and Co., 1902), pp. 499–500.

39 H. G. Schenk, *The Mind of the European Romantics* (Garden City, N.Y.: Doubleday Anchor Books, 1969), pp. 49–122.

40 Cf. Philip Appleman, William A. Madden, Michael Wolff, eds., *1859: Entering an Age of Crisis* (Bloomington: University of Indiana Press, 1959); Gertrude Himmelfarb, *Darwin and the Darwinian Revolution* (London: Chatto and Windus, 1959), pp. 373–374.

41 Pater, "Coleridge," p. 68.

42 Philip Appleman, "Darwin, Pater, and a Crisis in Criticism," in *1859: Entering an Age of Crisis,* ed. Appleman *et al.,* pp. 81–95; David J. DeLaura, *Hebrew and Hellene in Victorian England: Newman, Arnold, and Pater* (Austin: University of Texas Press, 1969).

43 Routh, *Towards the Twentieth Century,* pp. 12–13.

44 John Stuart Mill, *On Liberty,* in *Autobiography and Other Writings* (Boston: Houghton Mifflin, 1969), pp. 403, 409–410, 441.

45 See Jacques Barzun, *Darwin, Marx, Wagner: Critique of a Heritage,* rev. ed. (Garden City, N.Y.: Doubleday Anchor Books, 1958).

46 W. H. Mallock, *The New Republic* (New York, 1878), pp. 56, 15 (first published, 1877).

47 Graham Hough dates "the foundations of modern literature" to 1880 on the grounds that, along with the importation of French realistic literature, "the influence of Pater on style and feeling" had become "decisive" in the late 1870's. "George Moore and the Nineties," in *Edwardians and Late Victorians,* ed. Richard Ellmann (New York: English Institute Essays for 1959, 1960), p. 2.

48 Pater, "Coleridge," p. 104.

49 Pater, *The Renaissance: Studies in Art and Poetry,* in *Works,* I, 227, 231.

50 Pater, "Wordsworth," in *Appreciations, Works,* pp. 60, 62.

51 Pater, "Mérimée," in *Miscellaneous Studies, Works,* VIII, 14.

52 William Butler Yeats, *Autobiography* (New York: Macmillan, 1965), pp. 323, 201.

53 Kenneth Graham, *English Criticism of the Novel: 1865–1900* (London: Oxford University Press, 1965), p. 19; see also pp. 61–70.

54 Justin McCarthy, *A History of Our* [...] n.d.), II, 656.

55 Graham, *English Criticism of the No* [...]

56 Gordon Haight, *George Eliot* (Londo [...] 1968), p. 458.

57 Henry James, review of *Middlemarch,* [...] *Essays on the Art of Fiction,* ed. Leon Edel [...] 1956), p. 89.

58 R. H. Hutton, *Sir Walter Scott* (London [...]

59 John Ruskin, *Fiction, Fair and Foul,* in [...] 284.

60 H. G. Wells, *Experiment in Autobiograph* [...] 1934), pp. 415–416.

61 Matthew Arnold, "Count Leo Tolstoi," in [...] ser., reprinted with 1st ser. (London: Dent, 196 [...]

62 Edmund Gosse, "The Limits of Realism in [...] *Modern Literary Realism,* ed. George J. Becker [...] ton University Press, 1963), p. 386.

63 Émile Zola, "Naturalism in the Theatre," [...] mental and reprinted in *Documents,* ed. Becker, p [...]

64 Émile Zola, *The Masterpiece (L'Oeuvre),* tr. [...] don: Paul Elek, 1957), pp. 379–380.

65 Quoted in *Pernicious Literature,* published by [...] Association in 1889 and reprinted in *Documents,* e [...]

66 W. S. Lilly, "The New Naturalism," in *Docu* [...] 289.

67 Meredith, *Letters,* II, 890.

68 James, "George Sand," in *French Poets and Nov* [...] *Letters,* I, 104–105.

69 Unsigned review, *British Quarterly Review,* LXX [...] 530; reprinted in *James: The Critical Heritage,* p. 78.

70 Charles Dudley Warner, "Modern Fiction," [...] 1883), 467.

71 Hamilton Wright Mabie, "A Typical Novel," i [...] Becker, p. 304.

72 William Dean Howells, "Henry James, Jr.," *Cen* [...] 1882), 28–29.

73 H. Rider Haggard, "About Fiction," *Contempor* [...] (Feb. 1887), 175.

74 James, "Anthony Trollope," in *Partial Portraits,* p. 1 [...]

75 George Gissing, *New Grub Street* (Boston: Houghton [...] p. 348 (first published, 1891).

76 Michael Sadleir, *Trollope: A Commentary* (London [...] versity Press, 1961), p. 14.

[33] Pater, "Coleridge," in *Appreciations, Works,* V. 66.

[34] Burckhardt, *Judgments on History and Historians,* p. 218.

[35] H. Stuart Hughes, *Consciousness and Society* (New York: Knopf, 1958), ch. ii; Moore, *Confessions of a Young Man,* in *Works,* IX, 464 (first published, 1888; revised, 1916).

[36] Johann Eckermann, *Conversations with Goethe,* tr. John Oxenford (London: Dent, 1930), pp. 126, 313–314.

[37] Erich Heller, *The Artist's Journey into the Interior and Other Essays* (London: Secker and Warburg, 1966), pp. 84, 132–133.

[38] William James, *The Varieties of Religious Experience* (London: Longmans, Green, and Co., 1902), pp. 499–500.

[39] H. G. Schenk, *The Mind of the European Romantics* (Garden City, N.Y.: Doubleday Anchor Books, 1969), pp. 49–122.

[40] Cf. Philip Appleman, William A. Madden, Michael Wolff, eds., *1859: Entering an Age of Crisis* (Bloomington: University of Indiana Press, 1959); Gertrude Himmelfarb, *Darwin and the Darwinian Revolution* (London: Chatto and Windus, 1959), pp. 373–374.

[41] Pater, "Coleridge," p. 68.

[42] Philip Appleman, "Darwin, Pater, and a Crisis in Criticism," in *1859: Entering an Age of Crisis,* ed. Appleman *et al.,* pp. 81–95; David J. DeLaura, *Hebrew and Hellene in Victorian England: Newman, Arnold, and Pater* (Austin: University of Texas Press, 1969).

[43] Routh, *Towards the Twentieth Century,* pp. 12–13.

[44] John Stuart Mill, *On Liberty,* in *Autobiography and Other Writings* (Boston: Houghton Mifflin, 1969), pp. 403, 409–410, 441.

[45] See Jacques Barzun, *Darwin, Marx, Wagner: Critique of a Heritage,* rev. ed. (Garden City, N.Y.: Doubleday Anchor Books, 1958).

[46] W. H. Mallock, *The New Republic* (New York, 1878), pp. 56, 15 (first published, 1877).

[47] Graham Hough dates "the foundations of modern literature" to 1880 on the grounds that, along with the importation of French realistic literature, "the influence of Pater on style and feeling" had become "decisive" in the late 1870's. "George Moore and the Nineties," in *Edwardians and Late Victorians,* ed. Richard Ellmann (New York: English Institute Essays for 1959, 1960), p. 2.

[48] Pater, "Coleridge," p. 104.

[49] Pater, *The Renaissance: Studies in Art and Poetry,* in *Works,* I, 227, 231.

[50] Pater, "Wordsworth," in *Appreciations, Works,* pp. 60, 62.

[51] Pater, "Mérimée," in *Miscellaneous Studies, Works,* VIII, 14.

[52] William Butler Yeats, *Autobiography* (New York: Macmillan, 1965), pp. 323, 201.

[53] Kenneth Graham, *English Criticism of the Novel: 1865–1900* (London: Oxford University Press, 1965), p. 19; see also pp. 61–70.

[12] George Gissing, *Demos* (London: Dent, n.d.), p. 312 (first published, 1886); Gissing, *Thyrza*, p. 14.

[13] Carlton J. H. Hayes, *A Generation of Materialism: 1871–1900* (New York: Harper and Brothers, 1941), pp. 175–176.

[14] Henry George, *Progress and Poverty* (New York: Modern Library, n.d.), p. 10 (first published in America, 1879).

[15] Helen Merrill Lynd, *England in the Eighteen-Eighties* (London: Oxford University Press, 1945), p. 9.

[16] Herman Ausubel, *In Hard Times: Reformers Among the Late Victorians* (New York: Columbia University Press, 1960), pp. 170, 149.

[17] *Annual Register* for 1887 (London, 1888), Pt. I, 190.

[18] Meredith, *Letters*, II, 964.

[19] *Annual Register* for 1883 (London, 1884), Pt. I, 69.

[20] See Clark, *The Making of Victorian England*, ch. vi; Hayes, *A Generation of Materialism*, pp. 135–136; Walter E. Houghton, *The Victorian Frame of Mind* (New Haven, Conn.: Yale University Press, 1957), see esp. chs. iv, vii, and x.

[21] Quoted in the *Annual Register* for 1880 (London, 1881), Pt. I, 75.

[22] Gissing, *Thyrza*, p. 93.

[23] *Journal of the Statistical Society, 1880–1890*, Vols. 44–54 (London, 1881–1891); Thomas Hardy, "The Profitable Reading of Fiction," in *Life and Art*, ed. Ernest Brennecke, Jr. (New York: Greenberg, 1925), p. 62.

[24] Edward Bellamy, *Looking Backward* (New York: Modern Library, 1951), p. 36.

[25] John Morley, *On Compromise* (London: Macmillan, 1903), p. 217 (first published, 1874); James, "Ivan Turgénieff," in *French Poets and Novelists*, p. 233.

[26] Alfred North Whitehead, *Science and the Modern World* (New York: Macmillan, 1925), p. 143.

[27] G. K. Chesterton, *The Victorian Age in Literature* (London: Oxford University Press, 1966), p. 93.

[28] J. A. Froude, *Thomas Carlyle: A History of His Life in London*, 2 vols. (New York, 1884), I, 248.

[29] See U. C. Knoepflmacher, *Religious Humanism and the Victorian Novel* (Princeton, N.J.: Princeton University Press, 1965).

[30] Friedrich Nietzsche, *Twilight of the Idols*, in *The Portable Nietzsche*, tr. and ed. Walter Kaufmann (New York: Viking Press, 1954), pp. 521, 530.

[31] Walter Kaufmann, *Nietzsche: Philosopher, Psychologist, Antichrist* (Princeton, N.J.: Princeton University Press, 1968), p. 418.

[32] Friedrich Nietzsche, *The Will to Power*, tr. and ed. Walter Kaufmann, assisted by R. J. Hollingdale (New York: Random House, 1967), p. 452; Pater, "Style," in *Appreciations, Works*, V. 18.

[77] Asa Briggs, *Victorian People* (London: Odhams Press, 1954), p. 102.

[78] Harry Levin, *Refractions* (London: Oxford University Press, 1966), p. 268.

[79] Anthony Trollope, *Autobiography*, ed. Bradford Booth (Berkeley: University of California Press, 1947), pp. 29, 28 (first published, 1883).

[80] Robert M. Polhemus, *The Changing World of Anthony Trollope* (Berkeley: University of California Press, 1968), pp. 187, 2–3.

[81] Anthony Trollope, *Dr. Wortle's School* (London: Oxford World's Classics, 1928), p. 242 (first published, 1881).

[82] Anthony Trollope, *The Land Leaguers* (New York, 1883), p. 3.

[83] Anthony Trollope, *Lord Palmerston* (London, 1883), p. 104.

[84] Briggs, *Victorian People*, p. 113.

[85] Anthony Trollope, *Thackeray* (London: Macmillan, 1925), p. 57 (first published, 1879); Trollope, *Autobiography*, pp. 100–101.

[86] Moore, *Confessions of a Young Man* and *Avowals* (in same vol.), in *Works*, IX, 455, 88.

[3] The Freeing of the Ego

[1] Jean Jacques Rousseau, *Confessions* (New York: Modern Library, n.d.), p. 3; John Bunyan, *Grace Abounding to the Chief of Sinners* (in same vol. with *The Pilgrim's Progress*) (Boston: Houghton Mifflin, 1969), p. 7; Pater, "Pascal," in *Miscellaneous Studies, Works*, VIII, 80; George Moore, *A Mere Accident* (London, 1887), p. 86.

[2] Walter Pater, *Letters*, ed. Lawrence Evans (London: Oxford University Press, 1970), p. 52.

[3] Dostoevsky, *The Brothers Karamazov*, tr. Constance Garnett (New York: Modern Library, 1937), pp. 317–318.

[4] Harry Levin, *The Gates of Horn* (New York: Oxford University Press, 1963), p. 127.

[5] See Jerome Hamilton Buckley on the Victorian "Passion of the Past," in his *The Triumph of Time*, ch. vi (Cambridge, Mass.: Harvard University Press, 1966).

[6] Anthony Trollope, *Autobiography*, ed. Bradford Booth (Berkeley: University of California Press, 1947), p. 1.

[7] G. K. Chesterton, *Heretics* (New York: John Lane, 1905), p. 132; Friedrich Nietzsche, *Beyond Good and Evil*, tr. Walter Kaufmann (New York: Vintage Books, 1966), p. 92.

[8] Samuel Butler, *The Way of All Flesh*, in *Works*, Shrewsbury Ed., 20 vols. (London: Jonathan Cape, 1925), XVII, 62.

[9] U. C. Knoepflmacher, *Religious Humanism and the Victorian Novel* (Princeton, N.J.: Princeton University Press, 1965), p. 255.

[10] Butler, *The Way of All Flesh*, p. 387.

[11] John Ruskin, *Praeterita*, in *Works*, Library Ed., 39 vols., eds., E. T. Cook and Alexander Wedderburn (London: Allen, 1903–1912), XXXV, 166, 279, 119, 220.

[12] Butler, *The Way of All Flesh*, pp. 410, 192, 387.

[13] Walter Pater, "Aesthetic Poetry," in *Sketches and Reviews* (New York: Boni and Liveright, 1919), p. 2.

[14] Pater, "The Child in the House," in *Miscellaneous Studies, Works*, VIII, 176, 181.

[15] Pater, *Renaissance*, in *Works*, I, 238, 237.

[16] T. S. Eliot, "Arnold and Pater," in *Selected Essays*, rev. ed. (New York: Harcourt, Brace, 1950), pp. 392–393.

[17] Pater, *Letters*, pp. 52, 64.

[18] Pater, *Renaissance*, pp. 235, 237.

[19] Pater, *Marius the Epicurean*, in *Works*, II, 147.

[20] *Ibid.*, pp. 142–143.

[21] Knoepflmacher, *Religious Humanism and the Victorian Novel*, p. 223.

[22] Moore, *Confessions of a Young Man*, in *Works*, IX, 299.

[23] James, "A New England Winter," in *Collected Tales*, VI, 115.

[24] Pater, "Sebastian Van Storck," in *Imaginary Portraits, Works*, IV, 115.

[25] Pater, "A Prince of Court Painters," in *Imaginary Portraits*, p. 44.

[26] Ramon Fernandez, *Messages*, tr. Montgomery Belgion (New York: Harcourt, Brace, 1927), p. 295.

[27] Jacob Korg, *George Gissing: A Critical Biography* (Seattle: University of Washington Press, 1963), p. 177.

[28] William Hale White, *The Autobiography of Mark Rutherford* (New York: Jonathan Cape, 1929), pp. 9–10 (first published, 1881).

[29] André Gide, *Journals*, 4 vols., tr. and ed. Justin O'Brien (New York: Knopf, 1948), II, 101.

[30] Irvin Stock, *William Hale White (Mark Rutherford): A Critical Study* (New York: Columbia University Press, 1956), p. 80.

[31] *Ibid.*, pp. 21, 77.

[32] William Hale White, *The Deliverance of Mark Rutherford* (New York: Jonathan Cape, 1929), pp. 40, 88, 115 (first published, 1885).

[33] Joseph Henry Shorthouse, *John Inglesant*, 6th ed., (New York, 1886), p. 273 (first published, 1880).

[34] Paul Elmer More, *Shelburne Essays*, 3rd ser. (New York: Putnam, 1907), p. 227.

[35] Henry James, "Mrs. Humphry Ward," *Essays in London and Elsewhere* (New York, 1893), p. 253. James describes *Robert Elsmere* as "the most serious, the most deliberate, and most comprehensive attempt made in England in this later time to hold the mirror of prose fiction up to life" (p. 255).

[36] Mrs. Humphry Ward, *Robert Elsmere* (London: Nelson, 1952), p. 7 (first published, 1888); Mrs. Ward, *A Writer's Recollections*, 2 vols. (New York: Harpers, 1918), II, 67.

[37] Richard Jefferies, *The Story of My Heart* (London, 1883), pp. 137,

125. Appreciations of Jefferies can be found in Edward Thomas' *Richard Jefferies: His Life and Work* (London: Hutchinson, 1909) and in Q. D. Leavis' brief essay, collected in *A Selection from Scrutiny*, 2 vols., ed. F. R. Leavis (Cambridge, Eng.: University Press, 1968), II, 202–211.

[38] Richard Jefferies, *Amaryllis at the Fair* (London, 1887), pp. 74–75.

[39] Olive Schreiner, *The Story of an African Farm* (New York: Modern Library, 1927), p. 262 (first published, 1883).

[40] *Ibid.*, p. 162.

[41] Philip Magnus, *Gladstone* (London: John Murray, 1954), p. 270.

[42] Herman Ausubel, *In Hard Times: Reformers Among the Late Victorians* (New York: Columbia University Press, 1960), p. 253.

[43] John Gross, *The Rise and Fall of the Man of Letters* (New York: Macmillan, 1969), p. 132.

[44] See Richard Burton's Foreword to *The Book of the Thousand Nights and a Night*, 10 vols. (London, 1885–1886), I, ix.

[45] H. Rider Haggard, "About Fiction," *Contemporary Review*, LI (Feb. 1887), 180.

[46] Quoted in Malcolm Elwin, *Old Gods Falling* (New York: Macmillan, 1939), p. 193.

[47] Olive Schreiner, *The Story of an African Farm*, ix; Haggard, "About Fiction," p. 173.

[48] Henry M. Stanley, *In Darkest Africa*, 2 vols. (New York, 1891), I, 4.

[49] H. Rider Haggard, *King Solomon's Mines* (London, 1885), pp. 224, 308.

[50] *Henry James and Robert Louis Stevenson: A Record of Friendship and Criticism*, ed. Janet Adam Smith (London: Rupert Hart-Davis, 1948), p. 184.

[51] Quoted in Robert Kiely, *Robert Louis Stevenson and the Fiction of Adventure* (Cambridge, Mass.: Harvard University Press, 1964), p. 41.

[52] Robert Louis Stevenson, "A Gossip on Romance," in *Works*, South Seas Ed., 32 vols. (New York: Scribner's, 1925), XIII, 136.

[53] James, "Robert Louis Stevenson," in *Partial Portraits*, p. 144.

[54] Robert Louis Stevenson, "A Humble Remonstrance," in *James and Stevenson*, ed. Smith, p. 91.

[55] Robert Louis Stevenson, *Dr. Jekyll and Mr. Hyde*, in *Works*, X, 8, 19, 88.

[56] *Ibid.*, p. 88.

[57] Kiely, *Stevenson and the Fiction of Adventure*, pp. 209–210.

[58] Robert Louis Stevenson, *The Master of Ballantrae*, in *Works*, XVIII, 73, 112.

[59] *Ibid.*, p. 155.

[60] Elwin, *Old Gods Falling*, pp. 180–181.

[61] Kiely, *Stevenson and the Fiction of Adventure*, p. 149.

[62] Max Beerbohm, "1880," in *Works* (London, 1896), p. 46.

[63] Walter Pater, "A Novel by Mr. Oscar Wilde," in *Sketches and Reviews*, p. 132.

[64] Holbrook Jackson, *The Eighteen Nineties* (New York: Knopf, 1922), p. 64.

[65] Oscar Wilde, *The Picture of Dorian Gray*, in *Works*, ed. G. F. Maine (London: Collins, 1948), pp. 69, 17.

[66] *Ibid.*, p. 32; Henry James, *The Ambassadors*, in *The Novels and Tales of Henry James*, New York Ed., 24 vols. (New York: Scribner's, 1907–1909), XXI, 217.

[67] George Bernard Shaw, *An Unsocial Socialist*, in *Selected Non-Dramatic Writings*, ed. Dan H. Laurence (Boston: Houghton Mifflin, 1965), p. 61.

[68] George Bernard Shaw, "A Degenerate's View of Nordau," in *Selected Non-Dramatic Writings*, ed. Laurence, p. 358.

[69] Shaw, *An Unsocial Socialist*, pp. 203, 83.

[70] Jerome Hamilton Buckley, *The Victorian Temper* (Cambridge, Mass.: Harvard University Press, 1951), p. 225.

[71] Reprinted in James McNeill Whistler, *The Gentle Art of Making Enemies* (London, 1892), pp. 154–155. Cf. Roger Fry, "Art and Life," in *Vision and Design* (London: Chatto and Windus, 1920), ch. i.

[4] Artists of Change

[1] George Gissing, *The Private Papers of Henry Ryecroft* (New York: Dutton, 1927), p. 54 (first published, 1903).

[2] See Philip Henderson, *Samuel Butler: The Incarnate Bachelor* (London: Cohen and West, 1953), p. 92.

[3] William Gaunt, *The Aesthetic Adventure* (New York: Harcourt, Brace, 1945), p. 80.

[4] Malcolm Brown, *George Moore: A Reconsideration* (Seattle: University of Washington Press, 1955), p. xi.

[5] Arnold Bennett, "Mr. George Moore," in *Fame and Fiction* (London: Grant Richards, 1901), pp. 257–258.

[6] George Moore, *A Modern Lover: A Realistic Novel* (New York: Lipkind, n.d.), pp. 38, 83 (first published, 1883).

[7] Moore, *A Mummer's Wife*, in *Works*, II, 98 (first published, 1885).

[8] Anthony Trollope, *Autobiography*, ed. Bradford Booth (Berkeley: University of California Press, 1947), p. 198.

[9] Oscar Wilde, "The Critic as Artist," in *Works*, ed. G. F. Maine (London: Collins, 1948), p. 961.

[10] George Moore, "Literature at Nurse, or Circulating Morals" (London, 1885), p. 19.

[11] Gissing, *Letters to Family*, p. 166.

[12] Gissing, *The Private Papers of Henry Ryecroft*, p. 19.

[13] *Ibid.*, p. 89.

[14] Q. D. Leavis, review of Gissing, reprinted in *A Selection from Scrutiny*, 2 vols., ed. F. R. Leavis (Cambridge, Eng.: University Press, 1968), II, 88.

[15] Gissing, *Letters to Family*, p. 53. Frederic Harrison, who had provided encouragement and financial support for Gissing, justifiably wondered: "Where are the 'Workers in the Dawn'?" (p. 79).

[16] George Gissing, *The Unclassed* (London, 1895), p. 212 (first published, 1884).

[17] Walter Allen, *The English Novel* (London: Phoenix House, 1954), p. 278.

[18] Jacob Korg, *George Gissing: A Critical Biography* (Seattle: University of Washington Press, 1963), p. 66.

[19] Henry James, *Notes on Novelists* (New York: Scribner's, 1914), pp. 436–443.

[20] Forrest Reid, "Minor Fiction in the 'Eighties," in *The Eighteen-Eighties*, ed. Walter de la Mare (Cambridge, Eng.: University Press, 1930), p. 113.

[21] Gissing, *The Unclassed*, pp. 165, 116–117, 211, 290.

[22] George Gissing, *Demos* (London: Dent, n.d.), pp. 365, 311 (first published, 1886).

[23] *Ibid.*, p. 39.

[24] George Gissing, *Thyrza* (New York: Dutton, n.d.), pp. 68, 67, 108 (first published, 1887).

[25] Gissing, *The Private Papers of Henry Ryecroft*, p. 101.

[26] Frank Swinnerton, *George Gissing: A Critical Study* (Port Washington, N.Y.: Kennikat Press, 1966; reprint), pp. 61, 96.

[27] Gissing, *Letters to Family*, p. 315.

[28] Gissing, *The Private Papers of Henry Ryecroft*, p. 95.

[29] Quoted in Florence Emily Hardy, *The Life of Thomas Hardy* (London: Macmillan, 1962), pp. 50, 184.

[30] *Ibid.*, p. 182.

[31] Thomas Hardy, "The Profitable Reading of Fiction," in *Life and Art*, ed. Ernest Brennecke, Jr. (New York: Greenberg, 1925), p. 65.

[32] Thomas Hardy, "Candour in English Fiction," in *Life and Art*, ed. Brennecke, pp. 79, 84.

[33] Mrs. Hardy, *The Life of Thomas Hardy*, p. 150.

[34] See Laurence Lerner, *The Truthtellers: Jane Austen, George Eliot, D. H. Lawrence* (New York: Schocken Books, 1967), pp. 118–119.

[35] Irving Howe, *Thomas Hardy* (New York: Macmillan, 1967), p. 66. For interesting, differing views on Hardy, see, for example, Raymond Williams, *The English Novel: From Dickens to Lawrence* (New York: Oxford University Press, 1970), pp. 99, 109–110; John Holloway, *The Victorian Sage* (New York: Norton, 1965), p. 252; Albert Guerard, *Thomas Hardy*, rev. ed. (Norfolk, Conn.: New Directions, 1964), pp. 3, 82. A suggestive recent book on Hardy is J. Hillis Miller's *Thomas*

Hardy: Distance and Desire (Cambridge, Mass.: Harvard University Press, 1970).

[36] Mrs. Hardy, *The Life of Thomas Hardy*, p. 362.

[37] Thomas Hardy, *Two on a Tower* (London: Macmillan, 1952), pp. 31–32.

[38] *Ibid.*, p. v.

[39] Howe, *Thomas Hardy*, p. 101.

[40] Meredith, *Letters*, II, 1068–1069.

[41] Mrs. Hardy, *The Life of Thomas Hardy*, p. 171.

[42] G. K. Chesterton, *The Victorian Age in Literature* (London: Oxford University Press, 1966), p. 60.

[43] Meredith related this to Edmund Gosse, who could not resist writing to Hardy: "I wonder whether you were not saddened by his optimism? There is something almost flighty in his cheerfulness. You know he has broken his ankle? He appears to be quite cheerful about that too. What a very curious thing temperament is—there seems no reason at all why G. M. should be so happy, and in some irrational way one almost resents it." Quoted in Siegfried Sassoon, *George Meredith* (New York: Viking Press, 1948), pp. 255–256.

[44] "The pretence of 'sexuality' is only equalled by the absence of it," James complained (*Letters*, I, 200). Hardy himself ridiculed James by referring to his "ponderously warm manner of saying nothing in infinite sentences"; but he admitted, late in life, that for "a writer who has no grain of poetry, or humour, or spontaneity in his productions," James "can yet be a good novelist. Meredith has some poetry, and yet I can read James when I cannot look at Meredith" (Mrs. Hardy, *The Life of Thomas Hardy*, pp. 181, 370).

[45] Henry James, review of *Far from the Madding Crowd*, in *Literary Reviews and Essays*, ed. Albert Mordell (New Haven, Conn.: College and University Press, 1957), p. 297.

[46] Mrs. Hardy, *The Life of Thomas Hardy*, p. 211.

[47] D. H. Lawrence, "Study of Thomas Hardy," *Phoenix: The Posthumous Papers*, ed. Edward D. McDonald (New York: Viking Press, 1936), pp. 438–439.

[48] Henry James, "French Pictures in Boston," in *The Painter's Eye*, ed. John L. Sweeney (London: Rupert Hart-Davis, 1956), p. 48.

[49] Henry James, *Hawthorne*, English Men of Letters series (New York: Harper, 1894; reprint), pp. 139–140 (first published, 1879).

[50] Henry James, *A Small Boy and Others* (New York: Scribner's, 1913), p. 216.

[51] F. W. Dupee, *Henry James* (Garden City, N.Y.: Doubleday Anchor Books, 1956), p. 161.

[52] James, "Ivan Turgénieff," in *French Poets and Novelists*, pp. 250–251.

[53] James, "Guy de Maupassant," in *Partial Portraits*, p. 247.

[54] Wylie Sypher, *Loss of the Self in Modern Literature and Art* (New York: Random House, 1962), p. 44; José Ortega y Gasset, "Point of View in the Arts," in *The Dehumanization of Art and Other Writings on Art and Culture* (Garden City, N.Y.: Doubleday Anchor Books, 1956), p. 113.

[55] Ramon Fernandez, *Messages*, tr. Montgomery Belgion (New York: Harcourt, Brace, 1927), pp. 293–295.

[56] James, *Letters*, I, 222.

[57] F. O. Matthiessen, *Henry James: The Major Phase* (New York: Oxford University Press, 1944), ch. vi.

[58] James, *Notebooks*, pp. 40–41.

[59] James, *Letters*, I, 100–101.

[60] James, "The Letters of Eugène Delacroix," in *The Painter's Eye*, p. 183.

[61] Ernest A. Baker, *The History of the English Novel*, Volume IX (New York: Barnes and Noble, 1966; reprint), p. 243. And see William C. Frierson, *The English Novel in Transition: 1885–1940* (Norman: University of Oklahoma Press, 1942), pp. 110–111, 115.

[62] Jacques Barzun, *Classic, Romantic, and Modern* (Garden City, N.Y.: Doubleday Anchor Books, 1961), p. 133.

[63] Williams, *The English Novel*, pp. 135–136. See Leon Edel, *Henry James: The Conquest of London* (Philadelphia: Lippincott, 1962), p. 168.

[64] James, "The New Novel," *Notes on Novelists*, p. 320.

[65] W. C. Brownell, "Henry James," originally in *Atlantic*, XCV (April 1905), 496–519; reprinted in *James: The Critical Heritage*, p. 423.

Part II. George Meredith at the Victorian Crossways—Introduction

[1] James, *Letters*, II, 252, 251, 257.

[2] Edith Wharton, *A Backward Glance* (New York: Appleton-Century, 1934), pp. 232–233.

[3] James, *Letters*, I, 219.

[4] Quoted in J. A. Hammerton, *George Meredith in Anecdote and Criticism* (London: Grant Richards, 1909), p. 154.

[5] Henry James, "The Lesson of Balzac," in *The Future of the Novel: Essays on the Art of Fiction*, ed. Leon Edel (New York: Vintage Books, 1956), p. 105.

[6] Virginia Woolf, "The Novels of George Meredith," in *The Common Reader*, 2nd ser. (London: Hogarth Press, 1932), p. 234.

[5] A Strange and Splendid Exhibition

[1] V. S. Pritchett, *George Meredith and English Comedy* (London: Chatto and Windus, 1970), pp. 120, 122–123.

[2] J. B. Priestley, *George Meredith*, English Men of Letters series (New York: Macmillan, 1926), p. 199.

[3] *Henry James and Robert Louis Stevenson: A Record of Friendship and Criticism,* ed. Janet Adam Smith (London: Rupert Hart-Davis, 1948), pp. 169–170.

[4] Quoted in Lionel Stevenson, *The Ordeal of George Meredith* (New York: Scribner's, 1953), p. 277.

[5] *Ibid.,* p. 237.

[6] E. M. Forster, *Aspects of the Novel* (New York: Harcourt, Brace, 1927), pp. 89–90.

[7] Meredith, *Diana of the Crossways,* in *Works,* XV, 19.

[8] Meredith, *Letters,* II, 876.

[9] George Gissing, *Letters to Eduard Bertz,* ed. Arthur C. Young (New Brunswick, N.J.: Rutgers University Press, 1961), p. 205.

[10] Cf. Joseph Warren Beach, *The Comic Spirit in George Meredith* (New York: Longmans, 1911), p. 205; Beach, *The Method of Henry James* (Philadelphia: Saifer, 1954; reprint), p. 161. More recently, Walter Wright has also written good studies of both Meredith (*Art and Substance in George Meredith* [Lincoln: University of Nebraska Press, 1953]) and James (*The Madness of Art* [Lincoln: University of Nebraska Press, 1962]).

[11] J. A. Hammerton, *George Meredith in Anecdote and Criticism* (London: Grant Richards, 1909), p. 69.

[12] Meredith, "Essay on the Idea of Comedy and the Uses of the Comic Spirit," in *Works,* XXIII, 39, 37.

[13] Jacques Barzun, "Henry James, Melodramatist," in *The Question of Henry James,* ed. F. W. Dupee (New York: Holt, 1945), p. 256.

[14] Arthur Symons, *Figures of Several Centuries* (London: Constable, 1916), p. 141.

[15] Oliver Elton, quoted in Hammerton, *Meredith in Anecdote and Criticism,* p. 310; Ernest Dick, quoted in Guy B. Petter, *George Meredith and His German Critics* (London: H. F. and G. Witherby, 1939), p. 23; Ramon Fernandez, *Messages,* tr. Montgomery Belgion (New York: Harcourt, Brace, 1927), pp. 155–190; William Ernest Henley, quoted in Lionel Stevenson, *The Ordeal of George Meredith,* p. 233.

[16] W. L. Courtney, "George Meredith's Novels," *Fortnightly Review,* CCXXIX (1 June 1886), 771; Percy Lubbock, "George Meredith," *Quarterly Review,* no. 422 (Jan. 1910), p. 224; Richard Le Gallienne, *George Meredith: Some Characteristics,* rev. ed. (London: John Lane, 1905), p. 176; G. M. Trevelyan, *A Layman's Love of Letters* (London: Longmans, 1954), p. 107.

[17] Oscar Wilde, "The Decay of Lying," in *Works,* ed. G. F. Maine (London: Collins, 1948), p. 915; Wilde, "The Soul of Man under Socialism," in *Works,* p. 1037.

[18] Meredith, *Letters,* I, 146. (A reviewer had called him the pupil of Browning.)

[19] *Ibid.*, II, 715, 661.

[20] Meredith, *The Shaving of Shagpat,* in *Works,* I, 302; Meredith, "Essay on Comedy," in *Works,* XXIII, 32.

[21] Meredith, *The Ordeal of Richard Feverel,* in *Works,* II, 288.

[22] *Ibid.*, pp. 483, 226.

[23] S. M. Ellis, *George Meredith: His Life and Friends in Relation to His Works* (London: Grant Richards, 1920), pp. 13–35.

[24] Priestley, *George Meredith,* pp. 4–5, 121.

[25] Meredith, *Letters,* I, 160–161.

[26] Meredith, *Sandra Belloni,* Volumes III and IV of *Works,* III, 215.

[27] *Ibid.*, III, 113–114; IV, 484, 528.

[28] *Ibid.*, III, 64.

[29] Meredith, *Letters,* I, 322–323.

[30] Lionel Stevenson, *The Ordeal of George Meredith,* p. 160.

[31] Jack Lindsay, *George Meredith: His Life and Work* (London: Bodley Head, 1956), pp. 138, 171.

[32] Meredith, *Vittoria,* Volumes VII and VIII of *Works,* VIII, 590, 378.

[33] Meredith, *Rhoda Fleming,* in *Works,* V, 412.

[34] *Ibid.*, V, 455–456.

[35] Paul Elmer More, *Shelburne Essays,* 2nd ser. (New York: Putnam, 1905), p. 150.

[36] Percy Lubbock, *The Craft of Fiction* (New York: Viking Press, 1957), pp. 137–138.

[37] Meredith, *Diana of the Crossways,* in *Works,* XVI, 12.

[38] Meredith, *Harry Richmond,* Volumes IX and X of *Works,* X, 417–418, 541.

[39] *Ibid.*, X, 682.

[40] Meredith, *Letters,* I, 485.

[41] *Ibid.*, II, 592.

[42] Meredith, *Beauchamp's Career,* Volumes XI and XII of *Works,* XII, 426.

[43] Meredith, *Letters,* II, 636.

[44] Meredith, *Beauchamp's Career,* in *Works,* XI, 38–39.

[45] *Ibid.*, XI, 39–40.

[46] *Ibid.*, XII, 327.

[47] John Morley, *On Compromise* (London: Macmillan, 1903), p. 258 (first published, 1874).

[6] The Last Victorian: Meredith in the 1880's

[1] Meredith, *Letters,* II, 581.

[2] Gabriel Marcel, "The Ego and Its Relation to Others," *Homo Viator: Introduction to a Metaphysic of Hope,* tr. Emma Craufurd (New York: Harper Torchbooks, 1962), pp. 13–28.

[3] Meredith, *Letters,* III, 1351.

[4] Meredith, "Essay on the Idea of Comedy and the Uses of the Comic Spirit," in *Works*, XXIII, 49–50, 3, 48, 15.

[5] *Ibid.*, pp. 16, 17, 10.

[6] *Ibid.*, p. 36.

[7] *Ibid.*, p. 46.

[8] Meredith, *The Case of General Ople and Lady Camper*, in *Works*, XXI, 185.

[9] Meredith, "Essay on Comedy," in *Works*, XXIII, 41; Meredith, *General Ople and Lady Camper*, in *Works*, XXI, 187.

[10] Siegfried Sassoon, *George Meredith* (New York: Viking Press, 1948), p. 137.

[11] Meredith, *The Tale of Chloe*, in *Works*, XXI, 253, 205.

[12] Meredith, *The Egoist*, Volumes XIII and XIV of *Works*, XIII, 5, 277. (All further page references to *The Egoist* will appear in the text of this chapter.)

[13] René Galland, *George Meredith: Les cinquante premières années* (Paris: Les Presses française, 1923), p. 351.

[14] Meredith, *Letters*, II, 569.

[15] Robert Louis Stevenson, "Books Which Have Influenced Me," in *Works*, South Seas Ed., 32 vols. (New York: Scribner's, 1925), XXVII, 71; William Ernest Henley, *Views and Reviews* (New York, 1890), p. 53.

[16] Meredith, "Essay on Comedy," in *Works*, XXIII, 47.

[17] Louis Auchincloss, *Reflections of a Jacobite* (Boston: Houghton Mifflin, 1961), p. 94.

[18] J. Hillis Miller, *The Form of Victorian Fiction* (South Bend, Ind.: University of Notre Dame Press, 1968), p. 95.

[19] Thomas Love Peacock, "The Four Ages of Poetry," in *Prose of the Romantic Period*, ed. Carl R. Woodring (Boston: Houghton Mifflin, 1961), p. 580.

[20] See Dorothy Van Ghent, *The English Novel: Form and Function* (New York: Rinehart, 1953), pp. 183–194.

[21] J. Hillis Miller also compares the two scenes in his suggestive chapter entitled "Self and Community" in *The Form of Victorian Fiction*.

[22] Meredith, *Diana of the Crossways*, in *Works*, XVI, 493.

[23] Ramon Fernandez, *Messages*, tr. Montgomery Belgion (New York: Harcourt, Brace, 1927), p. 160.

[24] Van Ghent, *The English Novel: Form and Function*, pp. 191–192.

[25] Henry James, *The Portrait of a Lady* (Boston, 1882), pp. 249–250.

[26] Gissing, *Letters to Family*, p. 156.

[27] Thomas Hardy, "George Meredith: A Reminiscence," *Nineteenth Century*, CIII (Feb. 1928), 148.

[28] See Gillian Beer, "Meredith's Idea of Comedy: 1876–1880," *Nineteenth-Century Fiction*, XX (Sept. 1965), 176. A brief account of Lassalle, which tallies with Meredith's description, is in Edmund Wilson's *To the Finland Station* (New York: Harcourt, Brace, 1940), pp. 232–253.

[29] Meredith, *Letters*, II, 614.

[30] Meredith, *The Tragic Comedians*, in *Works*, XV, 199–200. (All further page references to *The Tragic Comedians* will appear in the text of this chapter.)

[31] Quoted in Edward Clodd, "George Meredith: Some Recollections," *Fortnightly Review*, DXI (1 July 1909), 23.

[32] James, *Letters*, I, 219.

[33] Moore, *Confessions of a Young Man*, in *Works*, IX, 434–435.

[34] Sassoon, *George Meredith*, p. 158.

[35] Meredith, *Letters*, II, 876.

[36] *Ibid.*, II, 661; I, 412.

[37] *Ibid.*, II, 627.

[38] *Ibid.*, p. 675.

[39] *Annual Register* for 1883 (London, 1884), Pt. I, 78.

[40] See G. M. Trevelyan, *The Poetry and Philosophy of George Meredith* (London: Constable, 1906); Trevelyan, *The Reflections of an Historian* (London: Nelson, 1919); and Trevelyan, *A Layman's Love of Letters* (London: Longmans, 1954). G. K. Chesterton, *The Victorian Age in Literature* (London: Oxford University Press, 1966), pp. 63–64.

[41] Meredith, *Letters*, II, 743.

[42] Clodd, "George Meredith: Some Recollections," p. 24.

[43] Meredith, *Diana of the Crossways*, in *Works*, XVI, 252. (All further page references to *Diana of the Crossways* will appear in the text of this chapter.)

[44] Jack Lindsay, *George Meredith: His Life and Work* (London: Bodley Head, 1956), p. 268.

[45] James, "Anthony Trollope," in *Partial Portraits*, pp. 128–129.

[46] Meredith, *Letters*, III, 1573.

[47] Lionel Stevenson, *The Ordeal of George Meredith* (New York: Scribner's, 1953), p. 293.

[48] E. M. Forster, *Aspects of the Novel* (New York: Harcourt, Brace, 1927), p. 89.

[49] Meredith, *Letters*, II, 775.

[50] Quoted in J. A. Hammerton, *George Meredith in Anecdote and Criticism* (London: Grant Richards, 1909), p. 311.

[51] Meredith, *One of Our Conquerors*, in *Works*, XVII, 75. (All further page references to *One of Our Conquerers* will appear in the text of this chapter.)

[52] Fernandez, *Messages*, p. 177.

[53] Meredith, *Letters*, II, 1039.

[54] See Fabian Gudas, "George Meredith's *One of Our Conquerors*," in *From Jane Austen to Joseph Conrad*, ed. Robert C. Rathburn and Martin Steinmann, Jr. (Minneapolis: University of Minnesota Press, 1958), p. 232. Cf. Walter Wright, *Art and Substance in George Meredith* (Lincoln: University of Nebraska Press, 1953), pp. 189–195.

[55] Phyllis Bartlett, "The Novels of George Meredith," *Review of English Literature*, III (Jan. 1962), 38.

[56] Meredith, *Letters*, III, 1619.

[57] Constantin Photiadès, *George Meredith: His Life, Genius, and Training*, tr. Arthur Price (New York: Scribner's, 1913), p. 9.

[58] Meredith, *Letters*, II, 1034.

[59] J. B. Priestley, *George Meredith*, English Men of Letters series (New York: Macmillan, 1926), p. 189; Henley, *Views and Reviews*, p. 44; John Robertson, "Concerning Preciosity," *The Yellow Book*, XIII (April 1897), 101.

[60] Fred C. Thomson, "Stylistic Revision of *One of Our Conquerors*," *Yale University Library Gazette*, XXXVI (Oct. 1961), 70.

[61] Henley, *Views and Reviews*, pp. 44–45.

[62] Meredith, "Mr. Robert Lytton's Poems," *Works*, XXIII, 104.

Part III. Henry James and the Americanization of English Fiction —Introduction

[1] Quoted in Siegfried Sassoon, *George Meredith* (New York: Viking Press, 1948), pp. 232–233.

[2] Meredith, *Letters*, II, 720.

[3] Johann Eckermann, *Conversations with Goethe*, tr. John Oxenford (London: Dent, 1930), p. 126.

[4] André Malraux, *Museum without Walls*, tr. Stuart Gilbert and Francis Price (Garden City, N.Y.: Doubleday, 1967), p. 38.

[7] All for Art, or the World Well Lost

[1] James, "Greville Fane," in *Collected Tales*, VIII, 447.

[2] Henry James, *A Small Boy and Others* (New York: Scribner's, 1913), p. 103.

[3] James, *Selected Letters*, p. 11.

[4] See J. B. Priestley, quoted approvingly in Mario Praz, *The Hero in Eclipse in Victorian Fiction*, tr. Angus Davidson (London: Oxford University Press, 1956), pp. 170–171.

[5] Henry James, *Notes of a Son and Brother* (New York: Scribner's, 1914), p. 25.

[6] *Ibid.*, pp. 195, 5.

[7] *Ibid.*, pp. 26–27, 349.

[8] Leon Edel's introduction to Henry James, *The Ambassadors* (Boston: Houghton Mifflin, 1960), pp. viii–ix.

[9] James, *Notebooks*, p. 66.

[10] Henry James, "A French Critic," *Notes and Reviews*, ed. Pierre de Chaignon la Rose (Cambridge, Mass.: Dunster House, 1921), pp. 102–103; James, "Mr. Walt Whitman," in *The American Essays*, ed. Leon Edel (New York: Vintage Books, 1956), p. 136; James, "Miss Prescott's

'Azarian,' " "The Belton Estate," and "Fiction and Sir Walter Scott," all three in *Notes and Reviews,* ed. Chaignon la Rose, pp. 17, 23, 124–131, 1.

[11] Henry James, "Historical Novels," in *Literary Reviews and Essays,* ed. Albert Mordell (New Haven, Conn.: College and University Press, 1957), p. 279; James, "The Novels of George Eliot," in *Views and Reviews,* ed. Le Roy Phillips (Boston: Ball, 1908), pp. 1, 18; James, "The Noble School of Fiction," in *Notes and Reviews,* ed. Chaignon la Rose, p. 66.

[12] Henry James, unsigned review of *Dallas Galbraith, Nation,* VII (22 Oct. 1868), 330.

[13] James, *Letters,* I, 27.

[14] *Ibid.,* p. 22.

[15] Henry James, "Chester," in *Transatlantic Sketches* (Boston, 1875), p. 14.

[16] James, *Letters,* I, 55.

[17] Henry James, "James Russell Lowell," in *Essays in London and Elsewhere* (New York, 1893), p. 76.

[18] James, "Théophile Gautier," in *French Poets and Novelists,* p. 33.

[19] James, "Honoré de Balzac," in *French Poets and Novelists,* p. 86.

[20] Henry James, *Hawthorne,* English Men of Letters series (New York: Harper, 1894; reprint), pp. 3, 57 (first published, 1879).

[21] *Ibid.,* pp. 63–64. See F. O. Matthiessen, "Hawthorne and James," in *American Renaissance* (London: Oxford University Press, 1941), pp. 292–305; Marius Bewley, *The Complex Fate* (London: Chatto and Windus, 1952), pp. 1–10; F. R. Leavis, *The Great Tradition* (New York: George W. Stewart, 1948), p. 129; T. S. Eliot, "The Hawthorne Aspect," in *The Question of Henry James,* ed. F. W. Dupee (New York: Holt, 1945), pp. 112–119.

[22] James, *Hawthorne,* p. 99.

[23] James, "Gustave Flaubert," in *French Poets and Novelists,* p. 201.

[24] James, "Charles Baudelaire," in *French Poets and Novelists,* p. 61.

[25] Richard Poirier, *The Comic Sense of Henry James* (New York: Oxford University Press, 1960), p. 55.

[26] Henry James, *Parisian Sketches,* ed. Leon Edel and Ilse Dusoir Lind (New York: New York University Press, 1957), pp. 23–24, 129–131; James, "An English Easter," in *Portraits of Places* (Boston, 1884), pp. 197–198; James, *Letters,* I, 114.

[27] James, "London at Midsummer," in *Portraits of Places,* p. 226; James, *Letters,* I, 310–311; see also *The Legend of the Master,* ed. Simon Nowell-Smith (London: Constable, 1947), p. 100.

[28] James, *Letters,* I, 36–37; James, "In Warwickshire" and "Italy Revisited," in *Portraits of Places,* pp. 258, 68.

[29] James, "Roman Neighborhoods," in *Transatlantic Sketches,* pp. 179, 161; James, "Italy Revisited," pp. 52–53.

[30] James, "Théophile Gautier," p. 56.

[31] Henry James, *Watch and Ward* (Boston, 1879), p. 100 (serialized in 1871, but not published in book form until 1878).

[32] James, "At Isella," in *Collected Tales*, II, 327.

[33] James, "A Passionate Pilgrim," in *Collected Tales*, II, 248, 245.

[34] James, "The Madonna of the Future," in *Collected Tales*, III, 16, 15.

[35] James, "Madame de Mauves," in *Collected Tales*, III, 129, 162, 140.

[36] Leon Edel, *Henry James: The Conquest of London* (Philadelphia: Lippincott, 1962), p. 178.

[37] Henry James, *Roderick Hudson* (Boston, 1876), pp. 128, 253.

[38] Henry James, "Preface" to *The Tragic Muse*, in *The Novels and Tales of Henry James*, New York Ed., 24 vols. (New York: Scribner's, 1907–1909), VII, xviii.

[39] Henry James, *The American* (Boston, 1877), pp. 473, 44.

[40] James, "An English Easter," in *Portraits of Places*, p. 186.

[41] James, *The American*, pp. 419, 196.

[42] James, *Selected Letters*, p. 69.

[43] Edmund Gosse, "The Limits of Realism in Fiction," in *Documents of Modern Literary Realism*, ed. George J. Becker (Princeton, N.J.: Princeton University Press, 1963), p. 385.

[44] James, *The American*, p. 44.

[45] Henry James, unsigned review of *Irene Macgillicuddy*, *Nation*, XXVI (30 May 1878), 357.

[46] James, "The Pension Beaurepas," in *Collected Tales*, IV, 382–384.

[47] *Ibid.*, pp. 376–377.

[48] James, "An International Episode," in *Collected Tales*, IV, 254.

[49] Henry James, *The Europeans* (Boston, 1878), p. 207.

[50] *Ibid.*, pp. 27, 116.

[51] Henry James, *Confidence* (Boston, 1880), p. 118 (first published in England, 1879).

[52] James, "The Diary of a Man of Fifty," in *Collected Tales*, IV, 419, 425.

[53] Joseph Warren Beach, *The Method of Henry James* (Philadelphia: Saifer, 1954; reprint), p. lix.

[54] James, "A Bundle of Letters," in *Collected Tales*, IV, 439–444.

[55] Henry James, "The Letters of Eugène Delacroix," in *The Painter's Eye*, ed. John L. Sweeney (London: Rupert Hart-Davis, 1956), p. 183.

[56] James, "Sainte-Beuve," added by Leon Edel to his edition of *French Poets and Novelists* (New York: Grosset and Dunlap, 1964), pp. 320, 341.

[57] Henry James, *Washington Square* (New York, 1881), pp. 244, 20, 30, 235–236.

[58] *Ibid.*, pp. 35, 200, 93, 246.

[59] James, *Selected Letters*, pp. 45–46.

[60] Matthiessen, *The James Family*, p. 191.

[61] Henry James, *The Tragic Muse*, 2 vols. (Boston, 1890), I, 392.

[8] Points of View and Pointed Views: James in the 1880's

[1] Unsigned review, *Literary World*, XII (Dec. 1881), 473–474; reprinted in *James: The Critical Heritage*, p. 106.

[2] Henry James, *The Portrait of a Lady* (Boston, 1882), p. 361. (All further page references to *The Portrait of a Lady* will appear in the text of this chapter.)

[3] Henry James, "Charles S. Reinhart," in *Picture and Text* (New York, 1893), pp. 67–68.

[4] Richard Poirier, *The Comic Sense of Henry James* (New York: Oxford University Press, 1960), pp. 212, 187.

[5] Quoted in Leon Edel, *Henry James: The Conquest of London* (Philadelphia: Lippincott, 1962), p. 383.

[6] James, *Letters*, I, 65, 67.

[7] Horace Scudder, "The Portrait of a Lady and Dr. Breen's Practice," *Atlantic*, XLIX (Jan. 1882), 127–128.

[8] William Dean Howells, "Henry James, Jr., *Century*, XXV (Nov. 1882), 26.

[9] Henry James, review of *Middlemarch*, in *The Future of the Novel: Essays on the Art of Fiction*, ed. Leon Edel (New York: Vintage Books, 1956), pp. 81, 83; James, "The Novels of George Eliot," in *Views and Reviews*, ed. Le Roy Phillips (Boston: Ball, 1908), p. 16.

[10] James, *Notebooks*, p. 15.

[11] James, "Daniel Deronda: A Conversation," in *Partial Portraits*, pp. 88–90, 82.

[12] Henry James, "Preface" to *The Portrait of a Lady*, in *The Novels and Tales of Henry James*, New York Ed., 24 vols. (New York: Scribner's, 1907–1909), III, xii.

[13] Poirier, *The Comic Sense of Henry James*, p. 217.

[14] See R. C. K. Ensor, *England: 1870–1914* (London: Oxford University Press, 1936), pp. 169–170.

[15] H. G. Wells, "Of Art, of Literature, of Mr. Henry James," in *Boon* (New York: Doran, 1915), p. 108.

[16] George Eliot, *Middlemarch* (London: Oxford World's Classics, 1947), pp. 205, 226.

[17] Henry James, *Hawthorne*, English Men of Letters series (New York: Harper, 1894; reprint), pp. 82–83 (first published, 1879).

[18] Arnold Kettle, *An Introduction to the English Novel*, 2 vols. (London: Hutchinson's University Library, 1953), II, 22.

[19] James, "The Novels of George Eliot," p. 34. See Cornelia Pulsifer Kelley, *The Early Development of Henry James*, rev. ed. (Urbana: University of Illinois Press, 1965), pp. 62–63.

[20] Henry James, "Frances Anne Kemble," in *Essays in London and Elsewhere* (New York, 1893), pp. 117–118.

[21] Richard Chase, *The American Novel and Its Tradition* (Garden City, N.Y.: Doubleday Anchor Books, 1957), pp. 135, 119.

[22] Henry James, "Preface" to *The Spoils of Poynton*, in *The Novels and Tales of Henry James*, X, xvii.

[23] James, *Notebooks*, pp. 35–36.

[24] Oscar Cargill, *The Novels of Henry James* (New York: Macmillan, 1961), p. 118.

[25] See F. W. Dupee, *Henry James* (Garden City, N.Y.: Doubleday Anchor Books, 1956), p. 101; R. W. Stallman, *The Houses That James Built and Other Literary Studies* (East Lansing: Michigan State University Press, 1961), pp. 27–28; Edel, *Henry James: The Conquest of London*, p. 426.

[26] James, "The Poetry of William Morris," in *Views and Reviews*, ed. Phillips, p. 80.

[27] Henry James, *A Little Tour in France* (Boston, 1884), p. 237.

[28] F. O. Matthiessen, *American Renaissance* (London: Oxford University Press, 1941), p. 296.

[29] James, *Notebooks*, p. 18.

[30] Howells, "Henry James, Jr.," p. 26.

[31] James, *Hawthorne*, p. 139.

[32] James, "The Liar," in *Collected Tales*, VI, 406.

[33] Henry James, "An English Easter," in *Portraits of Places* (Boston, 1884), p. 186.

[34] Meredith, *Letters*, II, 607.

[35] Edmund Gosse, *Aspects and Impressions* (London: Cassell, 1922), p. 27; William James, quoted in Matthiessen, *The James Family*, p. 303.

[36] "American Novels," *Quarterly Review*, CLV (Jan. 1883), 214.

[37] Donald Murray, "Henry James and the English Reviewers: 1882–1890," *American Literature*, XXIV (March 1952), 1–20.

[38] Howells, "Henry James, Jr.," pp. 27–29.

[39] Rebecca West, *Henry James* (New York: Holt, 1916), p. 46; Henry James, quoted in Matthiessen, *The James Family*, p. 320.

[40] James, *Notebooks*, pp. 23–24.

[41] *Ibid.*, pp. 43, 27–28.

[42] *Ibid.*, pp. 40–41. Richard Poirier aptly speaks of "a theatricality of expression that death, any death, always brought from" James ("The Hunter and the Hunted; Leon Edel and Henry James," *Massachusetts Review*, IV [Spring 1963], 602).

[43] James, *Notebooks*, p. 42.

[44] *Ibid.*, p. 15.

[45] James, "The Point of View," in *Collected Tales*, IV, 479; James, *Letters*, I, 91; James, *Hawthorne*, p. 49.

[46] James, "The Point of View," pp. 500, 498.

[47] *Ibid.*, pp. 504–508.

48 See Matthiessen, *The James Family*, pp. 11–12.

49 James, "The Point of View," pp. 515, 512–513.

50 James, "The Siege of London," in *Collected Tales*, V, 72, 58.

51 George D. Painter, *Proust: The Early Years* (Boston: Little, Brown, 1959), p. 205.

52 James, "George du Maurier," in *Partial Portraits*, p. 370.

53 James, "Lady Barberina," in *Collected Tales*, V, 223, 249, 265.

54 James, "Georgina's Reasons," in *Collected Tales*, VI, 64, 85.

55 James, "A New England Winter," in *Collected Tales*, VI, 114, 118, 142.

56 James, "Pandora," in *Collected Tales*, V, 399, 370.

57 James, "The Author of *Beltraffio*," in *Collected Tales*, V, 309, 303. James's ambivalence of artistic intent in his depiction of Ambient as both model novelist and erring father is discussed by Viola Hopkins Winner in "The Artist and the Man in 'The Author of Beltraffio,'" *Publications of the Modern Language Association*, LXXXIII (March 1968), 102–108. Edwin T. Bowden curiously defends Mrs. Ambient on the grounds that, like Isabel Archer, she sees "the deadening evil of a life devoted to the esthetic and nothing more" (*The Themes of Henry James* [New Haven, Conn.: Yale University Press, 1956], p. 59).

58 James, "The Author of *Beltraffio*," pp. 331–335, 317, 307, 355.

59 Walter Besant, "Fiction as One of the Fine Arts," printed in America as "The Art of Fiction" (Boston, 1884), p. 34.

60 *Ibid.*, pp. 3, 18, 29.

61 James, "The Author of *Beltraffio*," p. 336; James, "The Art of Fiction," in *Partial Portraits*, p. 381.

62 James, "The Author of *Beltraffio*," pp. 331, 332; James, "The Art of Fiction," p. 398.

63 James, "The Art of Fiction," pp. 376, 394.

64 *Ibid.*, pp. 389, 390.

65 Henry James, "'The School for Scandal' at Boston," in *The Scenic Art*, ed. Allan Wade (New York: Hill and Wang, 1957), p. 14.

66 James, review of *Nana*, in *The Future of the Novel*, p. 94.

67 James, "The Art of Fiction," p. 406.

68 *Ibid.*, pp. 401–402.

69 James, "Anthony Trollope," in *Partial Portraits*, pp. 124, 116–117, 123–124, 132–133.

70 James, "The Life of George Eliot," in *Partial Portraits*, p. 62.

71 James, "Ivan Turgénieff," in *Partial Portraits*, pp. 296, 298–299.

72 Henry James, "Matthew Arnold," in *Literary Reviews and Essays*, ed. Albert Mordell (New Haven, Conn.: College and University Press, 1957), p. 353.

73 Henry James, "William Dean Howells," in *The American Essays*, ed. Leon Edel, (New York: Vintage Books, 1956), p. 152.

74 James, "Emerson," in *Partial Portraits*, p. 2.

75 James, *Notebooks*, pp. 73, 82.

76 Henry James, *The Reverberator* (London, 1888), p. 89.

77 *Ibid.*, p. 223.

78 James, *Notebooks*, p. 77.

79 James, "Preface" to *The Spoils of Poynton*, xv.

80 James, *Letters*, I, 74.

81 James, "A London Life," in *Collected Tales*, VII, 104–105.

82 *Ibid.*, pp. 101, 189, 198.

83 See Marius Bewley, *The Complex Fate* (London: Chatto and Windus, 1952), pp. 86–87; Wayne Booth, *The Rhetoric of Fiction* (Chicago: University of Chicago Press, 1961), pp. 347–354.

84 James, "The Liar," in *Collected Tales*, VI, 411.

85 James, *Notebooks*, p. 72.

86 James, "Daniel Deronda: A Conversation," p. 92.

87 James, "The Aspern Papers," in *Collected Tales*, VI, 327–328.

88 James, "The Death of the Lion," in *Collected Tales*, IX, 100.

89 Leon Edel, "Introduction," in *Collected Tales*, VI, 9.

90 James, "The Aspern Papers," pp. 299, 311.

91 James, "The Lesson of the Master," in *Collected Tales*, VII, 269, 261–262, 283.

92 James, "Brooksmith," in *Collected Tales*, VIII, 21, 15, 27.

93 James, "Mr. Kipling's Early Stories," in *Views and Reviews*, ed. Phillips p. 228 (originally written as the "Preface" to Kipling's *Mine Own People*, 1891).

[9] James among the Victorians

1 Edmund Wilson, "The Ambiguity of Henry James," in *The Triple Thinkers* (New York: Oxford University Press, 1948), p. 106.

2 James, *Notebooks*, pp. 44–45, 47.

3 "American Novels," *Quarterly Review*, CLV (Jan. 1883), 212.

4 Charles Dudley Warner, "Modern Fiction," *Atlantic*, LI (April 1883), 473–474.

5 James Herbert Morse, "The Native Element in American Fiction: Since the War," *Century*, XXVI (July 1883), 373–375.

6 James, *Notebooks*, pp. 46–47.

7 Alphonse Daudet, *The Evangelist*, tr. Olive Edwards Palmer (Boston, 1899), pp. 77–78.

8 Henry James, "George Sand," in *Notes on Novelists* (New York: Scribner's, 1914), p. 213; and see *The Legend of the Master*, ed. Simon Nowell-Smith (London: Constable, 1947), p. 74.

9 James, *Notebooks*, p. 47.

10 Joseph Warren Beach, *The Method of Henry James* (Philadelphia: Saifer, 1954; reprint), p. 41.

[11] Henry James, *The Bostonians* (London and New York, 1886), pp. 4–5. (All further page references to *The Bostonians* will appear in the text of this chapter.)

[12] William Butler Yeats, "The Tragic Theatre," in *Essays and Introductions* (London: Macmillan, 1961), p. 241.

[13] Matthiessen, *The James Family*, p. 329.

[14] *Ibid.*, p. 327.

[15] James, "Emerson," in *Partial Portraits*, pp. 17–18; James, "The Correspondence of Carlyle and Emerson," in *The American Essays*, ed. Leon Edel (New York: Vintage Books, 1956), pp. 42–44.

[16] James, "Emerson," pp. 26–27.

[17] James, *The Portrait of a Lady* (Boston, 1882), p. 210.

[18] Lionel Trilling, *The Opposing Self* (New York: Viking Press, 1955), p. 113.

[19] Horace Scudder, "James, Crawford, and Howells," *Atlantic*, LVII (June 1886), 852.

[20] Trilling, *The Opposing Self*, p. 117.

[21] James, *Notebooks*, p. 47.

[22] Irving Howe, *Politics and the Novel* (Cleveland, Ohio: World, 1957), p. 197.

[23] Henry James, Sr., "Some Personal Recollections of Carlyle," *Atlantic*, XLVII (May 1881), 597, 603.

[24] James, *Letters*, I, 123.

[25] Scudder, "James, Crawford, and Howells," pp. 851–852.

[26] Van Wyck Brooks, *The Pilgrimage of Henry James* (New York: Dutton, 1925), p. 99; F. W. Dupee, *Henry James* (Garden City, N.Y.: Doubleday Anchor Books, 1956), p. 129.

[27] James, *Notebooks*, p. 47.

[28] James, "Alphonse Daudet," in *Partial Portraits*, pp, 199, 237–238.

[29] Scudder, "James, Crawford, and Howells," p. 853.

[30] Nathaniel Hawthorne, *The Blithedale Romance* (New York: Norton, 1958), p. 58 (first published, 1852).

[31] James, "Nathaniel Hawthorne," in *The American Essays*, p. 19.

[32] Matthiessen, *The James Family*, p. 13.

[33] James, "The Life of George Eliot," in *Partial Portraits*, p. 62.

[34] John Stuart Mill, *The Subjection of Women* (New York, 1909), p. 108 (first published, 1869).

[35] James, *Notebooks*, p. 194.

[36] Matthiessen, *The James Family*, pp. 325, 329.

[37] Unsigned review (R. H. Hutton), *Spectator*, LX (Jan. 1887), 14–16; reprinted in *James: The Critical Heritage*, p. 175.

[38] James, *Letters*, I, 114.

[39] Henry James, "The London Theatres," in *The Scenic Art*, ed. Allan Wade (New York: Hill and Wang, 1957), p. 120.

[40] Henry James, "Chester," in *Transatlantic Sketches* (Boston, 1875), pp. 17–18.

[41] Henry James, "Rheims and Laon: A Little Tour," in *Portraits of Places* (Boston, 1884), p. 106.

[42] See W. H. Tilley, *The Background of The Princess Casamassima* (Gainesville: University of Florida Press, 1961), p. 10; Virginia Harlow, *Thomas Sergeant Perry* (Durham, N.C.: Duke University Press, 1950), p. 318.

[43] James, *Selected Letters*, p. 79.

[44] James, *Letters*, I, 104–105.

[45] James, *Notebooks*, pp. 69, 68–69.

[46] Henry James, *Notes of a Son and Brother* (New York: Scribner's, 1914), p. 210; Matthiessen, *The James Family*, pp. 49–58.

[47] James, "Ivan Turgénieff," in *French Poets and Novelists*, pp. 220, 233.

[48] Henry James, *The Princess Casamassima* (London and New York, 1886), p. 220. (All further page references to *The Princess Casamissima* will appear in the text of this chapter.)

[49] Henry James, review of *Virgin Soil*, in *Literary Reviews and Essays*, ed. Albert Mordell (New Haven, Conn.: College and University Press, 1957), pp. 191–193.

[50] Henry James, *A Little Tour in France* (Boston, 1884), p. 204; James, "Victor Hugo's Ninety-Three," in *Literary Reviews and Essays*, ed. Mordell, p. 140; James, *Parisian Sketches*, ed. Leon Edel and Ilse Dusoir Lind (New York: New York University Press, 1957), p. 31.

[51] James, "Madame de Sabran," in *French Poets and Novelists*, p. 293.

[52] See, for example, James, "An English Easter," in *Portraits of Places*, pp. 196–198.

[53] Henry James, "Preface" to *The Princess Casamassima*, in *The Novels and Tales of Henry James*, New York Ed., 24 vols. (New York: Scribner's, 1907–1909), V, viii.

[54] *Ibid.*, pp. xii–xiii.

[55] James, review of *The Spanish Gypsy*, in *Literary Reviews and Essays*, ed. Mordell, p. 289.

[56] James, "Preface" to *What Maisie Knew*, in *The Novels and Tales of Henry James*, XI, xx.

[57] Henry James, *A Small Boy and Others* (New York: Scribner's, 1913), pp. 175–176.

[58] Friedrich Nietzsche, *Twilight of the Idols*, in *The Portable Nietzsche*, tr. and ed. Walter Kaufmann (New York: Viking Press, 1954), p. 535.

[59] Howe, *Politics and the Novel*, p. 154.

[60] James, "London at Midsummer," in *Portraits of Places*, p. 214.

[61] James, *The Ambassadors*, 2 volumes in *The Novels and Tales of Henry James*, XXI, 119.

[62] James, *The Princess Casamassima*, 2 volumes in *The Novels and Tales of Henry James*, VI, 406.

[63] *Ibid.*, V, 362–363.

[64] Henry James, "The Novels of George Eliot," in *Views and Reviews*, ed. Le Roy Phillips (Boston: Ball, 1908), p. 22; "Epictetus," in *Notes and Reviews*, ed. Pierre de Chaignon la Rose (Cambridge, Mass.: Dunster House, 1921), p. 180.

[65] James, *Letters*, I, 252.

[66] Arthur Schopenhauer, *The World as Will and Idea*, in *Schopenhauer Selections*, ed. DeWitt H. Parker (New York: Scribner's, 1928), pp. 187–188.

[67] See Joseph Firebaugh, "A Schopenhauerian Novel," *Nineteenth-Century Fiction*, XIII (Dec. 1958), 177–197. This essay overstates in its intention, but it is undeniable that Schopenhauer's gloomy aestheticism was influential in the last decades of the nineteenth century in England (especially upon Gissing), and may even—minus the gloom—have affected James's beliefs.

[68] James, *Notes on Novelists*, p. 436.

[69] James, "Alphonse Daudet," pp. 220, 227–228.

[70] James, "Preface" to *The Princess Casamassima*, V, xxii.

[71] Yvor Winters, *Maule's Curse* (Norfolk, Conn.: New Directions, 1938), p. 205. Lionel Trilling argues that *The Princess Casamassima* "is a brilliantly precise representation of social actuality" (*The Liberal Imagination*, [New York: Viking Press, 1950], p. 74).

[72] James, *Letters*, I, 124, 121.

[73] Unsigned review in the *Edinburgh Review*, CXCVII (Jan. 1903), 59–85; reprinted in *James: The Critical Heritage*, p. 346.

[74] Walter Isle, *Experiments in Form: Henry James's Novels, 1896–1901* (Cambridge, Mass.: Harvard University Press, 1968), p. 5.

[75] See the extremely useful *Bibliography of Henry James*, 2nd rev. ed., ed. Leon Edel and Dan H. Laurence (London: Rupert Hart-Davis, 1961). While James's novels in the 1880's enjoyed considerably higher sales than, say, Gissing's novels during the same period and they were all reprinted (750 copies of *The Princess Casamassima*, for example, appeared in three volumes in 1886; the one-volume edition, for England and America, accounted for 3,000 additional copies; in 1888, 4,000 copies of the novel appeared in a two-shilling edition), they provided considerably less revenue than the novels of George Moore or H. Rider Haggard or Mrs. Humphry Ward. In the 1880's James's income was entirely dependent upon the sales from book publication and serialization.

[76] William Dean Howells, "Editor's Study," *Harper's*, LXXVII (Oct. 1888), 800.

[77] James, *Letters*, I, 135.

[78] James, "The Next Time," in *Collected Tales*, IX, 207.

[79] James, "Fiction and Sir Walter Scott," in *Notes and Reviews*, ed. Chaignon la Rose, p. 5.

[80] James, *Notebooks*, pp. 87–88.

[81] James, *Letters*, I, 138, 141–142.

[82] James, "Preface" to *The Tragic Muse*, 2 volumes in *The Novels and Tales of Henry James*, VII, v.

[83] Henry James, *The Tragic Muse*, 2 vols. (Boston, 1890), I, 52. (All further page references to *The Tragic Muse* will appear in the text of this chapter.)

[84] Leon Edel, *Henry James: The Middle Years* (Philadelphia: Lippincott, 1962), p. 261.

[85] James, "Preface" to *The Tragic Muse*, VII, xvii.

[86] See Quentin Anderson, *The American Henry James* (New Brunswick, N.J.: Rutgers University Press, 1957), p. 101.

[87] James, *Notes of a Son and Brother*, pp. 50–51, 195.

[88] Quoted in Edel, *Henry James: The Middle Years*, p. 31.

[89] James, *Notebooks*, pp. 63–64.

[90] Henry James, "Frances Anne Kemble," in *Essays in London and Elsewhere* (New York, 1893), p. 85.

[91] James, *Letters*, I, 207.

[92] Quoted in *The Legend of the Master*, ed. Nowell-Smith, p. 168.

[93] Henry James, "Honoré Daumier," in *Picture and Text* (New York, 1893), pp. 134–135.

[94] James, "John S. Sargent," in *Picture and Text*, p. 114.

[95] *Henry James and Robert Louis Stevenson: A Record of Friendship and Criticism*, ed. Janet Adam Smith (London: Rupert Hart-Davis, 1948), p. 185.

[96] James, *Letters*, I, 170.

[97] Quoted in Ralph Barton Perry, *The Thought and Character of William James*, 2 vols. (Boston: Houghton, Mifflin, 1935), I, 415.

[10] Conclusion: Two Novelists

[1] G. K. Chesterton, *The Uses of Diversity* (New York: Dodd, Mead, 1921), p. 43.

[2] Meredith, *The Amazing Marriage*, in *Works*, XIX, 511.

[3] Richard Poirier, *A World Elsewhere* (London: Oxford University Press, 1966), p. 124.

[4] Pater, *Renaissance*, in *Works*, I, 238.

[5] Henry James, *The Ambassadors*, 2 volumes in *The Novels and Tales of Henry James*, New York Ed., 24 vols. (New York: Scribner's, 1907–1909), XXI, 119–120, 245; XXII, 247, 253, 263.

[6] Stephen Spender, *The Destructive Element* (London: Jonathan Cape, 1935), p. 197.

[7] Sydney Waterlow, "The Work of Mr. Henry James," *Independent Review*, IV (Nov. 1904), 236–243; reprinted in *James: The Critical Heritage*, pp. 370–371.

[8] Moore, *Confessions of a Young Man, in Works*, IX, 432.

[9] E. M. Forster, *Aspects of the Novel* (New York: Harcourt, Brace, 1927), p. 89.

[10] Editorial (John Crowe Ransom?), *Kenyon Review*, V (Autumn 1943), 621–622.

[11] See Donald Fanger, "Joyce and Meredith: A Question of Influence and Tradition," *Modern Fiction Studies*, VI (Summer 1960), 125–130.

[12] James, *Notebooks*, p. 196.

[Index]